BEHIND THE OPEN DOOR
Foreign Enterprises in
the Chinese Marketplace

DANIEL H. ROSEN

BEHIND THE OPEN DOOR
Foreign Enterprises in the Chinese Marketplace

INSTITUTE FOR INTERNATIONAL ECONOMICS
Washington, DC

COUNCIL ON FOREIGN RELATIONS
New York, NY

January 1999

Daniel Rosen, *Research Fellow,* has focused on the economic development of East Asia, particularly emerging Greater China. He is now studying the commercial concerns of foreign invested enterprises in mainland China and the policy responses needed to address those concerns. Other areas of focus have included telecommunications negotiations, trade and environment linkages, and the limits of economic sanctions as a foreign policy tool.

INSTITUTE FOR INTERNATIONAL ECONOMICS
11 Dupont Circle, NW
Washington, DC 20036-1207
(202) 328-9000   FAX: (202) 328-5432
http://www.iie.com

C. Fred Bergsten, *Director*
Christine F. Lowry, *Director of Publications*
Brett Kitchen, *Marketing Director*

Typesetting by BMWW
Printing by Kirby Lithographic Co., Inc.
Cover Design by Naylor Design Inc.

For reprints/permission to photocopy please contact the APS customer service department at CCC Academic Permissions Service, 27 Congress Street, Salem, MA 01970.

Printed in the United States of America
00 99 98   5 4 3 2 1

Library of Congress Cataloging-in-Publication Data

Rosen, Daniel H.
  Foreign enterprises in the Chinese marketplace / Daniel H. Rosen.
    p. cm.
  Includes bibliographical references and index.
    ISBN 0-88132-263-6

  1. Corporations, Foreign—China.
2. Investments, Foreign—China.
3. China—Commerce.   I. Title.
HD2910.R67   1998
338.8'8851—dc21   98-29814
                                          CIP

The views expressed in this publication are those of the author. This publication is part of the overall program of the Institute, as endorsed by its Board of Directors, but does not necessarily reflect the views of individual members of the Board or the Advisory Committee.

The Council on Foreign Relations takes no institutional position on policy issues and has no affiliation with the US government. All statements of fact and expressions of opinion contained in all its publications are the sole responsibility of the author or authors.

*This book is dedicated to
my wife and partner, Anna.*

Contents

Preface

No nation is increasing its impact on the global economy as rapidly as the People's Republic of China at the close of the twentieth century. At the same time, few economies are as poorly understood. Hence the Institute has addressed priority attention to China in recent years with publications including Nicholas Lardy's *China in the World Economy* (1994); our recent *Measuring the Costs of Protection in China*, conducted in partnership with the Unirule Institute in Beijing; and a series of working papers by Marcus Noland and others. Richard N. Cooper is currently working on *China's Entry to the World Economy*, our next major release on China.

The availability and comparability of data on China have improved markedly in recent years, but much about the Chinese economy remains mysterious. The conditions of competition and business operation are especially obscure within China, behind its shrinking border barriers to trade. As Edward M. Graham and J. David Richardson chronicle in our 1997 study *Global Competition Policy*, these conditions have become the new frontier of commercial negotiation and frequently create international conflict because they lie outside the competence of the World Trade Organization (WTO). At the suggestion of Leslie Gelb, president of the Council on Foreign Relations, with whose cooperation *Behind the Open Door* was prepared, the Institute decided to address these questions by examining the experience of the foreign business community in China. This firm-specific approach is unusual for the Institute but is essential to the special challenges of gauging China's economic trajectory and judging, for example, whether it will more resemble open-market Hong Kong or dirigiste Japan in the future.

To conduct the study, the Institute and the Council identified nearly one hundred expatriates who provided the bulk of the data for this study. Institute Research Fellow Daniel H. Rosen then used this cohort to develop a comprehensive portrait of the challenges and opportunities facing foreign enterprises in China today. The analysis goes beyond the tricks of doing business, however, setting these foreign experiences in the broader context of both Chinese policy and corporate strategies themselves. The results provide food for thought for policymakers, including those in the United States, who have often mistaken commercial pitfalls encountered in China as policy problems caused by the central government and have underestimated the tendency of multinational firms to create their own difficulties.

Rosen's research also suggests that the positive social impact of foreign enterprises in China has been underestimated. His results depict, for example, a group of expatriates profoundly involved with virtuous reengineering of the employer-employee relationship in China, eager to augment with training and career development the ability of their local workforces to add value and expand the scope of operation.

Rosen's analysis provides both a rich and current picture of Chinese market conditions and responses to some of the most pressing questions facing Western decision makers in China today. Key issues addressed include the WTO negotiations, China's investment environment, and the balance between central and local authorities in directing the Chinese economy. In most cases, the views from the private sector differ significantly from those that permeate official channels and thus offer a fresh perspective on the US-China dialogue.

The book reaches four policy recommendations keyed to the United States: recognizing that some Chinese political reform may proceed faster without US prodding, refocusing policy initiatives on a narrower set of more practical concerns, expanding efforts to negotiate commercial agreements beyond the present WTO agenda, and designing a set of bilateral programs to assist China in building the institutions required to implement the many commitments that are being sought. In addition, Rosen's study raises important, hitherto understudied, questions about the Chinese marketplace itself that business and policy professionals alike will need to contemplate for some time.

Deep thanks go to the Council on Foreign Relations, and especially Les Gelb, for suggesting and contributing substantively to this study. The Council helped to identify and contact the expatriates to be interviewed, made a financial contribution to the project, and hosted formative planning sessions, an event to preview initial findings from the research, and a valuable session at their Hong Kong Forum to critique the penultimate manuscript. This partnership has been extremely rewarding and has greatly improved the final product.

The Institute for International Economics is a private nonprofit institution for the study and discussion of international economic policy. Its purpose is to analyze important issues in that area and to develop and communicate practical new approaches for dealing with them. The Institute is completely nonpartisan.

The Institute is funded largely by philanthropic foundations and private corporations. Major institutional grants are now being received from The German Marshall Fund of the United States, which created the Institute with a generous commitment of funds in 1981, and from The William M. Keck, Jr. Foundation and The Starr Foundation. The present study received generous support from the Freeman Foundation. The General Electric Fund provides financing for our extensive work on Asia. A number of other foundations and companies also contribute to the highly diversified financial resources of the Institute. About 18 percent of the Institute's resources in our latest fiscal year were provided by contributors outside the United States, including about 12 percent from Japan.

The Board of Directors bears overall responsibility for the Institute and gives general guidance and approval to its research program, including identification of topics that are likely to become important to international economic policymakers over the medium run (generally, one to three years), and which thus should be addressed by the Institute. The Director, working closely with the staff and outside Advisory Committee, is responsible for the development of particular projects and makes the final decision to publish an individual study.

The Institute hopes that its studies and other activities will contribute to building a stronger foundation for international economic policy around the world. We invite readers of these publications to let us know how they think we can best accomplish this objective.

C. FRED BERGSTEN
Director
November 1998

Acknowledgments

This book required the support and participation of an unusually large number of people. Director of the Institute for International Economics C. Fred Bergsten and Council on Foreign Relations President Leslie H. Gelb proposed the project and entrusted me to carry it out; for that I am deeply grateful. At various stages I benefited—particularly as a first-time author—from excellent guidance from business, academic, and China specialists too numerous to name. My colleagues at the Institute were a priceless resource, and I wish to thank in particular Gary Clyde Hufbauer, Edward M. Graham, and J. David Richardson. Hiroko Ishii and Erika Wada provided high quality research assistance, often under hectic time pressures. The editorial staff of the Institute worked hard with great patience, as usual. Special thanks to Erin Sullivan and Denise Groves who provided both the administrative support that an author juggling interviews on three continents dearly depends on and for their good cheer throughout the process. Most of all I must thank the hundreds of expatriate business professionals in China on whose experience this study is built: without their enthusiasm and trust, the project would not have been possible, and I regret that for confidentiality's sake I cannot thank each of them by name.

1

Gauging the New Chinese Marketplace

[Specialization] is not a good idea. We do not suggest this even with respect to our own provinces. We advocate all-round development and do not think that each province need not produce goods which other provinces could supply. We want the various provinces to develop a variety of production to the fullest extent. . . . The correct method is each doing the utmost for itself as a means toward self-reliance for new growth, working independently to the greatest possible extent, making a principle of not relying on others[.]

Mao Zedong (quoted in Riskin 1987, 206)

[We must] sail with borrowed boats, exit through other's borders, sing on rented stages, and make money on foreign land.

Qinghai provincial official (quoted in Yang 1997, 57)

Introduction

In the final years of the twentieth century, the United States has little choice but to formulate more practical and effective foreign and commercial policies toward the People's Republic of China. This imperative is made necessary by great economic, political, and social changes taking place in China in recent years. To succeed, the architects of this new strategy will need an accurate and nuanced understanding of the characteristics of today's China and of the directions in which China is most likely to evolve. Making those judgments from outside China is notoriously difficult, and it is not possible to do so unerringly. In the long-dominant strategic formula, China was seen as a transitional economy useful for its geopolitical weight but less critical from the perspective of US global eco-

1

nomic security; this view has become a poor guide for US policy as China has recast itself in the past two decades from totalitarian quagmire to looming capitalist (but still authoritarian) aspirant. Such transition has created contradictions, both within China and in the configuration of international economic and political power, leaving policymakers divided on how best to proceed. As a result, the evolution of US policy toward China largely stalled in the 1990s.

In order to help in crafting the commercial aspects of a dynamic policy toward China,[1] this study gets "inside" China in a novel way: by using the growing pool of expatriate professionals in China to uncover the country's development patterns. The time for exploring this group's insights is right. The Clinton administration has exhausted the utility of lambasting Beijing and moved toward a new strategic partnership. At the invitation of Jim Sasser, a former colleague turned ambassador, many members of Congress have visited China personally, and with the benefit of firsthand knowledge many have begun to tone down their annual indictments of China's trading status. At the same time, the need for US-China cooperation to address regional economic problems (especially the Asian financial crisis) and security problems (especially South Asian nuclear proliferation) provides a major impetus to find a new approach.

President Clinton's summit trip to Beijing in June 1998 marked a turning point in US-China relations. Though the visit achieved little in concrete terms, it worked to change perceptions of China in the United States and was used by Chinese leaders to demonstrate a new level of public openness in political debate. The results of the visit will require years to tally, but it is already clear that both countries have become much more open to compromise, negotiation, and cooperation.

A window for shaping a more constructive relationship has thus cracked open, but the strategic partnership remains a long way off. As the Chinese neglect public relations and US policy remains incoherent, popular misunderstandings continue to fester on both sides of the Pacific. In the United States, best-selling books such as *The Coming Conflict with China* (Bernstein and Munro 1997) are laden with alarmist predictions reminiscent of past red (and yellow) scares. In China, *Zhongguo Keyi Shou Bu* (China Can Say No), which apes a similarly titled Japanese book, illustrates how paranoid even younger Chinese writers can be about foreign interference in Chinese events.

In short, a new, better-informed strategy for dealing with emerging China must be devised to transcend these mutual misgivings and begin

---

1. Traditionally, it was maintained that foreign policy required little attention to commercial matters; however, US concerns about China, from human rights to nuclear proliferation, cannot be understood apart from international commercial realities. So whether one admits a commercial policy imperative or merely seeks greater economic understanding in the "realist" vein of traditional foreign policy, the relationship between commerce and policy must be studied.

to reconcile the outdated view of China common in the West with the reality of the surprising new China now taking shape. In the larger bilateral picture, the economic relationship between China and the United States is critical; it is the part on which the political and security demands of the region increasingly depend. Drawing on insights into the economic forces shaping the Chinese marketplace today, this study addresses pressing questions in US-China commercial relations (which requires a discussion of social and political topics as well).

Why Study the Expatriates?

For a number of reasons, China has long been poorly understood in the United States. First, China remains remote from the West linguistically, culturally, and geographically, with the hinterlands beyond the few largest cities more remote still. The difficulties of penetrating the complexities of Chinese society are heightened during this period of rapid change.

Second, Chinese officials often intentionally portray their governing regimes as more monolithic, orchestrated, and disciplined than they actually are, reflecting a long-held belief in the importance of presenting a unified front to foreigners. Too many Americans take this portrayal at face value—and thus mistake China for a bigger, badder Japan of "Rising Sun" vintage (never mind how quickly that bogeyman has fallen away in recent years). Third, even Western enterprises established in China sometimes misrepresent reality in order to curry favor, to talk up the markets or, conversely, to discourage potential rivals from following them into the market. The result is a distorted understanding of Chinese conditions, which can only lead to faulty US policy.

Because of these impediments to comprehending China by analyzing its formal economic regimes from the outside and by relying on normal government channels of interaction, this study brings non-Chinese eyewitness perspectives on present developments to the attention of Westerners. The eyewitnesses are primarily managers of foreign-invested enterprises (FIEs) in China, a growing group of dedicated observers as yet little surveyed for the purpose of policy analysis.[2] Their views will assist US policymakers in crafting more effective policies toward China, as well as helping analysts to review whether current policy adequately supports the endeavors of US firms in China.[3]

---

2. Although this cohort contributes to a literature on doing business in China, the foreign and commercial policy implications of their views are rarely explored.

3. That US outward foreign direct investment is beneficial for both the host country and the United States has been well established (see, e.g., Dunning 1958 for early work; Bergsten, Horst, and Moran 1978; Graham and Krugman 1995 on the reverse case of FDI in the United States; Graham 1996; and Rodrik 1997b for a discussion of the broader effects of globalization).

There are already many thousands of Americans (in addition to Europeans, Japanese, etc.) at work in China, managing as many as 250,000 Chinese employees on their payrolls.[4] By learning from the expatriates, many of the obstacles to a clear conception of China's position and direction can be avoided. It is not that the opportunity to draw on these experts was overlooked until now. Only recently has the pool of expatriate managers swelled to considerable numbers, and it is now time to exploit this new community of China expertise.

This study aims to reach a number of audiences. The policymaking community in the United States and developed-country capitals will find it useful to examine views from the private sector. Commonly, such views are filtered through so many parties that they have lost much substance by the time they get to policymakers; this study cuts out the filters. Corporate planners and other business professionals view aggressive policies from the US government as a key variable in their China operations, which is one reason why they too will find this analysis important.[5] Another is that despite their detailed knowledge of their own factories, they sometimes lose track of broader market trends addressed in this book. Academic readers with either general or business-related interests in China will find plenty of new questions worth pursuing, in addition to useful information in the interviews. Finally, Chinese government authorities will find here an honest appraisal of how well (or how poorly) their efforts to provide an attractive investment environment for foreign businesses are faring. The several reasons why Chinese authorities will read this study closely are the subject of one of the conclusions previewed in the executive summary and treated in depth in chapter 7.

A Methodology for Drawing upon Expatriates' Insights

The strategy of learning from the expatriates involved recruiting a set of firms willing to offer access to their managers in China and their frank opinions in return for anonymity. A core group of 13 firms participated; 48 managers from these firms were interviewed, while an additional 40 interviewees outside the core group were added ad hoc. Following their interviews, all reviewed the progress of the study.

---

4. American Chamber of Commerce in Beijing, "In China, the Twain Meet Almost Everywhere; Public's Association with US Industry, Culture, and Education Grows Daily," *Washington Post*, 24 June 1998, A26.

5. In interviews, several such planners identified US policy swings as the single greatest threat to their commercial success in the Chinese market.

These firms and individuals have unique insights, and the experiences on which they draw are extremely valuable. As the Beijing office director for one US conglomerate remarked in a 1997 speech to a US congressional delegation:

> The 17 people in the representative office of my company are in and out of more government offices, in and out of more state-owned enterprises, in and out of more private Chinese companies, and meet with more Chinese officials, managers, intellectuals, and workers in a month than the US embassy political and economic officers see in a year. I make that observation as a former military attaché (personal communication).

As useful as this methodology is, qualifications must be kept in mind. The views presented are oriented toward commerce, without pretense of disinterest. They can be expected to differ from the observations of political scientists, activists, or anthropologists. Moreover, expatriate investors in China and exporters on the other side of Chinese tariff barriers might disagree. For example, a German investor inside China may take comfort in the same external tariffs that are anathema to his exporting rivals in Bavaria.

The number of enterprises that can be involved in such a study is limited. Over 120 interviews were conducted, of which 88 were systematically explored for substance (the rest were culled for material as well, though somewhat less thoroughly). The sample was biased toward US manufacturing firms, but significant discussions with Europeans, Japanese, and overseas Chinese in Hong Kong and elsewhere were also included. A size bias is present, that is, most were large firms. While an effort was made to canvass as broad a selection of industries as possible, not all sectors were examined.[6]

Questionnaires and wide-ranging interviews were used to draw out information from interviewees. Though the study employs academic literature, press reports, and business analyses to flesh out and fill in parts of the story, these interviews were the primary source and determined all the "specific issues" identified. The participants, ranging from directors of China operations to plant managers to lobbyists, were asked to describe both the experiences of their firms in general and the focus of their daily work in particular.[7] Once the interviews were complete, remarks were grouped together by topic: for example, "comments about firm motivations," "importance of management control," "distribution," "legal issues," or "the role of relationships and connections." After related groups of comments and company documents were put together with

---

6. See further appendix B, on methodology, which also includes a descriptive list of interviewees.

7. Local Chinese employees also provided background information, but the study intentionally focuses on the expatriate perspective.

published and unpublished materials, principal business functions were assessed. These functions are

- negotiation and establishment (chapter 2),
- human resources and staffing (chapter 3),
- productivity and production management (chapter 4),
- ex-factory distribution and marketing (chapter 5), and
- legal obligations and privileges of ventures (chapter 6).

Though it was rare to find perfect consensus across industries and locations, the comments of expatriates revealed clear patterns and trends.

In addition to discussing broad themes, respondents described specific challenges. These groups of issues are listed in the concluding table to each chapter. The analytic section of each chapter examines the implications of these themes. How should these many topics be thought about, and which of them deserve the most prompt attention from readers concerned with policy? To answer this, four "drivers" of business problems are postulated: transitional problems, self-imposed problems, policy problems, and market structure problems. Distinguishing among these causes helps us to focus on those commercial concerns that foreign policy activism can affect and set aside those beyond the reach of policy intervention. Far too often, all issues regarding China have been seen as policy issues, and if this study does no more than uproot that tendency, then it will have succeeded.

Transitional problems reflect the adjustment of China's rapidly evolving economy from statism to the market. While Chinese authorities can marginally soften the impact of such problems, they are to a great extent inevitable and must be weathered.[8] For example, shortages of skilled labor will plague China for some time as a result of high growth rates and inadequate capacity for training key types of professionals. The solution is to develop greater training capacity and the market incentives to pull people into school and then match them with employers. It is important to recognize these transitional adjustments as such, because misdirected intervention on the assumption that they are policy problems could hinder efficient outcomes or make things worse.

One of the least-noted dimensions of the foreign commercial experience in China is the second category: *self-imposed problems*. For many reasons, foreign investors sometimes have entered the Chinese market hastily,

---

8. Though present (as opposed to past) policy cannot be blamed for transitional problems, it can play an important role in facilitating the process of transition.

sometimes recklessly. Often they have relied on data, partners, and assumptions that would never pass muster at home. The relative dearth of home-country analysts capable of second-guessing managers in China has contributed to these lapses.

But by arguing that they simply use the best information available and that the Chinese market is just too large to ignore, firms hardly answer these criticisms. Once established, foreign investors have often declined to scale the cultural walls that separate the expatriates in the special economic enclaves from the real expanse of the Chinese market. New "compradors"[9] often make this too easy for them. Therefore, many of the priority themes identified in interviews with foreign professionals in part originate with the firms themselves.

There is no question that many of the phenomena treated in this study involve *policy problems*. Government intervention, only partially lessened by the press of market forces, still pervades China's economy. New policy activity—some of it virtuous, some misdirected, and some simply bad— issues forth from the seat of power at Zhongnanhai (China's executive leadership compound in Beijing), as well as from lowly town rat-control boards.

Last come *market structure problems*. These problems are due not to policies in place but to the *absence* of procompetitive policies on the part (primarily) of central authorities. The preventive measures needed to support an open market include antitrust rules and a host of others as the Chinese economy becomes more sophisticated. The policies must address concentration of market power, public and private collusion in restraint of competition, and anticompetitive practices. In their absence, barriers to market entry naturally arise (as do similarly unhealthy efforts to bar *exit* from the market), harming consumers—especially the poorest—and foreclosing opportunities for new entrants both foreign and domestic (that is, other Chinese firms). While these problems are not specifically caused by policy, they cannot be remedied without policy reform.

Beyond identifying the proper drivers behind each business concern that the expatriates identified, this analysis indicates—where policy problems are involved (i.e., policy and market structure problems)—whether the policy problem is central, provincial, or local in nature, and whether the issue is considered high priority by foreign investors. This additional information will help Western policymakers separate policy issues that deserve focused pressure on central Chinese authorities from less immediate concerns.

---

9. Compradors (a mildly derogatory term from the pre-Communist era) are local Chinese agents of foreign merchants, used as a buffer between local markets and foreign business (see chapter 2).

Questions Needing Answers

This study provides busy policymakers with a comprehensive description of the real China experienced by expatriates living and working there today. Because policymakers do not have time to spend in the field (and, when they are in China, rarely have ample time for these business professionals), chapters 2 through 6 of this study bring the expatriate insights to them instead.

Building on its descriptive analysis, this study also seeks to provide answers to a set of China-related questions more relevant than those that have preoccupied the United States in recent years. Policymakers in Washington have fixed their attention on human rights, intellectual property rights, and the bilateral trade balance. More recently, concerns about inadvertent technology transfer to the Chinese military as a result of deeper engagement has become a hot topic, as have allegations of Chinese interference in US political campaigns.

These are all more or less valid areas of inquiry; but are they the most important questions bearing upon the long-term interests of developed economies, especially the United States? Many China specialists are frustrated that this narrow agenda crowds out a host of other questions that deserve serious attention. The answers to these questions will suggest no less rich an agenda for US policy toward China than have the recurrent politicized debates.

This section briefly lays out 10 questions that will be dealt with more completely in chapter 7. The reader should keep them in mind throughout the upcoming chapters on specific business functions.

How Compatible Is China's Present Investment Environment with International Expectations?

There is no one answer to the question of what level of Chinese economic openness is acceptable to the major trading nations today. The United States, Japan, and the European Union have expressed different opinions. The openness of the investment environment is clearly significant, though, because a local presence is often a prelude to selling goods and services in China.

The establishment process remains a tool to exclude foreign ventures deemed counterproductive to development in China, though the large volume of utilized foreign direct investment (FDI) does demonstrate extensive openness. The remaining impediments—and reasons why money continues to flow despite them—are explored in depth in chapter 2, while inequalities in the subsequent operating environment are explored in chapters 3 to 6. The process for many sectors is often more open than it first appears, and foreign investors can sometimes enjoy as many privileges as restrictions once their enterprise is set up. Moreover, in gauging the compatibility of the Chinese marketplace with international expectations, no one can insist that China come up to Hong Kong standards. Absolute levels of openness differ among nations, reflecting, in part, legitimate social choices.

What matters most is whether China passes the tests of national treatment and most favored nation status in the context of its investment environment. FIEs in China face noncommercial burdens ranging from partnering pressures to corruption to residual restrictions on scope of operation. But there is no one standard of treatment even for domestic firms; indeed, foreign firms can enjoy a level of independence from state intervention greater than does the typical Chinese *state-owned* firm, tempering the national treatment concern. The most favored nation principle is also hard to assess. It is difficult to find a pattern of specifically *country-oriented* investment privilege. Even US firms reported little discrimination based on their "Americanness," despite threats and tensions over bilateral political flare-ups. These key indicators suggest that the "openness" of the Chinese market in an investment context is minimally acceptable.

Why, Given Its Domestic Worries, Should China Care about the Concerns of Foreign Enterprises?

There are five reasons for Chinese authorities to attend to FIE concerns. First, they want FDI to keep coming, which necessitates a profound understanding of the needs of FIEs today (mere tax holidays are no longer sufficient). Second, the distinction between Chinese and foreign firms is disappearing. Third, a growing number of purely domestic firms are calling for many of the same reforms as do FIEs, in order to compete on a more even footing with them. Fourth, China needs to play by international rules in order to nurture its access to foreign markets, and that means attention to the concerns of trading partners. Fifth, the technocrats in Beijing know that they must deal with these problems if China's economy is to be competitive.

Has China Really Turned a Corner, and Should Foreigners React Differently to Its New Leadership?

There is considerable evidence that China has broken with past trends. Changes include a more open market, less emphasis on performance requirements (see chapter 2), more attention to smuggling and petty corruption (see especially chapters 4, 5, and 6), and an expected reduction in the size of the Chinese bureaucracy. Moreover, interviewees expressed strong confidence in Zhu Rongji's leadership. These developments coincide with the passing of Deng Xiaoping, return of Hong Kong, and ascension of Zhu Rongji to the premiership, all seminal political watersheds.

The tangible political and economic developments inside and outside China suggest that the "new" China seen during President Clinton's 1998 summit meeting is genuine. This break with the past can be for the good (more open and fair competition) or for the bad (more private collusion and asset stripping), but it must be understood before any policy actions are taken. A Chinese leadership serious about deep domestic liberalization and structural adjustment deserves more robust consideration from the United States than does leadership committed to an inadequate status quo, and such leadership is in evidence.

Will the Chinese Economy Be More Open to Foreign Participation in the Future?

This is among the most difficult of questions to answer; the verdict thus far is mixed. The comments of expatriate managers today, especially those recorded in chapter 5, make clear that traditional policies restricting FIEs from competition have eroded.[10] Some Chinese authorities saw the inevitability of this long ago, while others continue to resist domestic competition from foreign firms even today. Foreign firms have made alliances permitting them to penetrate the Chinese firewalls. They are, to varying degrees, actively involved in distribution, service, and even retail sales. In their eagerness to grow, in many sectors they are shaping the first nationwide markets. While the number of FIEs grows, the most important indicator of openness to foreign firms is expanded scope of operation. And as documented in the following chapters, such expansion is taking place in many places and in many ways, though mostly still informally (i.e., without unambiguous legal encouragement to do so).

As firms find their way forward inside the economy, external barriers continue to fall. Trade negotiators haggle over a simple average tariff that has fallen to less than 15 percent in 1998 from over 40 percent in 1994 (though tariff peaks in key sectors remain a problem). Moreover, the revealed average tariff rate is below 4 percent, owing to myriad leaks and loopholes in China's customs system.

But despite these encouraging signs, problems remain. First, informal central policy still plays a major role in distributing economic opportunities in China, no matter how low the external tariff may be. Until firms establish a presence in China and learn to do business effectively, the marketplace can seem quite impenetrable taken sector by sector. Chapter 2 provides a good look at the role of partners in finding opportunities to sell. Second, even as policy barriers fall, other difficulties worsen—for exam-

---

10. See also the section of chapter 2 titled "Keeping Up with the Joneses and the Yamamotos."

ple, the (ironic) scarcity of qualified local workers, hindrances created by the firm themselves (particularly by misjudgments during establishment), and market structure problems.

Are Foreign Corporations in China Influencing Social Trends in a Positive Way?

Chapter 3 of this study, on human resources, documents the array of mechanisms by which FIEs in China are transferring skills, opportunities, and benefits to workers. As Chinese authorities disassemble the remaining elements of a command economy, such as subsidized housing and free burial services, the superior model of employment at foreign-run facilities and their positive impact on China are increasingly apparent—to *Chinese* policymakers, who seek to emulate not only their mechanistic efficiency but their cultures of opportunity and social mobility. However, Washington policymakers seldom acknowledge the social benefits of foreign involvement in China. Those who know of such effects often predict virtuous results from commercial activity alone, irrespective of social agendas; those who are ignorant of them tend to condemn the economists as myopic. Policymakers have elected not to disrupt the ability of US firms to do business in China not *in light of* foreign enterprise's social impacts, but *in spite of* them—often arguing incorrectly that these effects are negative.[11] Isolated negative incidents have shaped opinion, dissuading policymakers from championing the presence of US firms in China.

Will World Trade Organization Accession Address the Commercial Priorities of China's Trading Partners?

Despite the broad competence of the World Trade Organization (WTO) to manage international trade, important Chinese policy problems remain outside its purview. The organization's agreement on investment (Trade-Related Investment Measures) opens the door to arbitration over performance requirements imposed on FIEs (discussed in chapter 2) but cannot prohibit several important types. The government procurement agreement is not required of China, nor are certain important sectoral agreements that are of keen interest to WTO members, including the United

---

11. For example, Rep. Chris Smith (R-NJ), in a 1996 missive, argues that the Clinton administration policy of "engagement" through "stronger economic and diplomatic ties" has led to worse human rights abuses (Smith 1996). Some members of Congress have taken the position, as did Sen. Craig Thomas (R-WY) on 12 September 1996, that "contact with the West through trade has let a genie out of the bottle that the regime in Beijing will never be able to put back" ("The Annual MFN Debate," Congressional Record 1996 (104th), page 510, 404). But even in those cases, the virtues of foreign business are depicted as abstract; the direct effects of employer-employee contact are not examined.

States. More important, the WTO does not yet squarely address the area of domestic competition—the problem of sales opportunities foreclosed not by public policy but by private actions.

I argue (especially in chapter 5) that as firms are transferred away from national ownership, local internal trade blockages will increase. These are not wholly private matters, given the involvement of lower-level governments in local enterprises and state policy lending among the remaining state-owned enterprises (SOEs). But the "corporatization" formula for shedding state ownership is afoot. This will create the sort of nationwide *private* foreclosure that foreign firms have complained about in Japan and have unsuccessfully tried to address through the WTO.[12] Therefore, rather than concentrate solely on the WTO, there should also be a discussion of commercial remedies in partnership with progressive Chinese leaders. This recommendation is bolstered by evidence that China is resigned to defer WTO accession until the dust of the Asian financial crisis is settled. The venue could range from the Asia Pacific Economic Cooperation (APEC) forum, to a bilateral competition discussion, and to a plurilateral "Competition Round" (or "Shanghai Round") initiated at Chinese suggestion.

Do Economic Trends Augur for Cooperation between US and Chinese Authorities, or Confrontation?

More trade between China and the United States will inevitably bring more commercial disputes but not necessarily more conflict. Canada and the United States have had as many trade disputes with one another as any other couplet of nations. That does not mean that their commercial relationship is not healthy. The rapid growth of new commerce portends transactional disputes, as explored in chapter 6. In fact, this analysis suggests a very significant role for cooperation between US and Chinese economic authorities.

The most problematic foreclosures of markets will increasingly involve private actions, not policy, actions that will probably harm Chinese firms even more than FIEs. Indeed, they are already producing harmful outcomes, and the United States and China share an interest in avoiding further development along these lines. The costs to China are high: exacerbated regionalism and urban-rural division. And the United States does not wish to face another marketplace that, like Japan's, is dependent on exporting because of rigid domestic trade impediments. That dependence would hamper China's ability to assume a regional or global external pol-

---

12. Importantly, this will be a concern not just for FIEs but for nonlocal Chinese firms as well, some of which already complain bitterly about being locked out (of the Shanghai auto market, for example).

icy, as the United States and other G-7 nations desire. Therefore, there is strong logic on both sides in favor of Sino-US cooperation to build capacity and a common agenda to support each other's procompetitive regulatory functions (see the "Competition Round" suggestion in the previous point). The blind eye turned toward Japan's domestic practices during the Cold War is not an option for China, and Chinese leaders understand that.

Will China's Central Government Remain the Conductor of Chinese Reforms?

Throughout this study (but especially in chapter 2), expatriates describe the tensions between central and local authorities and limits on Beijing's ability to compel local behavior. While FIEs initially welcomed local autonomy as allowing greater freedom from bureaucratic constraint, many interviewees have recently come to realize how the lack of national preeminence frustrates their desire to expand beyond compliant local partnerships. The US national interest is clearly in bolstering Beijing's regulatory power as well, as bilaterally negotiated agreements of all stripes are worthless without the ability to implement them locally.

This microeconomic study does not clearly predict how this tension will be resolved. Several interviewees judged the strong center and significant devolution of control scenarios to be equally likely. Central authorities are using FIEs to help train policymakers to deal with modern commercial regulatory tasks such as legal authorization, rescinding some licenses granted by localities that exceeded national guidelines, and providing more rational compliance mechanisms; these are essential for the strong center scenario. Moreover, both wealthier provinces (fearful of potential social unrest in a time of transition) and poorer provinces (still dependent on fiscal transfers from the wealthier regions) will continue to look to the center for help. Given the convergence of domestic, FIE, and foreign government interests in a robust central regulatory and security authority, the study concludes that the center will bear responsibility for China's reforms for some time, perhaps to an even greater degree in the future than today.

What Is the Prognosis for Foreign Firm Performance in China in the Coming Years?

In 1996 the Council on Foreign Relations' James Shinn edited *Weaving the Net*, a study on engaging with China. If this were concerned solely with the prospects for FIEs in China over the next five years, it might be titled *Leaving the Net*, a study in disengaging from Chinese partners. It is extraordinary how many expatriate managers in China still privately brag about their cozy relationships with local government entities, regulators, established firms, or other power brokers who made them adopted children and brothers in the fiercely contested Chinese market. But as the family grows, so do quarrels, which impede productivity (discussed in chapter 4). Will anyone be bragging about cozy relationships in five years?

Management analysts have observed "phases" of FIE development in the Chinese market.[13] In the first phase, businesses explore the Chinese market and make initial investments to get established and learn how things work. The second phase involves efforts to optimize productivity, to market brand names, and to identify distribution channels. The third phase brings acceptance as a local entity committed to China for the long term and, presumably, the right to compete aggressively within the Chinese market.

The number of foreign firms that have reached phase three is still small compared to those at earlier points. Most FIEs arrived in China in the first half of the 1990s, and many of them are experiencing difficulties dealing with sometimes intractable partners. The prognosis for future FIE performance is of course affected by market conditions, the resolution of the financial crisis across Asia, and a host of other factors. All other things being equal, however, many expatriate managers point to the relations between foreign firms and their Chinese partners as the most telling determinant of FIE performance for the coming years.

The dynamics of these relationships are discussed in chapter 2, particularly as regards venture format, and in chapters 4 and 5, regarding productivity and ex-factory issues respectively. Pertinent evidence includes a shift toward wholly owned foreign enterprises (WOFEs) and away from joint ventures (JVs), buyout or reduction of some Chinese partner shares in existing JVs, and increasing acceptance of Sino-foreign partnerships that limit foreign control only on paper. It appears that foreign firms increasingly will rise or fall on the basis of their own business plans, unhelped and unimpeded by shotgun marriages. Incumbents already stuck with indissoluble arrangements are likely to fare marginally worse, while the new wave of establishers will have a better chance of succeeding in the Chinese market. To genuinely separate commercial and political interests, and to deliver improved prospects for foreign and domestic firms alike, Beijing must ensure that public, centrally directed cronyism is not merely replaced with private or locally directed cronyism. As such wholesale privatization of business and government is a new phenome-

---

13. Several interviewees expressly rejected this three-stage model of business development in China, claiming that it offers a false trajectory and creates low expectations. They insisted instead that a firm should have its eyes clearly fixed on a path to profitability before ever signing a contract in China, denying the need to "bleed for some years" en route to success. Surveys by the EIU suggest that many successful firms turn profits in under three years, less time than the three-stage model would suggest is necessary. To many of the managers interviewed, however, the stage model did seem valid.

non on such a large scale and with so little market-oriented heritage, the outcome is naturally difficult to predict.

Is China a Source of Endless Excess Capacity That Will Threaten Other Economies?

China plays a leading role in the debate over the existence of a global capacity glut. It has even been suggested that new Chinese capacity, combined with a supposedly cheap renminbi policy after 1994, precipitated the Asian financial crisis in 1997.[14] Such misapprehensions arise because the situation within China is not understood.

Internationally, the shift of production to China reflects not so much an addition to capacity as a transfer of capacity along lines of comparative advantage. Economies that had some years ago lured lower-value-added industries away from nations such as the United States and France now were being forced to move up the value chain themselves (see Noland 1996, 14–19). Unwise capital allocation and insulation from the market, which blocked signals that capacity had to be shifted, led to problems.

But *within* China, overcapacity is a salient concern in competition to serve domestic markets, mostly because of naive local investment strategies and barriers to market exit. The result is more a Chinese "sectoral glut" than a global one, but the sectors affected are of particular interest to trade negotiators. Expatriates typically argue that their firms would survive were constraints on competition and bankruptcy in China lifted. So far, Chinese policymakers have tried to address their sectoral overcapacity problems with an approach less consistent with the WTO spirit, limiting entry to and exit from overcrowded markets. This is not an efficient way to use the scarce resources within the Chinese economy.

Results

The analysis presented here challenges assumptions about the scope of policy orchestration in China. It suggests that the frustrations of foreign firms can be self-generated, can reflect issues of transition, or can result from market structure problems—and thus may not be easily remedied by decree from Beijing. Once it is recognized that Beijing is incapable of delivering some of the policy concessions sought, finite negotiating energies can be redeployed. This point underscores the need to provide some

---

14. See Fernald, Edison, and Loungani (1998), Rosen, Liu, and Dwight (1998), and Noland et al. (1998) for arguments countering these incorrect views. China's renminbi actually appreciated in real terms following consolidation of the exchange rates at the end of 1994.

support for China's central authority, or at least to temper enthusiasm for the rapid devolution of authority away from Beijing.

By categorizing the obstacles to FIE operation, this study supports more accurate analyses than those focused on Chinese border barriers or negotiating positions alone. Formal positions lag behind developments in China—because policy takes time to formulate, as elsewhere, but also because China's central bureaucracy lacks capacity, is removed from the marketplace, and refuses to acknowledge some practices for ideological reasons (or out of embarrassment). By the time authorities liberalize distribution, for example, one can be assured that foreign participation will have had been taking place for some time: indeed, it already is.

The US government should not disregard Chinese official positions in setting its negotiating objectives: that is not how government-to-government negotiations work. But national strategy and negotiating objectives are not the same thing either; strategy should fully account for the realities on the ground, no matter how far removed from those realities Chinese negotiators insist on staying in the short term.

This study concludes by examining the implications of China's WTO membership, especially regarding aspects of market access that the organization cannot promise to address in its current form, and hence draws out an alternative strategy for progress. Efforts should focus on securing full scope of operation for FIEs in China up and down the value chain, a goal closely tied to dissuading China from relying on a Japanese or South Korean model of industrial policy for growth. The views of foreign managers regarding social trends and conditions suggest that political change in China is closer than widely believed. In light of these perspectives, how can US firms and the US government join efforts to influence this process positively when it comes? That is, how can they help China to achieve the most efficient economic governance possible, sacrificing the least liberty and entrepreneurialism for the greatest welfare gains to China's people: that is the question.

2

Foreign Enterprise Establishment in China

A contract? A contract is an excuse to have dinner.

Interviewee #18

Introduction

Chinese authorities are keen to lure foreign investors into the Chinese marketplace, and foreigners drawn by China's growth have been eager to leap into that market. These overlapping interests have led to huge flows in FDI into China (see figure 2.1), as exemplified by investments by General Motors, Motorola, and Kodak, each exceeding or pledged to exceed $1 billion. The trade flows have followed, as shown in tables 2.1, 2.2, and 2.3. For all the dollars (and yen, won, etc.) and all the projects, the process begins with the investment approval system and negotiations for permission to establish a business in China. By recounting the experiences of expatriates in dealing with that system, this chapter will help to determine the compatibility of China's implicit investment regime with international expectations. In addition, it examines the policy implications of those aspects that fall short of expectations.

The existing formal process does act as an entry barrier to many foreign firms, whether directly or indirectly. For many foreign producers, being denied a local presence in China is tantamount to being denied market access for their goods and services. This results largely from the intricacies of managing sales and distribution in China, and many of these com-

Figure 2.1 Foreign direct investment in China, 1991-97

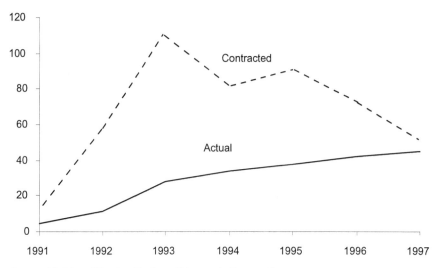

Billions of dollars

Source: Ministry of Foreign Trade and Economic Cooperation.

Table 2.1 US-China trade, 1980, 1985-97 (millions of dollars)

	US data			Chinese data		
	Exports	Imports	Trade balance	Exports	Imports	Trade balance
1980	3,754	1,058	2,696	na	na	na
1985	3,856	3,862	−6	2,352	5,090	−2,738
1986	3,106	4,771	−1,665	2,632	4,717	−2,085
1987	3,497	6,293	−2,796	3,037	4,831	−1,794
1988	5,021	8,511	−3,490	3,380	6,631	−3,251
1989	5,775	11,990	−6,215	na	na	na
1990	4,806	15,237	−10,431	5,179	6,588	−1,409
1991	6,278	18,959	−12,681	6,159	8,008	−1,849
1992	7,418	25,728	−18,310	8,594	8,901	−307
1993	8,763	31,540	−22,777	16,964	10,687	6,277
1994	9,282	38,787	−29,505	21,461	13,894	7,567
1995	11,754	45,543	−33,789	24,714	16,118	8,596
1996	11,978	51,495	−39,520	42,841	26,685	16,156
1997	12,805	62,552	−49,747	na	na	16,300

na = not available.

Note: US exports are valued free alongside ship (FAS), and US imports are valued on a customs valuation basis.

Sources: *U.S. Foreign Trade Highlights,* 1996, US Department of Commerce; *China Statistical Yearbook,* 1997, China State Statistical Bureau; http://www.uschina.org/press/trade5–6.html, July 1998, US-China Business Council.

Table 2.2 Japan-China trade, 1985-97
(millions of dollars)

	Exports	Imports	Trade balance
1985	12,477	6,783	5,694
1986	9,856	5,653	4,203
1987	8,250	7,401	849
1988	9,476	9,859	−383
1989	8,516	11,146	−2,630
1990	6,130	12,054	−5,924
1991	8,593	14,216	−5,623
1992	11,949	16,953	−5,004
1993	17,273	20,565	−3,292
1994	18,682	27,566	−8,884
1995	21,931	35,922	−13,991
1996	21,890	40,551	−18,661
1997	21,724	41,797	−20,073

Note: $1.00 = ¥121.10

Source: Custom Statistics, http://www.mof.go.jp/trade-st/199728c.htm#KUNI, July 1998, Japanese Ministry of Finance.

Table 2.3 China's top trading partners, 1996 (percentages)

	Share of China's exports	Share of China's imports	Share of total trade
Japan	20.4	21.0	20.7
NIEs-3[a]	9.3	23.2	16.0
United States	17.7	11.6	14.8
Hong Kong	21.8	5.6	14.0
European Union	13.1	14.3	13.7
ASEAN-4[b]	3.4	4.9	4.1
Rest of the world	14.3	19.3	16.7
Regional subtotals			
East Asia[c]	54.9	54.8	54.8
APEC[d]	75.4	71.6	73.6

a. NIEs-3 comprises Singapore, Taiwan, and South Korea.
b. ASEAN-4 comprises Philippines, Indonesia, Malaysia, and Thailand.
c. Japan, Hong Kong, ASEAN-4. and NIEs-3.
d. The 18 member economies of the Asia-Pacific Economic Cooperation forum.

Source: Australia Department of Foreign Affairs and Trade, East Asia Analytical Unit (1997a, 153).

plexities arise from central-level commercial policies. But the temptation to blame everything on policy is wrong: transitional, self-imposed, and market structure problems are present as well, and they cannot be attributed to present government actions (though they may reflect a lack of government intervention or past practice).

The process of establishing a business has evolved so significantly since reforms began in 1979 that the pioneers who stepped into the Middle Kingdom 20 years ago would barely recognize the process today. The snapshot presented later reflects mid-1997 conditions; a review of how the process evolved over the reform period can be found elsewhere.[1] While the regime will continue to change in years to come, this description should retain its relevance as a benchmark for some time.

Three groups of issues surface repeatedly for those establishing a presence in China. The first pertains to market information, as they need to accurately assess the Chinese market. Problems include gaps in pertinent market information—the economy is evolving so rapidly that accurate statistics are difficult to collect—and local firms' use of privileged information (such as bid selection criteria) to monopolize commercial opportunities. Potential investors are also uncertain about the behavior of other foreign firms in China, especially whether or not they are forming collusive business-government partnerships to foreclose markets.[2] Finally, foreign investors are hampered by ignorance and error as they try to understand Chinese politics, psychology, and culture.

The second set of issues involves the strategic choices foreigners make about their operations. These include questions of market proximity and geographic location. Investors must position themselves along various strategic continuums, as they decide to prioritize domestic market sales or to export; to employ high-level technology that must be guarded or, more timidly, to transfer outmoded equipment; to aggressively push to do things the foreign way under strong expatriate leadership or to pursue a more cooperative approach built around separate spheres of control; to begin with a loss-leader venture meant to make friends and collect local experience or to focus immediately on profitability. Often (but not always) these dimensions apply across sectors. As will become clear, they are interrelated; the choice about one may alter decisions about others. While the foreign investor must take responsibility for the final framework negotiated, authorities at various levels affect the choices through policy, informal pressure, or both.

---

1. See, e.g., IMF (1993), Shirk (1994), Lardy (1994), and Naughton (1996b) for a range of perspectives.

2. Susan Schwab, dean of the School of Public Affairs at the University of Maryland and a keen analyst of commercial conditions in China, observes further that information gleaned in one province has little value in other provinces (personal communication, 16 June 1998).

Third are the specific tactical details that must be considered during negotiations. These include structural decisions involving management (i.e., control), labor, finance, and phasing; bargaining over incentives (such as tax holidays) and obligations (such as requirements regarding exports or local content); and interpreting the sometimes ambiguous laws that provide the half-enforced, half-ignored guidelines for foreign investment.

There is much interplay among the three areas. For example, the careful selection of strategic partners will facilitate information gathering; but the better connected a partner, the greater the concessions that the negotiating authorities may seek to extract on its behalf. There is a traditional Chinese view, embraced by many FIE managers as well, that market information, a smooth negotiation, and prosperous operations naturally flow from the "right relationship." It is often contrasted with the preoccupation (characterized as Anglo-American) with legalities and due diligence. In the aftermath of the Asian financial crises of 1997, however, many Chinese authorities are showing a new interest in more Western modes of vetting investors. Market evaluations based on transparent macro- and microeconomic data, investment strategies judged against a matrix of commercial, regulatory, and demographic variables instead of a web of friendships, and finally negotiations guided by rules of law look increasingly like the way of the future in China.

The Investment Regime

Before turning to the issues that expatriates highlighted, a brief sketch of China's explicit investment regime and the basic steps FIEs pass through is in order.[3]

Foreign investment in China is today covered by laws, implementing regulations, and a variety of specific, though less formal, guidelines. The 1978 Law on Chinese-Foreign Joint Ventures was the first legal instrument to cover FIEs, followed by implementing regulations in 1983. Regulations extended the law to wholly owned foreign enterprises (WOFEs) in 1989 and 1990. In 1986 the State Council handed down the 22 Articles, which clarified details of FIE obligations and incentives. All along, circulars and notices have held forth on specific questions. In the mid-1990s, industry-specific guidance (discussed later) officially set down the government's investment priorities, which would-be investors previously had only been able to infer on an ad hoc basis.

---

3. This is by no means a comprehensive account. More details can be found in the publications of the US-China Business Council, the China-related publications of the Economist Intelligence Unit, and increasingly at Internet sites focused on China (e.g., the website of the US Embassy in Beijing, http://www.usembassy-china.gov/english). See also the commercial guide of the US Foreign Commercial Service available at National Trade Database (NTDB) websites such as www.flatrade.org/CCG/china.htm.

Thus today, unlike the early 1980s, most rules governing foreign investment and investors are published and known. The intentions of central authorities are generally clear, though to what lengths they will go to prevent local authorities from circumventing them is an important unresolved (if not untested) question. That foreign investors are denied rights of establishment for political or economic reasons in numerous important sectors is the subject of much contention. China's trading partners are not likely to concede them, and thus as China grows more eager for full integration with the world economy, these policies may change. For example, FIEs are involved in distribution to an extent seemingly at odds with policy, so while this sector is the focus of pivotal talks with China over accession to the WTO it is important to remember that often in China the official line and reality diverge substantially.

Guidelines for Investment

Prior to the central government's 1995 promulgation of Provisional Regulations for Guiding the Direction of Foreign Investment (hereafter called the Guidelines),[4] sectoral investment priorities were treated as internal information and were not formally available. The revised version of this significant document is included as appendix A of this book. For the first time, the Guidelines stated publicly a top-level design, by industry, for approving and disapproving the establishment of FIEs, including whether the WOFE or JV was preferred or required. They provide both prescriptions and proscriptions, with four categories of project: *encouraged*, *restricted*, *prohibited*, and *permitted*.

Encouraged ventures, such as manufacture of equipment for reclaiming wasteland, can expect a warm reception; management will enjoy greater freedom of control and access to incentives, with fewer performance requirements. Restricted sectors, such as manufacture of elevators, require that the foreign investor justify the enterprise by demonstrating some advantage to China (in the encouraged category, the benefits are assumed). Usually manufacturers are restricted because the sector already contains entrenched competitors not eager for more competition in the domestic market (and shielded to date by the external protection regime). Prohibited sectors include industries in which competition with domestic firms seems virtually unthinkable, such as in the area of traditional herbal medicines, as well as those sectors thought to concern national security (e.g., mainte-

---

4. Howson (1997) refers to them as the "Industrial Investment Catalogue Guiding Foreign Investment." They were issued jointly by the State Planning Commission, the State Economic and Trade Commission, and the Ministry of Foreign Trade and Economic Cooperation (MOFTEC).

nance of electric power grids) or to have the potential to harm the country (e.g., moviemaking, prostitution, casinos). Finally, the permitted category is a neutral catchall for any areas not assigned to the other three categories.

In practice, vague language in the restricted category permits central authorities (who automatically review some projects and have the final say on all) to arbitrarily reject projects they object to; ventures in encouraged sectors can also be blocked. Conversely, some ventures in prohibited industries have involved foreign investors despite the Guidelines: they do in fact function as *guidelines*, not absolute rules.

The real value of these categories for investors is not in declaring that casinos are prohibited and inland water treatment joint ventures encouraged; such patterns of approval and disapproval had already been widely recognized even though they were officially regarded as confidential matters of state, or *neibu*. Rather, by putting policy on the record the Guidelines temper the arbitrary character of approvals and disapprovals and preclude some local-central stalemates over technicalities. Moreover, promulgation of the Guidelines signals that the period of central government experimentation is winding down: the categories make clear which sectors, broadly speaking, should be closed off from foreign participation and which thrown open. That written commitment has given provincial officials the confidence to grant approval to some projects that previously would have waited for a wink from Beijing, thus reducing the time required for establishment.

According to official Chinese statistics for FDI by sector in 1996, the 24,556 projects approved that year had an average value of just under $3 million. Given the practice of requiring central approval only for projects larger than $10 million (or $30 million in designated areas, including most of coastal China, where investment is heaviest), and notwithstanding cases in which restricted-sector status made central approval necessary, local authority should have sufficed for the great majority of these projects. The significance of the $30 million cutoff (there are many $29.9 million projects in China) will be discussed later.

The Guidelines are not immutable; periodic adjustments should be expected, as occurred in December 1997. However, they do make abrupt changes in approval policy less common. Some changes would be welcome: important areas remain inadequately addressed by the Guidelines. Regarding distribution and services, for example, central authorities have agreed to open the door only slowly, mostly through a process of "creeping interpretation"—that is, a reliance on administrative guidance rather than laws and regulations. Thus foreign ventures are popping up in the casino gaming industry (unambiguously prohibited); there are wholly foreign-owned fuel service stations where there should not be (especially in Guangdong); foreigners are running distribution centers; and cellular giants quietly help manage phone networks even while they seek approval of the right to do so.[5] Cultural and media realms have also been infiltrated: foreign multiplex developers are pushing to establish movie theaters (interview #57) while financial news services, after a tussle with official Xinhua news, have been given the green light to operate (#86).[6]

It is broadly acknowledged that authorities do not really care about FIEs overstepping the guidelines in some areas. Dunkin' Donuts of the United States, for example, is registered in Beijing as a manufacturing joint venture, because foreign enterprises are supposed to be "productive": that is, they are supposed to make useful things (while doughnuts are useful, they are not what Deng Xiaoping originally had in mind) (#87).[7] Thus, exceptions are made to the Guidelines when it serves a special interest to do so. A handful of foreign retailers have been permitted to open "superstores," such as a Sam's Club in Guangdong. Other enterprises are founded on still shakier grounds. Though foreign participation in telecommunications network management is prohibited, it is widely believed to occur (##20, 28). Explicit identification of a participant would probably lead to a crackdown, but that risk has not stopped investors. Discretion is the better part of valor in some markets, where a "don't ask, don't tell" policy prevails.

Along with the informal factors, official interpretations trickle down and shape how investment guidelines are implemented. In the revision published by the Ministry of Foreign Trade and Economic Cooperation (MOFTEC) in December 1997, new inducements for high-technology investors were in evidence. Redirecting investment policies in China, like turning a large ship, takes much time and exertion. Only after central authorities have demonstrated commitment to a policy does implementation take place at the local level and in remote locales. But foreign enterprises, by contrast, react more quickly to changes in central guidance, as they are more eager for a legitimating basis.

From the perspective of a potential foreign investor, therefore, China is not wide open. Investment in some sectors is banned, because of both commercial and security concerns; other areas remain difficult to invest in. The flow of investment that would be attracted by such straightfor-

---

5. On gaming industries, see EIU's *China Hand* (1996b, chapter 14); on fuel stations, interviews ##12 and 14, and EIU (1997, chapter 6); on foreigners involved in distribution, interviews ##1, 21, 76, and 83; and on telecommunications, interviews ##20 and 28.

6. US Treasury Secretary Robert Rubin hailed the move to allow foreign news services greater latitude in China during his September 1997 visit to China: "It suggests to me that Chinese authorities appreciate that you cannot have financial markets without access to the latest and best financial information" (see *Lateline* report, 26 September 1997, http://china.muzi.net/news/q/2179.shtm).

7. John Fernald, a China specialist at the US Federal Reserve, points out that food is treated as part of manufacturing in the standard international classification (SIC) of products; that the retail points of sales where the doughnuts are sold are the exceptional matter is something of a fine distinction (personal communication, 16 June 1998).

ward factors as low labor costs is thus heavily influenced by central policy. Most developing countries encourage certain kinds of investment; China is not alone in its investment goals (see figure 2.2).

China is pondering whether to redouble or reduce its industrial policy activism, including the investment regime. The Asian financial crisis seems to be changing Chinese thinking on this question, which until mid-1997 had been leaning toward a Japanese- or South Korean-style conglomerate-building endeavor. At a minimum, Chinese industrial policy ambitions are likely to be more modest as a result of the crisis, with fewer sectors earmarked for complete closure to foreign competition. But the basic steps for approval will remain, though perhaps in a more streamlined and less capricious form.

The Approval Process: Basic Requirements

The steps required to establish an FIE in China vary, depending on form of venture (JV or WOFE), industry, location, and size. In the case of an *equity* joint venture, the most common investment vehicle to date (see table 2.4), there are roughly six steps to establishment. The process described is adapted from a successful negotiation in late 1995 between an American conglomerate and an entity carved out from a government agency to act as the Chinese business partner:

1. The potential partners sign a *letter of intent,* then a *memorandum of understanding* (the latter is not standardized). These explore the options for cooperation and the objectives of the parties in the business venture: the foreign investor and the Chinese joint venture partner(s), which can be governmental or nongovernmental. This agreement probably followed a period of informal exploration and mutual sizing up.

2. Once the parties are clear on their objectives, a more detailed *project proposal* is prepared; this will be submitted to the overseeing authority responsible for the Chinese partner, under the authority of MOFTEC (or another ministry with responsibility for the industry in question) or its provincial and municipal subsidiaries. The package may include a *preliminary feasibility* study and background materials on the foreign partner, including financial documentation. Additional materials might include a justification for foreign participation, a list of technology to be transferred to the venture, an assessment of the physical location and impact of the venture, the structure of the venture, and the schedule of development. The overseeing authority may request additional materials at this time, and after revisions are made it may approve the project to the next stage. The project can be approved in as little time as a month (as in the case adapted here), or it can languish indefinitely in administrative limbo.

Figure 2.2 Comparison of commercial regimes, APEC and China

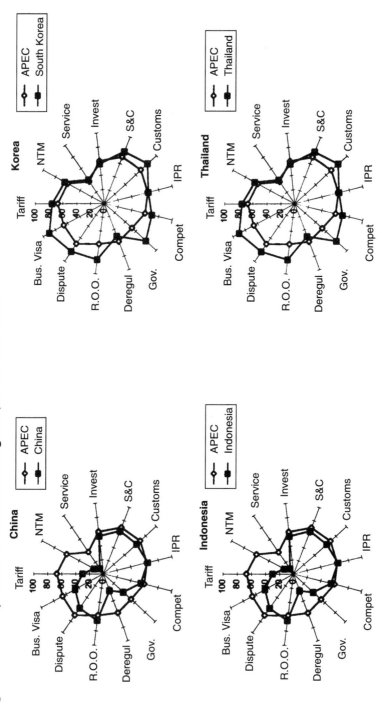

Note: These diagrams are based on final work by Ippel Yamazawa of Hitotsubashi University, Tokyo. The factors rated are (clockwise from top) tariffs, nontariff measures, service, investment, standards and conformance, customs procedures, intellectual property rights, competition policy, government procurement, deregulation, rules of origin, dispute mediation, and mobility of business people. Each is scaled from 0 (the worst regime) to 100 (a perfect regime).

Table 2.4 Number of FDI contracts by enterprise form, 1979-97

	Total	Equity joint venture		Contractual joint venture		Wholly foreign-owned venture		Joint exploration	
		Number	Percentage of total	Number	Percentage of total	Number	Percentage of total	Number	Percentage of total
1979-89	21,776	12,198	56.0	7,994	36.7	1,525	7.0	59	0.3
1990	7,273	4,091	56.3	1,317	18.1	1,860	25.6	5	0.1
1991	12,978	8,395	64.7	1,778	13.7	2,795	21.5	10	0.1
1992	48,764	34,354	70.4	5,711	11.7	8,692	17.8	7	0.0
1993	83,437	54,003	64.7	10,445	12.5	18,975	22.7	14	0.0
1994	47,549	27,890	58.7	6,634	14.0	13,007	27.4	18	0.0
1995	37,011	20,455	55.3	4,787	12.9	11,761	31.8	8	0.0
1996	24,556	12,628	51.4	2,849	11.6	9,062	36.9	17	0.1
1997	21,021	9,046	43.0	2,371	11.3	9,604	45.7	na	na

na = not available.

Note: Figures for 1997 are projections using MOFTEC and SSB data from October 1997.

Source: http://www.uschina.org/press/invest1.html, 15 July 1998, US-China Business Council.

3. Once approved by the overseeing authority responsible for the industry/sector (e.g., the Shanghai Tourism Bureau), the proposal and the authority's comments are passed on to the municipal (or other relevant) government, such as the Shanghai Municipal People's Government (perhaps to its "foreign investment office"), for *project registration*. Copies of the proposal must be circulated to all the pertinent departments in that government, such as the Bureaus of City Planning, Environmental Protection, and Fire Protection. Important decision makers in the government might be invited at this stage to visit demonstration facilities at the foreign investor's home operations.

4. Once the government grants registration of the project, the partners must prepare the *contract* and the *full feasibility study*. The feasibility study includes key information that affects the contract as well (it is not infrequently the main instrument for designing the venture).[8] These details include its structure (equity split in the case of a JV), employment and management (number and role of expatriates), local content to be used, export objectives if applicable, technology to be transferred, total investment and registered capital, source of financing, and expected rate of return. The feasibility study and contract will go through a comment and evaluation period during which the terms may be revised. They are then formally submitted to the government by the Chinese party for approval of *contract* and *articles of association*.

5. After the venture is approved, the partners apply for a *business license*, the legitimizing document granted by the licensing authority of the municipality, by the State Administration for Industry and Commerce (SAIC) at the national level, or by its subsidiaries at lower levels. The license formally establishes the venture and provides it with legal status.

6. Authorization to set up foreign exchange and other bank accounts, operating permits for facilities approved, residence permits for foreign staff, etc. are obtained by submitting the license to the respective authorities. The venture may begin operating.

Contractual joint ventures (CJVs) are less ambitious ventures used mostly for lower-value-added export-processing operations. They are considered to be short-term enterprises and have declined in number in recent years as other forms became more popular. Setting them up involves a similar set of steps; but because they are largely export processing, the occasionally contentious issues of performance requirements, management control, and finance and returns are not as complicated and the process is more streamlined. Furthermore, the definition of their op-

---

8. US firms might include certain terms regarding expropriation and third-party arbitration as well, as the United States and China do not have a bilateral investment treaty. Most of China's other major trading partners (Japan, Germany, and the United Kingdom) do.

Figure 2.3 Strategic trade-offs in the establishment process

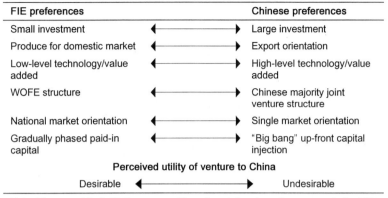

FIE preferences		Chinese preferences
Small investment	←——————→	Large investment
Produce for domestic market	←——————→	Export orientation
Low-level technology/value added	←——————→	High-level technology/value added
WOFE structure	←——————→	Chinese majority joint venture structure
National market orientation	←——————→	Single market orientation
Gradually phased paid-in capital	←——————→	"Big bang" up-front capital injection
	Perceived utility of venture to China	
Desirable	←——————→	Undesirable

Note: The more "desirable" a proposed investment, the closer it can come to the FIE preference side in each case. Most important, the obligations of the venture are somewhat fungible among the various trade-off areas.

eration is less statutory and more contractual. The matrix in figure 2.3 will clarify the trade-offs such firms might experience.

For WOFEs, as with JVs, the goal is approval by MOFTEC (or, better yet, its lower-level units).[9] In addition to the $30 million ceiling beyond which central-level approval is required,[10] WOFEs frequently trigger review by MOFTEC on other grounds.[11] In a number of sectors WOFE structures either are prohibited in the Guidelines or automatically require approval by the central authorities. Unlike those seeking joint ventures, potential WOFE investors must submit a lengthy assessment of the enterprise (known as a *baogao*) to the relevant people's government authorities (in the previous example, the Shanghai Municipal People's Government) *prior* to applying to the investment approval authorities. This report intends to establish accountability for the future requirements of the WOFE,

---

9. This discussion of the distinguishing characteristics of WOFEs owes a great deal to the trenchant analysis of Howson (1997).

10. Projects exceeding $30 million in total investment require central approval (by MOFTEC and the State Planning Commission); in the interior the limit is generally $10 million. Projects exceeding $100 million require State Council approval as well. These measures are ostensibly to deter profligate spending by local officials ill-prepared to negotiate with savvy foreign investors.

11. These include any reliance on allocation of state-distributed commodities, any impact on the national energy or transportation systems, an impact on the trade balance, a requirement for import licenses, etc.; in other words, there are almost limitless grounds for central review should the center wish to exercise that power.

and the local government must then certify that they can be met. This step presents foreign investors (and local authorities) with a substantial task, one that would be largely assumed by the Chinese partner in a JV.[12]

Differences in regulations governing the establishment of WOFEs affect their future operations in several ways, influencing management control, decision making, potential legal liability, and capital composition ratios. But the primary and defining difference is that WOFEs must satisfy one of two *performance requirements:* either a high export ratio (greater than 50 percent annually) or an advanced level of technology. As discussed later, these can be negotiated into JV contracts by Chinese authorities. For WOFEs, these requirements are theoretically a nonnegotiable statutory element, but in practice they are negotiated as well.

WOFEs, equity JVs, and contractual ventures represent the overwhelming majority of foreign ventures established in China today, and this study focuses primarily on the first two. However, the authorities are experimenting with a variety of new foreign investment structures, some of which will no doubt become more common. A Partnership Law was passed in early 1997, though it is being implemented slowly (Clarke, Howson, and Ganliang 1997). The recent Company Law now makes it possible for some foreign firms to more easily open branches. Joint stock companies, limited liability companies, holding companies, joint trading companies, and foreign retail, distribution, and captured finance companies are all forms being explored, though cautiously. Their proliferation reflects the maturation of China's economy, the deepening complexity of FIE needs, and the changing orientation of central authorities—increasingly outward—as they feel the effects of international economic events.

Challenges for Foreign Investors

The next topic is the concerns and observation of the expatriates interviewed for this study, most of whom have had considerable experience in grappling with the process of establishing a venture.

Market Information Issues

Why China Is Opaque

A foreign investor's first concern is market intelligence. While, as described already, the foreign investment regime and guidelines for investment promotion have become more transparent in recent years, the infor-

---

12. While this additional task is onerous, it can have a substantial payoff, as there will be fewer surprises down the road.

mation they provide barely begins to suffice. Surveys point to information gaps as primary FIE concerns. Several interviewees for this study described the need for inside information as the main reason why partnering with a favored Chinese entity is so important.

The difficulties of foreigners (and nonlocal Chinese, for that matter) in obtaining clear information on markets, economic trends, and other matters arise for a number of reasons. First, Chinese statistical data at all levels—local, provincial, and central—are subject to both intentional and unintentional biases. For example, production might be overstated to attract investors, or understated to avoid taxation: because the inaccuracies have so many causes, it is difficult to adjust for them.

Second, until recently private reporting on economic matters—which can help fill the gaps left by uncertain official statistics—was discouraged, and even prohibited. Seemingly mundane statistics were treated as state secrets, and reporters were threatened or occasionally imprisoned for violating national security when they provided basic economic information to mainstream media. Obviously, in such an environment good sources of market and economic analysis were hard to come by.

Third, in response to the growing demand for better economic information, the central government recently proposed to loosen its tight hold—but only to the extent of giving state-run Xinhua News Service a monopoly to disseminate official data. This idea did not go over well with the foreign community or with domestic businesses, long accustomed as they were to Chinese media that lied about even the weather. The initiative was rescinded, and economic consultancies both foreign and domestic are springing up to fill various needs.[13] Still, it will be some time before accurate information on basic economic indicators is freely available: information that ought to be provided as a public service gets held back so that government agencies told to be entrepreneurial might profit.

Fourth, the interviews for this study suggest that much of the information that firms depend on—to get approvals, learn about contracts, resolve disputes, appeal a customs duty rate, and the like—is gleaned from inside or "informal" sources. Inside information, in these cases, may concern the disposition of telecom purchasing authorities, or it may involve formal state policies that are *neibu*—that is, official policies not publicly promulgated but rather restricted to circulate among regulators. What could be called informal information reflects the ubiquity of *guanxi*, or "relationships" (the common English translation), and demonstrates how they shape commercial behavior. For example, the knowledge that a hypothetical Mr. Wang will oversee approvals for new licenses to distribute goods might tell a firm that partnering with Mr. Wang's cousin would secure

---

13. A number of consultancies have existed since the 1980s, distributing information from the outside within China (and thus unaffected by the Xinhua gambit). The concern, however, is good information on internal developments.

them a license, whereas partnering with that cousin's competitors would diminish their chances.[14] Other forms of informal knowledge include insight into a potential customer's creditworthiness: in the absence of modern credit rating agencies, hard-to-come-by local information is crucial.

Interviewees described the importance of having Chinese partner companies or sympathetic overseeing authorities provide them with the privileged information they needed to identify and exploit profitable opportunities and to avoid wasting time on chimerical ones. Such interaction is part of the nature of *guanxi*. To manage relationships and learn to profit from this information-processing landscape (which most Western executives would probably call corrupt on its face, as did several interviewees) is not easy, and it makes some uncomfortable. In many advanced economies, the same behavior would lead to charges of bid rigging, insider trading, and other transgressions too numerous to count. Adding to the difficulty, investors must navigate these information channels to reach agreement on the right venture, with the right partners, and in the right location, all before they even enter the Chinese market.

FIEs respond in several ways to these challenges. Many have introduced their operations in phases (discussed later), starting simply with a representative office to serve as a "learning center" and only gradually building up toward more value-added activities. Many firms enlist the services of overseas Chinese. These *huaqiao* (overseas) Chinese are more at ease casually plying clubs and corridors for information in local Chinese dialects; but they also have MBAs and engineering degrees and understand the psychology and imperatives of modern multinational firms. Throughout China today, and throughout the firms interviewed for this study, these multiculturalists make up an important share of management and represent a key strategy for dealing with information problems.[15]

A less successful information acquisition strategy is to rely entirely on joint venture partners, local authorities, or high-ranking patrons. Overly rosy analysis from these partners (combined with wishful foreign thinking, perhaps) regularly leads to trouble. Pro-China policies in neighboring countries can also create problems. For example, the government of Singapore has made large official investments in China and has strongly prompted Singaporean firms to set up operations in Singapore-bankrolled manufacturing parks. Bottom-line realism is dampening the enthusiasm of firms to oblige. *Business China*, a publication of the Economist Intelligence Unit (EIU), notes that Singaporean encouragement may have

---

14. Of course these same partners and authorities will have other relationships, too, and they will benefit from such knowledge as well, including proprietary information about an FIE, its pricing strategies, technology, and market share; so *guanxi* cuts both ways.

15. Weidenbaum and Hughes's *Bamboo Network* (1996) is a fascinating and readable account of the importance of the members of the Chinese diaspora in understanding Asia's modern business dynamism, with particular attention to their role in China.

harmed its firms: "[S]ome executives feel it may have made the companies even less prepared—complacent even—for the cutthroat competition in China" (15 September 1997, 9).[16]

The chairman of the China venture of a major Western agribusiness company observed that the responses of firms to the information problem varied by nationality: "Asian firms come in with a shotgun approach, and pare back to what works; [North American and European firms] tend to be much more about core competence" (#2). Interviewees with Japanese firms confirmed a greater inclination than most Western firms to negotiate and establish a larger number of FIEs (##65, 67, 68, 70). Many Asian respondents (both with Asian and Western ventures) thought it silly and self-defeating to react to poor information with hesitation and long, drawn-out due diligence. The preferred Japanese strategy, it seems, is to get in quickly; then, once the fog of uncertainty clears and it becomes apparent where the "money-spinners" are, poorly conceived ventures can be deprived of financial support and allowed to lie dormant. However, dotting the commercial landscape with moribund ventures has its downside: adverse effects on a firm's relationships in government and the private sector, on public perceptions, and on a firm's overall organizational structure.

Firms doing economic analysis are profiting from the FIE thirst for information. They have mushroomed along with FDI dollars, and restrictions on such operations are easing as Beijing becomes more aware of their importance. Chinese institutes both independent and quasi-independent now sell consulting services and analysis. Foreign and Sino-foreign companies are increasingly getting into this market (e.g., interviewee #79 heads a foreign-owned firm providing Western ventures with translations and analyses of stories related to their industries in the daily Chinese press).

Keeping Up with the Joneses and the Yamamotos

Interviewees for this study identified a second problem: poor information on the intentions of rivals from developed economies. This has fueled haste to establish commercial beachheads in China, leading to rushed agreements, poor planning, and excessive concessions on critical points such as control over management and distribution. The dash to the entrances was especially pronounced between 1993 and 1995, when contracted FDI went through the roof (see table 2.5), leading some observers to question whether investors had taken leave of their senses (#9).

Now, three to four years after that surge, the prevailing opinion is that this stampede was precipitated by foreign fears (reasonable at the time)

---

16. The same story notes that by contrast, Hong Kong investors who went into China without British hand-holding managed to keep expectations more closely in line with realities. Hong Kong entrepreneurs, however, rely on more immediate relationships than those characterizing the Singaporean industrial parks.

Table 2.5 FDI in China, 1991-97 and 1979-97 (millions of dollars)

	Total contracted	Total actual	US contracted	US actual	Japan contracted	Japan actual
1991	11,980	4,370	548	323	812	533
1992	58,124	11,008	3,121	511	2,173	710
1993	111,435	27,514	6,813	2,063	2,960	1,324
1994	82,680	33,767	6,010	2,491	4,440	2,075
1995	91,282	37,521	7,471	3,083	7,592	3,108
1996	73,210	42,350	6,920	3,440	5,131	3,679
1997	51,780	45,280	4,940	3,240	3,400	na
1979-97[a]	521,188	222,131	40,238	17,491	30,360	14,407

na = not available.

a. Cumulative.

Source: http://www.uschina.org/bas/invest.html, 24 July 1998, US-China Business Council.

that Chinese authorities would permit (or would not prevent) the efforts of the first movers to lock up markets. Limits on the availability of distribution channels needed to get one's product to markets (and restrictions on foreign entry into that critical sector) led to the belief that collusive arrangements could quickly blanket the marketplace; thus hasty establishment seemed necessary (a common view: e.g., ##7, 10, 12, 20).

In hindsight, those conclusions appear partly right and partly wrong; it is too soon to render a final verdict. In many sectors the number of distributors has actually increased, creating additional paths to market (see, e.g., #15). But few of these new agents can provide consolidated national coverage, and in the absence of national reforms to give FIEs control over their own distribution, producers in some sectors have made strides toward marketwide dominance. As the distributional foundations of concentrated market power solidify, Beijing leaders haggle in WTO talks over the very notion of foreigners' trading rights, while, ironically, big foreign players are already pushing into agreements with powerful local partners.

At the same time, the eroding ability of the center to reel in such players, together with the harsh wake-up call that has struck neighboring "tiger" economies practicing marketization without contestability, has increased Beijing's interest in moving against such collusion. Investors worry, however, that by the time Beijing perceives the damage that a collusive market structure can cause, first-mover companies will have secured unassailable positions.

Ignorance and Error

The two failures of information described already offer rational explanations for why investors establishing firms in China can misstep. Information lies at the heart of commerce today; denied adequate intelligence, any firm can falter. Yet foreign enterprises are not entirely blameless for their knowledge problems. A number of managers frankly identified simple ignorance and folly as also shaping their experiences (e.g., ##5, 26, 88).

Despite reams of evidence on mismanaged ventures, interviewees reported that they continue to observe new foreign applicants going through the establishment process badly, making errors such as ceding key control issues, negotiating with the wrong authorities, or greatly overestimating market potential (e.g., #46). These mistakes are not caused by the lack of available information or fears that competitors might achieve first-mover advantages: they are self-generated.

This study cannot accurately gauge the pervasiveness of such errors, but some respondents suggest they are very common. Reflecting on their own experience, managers often pointed to ignorance in the early stages of negotiation and establishment as the source of later operational problems ranging from difficulty protecting intellectual property to inability to set employee salaries. Even managers with sophisticated knowledge of the Shanghai or Guangzhou markets typically know little about the hinterlands.

Strategic Positioning Issues

Before entering into direct negotiations with Chinese authorities and partners, foreign firms must address a number of strategic questions. These reflect the investing firm's motivations and perceptions about the Chinese investment environment. The firm's success in grasping these questions and answering them is, of course, predicated on dealing successfully with the information challenges already described.

Foreign leverage to shape the venture varies by sector, size, and preferred location, which alter the calculus of approval. There are trade-offs, affected by how desirable the foreign investment is perceived to be (and how eager the investor is), that investors may make with the authorities. These choices determine the foreign firm's strategic position in the establishment process.

Figure 2.3 offers a rough model of how that strategic position can vary. It depicts six dimensions, each a continuum with a range of intermediate possibilities, on which foreign investors and Chinese authorities make trade-offs. Column I presents the preferences of FIEs, column II the preferences of Chinese approval authorities. To be sure, this is an oversimplification: for example, many FIEs strongly prefer to export, or start off with a big initial investment. Similarly, the preferences of Chinese authorities vary; especially at the local level, one finds authorities quite willing to cede management control and hence accelerate reform of the business culture. Nonetheless, these dichotomies are generally valid.

The Chinese authorities will choose their strategic position according to the desirability of the foreign applicant and the urgency of encouraging the investment in a given sector. Take the example of a foreign investor wishing to open a chopstick factory in Shanghai. Because this proposal would hold little marginal value for Chinese authorities, they might demand full concessions in each of the six trade-off areas (or block it altogether). But if a Silicon Valley computer company sought establishment, authorities might be much more willing to offer concessions; these could be either dispersed evenly across the trade-off areas or targeted (e.g., if the firm offered to use higher technology, the authorities might concede a great deal on the other factors).

The information gathering of the foreign investors focuses precisely on the question of how desirable the proposed venture seems to the authorities. That will provide an idea of the overall magnitude of the concessions that will have to be made. But where to make those concessions—finding the right mix on the different trade-off continuums—is the strategic positioning challenge. Each choice will be debated and fine-tuned during the negotiation ahead, yet it is essential to bring to the table some overall vision of the ideal result.

Moreover, the initial assessment by Chinese authorities is by no means scientific: a host of subjective influences can affect it. Patrons, sympathetic local authorities, or family connections can make them more willing to accede to the preferences of the foreign investor (column I); powerful entrenched competitors, bureaucratic overseers, or leaders with opposed views can shift them toward demanding more concessions (column II).

Expatriates indicate that in most cases an FIE can secure the factor most important to it, though it may be necessary to concede in other areas. For example, even a venture not deemed highly desirable might succeed in protecting its intellectual property interests (bringing in only a low level of technology) if it agreed to the authorities' preferences in most other matters. Again, while this may not be true in all cases (Chinese authorities might demand "all or nothing" as a way of denying establishment rights altogether), it reflects the experience of most firms consulted.

When interviewees discussed the strategic landscape, three themes dominated. First, locating successfully (i.e., proximity to markets or inputs) was a challenge; rapid development and economic change make optimal site selection difficult. Second, Chinese industrial policies attempt to steer foreign investors both toward specified locales and toward marriages with designated Chinese companies, regardless of the strategic interests of the foreign firm. These two are connected by a third factor: the role of partners. Each is considered later.

Locating Strategically

For some sectors in China, location remains beyond debate. Foreign financial-sector firms, for example, must establish operations in Shanghai's Pudong area if they wish to directly offer services anywhere else in the Chinese market; it is a statutory requirement.[17] In most sectors, however, the right site is not so obvious, and identifying the right location can be the difference between success and failure.

Interviewees stressed particularly proximity to markets and the character of local partners (along with the quality of inputs these partners contribute to the manufacturing process). Markets have expanded and potential partners increased across coastal China. The number of sites offering substantial incentives (which vary by locality) has risen dramatically, as competition to attract foreign investors intensifies and central authority relaxes.

In 1980 four special economic zones (SEZs) were opened: Shenzhen, Xiamen, Zhuhai, and Shantou; a fifth, Hainan, was granted SEZ status in 1988. In 1984, 14 more coastal cities were opened to foreign investment as "Economic and Technical Development Zones" (ETDZs), allowing them to grant SEZ-like incentives. In 1985 the first macroregions (such as the Yangtze River Delta) were given a status that permitted them to offer incentives as well. Through the 1990s special areas ranging from finance zones in Pudong to whole coastal provinces were authorized to extend attractive commercial terms to foreign investors, while special incentives for developing projects in the interior were created, especially for provincial capital cities. In reviewing the history of zone development, Yang (1997, 56) reported 111 development zones in 1991 (only 27 of which were centrally approved), 1,951 by September 1992, and as many as 8,700 by mid-1993. While the majority of these lacked full legitimacy, the surge demonstrated the embrace of the "zone idea" across China in the aftermath of Deng Xiaoping's reendorsement of reform after Tiananmen Square (during his famous "trip to the south"). The majority of those zones remain fields of dreams, but the number of viable locations has grown substantially. Though their novelty is fading, the zones remain important. They cover the most advanced areas of the country, their bureaucrats have extensive experience with the needs of FIEs, and the incentive packages they offer can be significant. Today, regions and zones are competing vigorously to attract investment. Although the foreign investor can benefit from such rivalry, zones sometimes offer incentives that they do not have authority to grant—thereby creating serious problems with central authorities.[18]

For firms primarily interested in positioning themselves to serve domestic markets, the choices have increased as well. While a few years ago only Beijing, Shanghai, and Guangzhou could attract foreign interest

---

17. Some private foreign investment consultancies open offices elsewhere to provide advice to clients. Moreover, a Shanghai presence is necessary but not sufficient: their services are regulated locally in each jurisdiction.

18. As many as 1,000 zones set up without the proper central government approval have been closed down in recent years by order of the State Council (Coopers & Lybrand 1996, 41).

based on local market potential, today an emerging middle class has buy-ing power in a growing number of cities. Recent surveys show half of large foreign manufacturers targeting sales to more than 50 different Chinese cities, and fully a third of these are selling in more than 25 provinces (i.e., nationwide) (USCBC 1998). Because internal trade block-ages still make it difficult to serve multiple markets from a single produc-tion site, local site selection affects *internal* market access for FIEs (just as it does for indigenous firms). Of course, the strategic importance of this factor is greater for FIEs that are oriented toward domestic sales.

Beyond the zones and high-growth cities is a vast marketplace. Some FIEs are seeking a clearer understanding of the "real" Chinese market; others, content to serve only the markets abutting the zones, have little taste for more exotic settings deeper in the hinterlands (especially given the limited buying power there thus far). Dispersing foreign know-how more broadly and quickly may be pleasing to those Chinese authorities concerned about the widening income and developmental gaps between the zones and the rest of China.

As discussed in chapter 5, problems and policies shaping the distribu-tion system complicate the question of where to site a domestic market-oriented facility. To facilitate exports, processors must be near the neces-sary port infrastructure, such as that found in Tianjin, Shanghai, Xiamen, and Guangdong Province; to target domestic consumers, ventures must be close to those markets, and probably to the rail system (the best of the poor options available for moving goods nationally). The most intractable of the distribution issues may be residual interprovincial trade protection. Foreign investors wishing to sell into neighboring local markets must lo-cate their enterprise with great care. If the market next door hosts a rival, it may not be so simple to do business there. As one interviewee said, "If you don't have manufacturing [in a jurisdiction], then you don't have godfathers" (#24). Investors can be assured that life in China without god-fathers can be difficult.

Another factor is the desirability of *clustering*—of setting up close to re-lated firms in an industry. Reliable suppliers and business partners are as critical to success in China as they are elsewhere. Thus textile industries are bunched in southern China and around Shanghai, microelectronics has bloomed around Tianjin, and a nascent computer industry cluster has emerged in Zhongguancun, near Beijing.[19]

It is widely observed among expatriates that the prevailing commercial culture of southern China is more entrepreneurial and freewheeling than that of the north (and, perhaps, more corrupt). Twenty solid years of mar-ketization, proximity to Hong Kong, and some distance from bureaucratic

---

19. For an excellent essay on Beijing's computer zone, focused on the now famous Stone Group, see Kennedy (1997).

Beijing have given southern China—especially Guangdong—a reputation as a commercial area. Many foreign investors therefore choose to base their establishment in the south, as figure 2.4 shows. In addition, many overseas Chinese investors trace their ancestry from the southern provinces, and thus choose to bring home their money and skills. Both groups are undoubtedly attracted by what has been referred to as the "inverse Beijing ratio": as distance from Beijing increases, the strict enforcement of regulations decreases. It is a new version of an old saying—"the mountains are high and the emperor far away" (Weidenbaum and Hughes 1996, 123).

Other siting considerations come into play as well. Amenities accessible to expatriate employees may be an issue, especially if they have spouses, children, or possible medical concerns (or if they insist on a ready supply of bagels and lox). Some industries may require that specific material inputs be locally available; others may have critical environmental requirements. Finally, there are claims that firms from a particular nation (Japan was identified), determined not to compete with one another in China, may orchestrate efforts to space their bases of operation. The evidence to date is purely anecdotal, but the question appears to be worth researching.

Clearly, the decisions that foreign investors make about location are far more important to their China strategy today than they were earlier in the reform period, when only a handful of sites were viable and authorities directed investor traffic with a much heavier hand. As the next section suggests, however, the hand of officialdom has not disappeared.

Steering Investors: Industrial Policy

In practice, the authorities overseeing investment often present an interested foreign firm with a short list of potential joint venture opportunities. The choice of local candidates may reflect some larger development goals or a desire to bolster a needy state-owned entity. Here, like many government practices in China, this one is not found in the regulations. The Guidelines require that FIEs in many sectors be joint ventures (sometimes Chinese controlled, sometimes not) rather than wholly foreign owned, but they do not instruct the investor to select from a list of offerings.

Larger firms are likely to deal with an entity of the central government, such as the ministry overseeing the relevant industrial sector, in courting specific partners. The chairman of a large American conglomerate's China holding company (#4) pointed out that the guidance of the central government in this regard is often a function of local interests. The authorities thus act like a matchmaker between foreign investors and state-owned enterprises (SOEs) that have expressed an interest in cooperation (or localities looking for investors, or sectoral authorities eager to improve their industries). The interviewee stressed that the views of the foreign investor and those of the central handlers on the competence of specific local enti-

Figure 2.4 FDI in China by location, 1996 (billions of dollars)

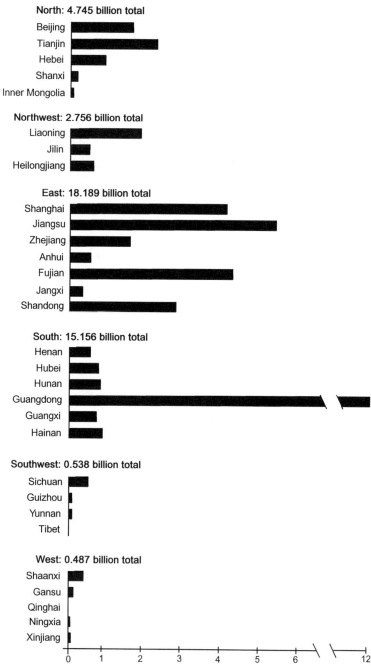

Source: *China Statistical Yearbook,* 1997 (page 608), China State Statistical Bureau.

40

ties are seldom the same, but that compromises were necessary for introducing foreign competition into the Chinese economy.

The senior attorney for another American firm (#14) was more critical. He argued that authorities intentionally steer FIEs toward partnership with low-quality SOEs in need of dramatic upgrading; similarly, successful domestic firms come under pressure to merge with weaker firms in their industries.[20] This interviewee was certain that in his sector (energy development and refining), Beijing authorities intended the best firms to be "national champions," insulated from foreign investor influence. His charge that the Chinese off-load poor performers onto stronger firms (including FIEs) is the obverse of Chinese complaints that FIEs often employ outdated technologies and products in China, and it demonstrates clearly why good market intelligence is essential: investors must be wary of buying a pig in a poke.

In addition to the industrial policy motive of strengthening and shielding certain industries, the central authorities also have geographical concerns. As already noted, economic growth has proceeded faster in the cities and SEZs than in the hinterlands, and faster along the coast than in the interior. Not only does unequal development raise obvious issues of equity and potential efficiency problems, but such a bifurcated marketplace may create social pressures that present real security concerns. The authorities worry above all about China's deep-rooted tendency toward fragmentation. Therefore, efforts to encourage more even development have long been an important plank in the Communist Party platform.

The official interest in promoting development can lead FIEs to choose locations other than those suggested by a purely market-driven calculus. Some firms are currying favor with central planners by putting plants in isolated interior areas. One firm interviewed for this study had worked out a quid pro quo with its overseeing ministry: it was developing a major factory in the interior in return for gaining market access for its goods back along the coast (#37). This is not how most FIEs wish to operate; but the success of such locational compromises (like others) is being judged in terms of long-term opportunities.

How important are Chinese industrial policy efforts to steer foreign investors in certain directions? A number of interviewees saw China as rife with competing provincial interests, claiming that the willingness of provincial officials to undermine one another and even national-level planners for the sake of local goals would preclude any concerted Chinese economic plan such as South Korea or Japan has fashioned. This may be true enough of the country as a whole. However, at the microeconomic level, such policies have a major impact on the strategic positioning of individual FIEs. Even when FIEs have worked within the system to gain

---

20. For example, Shanghai-area steel companies were forced to adopt weaker rivals; http://www.biztimes.asia1.com/btcommo/news25_4.html.

some short-run advantage (e.g., a protected market share) the contrived market structure poses difficulties for investors and authorities alike. To resolve them, central authorities must withdraw entirely from steering investors and matching them with partners. While authorities continue to express reluctance to stop intervening, the financial crisis of 1997, continuing WTO negotiations, and the apparent sophistication of new leaders all suggest that a change is possible sooner rather than later.

Partners

Expatriates in China constantly talk about partners and relationships, and anyone contemplating setting up an operation in the PRC will have had it drummed into his or her head that partners can make the difference between success and failure. The term *partner* has a number of referents. It might mean a high-level official willing to act as the FIE's patron, watching over its approvals and defending it against bureaucratic entrenched interests. Or it might mean a partner firm willing to fight the approval battles and then act in concert with foreign management. Very often, partners are sympathetic friends in the *local* government or in regulatory bureaus who can help push the project through higher-level hurdles or can get a vague statute interpreted in a manner favorable to the venture.

In each of these cases, one of the partner's most important roles, in the process of establishing the venture and after, is to help the foreign investors distinguish the practical from the impossible. As one executive in the air conditioner industry put it: "Partners are someone to help point you in the right direction; navigation—they help you to save time. Which projects are going to get approved; what can be done, what can't. A good partner is a critical source of good information" (#25).

Hundreds of officials can be involved in an FIE approval, representing not just the authorities but the firms and industries potentially affected by the new entrant. But typically, only a few will determine the outcome, and figuring out who they are can be critical. Partners can facilitate the brokering needed to finalize the deal or at least direct foreign investors toward those who are holding up the process. (Partners are key to getting contracts, too, as noted in later chapters.)

A partner firm with which the FIE forms a business alliance may be able to extract superior concessions and incentives for the JV from the approval authorities. It may be able to streamline and speed the approval process, leading to results far faster than a foreign investor pursuing a WOFE structure—and having to undertake the more complicated *baogao* process—could hope for. With their existing network of business contacts, local partner firms can assuage concerns about the competitive effects of the FIE establishment when foreigners on their own might fail. Furthermore, the pairing gives other locals someone within their traditional conception of relationships and *guanxi* to hold accountable (at least psychologically) if the foreign investor does harm their interests.

Take the case of a foreign firm that wants to set up an integrated operation in China and needs a bundle of licenses and favorable approvals in order to do so. Partners will be essential to this effort. A description of the operating strategy of the German chemicals firm BASF illustrates the point:

> BASF's target modus operandi in selling both its imports and domestic production is encapsulated in the slogans "One face to the customer" and "Direct to the end-user." In theory, these objectives are impossible to attain in China given that joint ventures may not sell either imports or the products of other joint ventures. . . . But despite all this, BASF is achieving remarkable success in presenting a united front to its Chinese customers. The reasons are two: first, an innovative agency arrangement[;] . . . second, a corporate culture in BASF China which both observes Chinese law and at the same time sidelines many of the obstacles regulations appear to place in a multinational's way. ("Right on It," *Business China*, 13 October 1997, 4)

This is exactly what everybody would *like* to be doing; somehow BASF *is* doing it. Surely its success is in part attributable to strong partners, including friends among the overseeing authorities and higher up. Should authorities wish, they could find something improper in these arrangements; they have not. BASF's setup is not viewed as illegal; the company is simply benefiting from a generous interpretation of statutes that can be imaginatively read and "sidelined." However, another firm might not be able to do the same—and in fact I interviewed managers of firms whose attempts to emulate BASF were meeting with resistance.

While approval or rejection by the examining authorities seems monolithic to many foreign investors, the internal processes are often complex and contentious.[21] The tumult of internal decision making is, in fact, what makes partners so important. The failure of seemingly good projects to survive the vetting process results in part from ministerial anxieties that industries they oversee will suffer as a result of foreign competition. The success of high-technology firms in getting approved can be explained not just by their inherent attractions but by the absence of domestic "clients" to oppose their application. All other things being equal, FIEs will lose these battles in China because they lack sophisticated knowledge of bureaucratic politics. With patrons of their own to provide them with domestic standing, they have a far better chance of success.

---

21. See Lieberthal (1995), chapters 9 and 12, and Lieberthal and Oksenberg (1988). The latter was conceived as a thorough analysis of decision making in the energy bureaucracy, but subsequently it was expanded to consider the broader nature of governance in China. Its principal finding: "Our study reveals a fragmented bureaucratic structure of authority, decision making in which consensus building is central, and a policy process that is protracted, disjointed, and incremental. . . . Put simply, the structure of authority requires that any major project or policy initiative gains the active cooperation of many bureaucratic units that are themselves nested in distinct chains of authority" (22).

The motives of patrons and partners are not altruistic: in FIEs they see technology, market access, exports, simple profits, or some other benefit. The problem is that while the marriage of partners can get a firm into China, there is no formula for divorce to get out.[22] The obligations binding one to a Chinese partner presumably bring mutual gains in the *current* business environment. But China—and its business climate—is changing rapidly. Most of the interviewees for this study had been involved in Chinese ventures for at least three to five years, and they were often finding their partners more a hindrance than an asset. Interlocking relationships among provincial and municipal ministries retard competition; firms that back home would be fierce competitors are cousins in China. Chinese firms may restrain their foreign partners from competing openly against rivals, because those rivals are under the protection of a powerful ministry from which the firm requires support. One American conglomerate with multiple business units in Shanghai has an unusual problem: the ministry that is the partner of one of its units is also the partner of the principal rival of another unit.

This story is repeated in a number of ways. There are regional jealousies: partners may prevent FIEs from optimizing operations by moving some production to another jurisdiction. While many of the FIEs are multinational corporations, with global interests and perspectives, their Chinese partners often have a far more parochial view of the venture's interests. Or the problem may be that the Chinese partner has run out of new equity to contribute and will not permit expansion that would entail erosion of its equity share. In many ways, FIEs can find that they lose flexibility once they are established.

A key determination that must be made by the FIE is whether the Chinese partner will remain a collaborator or will instead use transferred technology and know-how to become a competitor. Some management writers call this a "perception problem"—a fancy way of saying that the partners do not trust each others' intentions:

> Another perception may be any unstated fears of the foreign party that the Chinese enterprise is a potential competitor which would block their own involvement in a global strategic scale. With fundamental and far-reaching strategic issues at stake, it would be surprising if one or the other of the partners did not regard it as being in its interests to control the perceptions of the other. Such an approach merely perpetuates and institutionalizes the problem. (Guo and Akroyd 1996, 42)

Those interviewed for this study often gave evidence of such concerns about control, which contributed to the phenomenon of "same bed, dif-

---

22. Economist Nicholas Lardy of the Brookings Institution points out, as do others who focus on competition policy, that barriers to exit can be as big a problem as barriers to entry in achieving an efficient market (personal communication, 16 June 1998).

ferent dreams," or partners glossing over essential disagreements about their companies' direction in order to pursue short-term goals.

If things do go wrong, the partners cannot easily go their separate ways. A number of the firms consulted for this study tried to adjust by adding layer upon layer to their organizational structure, each intended to capture an opportunity the prior structure was not suitable for. The result can be a highly unwieldy company with multiple bureaucracies, partners, obligations, legal profiles, and lines of communication.

The tendency to make withdrawal from partnerships difficult will not dissipate quickly in China, though creating clear rules for easing the process would benefit foreign and Chinese firms alike. Rather than rely on Chinese enlightened self-interest, however, FIEs need to attend to this problem themselves by very careful partner selection: for the time being they have little outside recourse if their stable of partners proves unsatisfactory.

Conclusions on Strategic Issues

The head of an American company based in northern China (#36) provided an interesting perspective. In the Western model, he suggested, a business opportunity evolves from identification of what is permissible (legally), to the most logical manner to pursue that end, and finally to the question of what partners need be recruited to accomplish it. In the Chinese marketplace, he argued, the sequence is reversed. One takes stock of the assets and trust provided within one's relationships, then asks what opportunities could logically be pursued given those assets; and only then are the lawyers finally sent to find a legal loophole that will permit their pursuit.

As the Asian financial crisis enters its second year, it appears that the Western approach has demonstrated its superiority. Financial and investment arrangements predicated mostly on relationships have collapsed across the region, to the detriment of countless hardworking people. The rules-based prudential fraternities (the IMF, World Bank, and US Treasury) have been strained trying to restore enough confidence in the Asian markets to justify putting the savings of millions of others to work there. It would be easy to insist that the "Chinese/Asian" chain of thought must be inverted.

The foreign investors best able to function in the Chinese market, however, understand that they are not simply dealing with a competition between hierarchies. Chinese traditions run deep. History has left its scars on anyone old enough to remember the Cultural Revolution (1966–76), and millions more were marked by the turbulence of spring 1989. Low per capita incomes and little faith that legal regimes will guarantee social welfare and civil rights produce Chinese behavior that some expatriates see as foolish or odd; such views are misguided. China is in a transition that will take decades to complete. But those foreign investors able to accommodate and comfort Chinese sensibilities, while at the same time pressing for change and introducing new business skills, will not only profit from their effort but also hasten reform. Opportunities will remain for FIEs that prefer to be insulated from Chinese idiosyncrasies, in enclaves; increasingly, however, more dynamic foreign investors are going further afield and helping both sides to learn.

The Negotiation Process

The bulk of the issues with which foreign investors struggle in establishing a presence in China occur in and around the negotiating process itself. They are various and multidimensional; assembling them into an organizational framework is not a simple task, but it is essential.

The nature of a business determines a set of questions regarding structure, phasing, incentive priorities, and obligations, all of which must be negotiated. First are the terms of ownership that govern the enterprise, whether it is a minority or majority joint venture or a wholly owned foreign enterprise. A secondary question concerns management control, which can be negotiated even in the case of a minority-owned venture or effectively diluted in the negotiation even in the case of a WOFE. The specific labor and financial arrangements negotiated will have a profound impact on the latitude with which a firm can operate and thus on its efficiency. An important dimension increasingly negotiated at foreign insistence is phasing: that is, whether the foreign commitments in China will be met in installments contingent on performance by the Chinese side. All of these factors will require the potential venture to shop around for advantageous interpretations of governing regulations, as the permissible and impermissible can be fungible. A particularly critical point is the scope of business operation that the venture is permitted: for example, the degree to which it can control the distribution of its product. Also crucial are negotiating an advantageous slate of investment incentives and, on the other side, setting the performance requirements that will be expected of the firm (not least, any technology transfers). Each of these negotiating objectives is explored in this section.

A final introductory note: those interviewed for this study stressed above all the importance of thinking through at the earliest stage the human resources and professional needs of the venture to maintain control over management and personnel costs. Chapter 3 is devoted entirely to the topic of human resources, and one of the more serious problems it identifies is failure to take seriously enough the personnel needs of the venture while the establishment is being negotiated. Even minority foreign partners in JVs have been able to secure control over management, when that is made a priority in negotiations (recall figure 2.3). A general observation about successful businesses in China is that they have harmonious human resource profiles: the correlation does not prove causality, but it does provide food for thought.

Enterprise Type

The most basic structural question foreign investors negotiate is the type of venture to be set up: wholly owned, joint venture, or some other structure. Form of ownership is important because it affects control over the business. Chinese authorities have traditionally tried to limit foreign control, for several reasons. Originally the basis was an ideological response to the foreign commercial and military intervention the country suffered from the mid-19th century onward. In the reform period, the motivation was instead the desire to generate exports and gain technology transfers. Therefore, the preferred form of participation was the joint venture; until recently, WOFEs were approved only in a minority of cases.

As Chinese authorities have become less intent on control, foreign investors have become more so. WOFEs offer them better control over disseminating technology, providing incentives for staff, selecting distributors and other partners, and determining what share of returns to reinvest into operations. Because they are often built from scratch, the investors are less likely to inherit the onus of prior obligations. And of course they avoid the problems and acrimony that arise when foreign firm and Chinese partner interests diverge. As one executive looking ahead to a more flexible era noted, "Every joint venture has a divorce; it's just a matter of when" (#27). Starting with a WOFE structure precludes the need to go through that breakup (or, as noted already, inability to break up); it also prevents a foreign investor from delegating too much responsibility to Chinese partners who overstate their capacity to handle it, a common problem that is addressed later at several points.

In many sectors, however, foreign investors are prohibited from utilizing the WOFE structure (see appendix A). Indeed, in many, majority control must be ceded to the Chinese partner. These statutory obstacles are obviously difficult to circumvent, although with a big enough investment, good enough high-level contacts, or a special willingness to share technology it might be possible (though note that the last concession would negate one of the key benefits of the WOFE).

In addition to these formal limits, WOFEs receive extensive guidance from overseeing authorities—in some cases even more guidance than joint ventures under the aegis of appropriately disinterested authorities (or, it is alleged, those partnered with a passive People's Liberation Army entity).[23] In the approval process, they are subject to extensive scrutiny and they are required to submit extensive information on every aspect of their

---

23. In Summer 1998, the People's Liberation Army was instructed to divest itself of commercial enterprises.

Figure 2.5 Approvals for new FIEs by organizational form, 1990-97

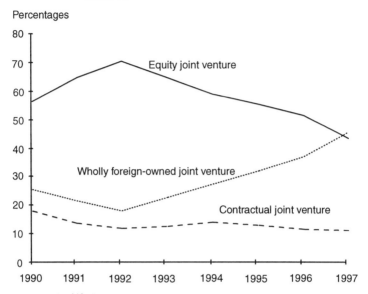

Percentages

Source: The US-China Business Council,
http://www.uschina.org/bas/economy.html, 15 April 1998.

operation and resource needs: this *baogao* report can be used to judge their performance, often more critically than that of JVs. Lacking a Chinese partner, they proceed through the negotiation without the same inside leverage that a potential JV would enjoy (although a WOFE investor with big dollars or big technology can obviously expect considerable support from the local government benefiting from its presence).

Despite the obstacles, the number of WOFE arrangements negotiated has grown sharply relative to the number of joint ventures, a shift that reflected both increasing wariness on the part of foreign investors and increasing permissiveness from approval authorities in order to maintain FDI volumes (see figure 2.5 and table 2.4). More recent data (see table 2.6) suggest that the shift to WOFEs has accelerated after holding steady for most of the 1990s. One could easily infer that the change is related to the Asian financial crisis; however, the trend shows considerable lead time, predating the crisis.[24]

---

24. Lardy dates the shift from the 1994–95 contraction in Chinese monetary policy, which prevented Chinese JV partners from matching new foreign contributions to venture capital and thus eroded their share—sometimes up to 100 percent. As noted elsewhere in this study, authorities tried to limit such indirect acquisition of WOFE status as well (personal communication, 16 June 1998).

Table 2.6 Enterprise forms, 1997

Foreign direct investment	Utilized	
	Billions of dollars	Percentage change from 1996
Total	45.28	8.51
Equity joint ventures	19.58	−5.68
Cooperative joint ventures	8.92	10.03
Wholly foreign-owned enterprises	16.15	28.11

Source: *China's Latest Economic Statistics, After EIU*, Business China, 16 March 1998 (page 11); China Monthly Statistics.

Clearly, what foreign investors want is a format that allows them freedom to staff, to organize production, to set prices and marketing strategies, to manage distribution and servicing, and to use proceeds as they see fit. From their perspective, productivity and ultimately profitability—not an imposed ownership and investment control structure—should determine the limits of the firm. Conscious of foreign sentiment, partly convinced of the advantages of greater corporate freedom, and feeling some pressure from the alternative investment destinations offered by neighboring economies whose currency devaluations (a step China has promised to avoid) made them more competitive as export platforms, Chinese leaders are slowly unveiling new ownership structures. These include the holding company, finally permitted by statute in 1995 after years of internal guidance and experimentation. Joint stock companies are also evolving in China in the late 1990s. As already mentioned, a Partnership Law has been promulgated, though its implementation is still unclear (Clarke, Howson, and Ganliang 1997). A few joint trading companies have been approved (three in Shanghai, two in Shenzhen) as have joint chain stores, perhaps presaging broader establishment forms to come for all FIEs. But at present the trade-offs and commitments required to get such rights are unacceptably high for all but a handful of firms, even if authorities were willing to extend them to all that met the criteria.[25] One of the largest American firms taking part in this study refused to accept a chance to set up a joint trading entity, failing to see adequate benefits in it (#6).

Through creative use of the approved formats, foreign firms are starting to organize in ways that allow them to coordinate decision making, sales, marketing, and even trading through a network of subsidiary ventures. This strategy is further discussed later.

---

25. Foreign investors with less than $400 million in total assets must have at least 10 preexisting production ventures in China; those with more, 3 such ventures. In either case, the preconditions are prohibitive for all but a very few firms.

Ownership Share and Management Control

Share of ownership affects foreign control over the venture, in terms of both long-term strategy and day-to-day management, but its effect can vary considerably. Interviewees pointed out that while in some joint ventures the Chinese partner is actively involved in the operation, in others they are almost entirely absent, acting merely as the partner of record (and taking a fee) when called on to legitimate the venture's status or ownership. Often the arrangement has the tacit assent of local governments. This option appears to be more popular with smaller foreign investors, preferring the risk of playing loose with the rules to that of having an activist partner wishing to run the show. It is also more attractive to these foreign investors than other possible trade-offs to gain management control: putting proprietary technology at risk or agreeing to forgo the domestic market and accept a high export ratio.

For larger firms, the risks of taking on an absentee partner are higher. For starters, larger ventures attract greater regulatory scrutiny; an FIE qualified for central-level approval attempting to use such a stratagem would probably not pass muster (unless protected by a powerful patron). Should a foreign firm with high brand-name recognition be found employing such tactics, the embarrassment could prove costly (at the least, putting the firm in a position to be shaken down for payoffs).

Nevertheless, several managers of large firms insisted that one should never choose partners who thought they knew what they were doing (i.e., who would seek to challenge foreign management of the business), and certainly should never give them veto power over the management. "The JV still works in China," said one (#24), "but if you do use it, do so with someone who is not in your industry—they are Neanderthals. Go with someone who just wants to make money, like SITIC [Shanghai International Trust and Investment Corporation]."

The foreign investment Guidelines specify sectors in which foreign investors are not permitted to be the majority shareholder ("the Chinese party will be the holding party or play a leading role"). But the EIU's *China Hand* (1996b, 14.45) points to foreigners with as little as a 5 percent stake (e.g., Nissan-Zhengzhou) securing effective management control of a JV, via high-technology contributions. Conversely, others with a majority share (e.g., Xerox Shanghai) faced problematic vetoes at their board of directors meetings because they had not negotiated effective board control. Again, statutory limits do not alone determine real control. As practice diverges from statute, foreign investors worry less about ownership share in the contract and more about de facto control. It can be secured with technology and export concessions, use of local patrons to protect the venture's independence, use of passive partners as described already, or (for larger investments) strategic phasing that offers a series of incentives for the Chinese partner to continue cooperating with the foreign management plan.

Many foreign investors, especially from the litigious United States, insist on adhering to a painstakingly negotiated agreement that sets out management control in relation to ownership shares. These businesses deserve respect for their commitment to the contract approach to establishment; a carefully negotiated contract can indeed provide greater management control at any given level of ownership. Business consultants sometimes suggest including a separate contract to take advantage of a loophole in JV guidelines that permits total foreign management when the alternative is "unsound," a convenient way to justify such a departure from statute (provided that authorities agree). Certain areas of enterprise management require special care in the contract—for example, control over export operations, so that the venture does not end up competing with the foreign firm in third markets. Forethought is needed to prevent headaches later on. But no firm can succeed in China today without recognizing that in this marketplace, management control is not determined by ownership share alone.

Labor Structure

Expatriates often identified careful structuring of the FIE labor profile as a primary element of a successful establishment. As chapter 3 will lay out, human resources success turns on stabilizing employee salary and non-salary costs, controlling workers' incentives, planning for training and retention needs, and ensuring against overstaffing or low-quality staffing (i.e., being able to fire people). The foreign investor's ability to meet these goals is largely a function of whether they are negotiated properly, early in the process. Interviewees confided problems arising in each of these areas because of negotiating failures.

Chinese FIE policy (like domestic policy) is oriented toward maintaining employment levels and allocating as much responsibility for workers as possible to firms, which, ostensibly, have sufficient cash flows to meet their needs. The aim is to stem social pressures created by layoffs and to bandage the hemorrhaging social welfare system (i.e., meet pension obligations). FIEs naturally have little interest in being stuck with fixed labor forces and unshakable welfare obligations. Many firms would prefer to start from scratch and do their own hiring, but such an outcome is unlikely unless the venture is a wholly owned greenfield enterprise (one built from scratch); therefore, careful negotiations over labor are necessary. Facing enormous potential pressure as well from special interests in the home country (especially in the United States, where there is much talk about labor rights), the foreign investor must proceed cautiously.

Specific complications attributed by interviewees to faulty negotiation included failing to secure power over salaries, permitting control over staff to alternate between foreign and Chinese representatives, providing no plan to monitor local staff with access to sensitive technology, and allowing poor labor practices (by subcontractors) to take place outside the control of foreign management. In addition, the question of moving employees geographically is difficult to revisit after the contract is agreed to; lack of initial clarity can stymie later expansion.

Overstaffing has been a major complaint of foreign investors in recent years, but FIEs are learning to manage this problem better. Some investors were inclined to accept staffing levels they did not need because they were in a hurry to set up their enterprise. They may have reassured themselves by observing that per worker costs were low, or by assuming they would be able to resize the venture over time. Such assumptions often led to disappointment; pruning staff after establishment is generally difficult. More than being just an incidental cost, redundant workers are a visible symbol of the failure of a venture to maximize productivity and give the venture adequate incentives.

Financial Structure

Negotiating a sound financial structure for the FIE is also critical. Pertinent financial setup questions to be addressed include the respective financial resources to be injected into the venture, by whom they will be injected, according to what schedule, and—especially for infrastructure investment projects—at what expected rate of return. Operating issues that must be addressed include expectations for cash flow growth, plans for collection of accounts receivable, selection of accounting and credit practices to be used by the venture, and choice of how and when to dispense dividends. These questions are urgent, for joint ventures suffer from a high incidence of internal conflict, have inadequate mechanisms for recourse, find it difficult to extend credit and collect on accounts in a volatile market, and face restrictions imposed on foreigners' rights to invoice and collect payment on all but the goods they produce locally.

In the detailed feasibility study presented to approval authorities, investors must supply the rate of return (ROR) the venture will generate. Officials use this information to plan for remittance flows, negotiate better terms on a national basis, and identify opportunities for high growth. To avoid tacit caps on their rates of return, FIEs have discovered alternatives to listing all gains in net profit. For example, an assembly operation might creatively use fees, pass-through costs, and other tricks to alter its ROR (though deploying such tactics conspicuously could land the venture in very hot water).[26]

For another example, consider the Shandong Rizhao Power Project, a 700-megawatt coal-fired facility that will cost $625 million and pay off

---

26. According to Sherwood et al. (1998), 70 percent of FIEs in China report tax losses. Sherwood also indicates (personal communication, 31 August 1998) that recent Chinese tax reforms imply that many of these losses are being used to disguise profits.

over a decade or longer on a build-operate-transfer (BOT) basis.[27] In a large project with no sovereign guarantees, investors want a high return to justify risk. But when the central authorities bargain, they want to have it both ways: in this case, the Ministry of Electric Power (MOEP) and overseers at the State Council refused to provide sovereign guarantees, which could justify the risk involved, but at the same time tried to hold down the return that investors demanded. Three years ago, when power industry investors eager to enter the market were frustrated by China's de facto ceiling on returns (supposedly 18 percent), the investment deal would have fallen apart. Today, the BOT basis for financing the project and sophisticated financial planning *may* provide a way forward (although as of mid-1998 this was the only BOT project to have made it through the approval process successfully; see also box 2.1).

Set alongside these financial innovations are "comfort letters": less formal promises from authorities who refuse to make sovereign guarantees while committing to defend the contract terms in principle. Foreign investors involved in such negotiations report that such soft guarantees have become an important part of financing large infrastructure projects in China.

Phasing

Unless investors intend to exploit an immediate opportunity in the Chinese market and then pull out, they may be inclined to increase their exposure gradually. Such incrementalism allows learning to take place and pitfalls to be identified. An investor who makes a large initial investment before gaining any experience may be left hostage to unanticipated forces, with an organizational structure incompatible with evolving opportunities. Authorities who are ready and willing to help resolve problems before an investment is made may suddenly have little time to spare once the money is sunk into the venture.

Many interviewees spoke of phasing investments in China, meaning two slightly different things. First, the term can refer to paying in the registered capital for a venture in installments. Such a venture can be a discrete undertaking of defined scope, and the phasing applies to fractions of its capital. For a WOFE, registered capital paid in installments must be fully transferred within three years, whereas for JVs there is no time limit (Howson 1997, 20–21). So this sort of phasing is at issue for JVs, not WOFEs.

Second, phasing can apply to the sophistication of the venture, which might be increased as commercial successes accumulate. In this framework, the initial investment might consist of opening a representative office, perhaps in Beijing. A rep office is a wholly owned entity intended to establish business connections or facilitate trade. Setting it up is not free

---

27. Frank Fang, "A Balanced Equation," *Independent Power*, October 1997, 29–31.

Box 2.1 Project finance and the approval authorities' perspective

Faced with an almost endless list of potential infrastructure investments, central authorities have parceled out approvals for big capital projects sparingly. Their actions are in stark contrast to the words of ministers, who actively drum up excitement among foreign investors on overseas tours touting infrastructure investment opportunities. Not only would the aggregate costs of all these projects deplete reserves and thus put in question Chinese ability to finance trade, but left to their own counsel less prudent local officials would squander a fortune: there are just not enough financial analysts available to perform the necessary "investment triage." Local leaders tend to overestimate their ability to repay, underestimate the consequences of default for China's long-term development, underestimate the constraints that profligate spending can force on sovereign governments, and overestimate their own negotiating prowess: as a result, foreign investors and suppliers enjoy higher returns and fees than necessary.

These factors help to explain the automatic review by central authorities of investment above certain levels ($30 million in most coastal special economic zones, $10 million in the less-advanced hinterlands and interior provincial areas). To further expedite responsible investment, new laws address the main concern in such projects: the need for recourse to sovereign guarantee in order to secure financing for these deals, which creates a liability that Chinese planners are reluctant to show on their books. One solution currently being implemented is the BOT (build-operate-transfer) law. It allows projects meeting certain conditions to be agreed to without central approval, with foreign investors permitted to collect its tariffs (such as highway tolls or power fees) for a period of time. After they have been paid off, the project would revert to state ownership.

Such arrangements leave some problems unresolved. Will the foreign exchange risk be assumed by the Chinese side, for example? And while foreign investment in choice projects is made easier, domestic capital is often invested at poorer returns; better and more efficient mechanisms to turn savings into domestic investment are sorely needed. Here again, technical expertise is lacking. One solution, proposed by Graham and Liu (1998), is to permit foreign financial professionals to operate in China's emerging bond market, providing not capital (under this scheme, China's capital account would remain closed at first) but service as they help to structure, grade, and market domestic development bonds. Such advisors are already operating informally to some extent; legitimizing their services seems reasonable indeed. Because China does not yet have its own pool of bond market professionals, now is the time to explore such ways of opening the new market—before a special interest emerges that would seek a monopoly and freeze out such efficiency-enhancing competition.

from bureaucratic hassles, but the process is simple compared to that required for other structures. A few interviewees complained about restrictions on hiring Chinese nationals for their rep offices (a government-assigned hiring agency must be used), but for China this is a minor hurdle (EIU 1996a, 12.3–8).[28]

---

28. Some foreign investors used the rep offices to do more than strictly permitted—i.e., as a de facto "cost center" for invoicing and coordinating distribution in the Chinese market, which is technically against regulations. They were most likely to grumble about having to take employees from government pools instead of hiring Chinese nationals directly.

The second phase of investment might involve a low-value-added assembly joint venture intended to establish production in the Chinese market and build a network of goodwill. Interviews revealed cases of FIEs *designed* to transfer technology and investment as a market-entry loss leader (#20); these might be located in the interior or some other needy locale (#36). The willingness to put "productivity before profitability," as one manager (#19) put it, or "bleed a while," in the words of another (#20), raises the possibility that the present gloomy wisdom on FIE profitability is misdirected. If a one- to three-year period of learning and reengineering is anticipated before foreign ventures can be expected to demonstrate profitability, then the fortunes of the "Deng Boomers"—the investors who surged in during the mid-1990s—can only now start to be judged (or, rather, could have been judged, had the Asian financial crisis not depressed the growth trend for the region significantly and thus diminished the normal performance that might have been observed).

Finally, a third phase of operation might involve a major investment of technology and money, with attention paid to profitability. At least a few foreign firms have reached this stage. Motorola, the American electronics powerhouse, is putting cutting-edge manufacturing in China, building on an established base of profitability and successful manufacturing. General Motors took a different approach: it will roll the first Buick off the line of its $1.5 billion facility in Shanghai in December 1998, having leapfrogged directly to a massive presence. Foreign willingness to move more rapidly to such large investments is of course conditioned by the dynamics of the industry in question: Buicks rely on a more mature technology than do semiconductors. Yet the importance of maturation in Chinese regulatory thinking cannot be overlooked either, for the strategic necessity of phasing investments—rooted partly in a defense against expropriation—is receding as China comes into conformity with international economic practice.

The foreign desire to negotiate latitude for ratcheting up exposure over time conflicts with several Chinese goals. Approval authorities, motivated both by the desires of the hopeful Chinese partner firm and by top-level encouragement of technology transfer, press the investor to commit to using as much technological sophistication as possible as soon as possible. To achieve this end, they offer various quid pro quos, including concessions on management authority, export targets, local content requirements, labor obligations, tax incentives, or other benefits. At the other bargaining extreme, they might point to specifications in the Guidelines and threaten to deny the applicant permission to establish. The sequence of increasingly complex phases of investment is determined by the importance of control in the sector, the availability of time to build up the China operation gradually, and the size of the up-front costs needed to enter the market. Technology and management control both matter, but to differing degrees in different industries.

Another dimension is the schedule on which capital is paid into the venture. Foreign investors have shown a preference to make installments of registered capital contingent on a designated set of benchmarks.[29] Subject to some conditions, JVs can generally draw out the period over which these financial injections will occur indefinitely (though even JVs typically are assigned a limited lifetime of perhaps 50 years); WOFEs, as already noted, must generally pay in within three years. In either case, investors are inclined to expand their phasing cautiously because registered capital cannot be withdrawn during the life of the venture; and few other changes can be made without the consent of authorities.

Not all respondents accepted the merit of the phasing strategy. Two contrarian perspectives emerged. One set of views (#22; #26) argued that successful companies need not accept a period of losses before reaching profitability in China. These interviewees stressed that profitability should be a primary concern from the outset and that to operate otherwise only delayed providing incentives to the workforce and invited graft and demand for loose credit. A well-regarded survey of multinational firms (EIU 1995, 5) supported this position: profitable ventures made money an average of two years after start-up, and 47 percent of those firms (in the survey) operating for two years or less were showing profitability.[30]

The second group of critics of phased evolution focused on the need to move fast. They were often primarily concerned about distribution channels, which are regarded as finite and as being snapped up right and left in the rush to control markets. One interviewee (#12) offered the metaphor of people partnering up at a dance; those who arrive at the party too late are left without options (or only "ugly" alternatives). These managers dismissed the idea of central authorities taking a procompetitive regulatory role anytime soon (i.e., a stance favoring competition and antitrust regulations). In their view, FIEs need to be bold or else stay home; gradualism is a waste of time.

Complicating the question of phasing is the size cutoff, which has affected many expatriates. Projects over $30 million in value have required central government approval; most under this level do not.[31] Local authorities are often far more malleable and willing to see things "the for-

---

29. Chinese authorities also worry that foreign investors may be padding their contribution with overvalued assets (old technology, for example).

30. Because some firms tend to negotiate many ventures and let most die slowly while concentrating their efforts on just one or two, these numbers may be misleading. The average time to profit of those ventures being *actively managed* is surely less than the average of all ventures.

31. As noted, in the Chinese interior the ceiling may be $10 million, depending on jurisdiction; unlimited liability companies always require central approval, as do investments in restricted sectors (Implementing Rules for the Law of the PRC on Wholly Foreign-Owned Enterprises, reproduced and analyzed in Howson 1997).

eign way" than are central officials. Therefore, if the value of a project is near this cutoff line, investors have good reason to get in below $30 million (see tables 2.7 and 2.8). This incentive can be potent: not only does Beijing drive a harder bargain, but it also follows up on the bargain it drives. In addition, the approval process often takes longer once Beijing and associated industrial potentates enter the picture.

Quite a number of FIEs, therefore, have explored creative ways to avoid Beijing's solicitude. The most common reported in interviews for this study (several firms had employed it) is to split a venture into two units, each under $30 million in value and ostensibly independent, although in fact they are two halves of the same factory. Another option is to establish

Table 2.7 Japanese enterprises in China

A. Initial capital

| Industry | Approved capital | | |
	Less than 30 million (percentages)	More than 30 million (percentages)	Average (millions of dollars)
Manufactures	96.9	3.1	6.8
Food	100.0	0.0	3.7
Textile	100.0	0.0	2.6
Wood	100.0	0.0	2.3
Pulp/paper	100.0	0.0	7.2
Publication	100.0	0.0	4.5
Chemical	100.0	0.0	5.4
Lumber	100.0	0.0	3.3
Pottery	73.3	26.7	16.0
Steel	93.7	6.3	7.6
Metal	100.0	0.0	4.2
Machinery	100.0	0.0	8.2
Electric machine	94.8	5.2	10.3
Transportation	86.4	13.6	13.0
Fine machinery	100.0	0.0	3.0
Other	100.0	0.0	5.4
Nonmanufactures	91.7	8.3	12.2
Agriculture	100.0	0.0	1.8
Mining	100.0	0.0	2.8
Construction	75.0	25.0	62.8
Retail/wholesale	81.8	18.2	9.6
Finance	85.7	14.3	12.3
Real estate	90.9	9.1	15.5
Carrier/ communication	100.0	0.0	3.6
Service	96.0	4.0	11.9
Other	0.0	100.0	30.0
Total	95.9	4.1	7.8

(continued)

Table 2.7 Japanese enterprises in China *(continued)*

B. After recapitalization, 1996

Industry	Approved capital		
	Less than 30 million (percentages)	More than 30 million (percentages)	Average (millions of dollars)
Manufactures	92.5	7.5	9.0
Food	100.0	0.0	4.1
Textile	100.0	0.0	3.1
Wood	100.0	0.0	2.4
Pulp/paper	100.0	0.0	7.0
Publication	100.0	0.0	5.8
Chemical	95.8	4.2	7.1
Lumber	100.0	0.0	5.6
Pottery	78.6	21.4	16.8
Steel	87.5	12.5	6.7
Metal	100.0	0.0	5.5
Machinery	91.3	8.7	10.4
Electric machine	83.6	16.4	15.9
Transportation	81.0	19.0	16.1
Fine machinery	100.0	0.0	2.5
Other	100.0	0.0	5.4
Nonmanufactures	89.2	10.8	17.6
Agriculture	100.0	0.0	1.4
Mining	100.0	0.0	0.8
Construction	75.0	25.0	63.0
Retail/wholesale	80.0	20.0	11.0
Finance	85.7	14.3	16.9
Real estate	77.8	22.2	42.2
Carrier/ communication	100.0	0.0	4.2
Service	94.7	5.3	17.2
Other	0.0	100.0	30.0
Total	91.9	8.1	10.7

Source: Japan-China Investment Promotion Organization (1997).

the venture in two investments, with the first under $30 million and the second treated as a nonexpansionary addition. Surely there are other such tactics as well. Local authorities sometimes even suggest these tactics: keen to get investment rolling in and to gain independence from the central authorities, they collude with investors or even try to compel the foreigners to shirk national regulations. Keep in mind that there may be nearly 10,000 municipalities now competing with one another and claiming to offer some sort of zonal incentive.

The downside to this game comes if a firm is caught; even if it is already up and operating, it can be shut down and made to begin the approval process (through the central government) all over again, while machinery

Table 2.8 Average capital of FIEs in China, 1979-97
(millions of dollars)

	Contracted		Utilized	
	Total	United States	Total	United States
1979-89 average	1.5	4.1	0.8	1.8
1990	0.9	1.0	0.5	1.3
1991	0.9	0.8	0.3	0.5
1992	1.2	1.0	0.2	0.2
1993	1.3	1.0	0.3	0.3
1994	1.7	1.4	0.7	0.6
1995	2.5	2.2	1.0	0.9
1996	3.0	2.7	1.7	1.4
1997	2.3	2.0	2.2	1.5

Note: Average utilized capital might be underestimated. It is calculated by dividing the total utilized capital by the total amount contracted, but many contracted ventures languish with little further capitalization.

Source: China Ministry of Foreign Trade and Economic Cooperation.

sits idle and loan payments and contracts go unmet. At the least, the venture would face fines and extremely close scrutiny when it seeks to expand or gain some future approval. The interviewees who had been in this situation found it regrettable and highly uncomfortable, though fatal to none of their firms. The general perception, however, is that for every firm that gets caught a multitude happily avoid detection. Central authorities threaten to crack down on the practice but have not done so consistently. Given the red tape in Beijing and the pace of market development (as well as the cover that the right partner can provide), this appears to have been a fairly successful coping mechanism.

Scope, Distribution Strategies, and Services

An important component of the FIE's negotiation concerns its *scope of operation:* will it be vertically integrated, or just a plant with an in door and an out door? In most marketplaces around the world, this question can be answered based on what makes sense in that market before the venture is set up. Moreover, firms can usually be expanded after start-up to adapt to developing business conditions. In China, however, the scope of business operations of non-Chinese firms is circumscribed by law. These restrictions reflect both anxieties about giving foreigners equal opportunities and parochial interests in cultivating domestic competitors. This issue is addressed in detail in chapter 5, as an operational problem; here, the concern is with how it affects establishment. The key point is that scope can, to an extent, be negotiated, just like ownership form, finance, and labor structure.

The business areas walled off from FIEs that came up most often in the case studies include domestic distribution, importing and exporting, logistical management, financial and credit management services related to sales, provision of maintenance services, and retailing. In many industries, all these functions can fall reasonably into a firm's in-house operations. For some firms involvement in these areas is not only desirable but essential. The globalization debate has highlighted an important reality: determining what activities a firm should make part of its operations and what are best subcontracted out is the central challenge to businesses today, requiring considerable sophistication. Placing arbitrary restrictions on a class of firms ("foreign invested") that deny them the chance to define themselves is outdated and inefficient; these limitations will increasingly dominate FIE establishment negotiations until either they are removed or they erode (through underenforcement) to the point of meaninglessness.

While FIEs are technically not prohibited from managing the distribution of goods they manufacture *in China*, they are prevented from directly distributing goods they make *elsewhere*, even if those are complementary to their China-made products. Moreover, FIEs *are* formally precluded from operating a number of attendant functions necessary for efficient distribution, such as financing and account collection.

Foreign investors are finding ways around the restrictions; the enormous efforts they are expending to this end indicate the importance of gaining broader business scope. Their circumvention is succeeding largely because more local and central authorities are recognizing the value for their localities of letting these firms have their way. The umbrella company that is emerging—recall the case of BASF, described already—exemplifies how larger firms are moving toward consolidating their finances, marketing, and distribution. In joint ventures that have passive Chinese partners, foreigners can manage distribution activities formally closed to non-Chinese, tacitly directing operations at the partner firms.

Negotiating such arrangements can provide a foreign investor with a certain amount of legitimacy, but this area of regulation is volatile. China's trading partners have made trading rights for their firms a key WTO objective, and in a few years this landscape will change. In the meantime, FIEs embrace a variety of stopgap solutions that involve some risk of the venture's being shut down. Such are the perils of doing business in China today: considerable gains in economic, political, and social freedom have not been matched by clear legal advances.

The greatest danger to FIEs negotiating their scope of business is not getting caught overstepping the rules; rather, it is failing to take distribution seriously enough. The interviews supply numerous examples of FIEs expecting to sell a product domestically but neglecting either to demand credible evidence of the distribution capacity of their Chinese partner or to ensure their right to manage this aspect of the business. Interviewees said that although the policy restrictions are a serious problem, foreign firms themselves are commonly to blame for not planning ahead for distribution (see chapter 5). Distribution and interaction with the Chinese market at the grassroots level are complicated by the policy environment, by the rapid transitions taking place across China, and by problems pertaining to market structure. Foreign investors only worsen their challenges if, after admitting those problems, in negotiations they cede responsibility for dealing with them to the Chinese side.

Interpretations

"Interpretation" here does not refer to the challenge of translating between English and Mandarin Chinese but rather to the translation between the letter of a law or regulation and the reality of what it permits and precludes. Every expatriate interviewed for this study involved in establishment negotiations emphasized the importance of eliciting a favorable interpretation of the regulations. It is a concern because of vague regulatory language, conflict among sources of authoritative guidance, arbitrary interpretation by approval authorities, changing opinions on the best way to use foreign investment, and shifts in the leverage that can be applied by investors and regulators. The issue is common to many emerging economies.

The hunt for favorable interpretations of the law is not limited to the process of establishing the venture; indeed, for enterprises in China it never ends. Everything from custom duty rates to qualifying as a technologically advanced venture (and hence gaining WOFE status or a lower export ratio) to permission to distribute depends on them. This phenomenon works in favor of FIEs as well as against them, at least on a firm-by-firm basis. Because it is inseparable from the development of China's legal system and overall transparency, it is discussed further in chapter 6. But especially at the point of establishment, before a firm understands the intricacies of Chinese approval processes, the need to secure favorable interpretations can be a potent nontariff barrier to entry and investment.

The interpretation game has the potential to aid incumbent firms, who have more sway with the authorities responsible for approvals, and stymie those firms that were not first movers. This has negative effects on Chinese economic welfare and presents a corruption trap to FIEs that must find alternative ways to counteract the power of incumbents.

Incentives

Before establishment the FIE may negotiate incentives as an inducement to invest. Depending on the size and nature of the investment, incentives can come from the national level, provincial level, or the local level. They may involve a combination of benefits at several levels. Some incentives are explicit and authorized by the central government; others are informal. In still other cases, localities provide incentives that actually *violate* central guidance on what should be extended to investors.

While eager to secure as preferential a deal as possible for their operations, foreign investors have had to recognize the risk that comes with accepting privileges that conflict with central regulations. If locally negotiated arrangements are subsequently reviewed at a higher level of authority, as they are when total value exceeds $30 million, concessions may be rescinded if thought too generous—whether they are technically permissible or not. The "permissible" is, as already shown, often ambiguous and highly dependent on interpretation and partner relations. Furthermore, it is common to hear expatriates describe a pattern of good cop, bad cop: localities offer incentives they know higher authorities will reject so that they might appear investor-friendly.

Any review of major incentives starts with tax rates.[32] Foreign investors face a maximum 33 percent tax rate (30 percent central, 3 percent local), which is lower than the rate for domestic private firms. In the various economic zones, the rate may be lowered to 24 or 15 percent if the venture is "productive"—that is, in manufacturing. Tax exemption in the first year or two following profitability is typical, with a 50 percent reduction through year five. In particular areas, such as the special investment area in Beijing and the Pudong new area, the tax holidays can be extended beyond five years (to six or ten years, respectively). The local tax portion of the liability can be independently reduced or waived by the locality. FIEs can qualify for further reductions by achieving export levels or by being "technologically advanced."[33] Firms that meet these qualifications may also gain a deduction for reinvesting profits in other enterprises in China.[34] These incentives are generally negotiable, not automatic, and they depend on the zone in question and the manufacturing firm's profile. Significantly, interviewees indicated that tax incentives tended to be honored over time, while other incentives were often subject to renegotiation.

Interviewees reported that the next most important incentive category was duty rates on materials to be imported by the venture. These apply to the plant and equipment the venture will use and the intermediates that go into the production process. Exemption from or reduction of duty on capital goods imported for use in manufacturing has been a high-priority issue for multinationals in recent years, as well as one of the most widely

---

32. This discussion draws on China's Foreign Enterprise Income Tax Law of 1991, that law's Detailed Rules for Implementation, and 1987 rules for encouraging foreign investment promulgated by MOFTEC, as well as on analyses of these in Howson (1997) and Coopers & Lybrand (1996).

33. See Coopers & Lybrand's *Tax Primer* (1996, 55–58) for a list of the tax inducements.

34 In balance of payment accounting terms, reinvested profits are tantamount to FDI and thus should qualify for incentivized treatment.

publicized.[35] When authorities attempted to rescind this duty exemption they faced heavy foreign opposition. After years of delay, and after grand-fathering some firms against the ill effects of the move, signs of decelerating FDI in 1997 (combined with the 1997 Asian financial crisis) led authorities to abandon this tack entirely. The capital goods duty exemption appears to be safe for now, at least for firms that bring a minimum level of technology.

How big a break do reduced duties provide? According to Naughton (1996a), imports into China under concessionary terms amounted to 30 percent of the total in 1988; by the mid-1990s, the figure exceeded 60 percent. Zhang, Zhang, and Wan (forthcoming) report that of $80 billion in customs duties that ought to have been collected in 1994 for 25 goods they examined, $27 billion wound up in government coffers. Negotiations can bring down considerably the duty rates on the mundane imports needed to set up an operation—cars, office equipment, furniture, and the like; minimizing them can be a major incentive.

The more the potential investors know, the better able they will be to negotiate for themselves; hence the importance of the information variable. Greater access to trading and distribution rights may ultimately prove more valuable than shaved tax and duty rates, but only a few of the expatriates interviewed recognized early in the process how critical it was to negotiate incentives in the former area. As chapter 5 notes, firms with 95 percent control over their ventures have ceded distribution responsibilities to Chinese partners and then been disappointed that they could not penetrate local markets. In order to take advantage of incentives, firms need to know what to ask for: investment incentives are valuable, but the best incentives are freedom to operate and an improved legal environment (see also box 2.2).

Performance Requirements

Performance requirements are stipulations to which foreign investors must agree in order to gain approval for establishment; like most developing countries, China has used them over the reform period. The three most common performance requirements pertain to exports, local content, and technology transfer. Each is discussed later.

Performance requirements imply a belief on the part of Chinese authorities that foreign investors can further the country's developmental objectives, that these objectives will not be met without intervention, and that government authorities have sufficient leverage to compel agreement

---

35. Pressure to end the exemption had come from domestic enterprises, which claimed that their ineligibility put them at a disadvantage. Evidence of "false foreign investment"—that is, Chinese money cycling out of the country and back in order to take advantage of such incentives—bolstered the perception among authorities that the policy should be changed.

Box 2.2 The incentive pendulum swings

After the terrific boom in FDI in the mid-1990s, Chinese authorities seemed to think they were making too many concessions and could reduce incentives without reducing foreign investment. But for a variety of reasons, in 1997 the rate of FDI growth fell markedly. A Hong Kong-based manager of an advisory and project finance firm with extensive operations in Beijing (a representative office) and Shanghai (a JV advisory company) explained the tail-off:

[Since] 1993–94 there was all sorts of crazy hype about the Chinese market; that's gone. It's probably good that it's gone. The froth is going away. There was a point when people said, "We have to be there"; now there is a return to realism. [There has been] a reduction in the number of players in infrastructure [investment], and those remaining are wiser. The infrastructure area is bright, with a new BOT law being passed . . . and better Chinese government understanding of the costs and risks [of foreign investment] (#9).

Although some see an FDI slowdown as healthy, Chinese authorities are anxious about the consequences for growth—especially in light of the Asian financial crisis of late 1997. Several interviewees involved in decisions about siting new factories echoed the remarks of a Shanghai government relations manager: "[They] asked us to come here. China is not the only place in the world. We don't give a damn about Chinese development; we need access to market share and profits" (#6). Comments like these and the slowing rise in foreign investment pushed the pendulum toward offering greater inducements to invest. At the beginning of 1998, wide-ranging duty exemptions were announced for high-tech capital goods, a major concession to FIEs. Competitive pressure from neighboring countries that devalued their currencies during their financial crises will encourage China to add to its incentives to keep the FDI flowing in, especially as the temptation to follow suit with the renminbi is resisted (Rosen, Liu, and Dwight 1998).

to the requirements. China's leverage over investors has diminished over time, and in response the use of these investment policies has shifted too. They have been aimed at economic goals (e.g., accelerating the absorption of technology, limiting balance of payments pressures, forcing formation of value chains), but they also have had a political aspect, quarantining the influence of foreign firms within limited enclaves. Clearly, this isolation has also begun to break down.

The performance requirements that FIEs face in China today range from the explicit and statutory to the informal and unwritten. They are a concern for many foreign managers, including some interviewed for this study, and pose a potential conflict with international governance. Nevertheless, the interviewees painted a picture of this issue considerably less baleful than generally presented, for reasons that will be discussed later.

Performance requirements arise during the approval process as the feasibility study and contract are prepared. They can also be pressed on an FIE as it evolves; for example, they may be upgraded during a contract revision, a review of approval to increase registered capital, or an application to open a new branch (#7). The baseline set during the initial negotiations is important, therefore, and especially dangerous, as the foreign investor bargains without prior experience in China. Investors making second investments appear to negotiate performance requirements with greater circumspection.

Export Performance

Chinese regulations stipulate that WOFEs must undertake to export more than 50 percent of the output value of their products;[36] this is known as the "export ratio." In the 1980s, firms negotiating such ventures often committed to export considerably more than 50 percent of production in order to secure sole control. For example, Sanyo's factories in Shenzhen and Shekou (Guangdong Province) were required to export 100 percent of their product (*Business China*, 13 May 1996, 7–8). (And not surprisingly, consistent with the theme of "exceptionalism" running throughout this study, some early WOFEs are reported to export *none* of their product.)

As more technocratic administrators came to power and potential foreign investors heard horror stories about Chinese ventures, the conditionality attached to wholly owned status has softened in practice. Regulations provide more official leeway as well. WOFEs producing import-substituting goods, as well as those using or producing high-technology goods, may be exempted from export performance requirements. Thus one performance requirement alone (exporting or technology transfer) can satisfy officials in industries to which authorities are particularly eager to attract investment.

FIE joint ventures, on the other hand, are bound by no *statutory* authority to export, but they often face informal pressure to include export performance targets in the contract. Such pressure can be applied during the comment and examination period of the approval process, when negotiations go back and forth among foreign investor, Chinese joint venture partner, and approval authorities (including parts of the bureaucracy with interests affected by the new enterprise, which can weigh in for or against it). Sometimes the target is implicit; for instance, the contract may state that the venture will "balance foreign exchange and receipts on its own," a euphemism for saying it must export to make hard currency (#54). The head counsel for a major American technology company noted:

> In our original 1991 JV in Beijing, the first signed version of the JVA [joint venture agreement] (i.e., pre-MOFTEC approval) had soft export targets, which were really noncommittal. This was encouraged by policy, but not statutory. The localization requirement was absent in the signed contract, but then made a condition of MOFTEC's approval, so the contract was modified to accomplish this (making it as noncommittal as possible). Again, this was without statutory basis. (#7)

---

36. See Detailed Implementing Rules for the Law of the People's Republic of China on Wholly Foreign-Owned Enterprises (1990), Article 3.

MOFTEC's leverage (or that of its local units) could lie in flat-out refusal to approve ventures, but usually its influence is wielded more subtly. In the case cited already, the firm accepted weak language pledging a "gradual increase" in exports "eventually" in exchange for gaining other contractual points dear to them. These included winning priority in getting VAT tax rebates, having products placed on "recommended products" lists maintained by a government agency (without which they could not sell in their sector), and gaining clearance to sell refurbished goods in China that would otherwise not be permitted. This FIE agreed to export goals that were very soft in order to get "carrots," not to avoid a "stick," thereby accomplishing its negotiating goals with relative ease.

Joint venture managers suggested that in practice local authorities do not strictly enforce these requirements, absent specific pressure to do so. Many reported that despite missing targets either "occasionally" (#16) or "commonly" (#4), they had not been adversely affected. Firms with WOFE structures are held more closely to their export commitments. Even here, however, in many cases failure to meet targets has not been treated as a punishable offense; one firm did apparently get close to real sanctions (#36).[37]

Other firms appeared to be meeting or close to export targets, which suited their intention that the venture serve regional markets in Asia. One of these was exporting 40 percent of its chemical production and trying to increase that share (#18). Another was at 80 percent—a difficult rate to maintain because domestic demand was even greater (#38). Another JV shipped out 50 percent of the production run but similarly was under pressure to raise production so as to better serve the domestic market while still exporting 50 percent (#40).

Even WOFEs, which have statutory requirements, report that approval authorities do not always insist on including export targets in the negotiations establishing the venture (#54). They can be avoided by generously interpreting the exemptions for FIEs engaged in import substitution or high-technology manufacturing. The WOFE law provides ample latitude for such an interpretation, and only one other ingredient is needed: sympathetic local authorities hungry for investment and willing to cooperate.

Many FIEs undoubtedly pay attention to export targets, though none in the case studies considered export performance a high-priority issue. At first, therefore, it might appear that export performance requirements are not a problem. However, that conclusion is incorrect for several reasons. First, many foreign firms (especially from the United States) try earnestly to comply with Chinese law, instead of comfortably taking advantage of the

---

37. The interviewee cautioned against taking chances with export requirements, especially if the company is dependent on China operations in a lean global structure and hence vulnerable to disturbed Chinese feelings. In this firm's case, the local government partner led the fight to protect the FIE from sanction from higher authorities.

gray areas of poor enforcement. Indeed, firms operating nationally cannot avoid scrutiny, and the closer to Beijing a venture is, the greater the compliance required. Furthermore, informal knowledge that authorities will not crack down on a firm is often insufficient to satisfy corporate officers back home in developed countries. As a senior attorney with an American firm noted, "In general performance requirements are not enforced, but it's tough to tell that to your board of directors [when seeking approval for the contract you have negotiated for the China operation]" (#14).

Second, failure to comply with export requirements can prove a firm's Achilles' heel. A change in enforcement patterns at the national or local level could leave the firm scrambling to meet obligations—not a far-fetched scenario. Moreover, even without a change in policy, failure to comply leaves the firm open to pressure from those in a position to enforce the regulations. For example, a venture seeking approval to increase branch offices may have its application held up for failure to meet export requirements that previously were largely ignored by officials (a typical worry of venture managers). FIEs have been pressured to ratchet up technology transfer to "compensate" for failure to meet export performance targets. "The teeth in the requirements come when you need to go to the authorities for [approval for an increase in] foreign exchange, or when you want to start a new venture," noted the financial director of a major US firm with both WOFE and JV structures (#30).

Third, the distribution of a number of subsidiary rights is at present based in part on export performance. For example, for buying and selling purposes, FIEs keep accounts in which they may hold reserves of foreign exchange that otherwise are supposed to be sold for Chinese currency at domestic financial institutions (depending on the terms they have negotiated). Lately, more and more FIEs are retaining control of their surplus hard currency: doing so offers them greater flexibility and a hedge against foreign exchange risk. The basic account used to hold this currency has a "ceiling" that is calculated based on the value either of the FIE's exports or of paid-in capital.[38] Thus the linkage of performance and financial management rights can be a powerful lever (if increasingly less so) for shaping FIE behavior; again, however, no interviewee considered this a central issue, especially as foreign exchange has become more readily available in recent years.

---

38. One Beijing-based finance director (#30) puts it this way:

The limit on the basic account is set relative to paid-in capital or a percent of exports. We have not had any problem, as the authorities are pretty generous in giving the limits and will give more than the formula if there is a business reason. Basically, they figure how many months' worth of foreign exchange you need to run smoothly. We have a generous limit that has never been a problem. Foreign exchange is very abundant and I do not think anyone has a problem in this area that affects their operations. Export requirements are still there, though not strictly enforced—again, mostly due to abundant foreign exchange.

More than one interviewee hoped that China's WTO accession would "obviate export performance requirements" (#32). Washington policy pundits sometimes feed such hopes by inaccurately stating that under the WTO China will be obligated to eschew these requirements (see, e.g., Mastel 1997, 151). While the WTO agreement on Trade-Related Investment Measures (TRIMs) made progress in proscribing some investment performance requirements (such as those pertaining to foreign exchange and trade balancing), it deliberately did not take on the questions of export performance (Schott and Buurman 1994, 113).[39] The North American Free Trade Agreement, by contrast, addresses the issue in acceptable fashion. The Multilateral Agreement on Investment (MAI), until recently under negotiation in the Organization for Economic Cooperation and Development, may prohibit "preestablishment performance requirements" (Graham 1996, 210), but it appears very unlikely that this agreement will get out of the gates and even more unlikely that China would assume its obligations. Nonetheless, it offers a model for progress.

Should export performance requirements made on FIEs during the establishment process be treated as an obsolescing, unenforced annoyance that requires little attention from China's trading partners, or are they rather a major source of subtle coercion and at the heart of needed reforms in China? Mastel makes his position clear:

> The enormous leverage the Chinese market provides and the Chinese government's willingness to use performance requirements on a sweeping scale create the potential that trade patterns and comparative advantage will be severely distorted by these requirements to the detriment of China's trading partners. No other single issue deserves more attention in trade negotiations than performance requirements in terms of both their immediate effects and the potential for future problems. (1997, 119)

This argument appeals to those looking for the "commie behind the bushes," but it is probably ill conceived. In practice, export requirements are far down the list of expatriate managers' concerns. Legally, they remain an enduring symbol of the presumption that a dynamic market needs government orchestration, thereby sending the wrong signal to trade negotiators whose attention should be elsewhere. Perhaps the greatest danger is that a mere 20 percent export requirement could, if the firm's future position in the Chinese economy is large enough, overwhelm production elsewhere, while the 80 percent not exposed still falls short of domestic demand. The statutory requirements are few, and the WTO as it is cannot fully address the issues arising from the Chinese regulations.

---

39. To the extent that export performance requirements are a violation of the national treatment provision, one can make an argument (though perhaps not successfully) that they *are* WTO-inconsistent.

Local Content Requirements

The local content requirement in China functions similarly to that for export performance—and thus it is not so onerous to foreign investors as some suggest. FIEs are even more interested in finding sources of domestic supply than in increasing exports. At the same time, they report that domestic content requirements are enforced more strictly than export requirements. Content is monitored not only on the central but also on local levels, which stand to gain jobs and manufacturing. Enforcement is often driven by local enterprises—the would-be suppliers—and their patrons. The higher-level Chinese authorities may strictly regulate local content pressure because they are suspicious of foreign firms' transfer pricing and fear they are being overcharged (#53). For FIEs themselves, increasing domestic content may be a strategy for reducing costs.

Domestic content issues arise at the same point that export requirements do: during the examination and comment period of the approval process. As their beneficiaries are more clearly defined, local content requirements may continue to be urged on ventures through the setup period and into the operational phase. Unlike export performance, local content obligations are not statutorily imposed on WOFEs or JVs but are pressed on investors informally. They are not a *transparent* statutory requirement but rather part of internal guidance for achieving a level of local sourcing in certain industries—especially so-called pillar industries. One interviewee remarked,

> I would not be surprised that a large assembly plant or one in a particular industry would be approached by the local government and pressure extended for them to increase local content of their product. The same sort of thing happened to Motorola vis-à-vis their establishment of joint ventures with their subcontractors, with pressure coming from the Tianjin municipality for the company to take equity stakes. Certain key industries focus more on local content (e.g., automotive) and encourage import substitution. With these I am sure that there are internal guidelines for localization of product (but no proof!). But pretty much all government-controlled industries have been affected by the philosophy of "Zili" [meaning "self-reliance": i.e., local authorities must shift from central support to finding customers themselves for their municipal enterprises]. (#53)

Expatriates reported that a wide set of actors encourage local content sourcing, including industry groups, examination and approval authorities, local governments, and local partners (#54). Several respondents suspected that their aspiring Chinese partners—and perhaps future competitors—were working behind the scenes with MOFTEC during the negotiations to ensure that localization was made a condition of approval (#7).

Interviewees provided several insights about agreeing to local content requirements. First, they saw local content issues (like export performance) as negotiable. Second, complying with these requirements demanded greater diligence than meeting export ratio targets. The finance director quoted already explains, "Local content rules are more strictly enforced or monitored [than export performance]. This is a challenge for us, but not insurmountable by any means. Like exporting, it makes good business sense" (#30).

Increasing local content serves several purposes beyond pleasing the planning ministries or other overseeing authorities. It can reduce input costs by avoiding duties and transportation fees.[40] In some cases, sourcing locally may ameliorate problems of unreliable distribution channels for inputs originating at a distance from the factory. Given the current tight profit margins, such cost-cutting and productivity-enhancing opportunities are significant.

Second, by increasing their share of local content, producers of intermediate goods are able to help customers meet *their* local content requirements, as FIEs are increasingly linked in value chains with other FIEs. For many firms the question is not whether to source locally but how to find local content that meets FIE quality specifications. FIEs that offer high local content *and* high quality make it possible for customers to satisfy their own content requirements and maintain quality at the same time, and such firms are doing very well (e.g., ##40, 46).

In other words, the FIEs themselves are often eager to increase local content. There are anxieties, however. Several firms suggested—quietly—that precisely what is local sometimes "gets mixed up." A southern China factory manager noted that tracking local content and sales to the domestic market is "tough, but I think we are OK. To be both ethical *and* profitable, you have to be creative" (#19). This firm (and thousands like it) sells products in the Chinese market as having local content that in fact are substantially imported material. Such circumvention is common in southern China. The "creativity" lies in making sure that such actions are acceptable to local government officials, usually willing to turn a blind eye if the firm is a dutiful contributor to the local economy (i.e., pays its taxes). In other cases, the firms instead have ready a strong defense in case their practices become an issue. It is not particularly comfortable to operate with such a sword over one's head, however.

Local content requirements, unlike export performance requirements, are on the "illustrative list" of investment measures noted in the TRIMs agreement as inconsistent with WTO policies (Schott and Buurman 1994, 167). Nevertheless, China's WTO accession will probably not spell the end of investors' complaints in this area. The TRIMs accord needs to be sharpened in order to make it effective; meanwhile, local content policies can be

---

40. Numerous managers noted, however, that many Chinese inputs remain less competitive than those from elsewhere in the region even though the latter are subject to these costs. Because of trade protection, a number of Chinese commodity prices stand above the world price. In many cases, the relative costliness of Chinese substitutes is due to the products' lack of service, their undependability, and the unpredictability of shipments.

hidden for some time behind other, more ambiguous regimes such as policies governing infant industries. Even after they are acknowledged and notice has been given,[41] these practices may be subject to lengthy phaseout schedules.

Therefore, it is imperative that FIEs take seriously local content obligations in the negotiation and—despite the low incidence of serious penalties for noncompliance—agree to commitments no more onerous than what would be incurred solely for commercial reasons. Demands that go beyond that level need not stop the deal; but neither should the foreign partner's insistence on language that permits flexible interpretation of what constitutes achievement of the local content targets.

Technology and Research and Development Requirements

It is the stated goal of the Chinese authorities that establishment should encourage the transfer and acquisition of technology from abroad. Regulations, including the Guidelines, are dotted with references to the need for investors to introduce technology in order to gain approval for their ventures. This implicit model of government activism claims four virtues: enhancing technological depth by accelerating local research and development, broadening the industrial base, promoting political autonomy, and providing greater national security (Moran 1998, 167–82).

Foreign firms in China have had their share of technology and intellectual property rights (IPR) problems. Recording, video, and software industry piracy has been very well publicized, though estimates of foreign losses have probably been overstated.[42] Other evidence abounds. Maskus, Dougherty, and Mertha (1998) provides a survey-based assessment of FIE IPR problems in China. Interviewees related instances of forced licensing (#7), reverse engineering (#20), trademark and patent infringement (##16, 18), trade name infringement (#22), and counterfeiting (#36). All firms participating in this study were concerned about IPR issues and were working to better protect their intellectual assets. In addition, all used their technology as a quid pro quo to secure desired objectives in the negotiation process and beyond.

As with other performance requirements, technology transfer policies are both explicit and informal; they most commonly arise as an inducement for the Chinese to cede greater management control and market access. For example, the Guidelines declare that foreign firms processing ethylene must be the minority party in Sino-foreign JVs. This may mean that their Chinese partners will have broad access to any technologies they employ (unless negotiated otherwise). No statute plainly mandates that

---

41. In the working parties on WTO accession, it has become clear that China was ill prepared to meet even the notification requirements for such practices.

42. See Noland (1996) for a critical look at how these losses were calculated.

foreign enterprises must transfer technology. The rules do require technology considerations for a firm to qualify simultaneously for WOFE status (or in some cases gain majority status in a JV and hence management control) *and* market access. Statutorily, technology transfer is thus "required" only for those firms bent on gaining both. This exchange is a prime example of the trade-off model of establishment offered in figure 2.3.

In practice the pressure for technology transfer is felt from approval authorities during the notice and examination period. How much pressure, and how the technology is shared (e.g., by compulsory licensing at local institutes specializing in reverse engineering and dissemination), differs by sector. The Guidelines make quite clear which sectors are candidates for technology requirements, formal or informal, in negotiations. Again, it is common for the potential Chinese partner and the approval authorities to play good cop, bad cop to elicit an agreement on transfer from the foreign partner in exchange for approval.

Managers interviewed for this study made a number of observations that mitigated the standard depiction of the Chinese as blatant technology outlaws. The most cynical suggestion was that incumbent firms see no reason to make potential competitors think it easy to do business in China: fear of IPR factors works to their advantage.[43] Other points were less conspiratorial, and taken together they somewhat moderate the usual analysis of the technology transfer performance requirement.

First, some argued that firms can rationally balance technology and control if they think ahead. When there is loose venture control in sectors prone to reverse engineering, foreign investors can anticipate this behavior and accordingly select the appropriate technologies to transfer. Interviewees *expected* misappropriation of technology by both private and public parties. They understand that using a technology means giving it away to potential local competitors, and therefore they bring to China only what they can part with comfortably. In some cases, the foreign side proposed the arrangements (knowing the technology would be pirated) as a device to secure market access.

This tactic has led to some complaints from Chinese authorities that foreigners are bringing too much "junk"—low-tech products or outdated models—to the market. But increasingly they understand that foreigners cannot be expected to bring their "crown jewels" to China without assurances of protection. As the number of WOFEs (and JVs with strong foreign control) approved in China is increasing, a few multinational corporations (e.g., Motorola, General Motors) are starting to install jewels (albeit lesser ones) in their operations (##4, 20, 27, 43).

Second, interviewees noted that to a significant degree, central administrative efforts to coerce technology transfer, like local content require-

---

43. For very similar behavior among foreign firms in the Japanese market, see Christopher (1986).

ments and export performance targets, go unenforced or only partially enforced, because local authorities often align themselves with the foreign investors. FIEs, in contrast, have managed in some cases to force stronger implementation of intellectual property laws, such as those governing copyright and trademark infringement, in more cooperative jurisdictions.

Third, FIEs have found that in numerous ways, technology transfer makes good business sense. FIEs faced with local infringement are often told to negotiate technology transfers and subcontracting relationships with the entrepreneurial offender (#18). But many other FIEs voluntarily transfer know-how to build local suppliers into their value chains. Poor distribution infrastructure makes it highly desirable to have suppliers nearby. And for the time being, 25-year-old technologies are welcome at Chinese firms. Still other FIEs are already being driven upmarket by aggressive low-end competition and find that in their changing markets, more than the minimal technology transfer is essential if they are to move quickly in response to new pressures and opportunities (#8). All these factors suggest the utility to FIEs of providing technology transfers in China, beyond what would necessarily make sense in another emerging economy.

Fourth, managers of several FIEs reported that firms had explicitly decided to trade off more technology for accelerated access to market share in China. Recourse to such tactics demonstrates that the government does not have a sound procompetitive stance designed to foster dynamic benefits. As a means of spurring technological advance, competition is superior to bureaucratic orchestration, especially in such a complex policy environment as China's. In any case, firms with technology to offer are cutting their own deals with Chinese approval authorities (sometimes introducing advanced technologies without too much worry over control). They should make such choices with their eyes open. More than one foreign firm has thought that it knew how to control the technology it traded for market access, believing that Chinese partners were not advanced enough to use it on their own—and gotten burned (#20; and see box 2.3).

Finally, the fifth common observation was that Chinese firms were poor utilizers of technology and thus posed little threat in the long term. This conclusion rests on the industrial backwardness left from China's statist past. It is still apparent in many quadrants in China, especially outside the developed cities. Peter Evans, an MIT-based expert on technology promotion in the energy sector, visited a Japanese Overseas Development Agency project in Dalian:

> The energy efficiency testing equipment—worth over $150,000—was still in the bubble wrap. The Japanese on site wanted to use the equipment, but couldn't get Chinese firms to pay for the energy efficiency audits, partly because they thought the Japanese should do it for free and partly because there was a rival Chinese energy efficiency unit in the same town that considered energy efficiency audits its own turf and didn't want any competition from Japanese upstarts. (personal communication, 23 November 1997)

Box 2.3 Technology Digestion and Acquisition
(from Gilboy 1997, chapter 2)

In 1995, Chinese large and medium-sized enterprises spent about $4.45 billion on technology imports, but only about $160 million on technology *xiaohua xishou*—"digestion" and "assimilation." Technology indigenization projects comprise only about 10 percent of all technology import activities, and spending on indigenization comprises only about 3.5 percent of all technology import spending. In its 1996 *Industrial Development Report,* China's Institute for Industrial Economics contrasts this with the case of Japan, where for every one dollar spent on buying "hard" technology, 10 dollars are spent on indigenization and innovation, calling China's indigenization efforts "pitiful."

In general, Chinese firms do not pay for extensive training for their staff on the new machines they import, nor will they pay for spare parts or replacement parts. Chinese firms tend to see technology transfer as simply the purchase of a lump of metal and its subsequent installation in the factory. Indigenization is defined as successful when plans and blueprints are translated, and operators know how to use the machine. But this attitude toward technology is far different from the "technology ideology" of Japan and "technological learning" of South Korea, "miracle" countries with which China is increasingly compared. In those countries engineers, managers, and policymakers were not satisfied with knowing the "how" of machines, they also wanted to know "why"—that way, they could make the next series of technological improvements and new products themselves. Chinese firms do not display a similar attitude toward technology.

Technology import vs. technology assimilation, 1990–95 (100 million RMB)

	1990	1991	1992	1993	1994	1995
Technology import (total)	92.5	90.2	116.1	159.2	266.7	360.9
Xiaohua xishou	5.7	4.1	5.4	6.2	9.3	13.1

Sources: Adapted by Gilboy (1997) from the National Science and Technology Commission's *China's Science and Technology Indicators 1996,* and National Statistics Bureau's *China Science and Technology Yearbook 1995.* Reproduced with permission from the author.

Chinese scholars supply further evidence. For example, three researchers from the Department of Industrial Science and Technology of the State Science and Technology Commission wrote:

> Because of the failure to accord central importance to the absorption, assimilation, and innovation of imported technology, both the government and enterprises handle absorption and assimilation funds in a most haphazard unplanned manner and fail to make them actually available. Hence the severe underinvestment in the absorption and assimilation of technology. In 1991, the ratio between import funds and absorption and assimilation funds was 17:1. In contrast, the ratio in Japan, a success story in absorption and assimilation, was 1:7. (Shi, Yang, and Mu 1997, 10)

Thus many foreign investors in China do not take seriously the threat of local technological prowess. The most modern enclaves in China's economy, such as Motorola's WOFE plants in Tianjin or GM's new facility in Shanghai, may make such thinking obsolete. For now, however, many foreigners continue to see Chinese technology piracy as a low-tech affair: serious for firms that expect 1998-vintage intellectual property protection for 1970s-era technologies, replicated with ease, but no challenge to fast-moving, technology-intensive industries.

In his survey study, Moran (1998) labels the standard model of technology licensing by emerging economies the "Japan-Korea model." It functions by blocking imports as much as possible, permitting domestic sales by firms that develop local technological know-how, and providing subsidies and incentives to foster the deepening of indigenous technologies. Moran finds evidence, however, that this model is not superior for the technological development or national security of emerging economies.

In important ways, China differs from the usual pattern described in the literature of technology transfer regimes, making it even less amenable to orchestrated efforts to extract technology from investors. China, compared to Japan and South Korea, is relatively open to foreign investment. Its investment environment is not monolithic, as myriad local bureaucracies (and firms) collude with foreign investors to circumvent the demands of central and provincial authorities. Economies with huge market scale and scope may not need to coerce technology transfer: many FIEs transfer more technology than required, not because of arm-twisting but because they want to cement relationships and (ideally) lock up markets. Moran observes that "wholly owned subsidiaries within highly competitive industries provide the most rapid vehicle for the transfer of technology into a given economy, with potentially significant spillovers to indigenous firms" (1998, 171). The present research certainly indicates that this is true in China and that Chinese authorities, recognizing it, are responding appropriately with more WOFE approvals.

Analysis

The 15 topics addressed in this chapter on establishment are presented in table 2.9. Each is assigned one or more of the four "drivers" described in chapter 1: transitional factors, self-imposed factors, policy variables, and market structure phenomena. These categorizations were first derived from the interviewees' comments and then refined after review by the interviewees.

Since the goal of this study is to illuminate the policy implications of the FIE experience in China, the table further breaks down those themes that have policy aspects. One column indicates the level or levels at which the policy in question is generated. More often than not the central government has a hand in the matters of concern to FIEs, but provincial and local

Table 2.9 Roundup of issues: establishment

Issue	Category	If policy . . . Level	Priority
Market information: China	Transitional, policy	Central, provincial, local	Medium
Market information: competitors	Transitional, market		
Ignorance and error	Transitional, self-imposed		
Locating strategically	Policy, market, transitional, self-imposed	Central, lower also	High
Chinese industrial-policy steering	Policy	Central, lower also	High
Partner issues	Market, policy, transitional, self-imposed	Central, lower also	High
Ownership forms available	Policy	Central	Medium
Share and management control	Policy	Central	Medium
Labor structure	Policy, self-imposed, transitional	Central	High
Financial structure	Policy, self-imposed	Central	Medium
Phasing investments	Self-imposed		
Interpreting a legitimate setup	Policy, self-imposed	Central, lower also	Medium
Scope of business	Policy, self-imposed	Central	High
Incentives	Policy, self-imposed	Central, lower also	Medium
Performance requirements	Policy	Central	Low

authorities play a role as well—sometimes at odds with central policy. The implications of such clashes for foreign responses to China's economic development are drawn out in chapter 7. In another column, each policy factor is assigned a priority, based on the case studies and follow-up surveys sent to FIEs.

It should be emphasized that while the concern here is the difficulties and problems FIEs encounter in China, the Chinese economy has made impressive progress toward compatibility with international norms (such as they are) since the end of the Cultural Revolution. If in 1978 Americans had set a 20-year target for China, few would have demanded the advances that have already been achieved. Chinese officials often complain that the more they accomplish, the more they are pressured about what remains to be done. Alas, such are the problems of success.

Transitional and Self-Imposed Problems

The issues reported by FIEs involve a range of factors. Transitional factors are common in the preestablishment phases of gathering market information and determining a strategic position for the venture, though they are never the only factors. The information deficit hampers all the players, including Chinese authorities (who recognize better than anyone else the difficulty of making decisions with dubious data). As China's transition moves along, therefore, one can expect these intelligence tasks to become less onerous. Transitional problems are also relevant in the case of negotiating the labor structure: as capacity to train skilled workers grows and the mobility and ability of unskilled workers to adjust to new conditions improve, dealing with the labor contract negotiation will become marginally easier.

Foreign investors are building information-handling capacity by training financial analysts and accountants, who provide the essential but now missing link required for good market appraisal. Though the market's growth will outstrip the supply of such professionals for some time, progress in this area will lighten the burden of market assessment and help to lift the veil of ignorance. As the gold rush of the mid-1990s slows to $30 billion a year or so of FDI, there will be fewer investors too panicked to gauge competitor behavior.

Location questions also have a transitional dimension. The incentive structure that has developed is highly volatile; depending on location one could pay nearly 50 percent tax or be virtually exempt from tax and duty for up to a decade. At the same time, viable markets are emerging all along China's eastern seaboard. Meanwhile the distribution infrastructure—needed to ship products out of those locales and intermediate materials in—remains poor. For the foreseeable future the optimal mix of market proximity and local incentives will keep shifting, presenting a challenge to new entrants to the Chinese market as they decide where best to set up shop.

Partners play a role that includes a transitional element, for they take part in information arbitrage and provide legitimizing fronts (e.g., in distribution; see chapter 5). Even where policy has been well developed, China's limited capacity to implement and enforce all the rules of a modern economy across its huge marketplace leaves a commercial vacuum, ensuring that FIEs still need to enlist the help of local partners.

Besides the transitional factors, a number of self-imposed problems arise in FIE negotiation and establishment. The personal ignorance and error to which a number of managers admitted is in part but not wholly a function of transition. Notably, many FIEs have erred by entering hastily, without paying sufficient attention to control of staff and scope of operations. Strategic decisions regarding partner choice, location, and the mix of incentives and obligations are all the responsibility of the FIE.

Susan Schwab of the University of Maryland further points out that foreign investors in China are often totally ignorant of or unconcerned about the degree to which their contract terms are compatible with international commercial rules and agreements (personal communication, 16 June 1998). Such inattention suggests that investors are missing an opportunity to help prompt reform in China, as well as contributing to their own future headaches when those rules are officially embraced by China and these inconsistencies come to light.

The identification of nonpolicy drivers behind FIE concerns itself has a policy implication: regardless of whether the commercial policy is "right," doing business in China will continue to be a challenge. The reader must be wary of the misguided tendency to presume that all of the roadblocks facing foreign enterprises in emerging China are mercantile. It is easy for outsiders to ascribe the Chinese business environment to a monolithic mercantilism on the part of the Communist leadership, and Chinese leaders can inadvertently contribute to this misapprehension through their strenuous efforts to project a unified front. Those who wish to better manage foreign commercial policies toward China (or better manage an FIE in China) must acknowledge the limits of the policy dimension. That said, the policy dimension is extensive, and these aspects are discussed next.

Policy Variables

Table 2.9 shows policy problems dominating the process of establishment. In fact, only three of the topics raised by expatriate managers do not involve the hand of government. The prominence of policy is nowhere greater than in the negotiation and establishment phase (though in legal issues it rises to almost the same level). In short, in the gatekeeper function policy appears to play its greatest role.

At the top of the table are market information problems that complicate the decisions that FIEs must face. Though transitional capacity inadequacies are being remedied, Communist Party control over media remains extensive. All newspapers must be registered and under the aegis of a state-sanctioned entity, and journalists are still occasionally jailed or fined for reporting unfavorably; in extreme cases, publications are shut down (Hazelbarth 1997, 14). Authorities have repeatedly attempted to place official agencies in charge of disseminating economic data and analyses. Foreign participation in financial services essential to information gathering and analysis, such as auditing and accounting, remains significantly limited. China has consistently treated market information as a service (whereas it has really become a part of business infrastructure in a global economy), and in service sectors the government intervenes and foreigners are restricted, reflecting an anachronistic understanding of modern business.

Policy interference in the ability of FIEs to research market conditions in China thus remains considerable, and it comes from the central authorities. But impressive progress toward a more open commercial information environment has also been made, with new providers appearing regularly. Increasingly, the problem for new investors will not be official restrictions on information flow but informal information hoarding by and collusion among private parties and provincial and local officials, who hope to preserve their own by protecting them from competition.

Explicit policy restrictions still affect site selection in a variety of ways. The foreign banks permitted to operate (on an experimental basis) must be established in Pudong, Shanghai; retail licenses have been handed out with only certain cities in mind; with the exception of AIG, the few foreign insurers allowed into the market have been made to select just a single city in which to operate. Provincial authorities, working below the central level, often have very specific locations in mind when they grant approvals. Official incentive policies—the special economic zones—of course also influence site selection. Finally, some FIEs have been required to establish facilities in interior provinces in exchange for access to the more attractive markets along the coast.

Policies designed to limit FIEs' choice of sites vary in importance by sector; they can be wholly determinative (as in banking) or nonexistent. As zones proliferate and competition for foreign investment dollars increases among provinces, restrictive policies seem generally to be waning. In specific industries, however—again, notably banking—they have become even more important. Depending on how vigorously Chinese leaders try to direct industrial policy, certain "pillar industries" may well face more geographic limitations in the future than they do today. Meanwhile, the emergence of markets across coastal China provides a motive (invest where the markets are, to make money) distinct from that driving the Party's geographic preferences (distribute development to ease social tensions); it is reasonable to guess that the logic of the market will win out over Party policy before too long.

The steering of FIEs toward specific partners is a related issue. Many interviewees recounted pressure to couple with weak domestic firms in need of bailouts. But unlike siting, which is influenced by a mixture of factors, this is solely a policy matter. The industry regulators manage these steering efforts, making proposals that are sometimes hard to refuse. Besides such specific matchings, the process of establishment more generally tends to force foreigners into partnering arrangements, if not with a firm then with local or higher-level patrons. Maneuvering within these partnerships, or someday separating from partners, has proven difficult and indeed sometimes impossible. Enforced cronyism is no strategy for economic health, whether for FIEs or for local Chinese firms. Foreigners will of their own volition partner with viable Chinese entities, and there are many such candidates: the time has come to outlaw shotgun weddings.

Policy factors are present in each of the specific negotiating areas, except for the decision about phasing. Structures and conditions of ownership are a matter of central policy, though like other negotiating issues they are adjusted at lower levels of authority. While Beijing authorities have experimented in recent years with new enterprise forms, the options continue to come up short. The share and management control limitations set by central policy also leave foreigners at a disadvantage in competing with ethnic Chinese nationals, often forcing them to build circumventions of the rules into their operations right from the start.

Policy plays an important role in the labor structure that the FIE will establish. It prevents representative offices from hiring locals directly, requiring instead that they accept assigned staff. FIEs that are industrial and commercial ventures are strongly pressured to absorb more staff than wanted during the examination period, when Ministry of Labor officials or their subsidiary agents attempt to set human resource policies (which are not transparent). Restrictions on the labor structure that the FIE will establish can prevent the foreign partner from providing incentives to managers and setting human resource policies. Ironically, one of the most frustrating consequences for FIEs is that they are unable to increase salaries as quickly as they would like for employees who perform well.

The financial structure is restricted by policies that prevent FIEs from moving money among subsidiaries effectively and from invoicing and managing credit in China for all but the goods they manufacture locally. Holdings of foreign exchange have been closely monitored in the past, with foreign enterprises allowed only limited control over hard currency holdings. If FIEs were not now generally inclined to want renminbi, this would remain a problem.[44] At present as in the past, however, the level of FIE control over foreign exchange flows varies greatly, and no definitive analysis is possible.

Policy explicitly prevents foreigners from setting up enterprises comprising sufficient scope: if a firm thrives on close management of distribution, marketing, or after-sales service, it may well be stymied by policy in China (unless high tech or high-level connections are involved). The biggest problem here is often the lack of qualified alternatives to doing it yourself, especially when firms wish to expand beyond the rich coastal enclaves.

The need to find an interpretation to legitimate the FIE—for example, in complex dealings whereby Chinese subsidiaries delegate certain invoicing responsibilities to a foreign holding company—is a problem created by policy. A personal note or interpretation from a senior leader, or a special dispensation from a central ministry or bureau, often means the difference between the doable and the illegal. Such fuzziness is echoed

---

44. As of late 1998, the problem is returning as investors look for dollars to hedge against the risk of a Chinese currency devaluation.

at provincial and local levels. Senior leaders have preserved this system of administration because it has provided comfort during a time of experimentation and uncertainty, and because it also greases the wheels (i.e., spreads enough money around to keep liberalization on track, so far). While the ends China achieved may have justified those means, a quick change of paradigm now seems to be in order.

These same points apply to incentives, both official and informal. Central policy encouraged local use of incentives to lure FDI, but now that they are allowed, Beijing has found it difficult to regulate their sometimes injudicious or illegal extension. These policies are temporarily aggravating inequitable distribution of wealth and opportunity between China's urban and rural areas, and between coast and interior. In response, leaders are contemplating how to level their domestic playing field. Foreign firms will be torn between supporting reform on the one hand and defending their special privileges on the other. In the end, businesses cannot be counted on to support the greater good: a fair bit of whining can be expected on the part of hitherto privileged FIEs before the process of dismantling uneven development is finished.

Finally, performance requirements are mandated or encouraged by central policy and echoed at lower levels. Though performance requirement policies do not appear prohibitively troublesome, these bureaucratic forays into the market are of dubious value. Firms might well provide better export performance, local sourcing, and technology transfer without them.

The interviewees' perspectives on these issues were used to determine priority for those matters that included a policy dimension. There are three rankings.

High: The handling of this issue will directly determine the success or failure of the venture.

Medium: The issue can substantially affect the success of the venture and consumes significant effort during establishment.

Low: The issue is important but manageable during establishment, and an undesired outcome is unlikely to undermine success.

Their comments suggest that the most significant issues for establishing a venture are strategic locational pressures, policies designed to steer FIEs into partnership with designated firms, the attendant partner issues, and the structural issues of labor control and scope of business operations (see table 2.9). To be sure, attention should not be limited to only this subset of themes stressed by one sample of managers. However, it does reflect the priorities of many (especially Western) foreign-invested enterprises seeking establishment in China. Their concerns center on the subtle relationships that the firm will depend on: with officials, managers, labor, and the distributors and sellers with which the venture interacts.

Market Structure

As shown, many of the concessions that FIEs make in order to establish in China are questionable. The reason most often given is overzealousness to get into the market, but there are other complex motivations. It is a common belief among foreign investors that after accepting a sufficient number of foreign firms to modernize their country, Chinese technocrats will then make establishment much more difficult for additional firms. And even if the center and localities were to agree to opening their borders further and eschewing industrial policy indefinitely, another problem partially validates the manic pace of foreign entry. China has shown little concern for procompetitive regulations that must be instituted at the central level. Without such a policy function, a tendency toward collusion and locking up distribution—already everywhere in evidence in China—may suffocate competition.

Market structure problems need not result from policy decisions; they only require that authorities fail to act. Three themes pertaining to establishment involve a market structure element, though never in isolation from the other factors. The first of these is uncertainty about the intentions of competitors.[45] Without a transparent regime for making commercial opportunities available to all bidders, managers are anxious that rivals will foreclose markets. Though many markets are unserved or remain underserved by existing domestic and FIE firms, new entrants can be held at bay. The fear—whether well founded or not—that markets are being locked up by competitors willing to make deep concessions has in some sectors led firms to make hasty decisions.

Second, market structure shapes the decisions that the FIEs must make regarding site selection and proximity to market. As an inducement to invest, local governments sometimes promise to protect "their" firms from competition. Such actions make markets available for some FIEs, but only within the bounds of the jurisdiction in which the venture is favored. Firms outside those bounds, whether elsewhere in China or abroad, find themselves on the wrong side of a wall—or at least with no local approval for establishment. The result is compartmentalization of market shares and reduced competition in some sectors.

Third, market structure problems lend partner relations much of their importance. The concentration of market power in a given sector may appear to be de facto evidence that partner relationships are at work, adding to the urgency for a potential FIE to join with partners of its own in order to find a way in. In an open, contestable market, partners are only necessary insofar as they add economic value to the enterprise. In a collusive

---

45. While all firms in market economies face this uncertainty, in a more mature market they can at least assume that their competitors will not attempt to achieve their ends by patently illegal anticompetitive means; this is not the case in China.

marketplace, they are needed because they have insider information, offer the way around a stranglehold on distribution or approvals, or are valued by someone with authority who controls access to the sector. A partnership entered for those reasons is liable to suffer a host of problems, including organizational discord and the misappropriation of shared venture assets such as intellectual property and technology. Thus the increasing prevalence of WOFEs augurs well for the future contestability of the Chinese market and for FIE performance as well (see chapter 7).

Failure to take into account the market structure likely to emerge absent competition policy in China is just as costly at the aggregate national level as at the microeconomic level. Because FIEs are restricted from a variety of economies of scope, including distribution and services, they are less able to combat a collusive market. Even FIEs that now enjoy a dominant position in China because of proprietary technology or the advantage of early entry will find that an uncontestable market structure works against them over time: local interests possessing marginally superior claims on local power brokers (never underestimate Chinese nationalism) or *guanxi* with local businesses will chip away at their positions.

3

Foreign Enterprises and Human Resources

The reasons why foreign firms generally tend to hire and fire on merit is that they must answer to owners who care first and foremost about the bottom line. . . . If they don't pay for performance, they will soon go out of business. By doing so they foster the radical notion—radical at least in China . . .—that individual merit matters and should be rewarded.

This sense of the value of the individual and of fairness is intrinsic to capitalism. It is, at the same time, an essential characteristic of a culture which respects human rights.

Business ethicist Michael Santoro
(*Asian Wall Street Journal*, 1 June 1998, 12)

Introduction

Having gotten its "chops,"[1] the FIE in China faces the first task of any business: securing the employees that will make it run. In examining the human resource issues that arise for FIEs in China today, this chapter makes three main points. First, by providing an overview of the day-to-day challenges of personnel management, from negotiating the labor contract onward, it demonstrates how deeply involved foreign firms have become in the development of the Chinese economy. Second, it makes clear that human resource problems account for many of the difficulties suffered by FIEs in the Chinese market: thus exclusionary Chinese

---

1. When an approved venture is formally registered, it is issued a set of chops, the carved stone seals used to imprint the red mark of the firm on official documents. This method of authentication has been employed in China since ancient times.

commercial policies create only some of the barriers that foreigners face. Third, it portrays foreign interactions with Chinese employees as nonexploitative. This study provides evidence of FIEs as agents for positive change in the employer-employee relationship in China today. To be sure, there are poverty-related abusive labor practices in many quarters, some involving foreign investors. But it is atypical of Western, certainly of US, FIEs, many of which are dramatically improving the social welfare (both material and intellectual) of the Chinese employees within their sphere of operation.[2]

It is unfortunate that in the rush to judge the inadequacies in China's human resources profile, American observers have largely missed the extraordinary, positive changes that have taken place in the 1990s. Not least, the exertions of foreign firms to reengineer the relationship between employee and employer have been underreported. Why? For one thing, cases of abuse draw more attention than examples of progress, and many of the innovations that FIEs have introduced in China would appear fairly mundane to most Westerners. Furthermore, few FIEs have chosen to showcase their efforts to date.

Many Western observers presume that Chinese labor is remarkable only for its cheapness and pliancy. In fact, the lure of "cheap labor" in China has turned into something of a cruel joke for many foreign investors: the time and effort consumed in managing labor resources are significant, and in many locations costs are ballooning. FIEs are raising staff levels in all major cities, as well as expanding into second-tier cities and beyond (a recent US-China Business Council survey indicates that half of large US firms in China are already serving over 50 markets; see USCBC 1998). Because the market is so large and physically disjointed, and because logistical tasks from advertising to distribution to marketing are in their nascent stages and are all areas that must be developed painstakingly with a hands-on approach, FIEs need the help of local talent. Labor costs have skyrocketed (especially for skilled and semiskilled workers), the relative size of the talent pool has dwindled as demand has grown, and competition among FIEs for competent English-speaking accountants, finance directors, marketing managers, and the like is fierce. These serious challenges are commercial; others come from governmental or quasi-governmental agencies, which press noncommercial labor agendas on both foreign and domestic firms.

One major reason for the urgency is easy to identify. In 1990 just over $4 billion in foreign direct investment (FDI) was placed in China by FIEs; in

---

2. In this chapter more than most, it must be stressed that the sample of firms and individuals in this study is not comprehensive. Those interviewed reflect the practices of American firms most of all, with important inputs from European and Japanese firms. Some would argue that a study of Taiwanese, Korean, and Singaporean firms might produce a very different set of findings on the "social footprint" of FIEs. That is so; however, the concerns of readers of this study are likely to revolve around the kinds of firms that are represented here.

Table 3.1 Employment of Chinese by foreigners, 1980-96 (thousands)

	Foreign-funded economic units[a]	Overseas-Chinese funded economic units[b]	Total labor force (rural and urban)
1980	na	na	423,610
1981	na	na	437,250
1982	na	na	452,950
1983	na	na	464,360
1984	na	na	481,970
1985	60	na	498,730
1986	120	10	512,820
1987	200	10	527,830
1988	290	20	543,340
1989	430	40	553,290
1990	620	40	639,090
1991	960	690	647,990
1992	1,380	830	655,540
1993	1,330	1,550	663,730
1994	1,950	2,110	671,990
1995	2,410	2,720	679,470
1996	2,750	2,650	688,500

na = not available.

a. Enterprises established by foreigners in China as joint ventures (cooperative and equity), wholly owned foreign enterprises, and other legal forms.
b. Enterprises established by overseas Chinese from Hong Kong, Macao, and Taiwan in mainland China.

Source: China Statistical Yearbook, 1997, China State Statistical Bureau.

1996 the total exceeded $42 billion; in 1997 it was over $45 billion. Chinese data (see table 3.1) suggest that the number of Chinese employed by FIEs rose from 660,000 in 1990 to 5.4 million in 1996. The actual number of Chinese under non-Chinese management may be higher.[3] This torrent of FDI has led firms to scramble for qualified people, not just for the shop floor but for management, marketing, sales, service, distribution, accounting, and advertising; there is substantial personnel pressure wherever FIEs are found. The task of managing this human resources revolution has been difficult for foreign investors and their Chinese partners.

These challenges are not unique to China, of course. However, they are unusually pervasive, because of the combination of rapid growth in a

---

3. FIEs are today managing Chinese directly through shell companies that are ostensibly independent. This stratagem allows foreigners to enter distribution and service markets that they would not be permitted to access directly.

large market, competition among foreign and domestic firms for a limited pool of skilled labor in the frontline commercial centers (i.e., Shanghai, Beijing), restrictions on employment practices, and lack of experience in grappling with the cultural nuances of staffing.

Management in general must fight against ancient culture and traditions, which diverge fundamentally from Western workplace habits. Child (1996, 33)—one of the foremost experts on foreign management in China—casts this difference in entrepreneurial terms (drawing on Boisot): "[T]he Chinese are not yet attuned to a 'Schumpeterian' kind of learning process based on disequilibrium models of innovation and opportunity; both their culture and governance systems are more attuned to an equilibrium model." Schumpeter, who championed the "creative destruction" of old patterns of thinking in order to make way for the new, would have found the apogee of conservatism in many Chinese enterprises as they hunker down against the prospect of competition and reengineering. (That this remains a fact is extraordinary given the violence and effort expended by Mao Zedong during the prior period to destroy traditional modes of thinking, and it says something of the tenacity of human belief.) With mixed success, foreign managers have worked to break through the reluctance of indigenous management and labor to accept change. While increasingly they can recognize kindred spirits in their younger Chinese counterparts, many expatriates still perceive themselves in isolated battle against a Chinese sea of statism.

Only a few years ago the purpose of all firms in China was to fulfill goals handed down by planning authorities; all had Communist secretaries and bureaucracies that shared management duties with the commercially oriented staff (most nonprivate firms still do, though to a far lesser extent).[4] Performance-based incentives were rare for either firms or individuals. How much power did Chinese managers traditionally have to balance their books? How much control did they have over transactions with suppliers and buyers? In each case, the answer is "very little."

While China's economy has been gradually introduced to new ideas, the FIEs typically turned old priorities on their heads from the moment of establishment—often in the face of considerable resistance. The level of control foreign managers wanted, the extent of change they intended to bring with that control, and the nature of the changes they sought all directly challenged conventional Chinese thinking. Given how deeply ingrained the old patterns are, the progress has been surprising. Foreign management in China has accomplished much in the years since it was first introduced; nonetheless, many challenges specific to assembling and managing FIE human resources remain.

---

4. Child (1996, 77) counted from 2 to 42 full-time Party staff at Chinese enterprises that were the subject of his case studies in 1985 and 1988; the average number declined markedly over those years. The average in 1988 for 12 ventures in Beijing and Nantong was 4, down from about 10 in 1985.

This chapter explores these challenges and considers why they are so acute and so important. The issues that FIEs face during establishment include the nontransparent approval process, pressures to overstaff, difficulties in obtaining the desirable mix of staff for the venture, and the fight to secure managerial control. The chapter also discusses the benefits of the FIE presence for the Chinese whom they employ. Operational issues after establishment is complete include availability of key professionals, wage pressures and changing labor patterns, worker mobility, nonwage costs, training and quality assurance, and retention. These concerns were identified through case studies and background interviews with human resource managers and other expatriates in China.

Several additional themes not directly discussed by interviewees could be discerned in their responses. First was the insulation of the foreign venture from corruption problems through loose affiliation with contractors or other indirect employees (including subcontractors). This is especially relevant to US firms, which are bound by the Foreign Corrupt Practices Act (FCPA). A related issue was the management of parts of the organization that must technically be independent to comply with Chinese restrictions on direct foreign participation (say, in distribution and service) while sometimes being in reality closely managed by foreigners. And there was another background theme against which expatriates made their comments on China's labor situation: the preoccupation in the West, particularly in the United States, with human rights and labor rights conditions.

A final introductory note: in general, interviewees reported that their ability to deal with personnel issues had improved considerably in recent years and that labor markets were stabilizing in places (Guangdong Province, for example). But while personnel issues have become less volatile (in terms of salary inflation, contract uncertainty, regulatory requirements, etc.), their scope increases relentlessly as ever broader swaths of the market are opened to FIEs, formally or informally. Therefore, even if 1998's decelerating trend in new FDI persists beyond the short or medium term,[5] the hothouse atmosphere enveloping human resource management in China will endure.

Human Resources and Establishment: Pressures Shaping the Labor Contract

Human resource issues start with the negotiations to set up a venture, as noted in the previous chapter. In law, FIEs enjoy broad freedom to hire

---

5. Financial upheaval in Asian markets in 1997 will likely curb the rate of overall Chinese growth, though this may be offset by announced fiscal stimuli of $750 billion or more over the period 1998–2000. The crisis' effects on the foreign-invested sector in particular are not clear as of this writing. It is foreseeable that a heavy impact would only encourage FIEs to focus that much more intensely on the Chinese *domestic* market instead of on glutted export markets, making demand for local personnel to serve the domestic business even more intense.

Table 3.2 Unemployment estimates

Source	Unemployment rate	Increase in unemployment	Timing
Chen Jinhua (State Planning Commission)	Target 3.5 percent		1998
Li Boyong (labor minister)	4.2-4.3 percent ("China could sustain 5-6 percent")	3.5 million (state sector)	1998
China Economic Times/Reuters		4 million (civil service)	1998
The Institute of Macroeconomics	5 percent		1998-2003
Wang Dongjin (senior state planner)		20 million (state sector)	1998-2000
Chinese Academy of Social Sciences		40 million (state sector)	na
All-China Federation of Trade Unions		8-10 million (state sector)	1998-2000

na = not available.

Sources: Reuters (8 March 1998; 27 February 1998); *China Daily* (16 March 28; 16 February 1998); *China News Digest* (1 March 1998; 7 May 1997).

and staff a venture as they see fit (USCBC 1996a, 23), choosing from the open market or among the staff available from a Chinese partner (in the case of a joint venture, or JV). The exception is the more timid foray into the market—the representative office—which must hire through an employment service company managed by the government; and even rep offices are finding ways to avoid these restrictions.

But despite these statutory rights and the evidence of pockets of flexibility in practice, considerable labor pressures are brought to bear on a potential FIE petitioning for approval. The authorities can withhold approval until the labor contract is suitably adjusted, or else until management control is structured in a way that will permit the Chinese representatives in the venture to control decision making on labor questions (e.g., salaries, hours, bonuses, responsibilities). Chinese motives for manipulating foreign investors' decisions on human resources are discussed later.

Official rhetoric fulminates against foreigners being permitted to hold imperialistic sway in China, but the immediate motives for shaping FIE labor profiles are more practical. First, central authorities have an interest in encouraging the use of Chinese personnel instead of expatriates, where possible, to promote managerial learning and to reduce high expatriate salary costs (which have the potential to add to remittances out of the country).

Moreover, the greatest political threat confronting Chinese reformers today is increased unemployment among unskilled labor. Table 3.2 cites some estimates of unemployment for the coming years: taken together, they suggest an astounding social dilemma. The figures included are both official and quasi-official; experience suggests that the reality will be worse, though some of these estimates (e.g., 40 million unemployed due to state-sector reforms) are fairly bold. Line ministries overseeing sectors of already high unemployment[6] (and their provincial and local subsidiary units) have an interest in FIEs' retaining as much surplus labor as possible, and they can try to force concessions on ventures. At local levels, officials may seek sinecures for specific individuals. Moreover, the bureaucratic inertia and difficulties caused by the *dang an* and *hukou* systems (described later) complicate the negotiation process for FIEs.

The Chinese partner firm (in the case of JVs) often has a similarly strong interest in maintaining employment levels and management control, even at the expense of performance. Chinese managers traditionally defined prestige in terms such as high head counts, even if that meant lower output per worker. One set of interviewees (##12, 14) related their difficulty in negotiating a partnership with a coastal petrochemicals refinery south of Shanghai. They laid out a plan to spin off the noncore elements of the business to subcontractors, and thus raise profitability. Their suggestions—for example, to divest the enterprise of its factory-owned crematorium—met with confusion and reluctance: why would anyone wish to reduce staff and scope of operations?

Nontransparent Approval

Despite the freedom provided by statute, FIE human resource latitude is constrained in practice. The appropriate labor bureaus (local, municipal, provincial, or central) must approve the labor contract of a joint venture (and of a wholly owned foreign enterprise, or WOFE, though that structure brings less potential for conflict on employment issues because downsizing is usually not involved), and they can therefore pressure FIEs to accept employment commitments. It is not unusual for a potential partner and the overseeing authority to collude to elicit employment concessions. It was reported that labor authorities may take the hard-line role on behalf of the Chinese partner (#7) or may work to compel the Chinese partners to accept some amount of downsizing (#53).

This process is largely nontransparent and prone to abuse. Dealing with such a system, which can clearly deny most favored nation or national

---

6. It was announced at the 15th People's Congress in March 1998 that many of these would be shut down or merged, including the Ministries of Chemical Industries, Coal, Electric Power, Electronics Industry, Forestry, Geology and Mineral Resources, Machine Building, Metallurgy, and Post and Telecommunications. Premier Zhu Rongji has staked his credibility on realizing this pledge; still, it might be too early to begin drafting obituaries for the ministries.

treatment to any given FIE,[7] is the first human resources challenge with which FIEs must grapple. China has not obligated itself to respect such principles, nor does the WTO yet reach into the area of rights of establishment deeply enough to address labor issues in particular. Still, capricious practices that do not offer predictability or recourse to investors will justifiably draw the attention of foreign trade negotiators until they are remedied. At a minimum, one could argue that the present nontransparent regime impairs or even nullifies the legitimate expectations of China's trading partners that their firms will enjoy the same commercial rights as other firms in China. FIEs unable to manage human resources with latitude equivalent to that enjoyed by private Chinese firms will lack the local presence needed to compete on an equal footing in, or sell goods into, the Chinese market.

As with other aspects of enterprise freedom, firms willing to establish ventures off the beaten path, especially in the interior, report greater leverage to stave off entreaties on the human resources front (#26). But regulatory disparities between the coast and the interior can be disadvantageous as well. Smaller foreign ventures without big-money leverage still face greater struggles with labor contract negotiations than do larger ones, especially when their operations cross jurisdictions. "Problems can arise from differences in labor regulations and practice from region to region, and ensuing uncertainty with interpretation," as one consultant noted (#53).

Pressure to Overstaff

Successful negotiation of a number of issues is key to running a profitable venture. Among the first to arise, for JVs, is the number of staff that will be absorbed from the Chinese partner. Earlier case studies of FIEs in China (e.g., Mann 1997) identified forced overstaffing as a major concern, and it continued to receive much attention in the literature of the 1990s. The problem is manifest in the state sector, as State Economic and Trade Commission Vice Minister Chen Qingtai recently conceded (remarks to the National People's Congress, 8 March 1998): "Within these [state-

---

7. The most favored nation principle requires that commercial rights offered to the interests of any one nation are no more advantageous than those extended to others, assuming all are parties to such an agreement. The national treatment principle stipulates that once goods have entered a market, discriminatory distinctions are not drawn between foreign goods and domestic goods. These concepts form the bedrock of the General Agreement on Tariffs and Trade, which anchors the WTO, and traditionally apply to trade in goods. Under the Uruguay Round, which established the WTO, progress was made extending the principles to services. Some, but far less, progress was made toward extending them to investment rights; this is a major task to which negotiators are now turning. China, which is not now a member of the WTO, is not bound by these principles. However, they are clearly the benchmarks against which its deeper integration with the international commercial regime will be judged in the immediate future.

owned] enterprises, if a third of the workforce was cut, these enterprises [could] still operate normally. If half of the workers were reduced, some could operate even better." As reforms progress, Chinese authorities have not been shy about pressuring FIEs to shoulder some of the burden of carrying excess staff. Over this period, firms unable to point to demonstrable technological contributions (or, just as usefully, powerful patrons) have experienced firsthand the difficulty of carrying on their payrolls a large share of redundant workers.

However, many respondents for this study suggested that the problem's severity is diminishing as they gain experience in negotiating labor arrangements. Foreign investors in some cases can now pay severance fees to shed staff,[8] insist on screening out unskilled workers or "lifers," and create retraining or placement centers to redirect unneeded staff. As the market for such services grows, capable human resource consultancies have emerged to help FIEs deal with overstaffing. Whether these adjustment mechanisms will successfully reallocate excess workers to new jobs, or just shuffle them out of the FIE's in box to an unspecified future, is not clear. It is a question that must be answered to gauge the potential for labor instability in China.

Increasingly, FIEs are pursuing a wholly owned format (WOFE) and build facilities from scratch. The desire to avoid the burden of excess staff plays an important part in this shift (as do other management control benefits, such as the chance to build a fresh corporate culture). Thus, while the problem of overstaffing remains widespread, FIEs are finding a variety of ways to cope. Perhaps in the future FIEs will continue to act surprised about the intractability of overstaffing problems, but they will have little excuse for not knowing what they were getting themselves into.

The Right Staff

Beyond the quantity of staff lies the question of quality. Foreign firms want to absorb the most capable personnel from Chinese partner organizations and avoid the burden of the less capable. Senior Chinese managers with critical connections are important; middle managers with demonstrated business skills are desirable; and younger staff with good language skills or exposure to foreign business culture are also sought after. Often firms prefer those workers with lower skills who have not grown accustomed to a state-owned enterprise (SOE) work environment. An additional complication is the massive "education gap" perceived among Chinese who were of school age during the Cultural Revolution

---

8. Other firms gain a credit or debt forgiveness in exchange for not letting people go. One investment banker helping to merge and reengineer industrial firms reported a credit against debt liabilities of 25,000 RMB per worker retained (#49).

(roughly 1966–76), when schools and universities were largely shut down so people could focus on their ideological convictions.

FIEs often deal with problematic realities in hiring. They are sometimes pressured to put friends or relatives of partners or approval authorities on staff whom they wish to refuse, either because of the expense or because such favors are a symbol of past practices that are at odds with the environment foreign managers are trying to create. Some labor agreements give hiring preference to spouses and siblings of current employees (#26). Interviewees almost uniformly desired young, untrained workers rather than older ones already inculcated with the local work ethic, but they recognized that nurturing good relations with local partners and authorities is critical to success.

In some sectors, foreign investors are required to meet quotas for Chinese employees. These restrictions can be found in the Guidelines on foreign investment and in the offers China is making to foreign trade negotiators in its WTO accession talks. For example, at joint venture medical clinics serving the foreign community, no fewer than 50 percent of the staff must be selected on the basis of Chinese nationality, a rather arbitrary criterion for declaring nurses and anesthesiologists qualified.

The number of expatriate managers staffing the venture and the payment of their costs are important negotiating issues. At least until Chinese markets and universities supply sufficient pools of managerial talent, FIEs will call on expatriate staff to oversee the rapid reengineering or development of their China operations. These individuals are the wellsprings of skill that nurture China's fragile markets. And yet, both Chinese policy and market forces argue for localizing management as quickly as possible (see box 3.1), and authorities may try to speed the process by discouraging ventures from budgeting for expatriate expenses. Therefore, according to confidential remarks by several interviewees, high expatriate costs (a possible cause for rejection by approval authorities) are sometimes borne offshore, offset (and disguised) with fees and payments to the parent company (a transfer-pricing phenomenon).

Securing Managerial Control

The foreign investor must also secure management control over the workforce in the negotiation process. In 1985 the top two concerns of SOE managers interviewed by a Western scholar (Child 1996, 94) were freedom to recruit and dismiss workers and freedom to set their salary and bonus levels; not surprisingly, these same issues were at the top of the list for foreign managers in 1997. Thus control over appointing the FIE's director of human resources is critical.

There are examples both of smooth Chinese acquiescence to foreign management leadership and of contentious wrangling that sinks ventures.

Box 3.1 The importance of localizing management

The World Bank claims to be satisfied with its loan performance in China, but its private-sector finance arm, the International Finance Corporation (IFC), has had less than stellar results in its 25 China projects (worth slightly under half a billion dollars in total). The IFC points to "extremely tough operating situations" in explaining a tendency to make investment decisions from headquarters in Washington, DC, using risk models not designed for the Chinese market (*Business China*, 15 September 1997, 12). Its share of equity in its China ventures is high, they are more costly than investments in other emerging markets. Scrappy local competitors outcompete them with cheaper production technologies in the tire, cement, and glass businesses. The IFC faces the same challenges as do other organizations: if management is not local, or if the firm insists on out-of-country decision making, it will likely be disappointed in China.

Expatriates stress that locating management in China is essential to success. This is why FIEs are scrambling to groom local Chinese, with marginally lower salary and overhead costs than imported managers and better local knowledge, to fill decision-making positions. While expatriates do report pressure from overseeing authorities to localize management as much as possible, in practice internal commercial logic argues even more strongly for localization. Those on the ground know, for example, that many Chinese enterprises will simply write off suppliers if they get far enough ahead on credit terms. Because local savvy is so crucial, relations between field managers and home-country officers are frequently tense. Local managers often point to underdelegation as an important reason for poor venture performance.

The widely read account of the Beijing Jeep venture was strewn with battles over management that nearly destroyed the business (Mann 1989). The official regulations themselves are only marginally useful in determining the extent to which foreign management control is possible in a given industry. The Guidelines broadly signal the level of foreign control Chinese authorities are prepared to countenance, by way of ownership and share structure. But minority or majority ownership only partly correlates with foreign control. Other factors reported by firms include the closeness of the Chinese partner firm to the core business lines, the presence of higher-level partners intent on forcing reform in the sector, the decision of the foreign negotiator to make control a priority, and the leverage provided by the technology the foreign firm brings or other strategic tradeoffs it can make (recall the discussion of strategic positioning in chapter 2).

An example of a management control pitfall is the inability of foreign managers to set salary incentives. Howson (1997, 30) notes that until recently, JVs were required to pay workers at least 120 percent of the average wage at comparable state enterprises, *but not more than 150 percent*. Statutes required that the FIE receive permission from examination and approval authorities to go outside these parameters. Several interviewees (##20, 26) were prevented from raising salaries to a competitive level, because they failed to negotiate control over this point during establishment and their Chinese partner was uncomfortable paying higher salaries to productive employees than to average ones. Though the statutory ceiling on wages has apparently been removed (for purposes of contracts henceforth), in practice FIEs must still secure management control over incentives, including salaries.

The authorities' veto power over incentive decisions is a major limitation on foreign management control. Others important limits involve appointing and appraising venture managers, supervising the recruitment process, assigning production targets and overtime limits, setting training allotments and priorities, determining gift-giving and travel policies, and other matters of daily operation. The Chinese regulations provide grounds (i.e., that the venture would otherwise face "serious losses") that permit foreigners to negotiate far-reaching control over all these issues of human resource management. Many foreign firms are learning to take advantage of these regulatory loopholes; others are opting for the do-it-yourself WOFE solution. Both of those stratagems depend on the blessing of local authorities, however.

Interviewees were aware that JV partners had preexisting patterns of management that could not be changed overnight. Child (1996, 90) notes the extent to which planning officials withheld management control from state-owned enterprises even recently. Solely in the personnel area, the SOEs studied by Child commonly lacked decision-making authority to recruit managers, determine enterprise size, set workers' basic salaries, and set compensation for the mandated Party employees; for several, dismissing workers was off-limits, too. The abrogation of management control inherent in the SOE system underscores the importance for FIEs of selecting partners wisely and then negotiating authority to reengineer these issues where need be.

After the Contract: Just the Beginning

While poorly negotiated labor arrangements are trouble, much is worked out despite or sometimes in violation of the contract—provided things are otherwise going well for the venture. For example, in many JVs, especially in southern China, hours worked commonly exceed the limits set out in the labor contract. Local authorities and partners are often complicit in this violation (see table 3.3). Reportedly, local authorities take a pragmatic position: "as long as you have worked this out in a manner acceptable to your employees, and we don't hear complaints, then we don't care how many hours overtime they work" (#19).

This illustrates an important point: as much as FIEs sometimes complain about legal ambiguities and unenforced contract terms, they routinely benefit from these conditions as well. For larger Western firms with a stated commitment to the letter of the law, the attitude of both Chinese

Table 3.3   Overtime at a southern China FIE, 1997 (hours)

	Driver	Guard	Cook	Cleaner	Contractor
	Position				
January	*40*	*40*	9	26	33
February	18	*42*	2	14	20
March	*43*	30	5	32	26
April	27	7	4	*52*	*69*
May	*67*	29	0	35	*48*
June	*43*	*56*	0	28	32

Note: Chinese law limits overtime to 36 hours per month. Numbers in italics indicate employees working over the regulatory limit.

Source: Author's interviews.

and other foreign investors, and even authorities, presents a dilemma. Absent credible enforcement, domestic rivals scoff at the notion of complying fully with labor regulations. Chinese partners discourage (and occasionally almost forbid) foreign managers from naively following the rules. This creates tension within firms over labor practices. For Western firms trying to showcase their ability to implement a corporate code of conduct worldwide, these tensions are not only ethically but commercially worrisome (consider the massive bad press directed at Nike over Chinese labor conditions in recent years). China is increasingly porous to foreign journalists and "social auditors," and the power of publicity about China operations to affect global sales is now clear.

The contract negotiation only foreshadows the human resource challenges to come. A well-negotiated labor structure can reduce sources of contention, but it cannot eliminate them. Conversely, while problems built in during the process of establishment will create headaches for the foreign manager trying to reengineer his or her corner of the vast Chinese marketplace, they do not present an insurmountable problem if the parties are open to learn—and if the potential for profitability is fundamentally sound.[9] And, of course, one must consider the leverage the foreign investor possesses (a function of sector, technologies involved, etc.). Like other factors, trades can be made affecting control over labor, depending on what other chips are on the table for China (exports, technology transfer, jobs) and what the gains are for the investor (market access, profits, market share).

---

9. Numerous expatriates commented that the performance of the venture was the best indicator of whether such issues could be resolved. It appears that as long as there is a good cash flow, anything can be worked out—a very practical perspective.

Human Resources after Establishment

FIEs face various operational human resource challenges once they are up and running in China. Many are common to other high-growth emerging economies where multinational firms operate. What is unusual (and thus may make these problems themselves appear unusual) is the intense criticism in the West of China's labor profile in recent years. The key topics interviewees discussed are wage pressures and patterns, mobility, nonwage costs, training, and retention. Two supplemental themes distilled from the interviews are insulation from dubious business practices through comprador relationships with local Chinese partners and the background concerns about human rights and labor rights that echo through debate about China in the United States. Each of these issues remains important over the life of the venture. The interviewees described deep interaction between foreign firms and Chinese employees, in stark contrast to the depiction offered by many human rights groups of penniless laborers, alienated and exploited.

Availability, Wage Pressures, and Changing Labor Patterns

Surveys of FIEs consistently identify "local management and skills shortages" as among the greatest impediments to productivity growth in China operations (EIU 1997, xv).[10] Shortages in the pool of labor clearly lead to difficulties in filling critical roles in finance, accounting, marketing, human resource management, and other important business fields, which frustrate FIE operations. And, naturally, because these resources are scarce their cost has risen.

Expatriate managers are increasingly aware of rising wage pressures, along with the changing expectations among staff that accompany increasing salaries. Table 3.4 and figure 3.1 offer illustrative recent wage increases for local managers at a Sino-American firm in China, with projections (1998–2000). Four sites are included: Beijing, Shanghai, Guangzhou, and Tianjin. Table 3.5 shows the variation in average annual compensation at joint ventures in locations in coastal China for positions ranging from deputy general manager to unskilled production worker.

The data in these tables suggest several important points. First, while wages are climbing across the board, there is a widening gap between salaries of high- and low-skilled workers. This is a promising sign of a

---

10. As with many issues addressed in this study, China is not unique in this regard, although the problem may be most pronounced there. Manager polls indicate that fewer than half the firms in East Asia feel they have enough skilled managers to meet company growth over the next 10 years in Taiwan, Hong Kong, Singapore, South Korea, Malaysia, Thailand, and Indonesia ("Asia Executive Poll," *Far Eastern Economic Review,* 28 August 1997, 28).

Table 3.4 Local managers' salary increases, 1996-2000
(percentages)

	Location			
	Beijing	Shanghai	Guangzhou	Tianjin
1996	24.0	24.1	21.8	16.5
1997	18.6	17.6	17.3	12.5
1998	17.1	16.7	15.3	12.5
1999	16.6	16.2	14.7	12.3
2000	16.1	15.7	14.1	12.1

Note: The numbers after 1998 are forecasts.

Source: Author's interviews.

change in the culture of the Chinese firm, moving away from a focus on nominal equality and toward efficient use of incentives and increased productivity. Increasing productivity is the real source of wage growth, as the second point demonstrates: the average wage earnings of even the lowest-paid workers in these joint ventures are higher than the national average manufacturing wage of 5,642 RMB reported for 1996 (China State Statistical Bureau, *China State Statistical Yearbook* 1997, 124). In Shanghai, where interaction between Chinese workers and FIEs is quite advanced, the wages of unskilled workers are almost *double* the national average and rising precipitously.

Perks to retain good employees are also more common. The most re-markable example may be the home mortgage financing programs initi-ated by many of the firms involved in this study. In these programs, the employer uses its financial power to finance low-cost, typically 10-year mortgages for employees (in some cases for only the best employees, in others for all employees). This creates a disincentive to leave the firm, be-cause doing so would lead to foreclosure. The firms that introduced this practice find also that the work ethic and psychology of employees who own their own homes is superior. These FIE home acquisition projects have attracted copious positive attention in China, yet are barely known in the United States.

Ironically, this acceleration both in wage growth for capable individu-als within firms and in wage differential between FIEs and domestic firms is creating hostility and resistance in some quarters. Bureaucrats are anx-ious about the social implications of these increasing disparities. While the solution employed until recently—chaining the compensation of the most productive workers to that of the lowest (or to the industry aver-age)—is being abandoned, several foreign managers interviewed for this study described how their Chinese board partners were still preventing raises that would result in more venerable employees making less than their aggressive, productive juniors. The Chinese partner was able to

Figure 3.1 Managers' salary increase, 1996-2000

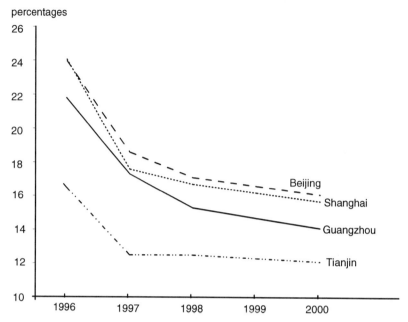

percentages

Note: The numbers after 1998 are forecasts.

Source: Author's interviews.

block the salary increases because the investor tolerated a weak position on labor control when the venture was first established, quite possibly in order to accelerate approval. The debate over income distribution and globalization is now heating up in the United States as well (see Cline 1997, Rodrik 1997b); but there is no question that for the time being, in China greater variations in income are necessary.

Third, tables 3.4 and 3.5 indicate that there still exist major locational differences in salary. An accountant's salary in Shanghai is double that in Hangzhou. Given that the two cities are only a few hours apart, why don't people simply move to meet demand? The answer is threefold. First, living costs vary significantly between cities, accounting for some of the differences in compensation. Second, labor mobility in China remains limited, as noted already, because of bureaucratic impediments to changing residence and because of the difficulty of carrying over benefits for dependents.[11] Third, there are simply not large pools of professionals in any

---

11. Most young Chinese do not want to move from Shanghai to the hinterlands any more than a New Yorker would relish an assignment in Arkansas. Andrew Jackson, human resources manager for Ford China, recently put it this way in an interview: "No one is ever going to give up living in Shanghai or Beijing and yell, 'Yes! I want to go and live in Nanchang!' You would need your head examined to do that" (Weir 1997).

Table 3.5 Average annual pay at FIEs, October-December 1996 (renminbi)

Position/title	Salary (cash) HWN[a]	Salary (cash) Shanghai	Total earnings[a] HWN[b]	Total earnings[a] Shanghai
Deputy general manager	83,593	104,394	103,653	115,538
Accounting supervisor	22,912	58,450	31,620	72,441
Receptionist	12,350	16,722	16,232	24,406
Line supervisor	18,100	48,360	27,832	59,968
Unskilled production worker	6,000	14,241	13,580	23,833

a. The source for this table does not define the composition of total earnings, but presumably it includes bonus and other in-kind payments.
b. HWN = Hangzhou, Wuxi, Nanjing.

Source: China STAFF (1997).

location, and reaching them through advertising and recruitment is not always easy; securing their release from current employers (i.e., release of their *dang an*, discussed later) may be complicated as well.

Somewhat shell-shocked by the sudden onset and pace of new labor pressures, authorities have been slow to fashion a comprehensive response to the human resource regulatory needs of dynamic firms. The *dang an* and *hukou* systems have not been overhauled, only tinkered with (eroded mostly *despite* government, not because of it). Unfunded pension and welfare systems and state-allocated housing diminish labor mobility. Greater flexibility is required to permit firms to fashion modern organizational structures in China to serve the growing market, streamline production, and operate productively. But firms, including FIEs, will not wait forever for reform; they are contributing to making the government's role over human resources marginal—albeit by moving forward in the dark, interpretation by interpretation.

Mobility and the *Dang An* and *Hukou* Systems

Markets that are segmented—that is, disconnected from national distribution patterns—are emerging across China, particularly but not solely along the Pacific coast. To serve these burgeoning centers in spite of internal barriers to trade, shortages of local expertise, and other complications, firms foreign and domestic in many sectors must rely on increasingly mobile management teams. Now is the time to hit the ground running in the 11 "first-tier" cities (population more than 2 million people), the 23 "second-tier" cities (1–2 million), and 239 more cities with between 200,000 and 1 million residents (the numbers would swell if the "unregistered population" were included). A primary constraint for many firms as of summer 1997 was availability of upper-level personnel. If a general manager for a regional office in Xinjiang cannot be found locally, then the question is whether someone with the needed skills can be dispatched from Shanghai, or Beijing, or Tianjin.

Two inevitabilities of postwar life in China, nowadays waning in importance yet still essential, are the *dang an* and the *hukou*.[12] The *dang an* is a personnel file, a dossier on each employee, established as early as primary school and maintained by employers thereafter. It tracks an individual's political and professional record, from academic grades to performance reports, problems with authorities to marriage and childbearing. This dossier is an essential record needed before an employer can hire or provide pension or insurance benefits for the individual. One employer might demand a payment before releasing the *dang an* to a new employer. The *hukou* is a residence permit, entitling the bearer to social services and rights (including not being removed to the countryside) available to local residents only. Without this permit, an individual has no access to the subsidized housing, medical care, schooling for dependents, and social security that urban China was organized around over the past 40 years.

These bureaucratic devices were the keys to controlling Chinese society under communism. They have less force today, as increasing numbers of Chinese join private enterprises and become less beholden to government, yet many potential employees still resist changing localities or employers if it means compromising their *dang an* and *hukou* status. Fearful of being burdened with new residents without an accompanying transfer of their pension benefits from the old jurisdiction, many localities are fiercely reluctant to hand out new *hukou*s, at least until the social welfare system is revamped.[13] The US-China Business Council (1996a, 24) estimated that Beijing Municipality handed out only 2 new *hukou*s per 10,000 residents in 1996 (thus merely 2,100 or so in a city with an official population of 10 million).

Freelance service companies have emerged as valid depositories for the *dang an*, giving greater employment flexibility to foreign firms that are not permitted to hold personnel files directly for Chinese workers. Temporary residence permits are supplementing the *hukou* for some staff on assignment away from their home municipality. However, these remnants of totalitarianism and the intractable problems of the existing social system remain challenges to foreign investors concerned above all with building

---

12. In the state-owned sector the bureaucratic apparatus is far more complex; the *dang an* and *hukou* elements discussed here are only part of the story, but are the parts most relevant to FIEs. See Child (1996) for more background on labor markets and rigidities in China.

13. Such transfers are unlikely on a large scale, because obligations are largely met out of current revenues: that is, there is no funded lump sum to be transferred (see World Bank 1997h, 18–25).

Table 3.6　Per capita income by area, projected

Area	1996 (RMB)	2000 (RMB)	2010 (RMB)	Annual growth rate (percentage)
Urban residents	4,839	8,508	29,162	13.7
Rural residents	1,926	3,278	10,707	13.0

Source: State Information Center, Reuters,
http://biz.yahoo.com/finance/971214/china_gap_l.html,
14 December 1997.

Table 3.7　Per capita GDP by province, 1996 (dollars)

Province		Province	
Shanghai	2,679.2	Inner Mongolia	512.3
Beijing	1,809.4	Hunan	496.7
Tianjin	1,475.8	Guangxi	490.8
Guangdong	1,144.2	Henan	485.0
Zhejiang	1,137.2	Anhui	466.8
Jiangsu	1,016.0	Sichuan	452.6
Fujian	978.6	Qinghai	450.8
Liaoning	929.7	Ningxia	448.8
Shandong	822.0	Yunnan	446.8
Heilongjiang	777.9	Jiangxi	446.8
Hainan	661.5	Shanxi	398.5
Hebei	642.9	Shaanxi	398.5
Xinjiang	621.5	Gansu	348.9
Jilin	621.0	Tibet	328.6
Hubei	616.1	Guizhou	251.7

Note: $1 = 8.3RMB, the average market exchange rate in 1996.

Source: State Statistical Yearbook, 1997, China State Statistical Bureau.

flexible organizations. It will take some time for these bureaucratic hold-overs to disappear.

To better understand the source of government anxiety and hence its sluggishness to engage in reform, see tables 3.6 and 3.7 and figure 3.2. It is predicted that the sizable income gaps between dynamic commercial centers and poor hinterlands will widen, continuing to separate Chinese into the well situated and the unfortunately placed. These disparities are spawning intense migratory pressures that, without the presence of the

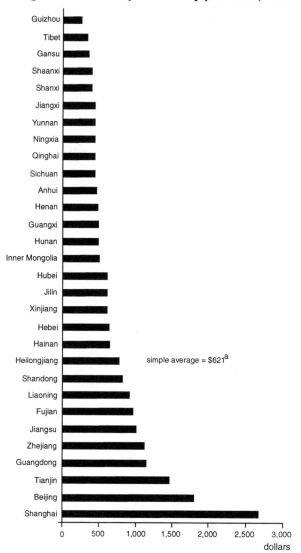

Figure 3.2 Per capita GDP by province, 1996

simple average = $621[a]

a. Average of all 30 provinces, not adjusted for population.

*Source: State Statistical Yearbook,*1997, China State Statistical Bureau.

old checks on movement, could quickly lead to serious and violent social deterioration. Of course, masking these pressures will not make them go away; but Chinese leaders are buying themselves time, hoping that in the future they will be able to bring to bear greater resources and more policy acumen on these problems.

Nonwage Costs

Foreigners have seen many changes in the social obligations that stand alongside wages as major worker-related costs.[14] When they arrived in the early 1980s, FIEs faced nonwage obligations modeled on those prevailing in the state sector. In 1978 SOEs were reported to pay out nonwage benefits valued at 14 percent of wages; in 1994 the amount was 30 percent on average for all enterprises, according to the US-China Business Council (1996b, 3). The World Bank calculated pension contribution expenses of about 25 percent on average for all firms in the 13 provinces and 12 municipalities it has studied, a figure it judges "well above the international norm" (1997g, 2).

The total nonwage overhead costs (including pensions) for foreign enterprises reported by managers interviewed for this study were as high as 65 percent of salary. Recall the discussion of incentives in chapter 2: less attractive locales can waive many (if not all) nonwage costs, while more popular destinations have the leverage to make more demands. The range of nonwage costs identified here is consistent with the US-China Business Council surveys.

In the mid-1990s, authorities attempted to provide a new basis for social security, moving toward a government-managed system (to be based at the local level) instead of an enterprise-based regime. The new framework was an improvement over past practice; however, there remained ambiguity about local implementation of fee schedules and obligations, requirements to keep longtime employees on staff, and many other labor factors. Today, municipally managed pension funds coexist with old, enterprise-based funds in many jurisdictions, and ultimate obligations are unclear. In some cases pensions are being pooled provincewide; in others enterprises are still pooling by industry or by a particular set of firms (World Bank 1997g, 2). As in the past, compliance of FIEs with local obligations varies and is commonly settled by negotiation, a situation the World Bank describes as a "hornet's nest." It appears that southern FIEs tend to contribute to fewer funds, while WOFEs, especially in the north, are compelled to comply more closely than JVs with the overlapping obligations set out in law (USCBC 1996b, 2).

An illustrative list of common nonwage costs an FIE might face (by statute) includes

- pensions (local and/or provincial),
- unemployment insurance,

---

14. A review of the evolving social welfare regulatory environment and its implications for FIEs can be found in USCBC (1996b). For an assessment of China's policy choices, see World Bank, *Old Age Security* (1997g).

**Table 3.8 Personnel overhead expenses:
contribution of an FIE in Shanghai**
(percentages of total wages)

Overhead expense	Employer contribution
Pension	30
Housing fund	15
Medical insurance	7
Matching fund	5
Union fee	2
Housing allowance	2
Unemployment insurance	1
Birth insurance	1
Total	**63**

Note: In the pension category, 17 percent goes to the government while 13 percent goes to insurance.

Source: Author's interviews.

■ accident and disability insurance,

■ maternity fees,

■ health insurance,

■ housing (subsidies or direct obligations),

■ enterprise-based welfare funds,

■ bureaucratic administration funds,

■ union fees, and

■ vacation allowances, funeral subsidies, education allowances, etc.

Table 3.8 presents the cost over wages that some of these fees represent to an American joint venture in Shanghai. Some readers might find these obligations excessive; others will find them comparable to those in many OECD economies. But that is the point: FIEs do not avoid all labor costs in China.

In addition to these payments, workers must be granted paid leave for a host of eventualities including funerals, sickness, paternity, maternity, miscarriage, "home leave" of up to 45 days every two years to visit family, and public holidays. State enterprises often provided services including schools, doctors, movie theaters, festival halls, funeral homes, restaurants, and many other aspects of civil life—most particularly housing. These all added to the value of the enterprise's contribution to the individual's compensation. It has been common, though the matter is negotiable, for FIEs to be asked to make funds available to offset their savings from not having to meet such expenses. It is important not to ignore these expenditures when debating Chinese labor issues in the West. Too often, low daily pay figures are bandied about with cries of "How is anybody supposed to live on that?" with no mention of the value of room and board, as well as medical, holiday, and other in-kind payments.

The imprecise obligations of the FIE and the ad hoc nature of setup negotiations have led to widely differing nonwage costs in different municipalities. The US-China Business Council (1996b, appendix C) found overall nonwage costs per worker to range from as little as 22 percent of the value of wages in Shenzhen to as much as 98 percent in Wuxi. Not only is this variability confusing but it can also serve as a barrier to mobility, as noted already. While today's crazy quilt of regimes is problematic, FIE human resource managers also fear that nonwage obligations could increase unpredictably in the future as China struggles to cover the rising tide of social obligations.

Setting aside the question of whether the social insurance revenues garnered from FIEs are managed responsibly on behalf of workers (generally they are not), these requirements impose discriminatory fee burdens on foreign investors that domestic companies do not face. Firms in different cities face different assessments, but similar firms in the same city might also pay different amounts, depending on their negotiating skills and the influence of their partners. Foreign enterprises pay larger tuition "reimbursements" to Chinese colleges when employing graduates than domestic employers do, for example. This violates the spirit of the national treatment principle: the full catalogue of differential payments could be questioned within the WTO accord.

On the other side of the equation, many domestic firms in the state sector receive subsidies so many and so varied that the Chinese government itself has said it has no idea what the total value is, or even what all the subsidies are. Communist rule in China has been marked by the transfer of resources from productive to less productive elements, a practice that thoroughly eroded Chinese productivity. The next 20 years, like the past 20, will witness the unraveling of this knot of transfers. A closer accounting of where the nonwage costs paid by FIEs actually go is long overdue. Increasingly, FIEs are treating these cash flows as owed directly to their workers instead of as a cover charge to operate in China, and they are more aggressively trying to control the use of these moneys.

As traditional barriers to competition between FIEs and domestic firms come down, preferential or discriminatory nuances such as those characterizing nonwage labor obligations will draw careful scrutiny because they may violate national treatment provisions of international economic regimes. At a minimum, statutory clarity will be required, including legal means of recourse to challenge unfair practice under the current regime. More important, central authorities must take the initiative in making labor practices around China uniform in order to nurture a more efficient, modern labor market.

The World Bank (1997g) argues that the present social welfare system fails to serve its purpose (provident savings to meet the needs of the unemployable) and is unsustainable (if current trends prevail, it will soon go bankrupt). It also fails to intermediate effectively between long-term savers and users of investment, thereby missing the opportunity to contribute to strengthening the financial sector.[15] Furthermore, the Bank recognizes that the present arrangement hampers structural adjustment:

> If a nonviable mill closes down in one city, laid-off workers need to be able to move to areas where similar industries might be expanding. For that to happen, the pension benefits of workers must be portable. The division of the national system into many separate unfunded municipal pools makes portability difficult and will become an increasingly serious impediment to labor mobility. (1997g, 3)

Should unmet pension needs lead to fiscal deterioration, FIEs will likely be forced to assume an even larger share of these obligations. Already, many are going beyond the letter of the law in providing for the well-being of their employees (e.g., by financing housing, education), recognizing that current arrangements fall short.

Training and Quality

Most FIEs must to some degree systematize production, operational style and management, and quality across their operations. The trick is doing it while retaining the flexibility needed to succeed in the diverse markets around China. The CEO of United Technologies, George David, has called this the imperative of "disciplined decentralization" in his speeches.

Training is crucial, as well as attention to objective metrics—first and foremost, *quality*. The *People's Daily* reports that *half* of all Chinese output is "substandard" (21 January 1998). Not surprisingly, therefore, in a mid-1996 survey only 7 percent of Chinese considered Chinese products to be of very good or excellent quality.[16] Such figures indicate where the battle for dominance of the Chinese market is likely to be fought and won in coming years, underscoring how important it will be to inculcate in workers a consciousness of quality.

Expatriate managers emphasize training within the firm, preferring to teach young staff to do things right the first time instead of retraining staff accustomed to outmoded practices. By schooling raw staff in-house, they can also help to moderate labor market constraints. However, managers worry that their good employees will take their new training to other jobs

---

15. Eighty percent of pension funds must, by regulation, by invested in government bonds, the remainder in bank balances, despite piteously low returns—below the rate of inflation, in recent years (World Bank 1997g, 3).

16. Gallup/Bozell, cited in EIU's *Business China* (7 July 1997, 3).

(a problem in developed markets too, of course). The US-China Business Council describes higher turnover and increased poaching of employees as undesirable side effects of training (1996d).

Fears of poaching notwithstanding, the larger firms examined in this study have developed extensive in-house training programs to build their China organizations. Making a considerable investment of time, they send employees, regulators, potential suppliers, and other partners back to the home country (or to hubs in China or Asia) for training and exposure. Some even sell their training expertise to outside companies too small to have training functions themselves (#34). Smaller firms can use the services of private human resources training consultancies, a number of which have emerged in China (##44, 61). An article in *Business China* (4 August 1997, 8) describes the expansion of Hewitt East Gate, a successful wholly foreign-owned training consultancy (able, as a local company, to invoice other FIEs directly in RMB) and profiles other new entrants to this rapidly growing market.

New opportunities for training are appearing regularly. In recent years numerous Sino-foreign MBA programs have opened their doors. With growing backing from FIE corporate members (and local Chinese companies), China-Europe International Business School (CEIBS) at Jiaotang University in Shanghai is graduating MBA students with concentrations in marketing, human resources, finance, and corporate restructuring. The main constraint on growth for CEIBS is the availability of foreign business professors willing to spend extended periods of time in China. In March 1998, New York's Fordham University announced that it is leading a consortium of 24 American colleges that will join Beijing University in running an MBA program. Official Chinese estimates suggest that 300,000 MBAs are needed to help privatize SOEs and revitalize the economy,[17] so many more such cooperative programs seem likely.

Quality is an important foreign enterprises comparative advantage. Foreign firms seek to use the reputation of being more reliable than their Chinese competitors to bolster their market position.[18] But the potential for loss of that reputation is a serious threat. For example, streetside "fountain" (not prebottled) Coca-Cola is frequently made with unpurified water direct from the water system, water that often fails to meet drinking standards.[19] If children were to die drinking contaminated Coca-Cola,

---

17. United Press International, "MBA in China," 10 April 1998.

18. The consumers' strong beliefs can have amusing consequences. A manager for a major American manufacturer whose products involve prerecorded announcements demanded that his factory manager explain why the recordings were made in English. The response was that Chinese purchasers of the product prefer the English announcements—even though they cannot understand them—because they are a sign of Western quality.

19. This is true in major hotels in some cities as well, where the water lines feeding the hotel bars and kitchens are the same ones marked "NON-POTABLE" in guests' rooms.

hypothetically speaking, the brand's good name could be threatened not just in China but worldwide. Adequate training—for the bottlers, the installers of lines to soda fountains, and retailers—is critical to make sure that does not happen. Foreign firms are devoting enormous energy to building quality management around their branded products in China, ensuring first of all that workers can judge what is safe and what unsafe.

FIEs must also use training and quality to respond to anticompetitive practices directed against foreign products. Such practices include deliberate acts of sabotage (such as induced spoilage) and besmirchment (starting libelous rumors about competitors). They are not unique to China by any means. Unfortunately, in the Chinese case they often coincide with official or quasi-official endorsements of the superiority of "glorious Chinese brands," a display of partiality worrisome when shown by industry regulators.[20]

By focusing on modern management, training, and quality, FIEs are engaged in a form of technology transfer that is reshaping business enterprises in China. Young Chinese are eager to work for foreign ventures, and this soft technology is spilling over to domestic firms that increasingly emulate their foreign rivals. Indeed, the culture of the foreign firms in their midst is affecting Chinese society more generally; as Lieberthal notes,

> Technology doesn't develop in splendid isolation. Its use also transmits values, and it has wide-ranging, complex effects on those who seek to absorb and utilize it.... How far to open this window [to foreign technology and the culture attending it] has been an issue of contention in China since the 1860s. (1995, 23)

Retention

That retention of staff is a problem for FIEs in China today reflects a quite radical change: staff are now free to choose their career paths. Until recently, careers were largely assigned by state authorities, and urban jobs were for life.[21] Job mobility also indicates that there are opportunities available: people with business skills or knowledge of foreign languages

---

20. Chen Zili, deputy secretary of the Shanghai Communist Party, endorsed the revival of the Peony ink brand in the *Shanghai Wenhui News* (14 May 1997). The entrepreneurs in question had established themselves by unilaterally breaching their contract with a foreign firm, which the newspaper insinuated was unscrupulously trying to cheat the patriotic Chinese businessmen.

21. Such rigidity was institutionalized during efforts to force peasants who had moved to the cities back to the countryside after the failed harvests of the Great Leap Forward (1958–61). By giving factory staff lifetime employment in exchange for no labor mobility, the Party hoped to check migratory pressures on the cities and to spur agricultural output. As a result the work unit, or *danwei*, became the focal point of the individual's labor existence (Lieberthal 1995, 109).

have choices. From the perspective of the liberal West, where freedom is gauged by the ability of individuals to act on their choices, this is extraordinarily good news.

Though the majority of Chinese do not yet fully enjoy such skill-based mobility, an emergent middle class offers powerful evidence of social and cultural change in China, with important implications for the economic—and ultimately political—behavior of younger generations of Chinese. What's more, interviews did suggest that even in low-skill industries such as garment manufacturing in southern China, staff turnover is very high. Rural peasants reportedly leave urban factories within a year of arrival, more often to work elsewhere locally than to return home (annual turnover at a textile firm with headquarters in Hong Kong and factories in Guangdong approached 100 percent; #8).

Human resource managers for FIEs do not always see the turnover trend in such a rosy light: for them, it threatens company growth and leaves some firms unready for market while ventures that were established earlier build an unassailable advantage. The temporary surge of demand for young Chinese professionals has put tremendous leverage in the hands of people in urban areas whom Margaret Pearson (1997) calls "China's new business elite." That leverage is largely a function of the arrival of foreign investors.

Insulation

By the standards of the Organization for Economic Cooperation and Development, the Chinese marketplace is not particularly "clean" in its commercial practices. Virtually anyone who has done business in China says that playing entirely by the rules is not an option: kickbacks, bribes, favors, rough collection tactics, and other irregularities are ubiquitous.[22] Informal affiliation with local Chinese staff is sometimes used to insulate FIEs from disreputable practices, ensuring distance (and deniability) while at the same time providing a modicum of foreign control. Foreign managers can point to the "complexities" of local markets and claim to prefer dealing with buyers and sellers through an intermediary (thereby also acknowledging the importance of personal connections in Chinese business culture). Such "subcontractors" ostensibly form a barrier between foreign investors and operations that dispose of toxic or hazardous wastes, "convert" imports across the Hong Kong border at low tariff rates (see chapter 5), manage factories with substandard labor conditions, and so on. These arrangements conveniently shield foreign managers (who, if American, are liable to the FCPA) from blame for dubious practices.

---

22. There will always be a few who insist that they have found a magic way to insulate themselves from these pressures.

FIEs are also using loose organizational affiliations to expand their scope of business beyond the restrictions set by Chinese law. Central authorities have withheld distribution and service rights from non-Chinese firms, partly under pressure from local industries. But in alliance with Chinese firms legally permitted to exploit such areas, FIEs circumvent the rules, often controlling the Chinese "front" company. In many cases this is done with tacit approval from local authorities. Central authorities no doubt are generally aware of these practices as well, but still the ruse of insulation is important. The FIE needs a defense should it attract too much bureaucratic attention, and authorities need an appearance of propriety to retain "face": that is, to avoid appearing impotent to enforce the law.

All this is reminiscent of the comprador phenomenon. Foreign businesses operating in China prior to the Communist era used Chinese merchant-middlemen, known as compradors (a term borrowed in the mid-19th century from the Portuguese word for "buyer"), as intermediaries to the markets for many of the same reasons: they provided knowledge of the language and culture, some political protection, and insulation from corrupt practices. Some expatriates describe the present business environment as "the return of the compradors."

Some Western firms (e.g., Nike and Reebok in the footwear and garment industries), criticized for such arm's-length stratagems, have responded by trying to manage the work environments of their subcontractors more closely (Chan and Senser 1997).[23] Clothing conglomerate Liz Claiborne now requires all subcontractors to meet the "Liz List," a checklist that takes account of a broad set of labor conditions. The CEO of one textile firm subject to the checklist (#8) suggested that such voluntary standards (in large part devised for good public relations) are having real, beneficial effects in factories in southern China.

However, these voluntary regimes are not likely to satisfy labor advocates. Although it has had a "standards for vendors" program in place since 1992, Wal-Mart Stores of the United States continues to skirmish with activists over its "Kathie Lee" clothing line, partly manufactured in China.[24] The National Labor Committee, a watchdog group, claims that Wal-Mart is incapable of monitoring Chinese subcontractor practices and calls their certification program ineffectual. Judging compliance with labor standards is highly inexact, and debates about the efficacy of certifications and checklists will be determined by public relations concerns as much as by anything else. Irrespective of their other merits, however, such scuffles do raise awareness of labor issues. Labor advocates believe that any pub-

---

23. See also Anita Chan, "Boot Camp at the Shoe Factory," *Washington Post,* 3 November 1996, C1; Dana Canedy, "Peering into the Shadows of Corporate Dealings," *New York Times,* 25 March 1997, B1; and "Group Faults Reebok, Nike on Child Labor," *Journal of Commerce,* 22 September 1997, 3A.

24. Reuters, http://biz.yahoo.com/finance/980318/walmart, June 1998.

licity is good publicity, and businesses' voluntary programs—even if undertaken solely to forestall bad press—may have virtuous results.

In the Background: Human Rights

FIE managers in China have a strikingly low opinion of the fixation on human rights back home (especially in the United States), which is seen as hopelessly misdirected in light of the epochal social changes taking place across China today. Expatriates see misunderstanding of common Chinese attitudes about government, failure to grasp the connection between these attitudes and per capita income growth, and ignorance of the scale and scope of the reforms with which authorities are wrestling. They focus instead on the rapid growth of social and economic freedom in China over the reform period and the government's relative success to date in managing these changes since 1978.[25] Indeed, China has achieved far more than anyone could have reasonably predicted before reform began. Thus when talk turns to human rights, many expatriates tend to lecture their Western compatriots.

However, the interviewees realize that this perception could destroy the hard-won beachheads established by FIEs, regardless of their capacity to function as catalysts for social change, and therefore it must be taken seriously. The more thoughtful managers were also aware that, as Bette Bao Lord of New York's Freedom House has remarked, China does not have a suitable safety valve to harmlessly vent the steam building up from civil dissatisfaction (personal communication, 23 April 1998). Though FIEs are doing much to facilitate a change in culture by demonstrating a new sort of employer-employee social contract, based on individual rights and responsibilities, they must do more, this argument goes, to ensure the safety of their golden goose. But what is the "more" that the virtuous company can do?

A significant number of the firms involved in this study have instituted voluntary standards programs designed to assess their performance concerning human and labor rights, and many hosted visits and factory tours for US members of Congress in 1997. These programs and exchanges have been useful steps toward giving Western opinion makers a better understanding of Chinese conditions. However, most FIEs still have not sufficiently communicated to home audiences their labor experiences in China.

There is evidence of reasoned thinking in this debate on China. Models of fair allocation of responsibilities to press human rights concerns in China (Santoro 1998 is a good example) distinguish between, on the one

---

25. Commentators usually remark on the opposite: the imbalances in development taking place in China. But social imbalances plagued Chinese society long before the market was introduced; the difference now is that more of the problems are related to prosperity, not simply poverty.

hand, the FIEs' responsibility for the conditions found under their roofs, in the course of their business, and among their subcontractors and, on the other hand, general levels of human rights in China outside their scope of business. Such differentiation is practically as well as ethically sound. If firms were expected to pressure the Chinese on questions of human rights outside their operations, they would be so distracted from the tasks of doing business that most would be bankrupted and the opportunity to sow change even locally would be lost.

The Chinese authorities also bear blame for the unfavorable perceptions of their country, not only because they still resist political liberalization but also because they have failed to take seriously the importance of public diplomacy abroad. Beijing's disastrous neglect of its image suggests a lack of concern for the sensibilities and democratic political processes with which other world leaders must contend. Bad Chinese media management, in other words, has made the job of other foreign policymakers trying to build bridges to China more difficult.[26] This has begun to change in 1997–98, with the early release of prominent dissidents, a less bellicose dialogue with Taiwan, and a more tempered reaction to the cacophonous anti-China rancor in the US Congress.

Nonetheless, ultimate responsibility for a sound policy toward China rests with the foreign nation itself. Richard Latham, president of United Technologies Beijing office, remarked to members of Congress visiting Beijing in January 1997:

> We play a fool's game if we overplay our hand or misunderstand the stakes in the relationship. Fifty years from now, we'll find that our good intentions didn't secure much in the long term for a democratic China, but it will have cost us mightily in terms of our trading tradition. And here is the true irony: China will be a much more democratic society, albeit with Chinese characteristics. And people will be hard put to show any linkage with the US-China dialogues of the early 1990s. (Latham 1997)

Latham encapsulates the wisdom of foreign firms regarding the relationship between human rights and human resources. First, Westerners do have a hand to play—as major customers, they have the ability (and the right) to tell our merchant a thing or two; but they should not overestimate its value. Second, the aggressive unilateral tactics embraced to date have accomplished little for anyone other than the interest groups clustered around Capitol Hill. Third, and ironically, China is changing for the better on its own, by virtue of rising standards of living, increased daily caloric intake, movement of industrial facilities out of populated urban areas, and loosened controls over employment, residence, schooling, and ideology. Should threats to impose damaging sanctions on the Chinese

---

26. A conference on US-China media perceptions was cosponsored 6–8 May 1998 by the National Committee on US-China Relations, Harvard University, and American University; the proceedings can be accessed at http://chinamedia.soc.american.edu.

economy be carried out, the results would undoubtedly be regressive. Once China does achieve the degree of liberality countenanced by the West, will the record show that it happened because of economic sanctions, or despite them? The evidence of narrow limits on the utility of sanctions is nearly conclusive (see Hufbauer, Schott, and Elliott 1990).

Analysis

The view of FIEs and the Chinese labor market that emerges from this chapter has a number of implications. First, foreign economic officials should recognize that human resource constraints not related to policy explain many difficulties encountered by foreign firms in China. This deflates somewhat the thesis that trade policy pressure can compel the Chinese government to remedy all foreign investor woes. Thus, a better understanding of Chinese personnel challenges can both temper the appetite for aggressive trade policy that many Westerners have worked up and redirect attention to those areas where policy pressure is more likely to have beneficial effects.

Second, there are indeed policy dimensions to the labor situation in China today: roughly half the concerns raised by interviewees do have a policy aspect. Some of these are amenable to pressure from China's trading partners, and chapter 7 offers a prescriptive agenda for addressing them.

Third, in light of this analysis, groups fighting for human and labor rights might reconsider their dark depictions of FIEs' impact on labor and civil society in China—that is, if their interests are genuine and not merely protectionist. If the goal of developed-country labor advocates is really solidarity with workers in China, not just protection from foreign competition, then they must distinguish between the many foreign firms contributing positively to Chinese development and the notorious cases in which investors are involved in abuse. If standards are ratcheted up so high that FIEs are made to pull out of China, Chinese workers will be deprived of the beneficial impacts of the foreign presence while receiving little real help in its place. Human rights activists, too, must respect the extent to which economic changes, including—if not especially—those brought about through foreign investment, drive progress; and foreign withdrawal would unquestionably slow that progress.

The four drivers behind the human resource issues described in this chapter are examined next. Table 3.9 summarizes the 14 human resource themes treated in this chapter, the categories of problem at issue, and the level and importance of the policy dimensions.[27]

27. The question of labor unions in China has not been discussed in this chapter; somewhat surprisingly, the topic rarely arose in the interviews.

Table 3.9 Roundup of issues: labor

Issue	Category	If policy . . . Level	If policy . . . Priority
Nontransparent approval	Policy	Central, provincial, local	Medium
Availability of skilled, semiskilled labor	Transitional		
Pressure to overstaff	Policy	Central, provincial, local	Medium
Selecting the "right" staff	Self-imposed, policy	Local	Low
Securing managerial control	Self-imposed, policy	Central	High
Ability to employ expatriates	Self-imposed, policy	Central	Low
Wage pressures and patterns	Transitional, self-imposed		
Mobility	Transitional, policy	Central	Medium
High nonwage costs	Transitional, policy	Central	Low
Training capacity issues	Transitional		
Quality management	Transitional		
Retention problems	Transitional		
Comprador employment	Transitional, policy, self-imposed	Local	High, medium
Human rights, labor rights	Transitional, policy	Central	Low

Transitional and Self-Imposed Factors

Many problems in the human resources area have transitional or self-imposed aspects. Availability of skilled staff, a first-order concern for FIEs, is transitional in nature. Wage pressures are obviously related to this undersupply and share a transitional dimension, although a reckless tendency to poach others' employees by offering bloated salaries rather than training one's own staff represents a self-imposed problem. Reaching an equilibrium of demand and supply for skilled and semiskilled workers will require time and the reallocation of resources by the market; meanwhile, volatility in salaries and high staff turnover will continue. These are natural challenges on the road to a market economy, though the further a nation had departed from an efficiency-oriented model prior to reform, the greater they are (in China's case, this departure was epic).

Foreign investors and indigenous firms alike struggle to find the right people and impose predictability on their payrolls while the infrastructure necessary for adequate human resources (everything from schools to want ads) reevolves. Everyone has an interest in seeing these problems fixed, not least FIEs—which are making a disproportionately large contribution to building a functional labor market by adding training capacity and creating the benchmarks for effective human resource practices.

Many self-imposed problems stem from FIEs' recklessness as they rushed to enter the Chinese market. Many foreign investors have carefully built their Chinese teams, but others have set up without understanding local sensibilities, regulations, prerogatives, or economics. Following those poor starts, many firms try wrongheaded approaches to training and incentives, using managerial techniques ill suited to China or reacting to underdeveloped local conditions with disdain. A major problem is the failure to bridge the cultural divide between different languages and traditions that creates misunderstandings between partners from different backgrounds. Remedying those misunderstandings requires time, exposure to one another, and a willingness to learn. It is the need to bridge these divides that has led to the widespread employment of overseas Chinese to help in managing Western ventures, a trend that is mutually beneficial as long as it doesn't decay into mere dependency on new age compradors instead of real marketplace learning.

Policy Issues

Policy issues remain a significant problem in the human resources area as well. They begin before the firm exists: the nontransparency of establishment, a policy-related problem in part, affects human resources as it does every negotiated area. Approval of a foreign venture is conditioned on the labor authority accepting the human resources contract. These authorities operate with wide discretion to require changes and concessions, and they leave the FIE little avenue for formal recourse (and little chance that investors would be wise to seek such recourse when it is available). Resolving these matters rests primarily with central authorities, who have the power to streamline labor-related approvals, especially by restricting the scope for arbitrary action by local officials captured by special interests. Some progressive local areas and certain economic zones have blazed the trail by basing approval of labor agreements entirely on well-defined criteria.

Lack of transparency affects foreign investors in China generally; but pressure to overstaff is a very specific policy-related labor problem. As already noted, the overstaffing problem is today better managed by foreign enterprises, thanks to experience and new mechanisms for shifting surplus workers elsewhere (including buyouts and the use of retraining agencies). Nevertheless, there remains policy pressure to overstaff foreign enterprises (just as for domestic enterprises), especially in sectors undergoing deep adjustments. It arises because of high-level anxieties about employment, and it affects FIEs at all levels of approval. While overstaffing pressure has a transitional aspect, the problem will not go away until central authorities, changing their policy, decide to stop trying to deal with unemployment through imposed labor rigidity.

Rhetoric at the National People's Congress meetings of March 1998 suggests that leaders are aware that this is the way forward. At the 15 September 1997 Congress opening, President Jiang Zemin had focused on reform of the social safety net to facilitate labor adjustment. However, some expatriates are concerned that the increase in unemployment stemming from quickened SOE reform in 1998–2000 and the Asian financial crisis will lead to renewed pressures to overstaff.

Restrictions on the foreign enterprise's ability to select what it considers the right staff are self-evidently related to policy. However, this problem is typically expressed at the local level, as overseeing authorities try to secure positions for friends or Chinese partners attempt to pad the payroll with cronies: central authorities do not generally support or defend such practices. But central officials have interfered with FIEs' ability to hire expatriates, reflecting an enduring suspicion that each foreign employee represents a high cost and the loss of one more local management job. Local authorities seem to rely on more highly placed officials to tell foreign negotiators seeking approval to cut back on the number of expatriate employees. Increasingly, this is more a financial question of whether a JV should be expected to pay all the costs of expatriate staff than an ideological worry about foreigners running the show (although that has not entirely disappeared).[28]

Foreign enterprises' managerial control over their ventures is hampered by central policy. The Guidelines on foreign investment forbid using the WOFE structure or require Chinese majority control in many industries. If foreign investors cannot control the company board, they cannot freely manage human resources. Even foreign majority JVs and WOFEs can be pressured to share control. They may have to return to examination and approval authorities if they wish to change labor practices. FIEs can also be subject to greater labor union activity than domestic firms are. Although in practice the authorities responsible for limiting foreign control often remain silent *unless* a Chinese interest beseeches them to do something, the potential to restrict the rights of foreign management remains and raises issues of national treatment.

While the wage costs that many FIEs face are increasingly market-driven, the nonwage bill—a policy-related factor—remains significant. The central government must lead in reforming the Chinese social security system. At present a mosaic of experimental policies stretches across the country. These costs appear to be marginally higher for FIEs than for domestic enterprises. Far more serious, however, is the difficulty caused

---

28. A number of Chinese sources argued that covering the costs of foreign staff was sometimes a surreptitious means of extracting gross cash flow from the venture without attracting attention from authorities. Expatriates also described the use of various fees to compensate the parent for costs that the JV did not want to pay directly.

by conflicting or incompatible obligations across jurisdictions; these thwart a firm's efforts to operate regionally or nationally and aggravate the labor rigidities that hamper staff adjustment.

The inchoate state of social security reform is just one source of difficulties faced by FIE staff (and by dynamic domestic firms as well); the bureaucratic *hukou* and *dang an* systems also impede reform. Like many problems connected to the immobility of the labor force, these are partly transitional matters that will lessen with time and market reallocation; but if this reform is to take root, they must also be addressed on a policy level.

A final policy matter is the phenomenon of comprador employment used to skirt either Chinese regulatory blockades or US laws governing corrupt practices. Central authorities promulgate vague statutes in order to mask their uncertainty about regulatory direction, and then they tolerate the extraordinary interpretations that proliferate. Ambiguities in their policies buy leaders time to adjust course while maintaining a consensus favoring reform; they also foster a commercial environment in which compradors are everywhere and respect for law is hard to find.

Nine of 14 labor issues in this chapter included a policy aspect, but in only two cases—securing managerial control and dealing with compradors—did they strike the interviewees as high priority. Regarding compradors, policy shapes the FIEs' problems in fairly indirect ways; it is just as much a problem that the FIEs bring on themselves.

In most cases the policy element derives from central authority, either the Ministry of Labor (which is slated for future merger with the Social Security Administration) or the line ministries that also have a say about the employment contracts. Operationally, however, labor issues and policy clash entirely at the local level.

Market Structure

None of the problems addressed in this chapter necessarily result from competition policy, but the overall situation does have a market structure aspect. An inefficient market structure, which is likely when governments tolerate monopolies or oligopolies, lowers the quality of the labor market and diminishes leverage for labor as well (Graham and Richardson 1997c, 36–37). Such market conditions reduce competitiveness and erode productivity.[29] Through their inaction, central authorities fail to restrain lower levels of government from dampening competition. Labor contracts require approval from local authorities with parochial priorities, and the results serve Chinese workers poorly in the long run. Social insurance

---

29. Ironically, in a rare exception to the protection of competition under US antitrust law, the Clayton Act specifically permits workers to collude together to bargain over wages—that is, to form unions; but in negative symmetry, this is one area in which Chinese authorities have certainly *not* permitted collusion (Fox and Pitofsky 1997, 261).

schemes are still funded haphazardly and the profession of pension fund management barely exists. Until the central authorities enforce the rights of FIEs and local firms alike to choose labor solutions, as well as create the conditions and regulatory framework necessary to support the pension and benefit needs of a national labor market (instead of innumerable local ones), labor problems rooted in competition policy will worsen.

A Concluding Note

This review of FIE labor experiences in China underscores the importance of developing the human assets of the firm in order to succeed in China. Though Chinese government policy hampers the ability of FIEs to meet the challenge, firms are playing an important role in building China's human resources capacity. Cooperative efforts to increase training and educational programs (e.g., producing MBAs) also increase the supply of skilled labor at the margins. Bilateral and multilateral government interactions that address the centrality of building human capacity to China's development could support several agendas (much more effectively than simply complaining about policy impediments).

That foreign firms engender a model of greater firm reinvestment than domestic enterprises has a macroeconomic significance worth considering. Recent efforts to measure household income in China (Khan and Riskin 1998, 235) suggest that the growth of personal income has lagged behind GNP growth considerably between 1988 and 1995. The explanation lies in relatively greater income accumulation by businesses than by the government or household sectors. Because personal income is a better indicator of poverty than GNP, analysts should be concerned with developing a marketplace in which profits are distributed and invested as productively as possible.

The human resources puzzle clearly has a human rights dimension. The relatively high salary and benefits, intensive training efforts, home financing experiments, and corporate culture of many (especially Western) FIEs have a virtuous impact on workers in China; as noted in chapter 7, foreigners create more of these higher-value-added opportunities as they become more deeply involved in the Chinese market. American firms, perceived to be most socially conscious in terms of the employer-employee relationship, are ironically under the greatest pressure from home-country special interests to delay deepening their operations in China. Indeed, probably only the withdrawal of foreign participants from China's marketplace could reverse the current positive trend; it would be ironic if that came to pass *because of* a concern for human rights. To be sure, the Chinese human rights and labor conditions do not resemble those in Japan, Europe, or the United States. But the improvements in labor practices in China since reforms began are manifest to most foreign observers who live and work there, and they themselves have something to do with the change.

4

Running a Productive Plant

The biggest problem in China is 50 years of socialism; who cares about doing a good job after that? In Russia it's worse; here [in China] at least there are people who were already living the last time productivity mattered.

Chairman of an American corporation's China
holding company, Beijing

There's a pattern: we try to do something our old way; we fail. We give the job to locals so that they can do it for us, "the Chinese way"; that fails. Finally, we roll up our sleeves and learn how to do it ourselves, our way, but a new way suitable to the situation in China. Either learn to do that or get out of China.

Chief counsel for an American firm's
operations in China, based in Hong Kong

Introduction

After the goals are set out, the contracts negotiated, and the venture staffed, it is time to run the business: for most foreign-invested enterprises (FIEs), that means running a production process—a plant. The second half of the job is *ex-factory*—distribution, marketing, and so on—addressed in chapter 5. This chapter examines the experiences of expatriates managing production in China. In particular, it is concerned with the impediments they face to raising *productivity* (defined later). Although it focuses on the problems that continue to require consideration by policymakers and students of China's reforms, remarkable progress has been made during the reform period. China is moving toward an economy better able to allocate resources productively and toward the modernity that distinguishes FIE operations.

Foreign investors have much to offer to the Chinese economy, demonstrated by their placement of over $45 billion in foreign investment in 1997. Foreign investors are refurbishing, recapitalizing, and reorganizing existing ventures, as well as creating new enterprises from greenfield sites. They are contributing to China's ability to produce goods and services for domestic consumption and for export. They are building new markets and developing old ones, both directly and indirectly—by the force of competition they bring to bear on a still-sluggish business culture. They are diversifying both the production base and financial risk allocation.

The chapter begins with a brief discussion of productivity, both in general and in China in particular.[1] The problems examined later are then grouped according to the "factors" that determine productivity and thus ultimately profitability: labor (human resources), intermediate goods, and capital. Also considered are institutional factors, such as corruption, that transcend these categories and provide the background against which productivity is examined. While FIE productivity is generally superior to that of indigenous competitors and partners, achieving productivity growth remains a major trial. Some impediments to that growth can be attributed to Chinese policy, whose possible implications for China's trading partners are therefore sketched.

Productivity

What Is Productivity?

Business professionals use the term *productivity* broadly. They mean a measure of the firm's ability to create or add value to their product. It makes no difference whether that product is petroleum, telephones, or candy (or legal services, for that matter). Porter (1990, 6) provides a definition with which the typical expatriate would agree: "Productivity is the value of output produced by a unit of labor or capital. It depends on both the quality and features of products (which determine the prices they can command) and the efficiency with which they are produced."

Economists rely on a definition that is a bit sharper, but essentially the same. The productivity charted by the US Bureau of Economic Analysis refers specifically to *labor productivity*, the amount of output gained per unit of labor. Economists are also interested in *capital productivity*—the marginal output achieved per unit of capital devoted to an enterprise (i.e., the rate of return on capital)—and the *intermediate goods* that go into

---

1. Some observers are hostile to the very idea of reducing human endeavor to a quantitative calculus of productivity. But this is merely a tool to determine whether work habits can be sustained or whether adjustments might be needed to protect an enterprise from extinction.

the production process.[2] These factors may fail to fully explain an increase (or decrease) in output, leaving a residual element referred to as "total factor productivity" (TFP). TFP is explained either by an improvement in the use of the given mix of capital, goods, and labor (a dimension referred to as "x-efficiency") or by an evolutionary improvement in the level of technology.

A monopolistic market structure such as existed in China until recently (and that persists in some sectors) leads to "x-inefficiency" (see, e.g., Scherer and Ross 1990, 668–70). For example, excessive portions of capital resources earned as monopoly rents by protected firms might go to executive salaries, instead of to reinvestment or to shareholders, because there exists little competitive threat to motivate such thriftiness. Although the firm could achieve its level of performance with fewer capital inputs, it does not. With each such unnecessary application of resources, the firm lags further behind its possible achievements. Even if the firm behaves "ethically," under monopoly or oligopoly conditions managers misjudge what is necessary and what inessential. Thus firms misallocate resources and productivity suffers.[3] As the plant-related issues that expatriates deal with in China are explored, it will become clear that many of them are x-efficiency issues.

The second factor influencing productivity enhancement (and hence profitability, leisure, or whatever else the gains are directed toward) is technological progress. As technology changes, it enables an enterprise to be more productive at a given level of input than it was before. In the long term, technology is the more important determinant of productivity, because it continues to advance after the slack in x-efficiency is taken up. Unless underlying productivity (TFP) improves, the only means to increase output is to provide more input, whether of labor, capital, or intermediate goods.[4]

What is most productive can be a complex and sometimes controversial question, with different long-term and short-term answers. For example,

---

2. "Intermediates" could instead be termed "previously utilized capital and labor"; but it is more useful for us to treat them as a third type of input.

3. X-efficiency is endogenous to the firm: it does not hinge on the matter of price signals. Even if price signals are dead wrong, the firm can be said to maximize productivity under those circumstances.

4. Economist Paul Krugman caused a stir in 1994 by arguing that Asia's economic gains resulted mostly from increased investment into the economies, not underlying productivity growth (see, e.g., Krugman 1994). The distinction is important, as over time wages rise as productivity increases. This insight might defuse the charge that wages alone lure American jobs to Malaysia or Mexico, because lower productivity translates into a need for more workers, capital, or inputs to achieve the same output. Hsieh (1998), with considerable econometric effort, argued that TFP growth was at work, at least in the cases of wealthier Asian states such as Singapore.

Table 4.1 Total factor productivity growth in China's state and collective industries, 1980-92 (annual percentage increase)

		Collective	
	State	**Initial**	**Revised**[a]
1980-84	2.24	3.29	2.80
1984-88	3.68	8.73	4.52
1988-92	1.58	9.44	2.98
1980-92	2.50	7.15	3.43

a. The revision stems from the authors' concern that poor price and output data for the collective enterprises were swelling. The adjusted results apply the price index for the SOEs to the COEs, reducing the margin in performance dramatically.

Source: Jefferson, Rawski, and Zheng (1996, 155).

short-run productivity may not take into account the need for research and development, while these activities are inherent in the long term. Environmental impacts are also often omitted. Although environmentalists insist that pollution "externalities" must be internalized in order to accurately measure productivity, the proper long-term value of many environmental harms is uncertain (because of methodological problems with measurement and prediction, and also because the values attached to environmental assets differ and change with per capita income) because the criteria of the productivity balance sheet is debated (see Grossman and Krueger 1993).

Third, in a marketplace as quickly changing as China's is, adaptability may be as important a question as productivity. While productive enterprises might be expected to be better able to change with commercial conditions—in both cases quality management is a major factor—this is not necessarily the case.

The Chinese Context

Much energy has been spent debating China's productivity growth performance during the reform period, but no consensus has been reached. The best guess is that state- and collective-sector productivity have improved modestly over the past two decades, slowing somewhat in the early 1990s. Table 4.1 summarizes TFP estimates for the state and collective sectors prepared by several economists who have extensively researched productivity in China (Jefferson, Rawski, and Zheng 1996).

This table suggests several points. First, the famed Chinese lack of reliable data has a major impact on the productivity conclusions, as seen in the difference between the initial and revised calculations of collective-sector TFP growth. Not only do they yield different paces of growth but the *sign* of the change reverses as well: recent collective-sector performance either climbs or falls by nearly half, depending on the adjustments made. So while these data offer fascinating grist for the mills of forensic statisticians, they fail to give an unambiguous picture of the Chinese economy under reform. Jefferson, Rawski, and Zheng do, however, feel that the state-owned enterprises (SOEs) show robust performance, even if the numbers for collective enterprises are contentious.[5]

Second, regardless of revisions, the table shows a pattern of accelerating TFP improvement in the early 1980s and decelerating, or more likely reversing, TFP growth more recently. One might posit that the easy steps for increasing productivity have been made, and future progress will be slower.

Third, different sectors of the economy have performed quite differently over the reform period, with collective enterprises consistently outperforming state enterprises in productivity growth (albeit to a questionable extent—3.5 percent annually to 2.5 in the adjusted calculations).

Important questions about the validity of these results and the causes of the differences observed in productivity growth remain. For example, Sachs and Woo (1997) challenge the usefulness of the data underlying these calculations. In particular, input prices and output values are shaky. Bai, Li, and Wang (1997) ask whether productivity is the best indicator of gain for China's SOEs, in that the firms may be maximizing *production* rather than *profit*. That is, if a firm produces goods that nobody wants (because it is geared toward not profit but maintaining employment)—say, statues of Vladimir Lenin—then productivity could rise, with more inputs consumed and greater amounts of output produced, but all to the detriment of the economy. Both of these critiques involve the critical signaling mechanism of a market economy: prices. But a plant can operate "productively" given a set of prices, even if those prices are wrong—provided that sufficient subsidies insulate the microeconomic choices of the firm from the "wrongness" of the prices in the marketplace. This has widely been the case in China under state planning, and the price-distorting effects of subsidies to state-sector enterprises remain significant. Not only are direct monetary subsidies employed, but protection barriers to competition of all sorts provide an implicit subsidy to SOEs and collective enterprises, as well as to private firms. Even FIEs are in effect "subsidized" by tariffs that foreclose import competition to their operations in China.

The trend in the national data offers little insight into differences in productivity performance at individual firms, and hence little direction for those wishing to fine-tune policy. Jefferson, Rawski, and Zheng (1996,

---

5. Collective enterprises, which include township and village enterprises, are firms for which responsibility has been shifted to local authorities. Unable (in principle) to rely on national subsidies, they ostensibly work in a more competitive operating environment.

171) note "the importance of performance differences among enterprises bearing the *same* ownership labels" (i.e., within the state-owned category). They go on:

> If ownership categories conceal important heterogeneity, we need micro-level studies to identify specific institutional innovations that enable some firms to succeed in harnessing their productive potential while others fail. To appreciate these differences and possibilities, we need a new generation of research that investigates the distribution of performance outcomes and their determinants rather than debating trends and averages based on the standard statistical aggregates.

These authors are concerned with Chinese enterprises and especially with those parts of the economy most affected by government reform policies, hoping to aid in achieving greater productivity gains through a better understanding of the forces shaping China's economic productivity development.

The microlevel "institutional innovations" employed by wholly owned foreign enterprises (WOFEs) and by Sino-foreign joint ventures (JVs) are also important to understanding the forces at work in the Chinese economy. FIEs are providing much of the trend-shaping competition that affects state- and collective-sector performance. The necessity of meeting their challenge is proving to be the mother of invention, especially as the compartments that Chinese planners first employed to separate FIEs from the domestic marketplace erode. Part of the domestic productivity story (i.e., diminishing TFP growth) has resulted from the best of the SOEs leaving that category to form joint ventures with foreign firms. As they depart, the *average* fitness plummets among those left behind. Finally, productivity increases in the domestic economy are fueled by the spillover of business know-how and the transfer of hard technology from foreign enterprises.

Thus foreign investors have an impact on domestic productivity in a variety of ways beyond their own firms' output. While the natural complementarity of high-productivity FIEs helps to explain the rapid flow of FDI into China, it also helps to explain the Chinese government's apprehension about allowing FIEs unfettered entrance: they are perceived to have the potential to dominate the market.

The Foreign Experience

The productivity issues facing FIEs have become more numerous and complex over the reform period. Many early ventures were mere assembly sites, so-called "screwdriver operations" that pieced together parts made elsewhere, thereby adding little value to products. In 1983 and 1984, for example, contractual joint ventures (CJVs), which tended to be assembly operations, and "joint explorations," also involving practically no

Table 4.2 China's imports, first quarter 1998: SOEs vs. FIEs

Imports	Amount (billions of dollars)	Growth rate (percentage)
Total	29.57	2.6
SOEs	12.22	−2.0
FIEs	16.52	6.0

Notes: Growth rates are the changes from first quarter 1997. The average total growth in imports in 1997 was 2.5 percent

Source: China General Administration of Customs, as reproduced in China News Digest, 13 April 1998.

value added, together represented over 80 percent of foreign investments by number. By 1994 their share had fallen to 23 percent, with more ambitious equity joint ventures (EJVs) and WOFEs constituting the remaining 77 percent (recall tables 2.4 and 2.6).[6] In the early 1980s the "total knockdown" or "TKD kits" in the auto sector, such as American Motors devised for its Beijing Jeeps, epitomized foreign industrial facilities (Mann 1997). In more recent years FIEs have expanded into service, distribution, and operations outside the coastal enclaves.

This is not to say that foreign-run facilities are above using lower-cost Chinese labor to add modest value to more sophisticated intermediates crafted elsewhere. The continued dominance of FIEs in precipitating China's imports (see table 4.2) largely reflects their use of material to be processed (and presumably reexported, given that FIEs are still limited in their ability to distribute these imports domestically); indeed, the still relatively small foreign-invested community generates a surprising share of total Chinese exports (see table 4.3). But increasingly FIEs are using the materials they obtain to produce locally for the domestic Chinese market as well, relying on a web of local and foreign partners.

This chapter focuses on making goods; distribution and selling are discussed in chapter 5. But there are unavoidable overlaps: production efficiency is often a matter of reaching economies of scale, which may require that business scope include distribution and selling functions. So in talking about productivity, FIE managers often refer to sales and distribution functions. This would probably not have been the case 15 years ago, when the vast majority of FIEs were still focused on exporting and those with domestic sales were largely following the script that they were handed by Chinese partners or authorities.

---

6. CJV vs. EJV does not correspond exactly to low- vs. high-value-added operations, but it will suffice here. Pearson (1991, 84–85) notes that CJVs were characterized by lower levels of technology.

Table 4.3 Exports of FIEs, 1985-96

	Millions of dollars	Share of total exports
1985	297	1.1
1986	582	1.9
1987	1,208	3.1
1988	2,456	5.2
1989	4,913	9.4
1990	7,814	12.6
1991	12,047	16.8
1992	17,356	20.4
1993	25,237	27.5
1994	34,713	28.7
1995	46,876	31.5
1996	58,531	40.9
1997	59,720	32.6

Note: Exports are inclusive of those produced by equity joint ventures, contractual joint ventures, and wholly foreign-owned firms.

Sources: Australia Department of Foreign Affairs and Trade (1997a); US-China Business Council, http://www.uschina.org/bas/economy.html (30 April 1998).

The themes treated later fall into four categories of components that make up productivity.

- Labor factors:
    - human resource availability,
    - training,
    - deployment and management of staff, and
    - overstaffing.

- Goods factors:
    - intermediate goods inputs,
    - availability of local content,
    - trade policy,
    - technology application, and
    - scale and capacity.

- Capital factors:
    - financial efficiency within the organization and
    - cost control within the plant.

- Institutional factors:
  - existing culture and "resistance to change,"
  - corruption and graft,
  - conflicting organizational structures, and
  - scope of marketplace participation.

Labor Factors

Human Resources Availability

Labor is a key input to the production process. China is well known as a center of abundant *unskilled* labor, and many of China's strongest export sectors are highly labor-intensive (see table 4.4). The supply of available *skilled* labor is limited because of strong demand among foreign and domestic enterprises for local hires with specific expertise, language abilities, and management capabilities. Interviewees described the challenge of dealing with inadequate local human resources. The relative scarcity of these resources has pressured firms in many places to increase salaries and benefits. In addition to creating these added expenses, the tight labor market has meant high staff turnover, which strains organizational cohesion and culture. It can also incline some firms to hold back from optimally training their employees, fearing that these workers (taking the knowledge invested in them) might jump ship.

Consider the case of a Shanghai JV producing agricultural chemicals. The manager of this venture (#18) said that finding and stabilizing staff resources and costs are his *biggest* productivity challenges. In 1993 employee turnover was 17 percent: that is, nearly one in five employees was in the process of being trained at any given time, at a high cost to the operation. Turnover was lowered to 3 percent in 1996–97, improving productivity significantly. However, labor costs skyrocketed during this period. Of 121 permanent employees (the venture had about 50 contractors, too), over 70 percent had some postsecondary education by early 1997, and their higher qualifications contributed to annual wage bill increases well in excess of inflation. Nonsalary costs amounted to 65 percent of wages—but because most of these nonwage expenditures do not accrue directly to employees, they cannot be used as incentives. This US firm, which is giving top-level workers (nonmanagerial staff) 250,000 RMB interest-free housing loans in order to keep them at the factory, is still having trouble staving off poachers. The manager of the venture summed up by saying that FIEs like his had to either boost productivity rapidly or be prepared to move out of Shanghai to some location with lower wage costs, such as in China's interior (where practically no expatriate would be willing to now live). Meanwhile, he condemned newcomers to the Shanghai market, such as General Motors, for indiscriminately hiring em-

Table 4.4 China's trade: comparative advantage

	DRP[a] ratio 1995	Ranking	Change in DRP ranking, 1987–95	NEPR[b]	Ranking	Change in NEPR ranking, 1987–95
Coal	1.76	1	0	1.784	2	+1
Processed food	1.47	2	+4	0.933	3	+5
Animal husbandry	1.42	3	–1	0.727	5	–3
Textiles and clothing	1.40	4	–1	3.945	1	0
Building materials	1.36	5	0	0.921	4	+5
Wood	1.29	6	+5	–2.926	14	–3
Crops	1.16	7	–3	–0.357	10	–4
Paper	1.05	8	–1	0.652	6	–1
Machinery	0.94	9	+4	–1.843	13	0
Miscellaneous manufactures	0.83	10	–1	–0.246	9	+1
Chemicals	0.67	11	+3	–1.568	12	0
Refined petroleum	0.54	12	–2	–0.187	8	–1
Crude petroleum	0.46	13	–5	0.242	7	–3
Metallurgy	0.40	14	–2	–0.551	11	+3

a. DRP = domestic resource productivity. A DRP of greater than 1.0 means that China earns more than one dollar of foreign exchange for each dollar's worth of domestic resources used in producing exports in that sector.

b. NEPR = net export performance ratio. A positive NEPR means that China is a net exporter of the particular commodity; a negative NEPR means it is a net importer.

Sources: Zhang (1996); Australia Department of Foreign Affairs and Trade (1997a, 151).

ployees from existing FIEs at extravagant salaries in order to get their new operations up and running quickly.

The director of a large logistics company operating in China (#21), a service-sector enterprise, likewise identified human resources and training as the biggest impediments to increasing productivity. (The next two on his list were organizing a profitable financial structure and improving interaction with the licensing bureaucracy). On both the manufacturing and services sides of the FIE situation in China, therefore, availability of human resources can be the determining factor in raising productivity.

Training

Training can enhance the use of labor inputs going into a production process. That is, it can improve x-efficiency and thus get a plant closer to its optimal productivity. For example, increased labor productivity may mean more output per worker, fewer defects, and thus lower average costs. This is one reason why those US workers who are highly productive are not at risk from lower-productivity workers in developing countries. Training is also an essential prerequisite for introducing new technologies that enhance productivity. A worker with a powerful, appropriate machine stands to be far more productive than a pool of low-skill workers without such technology, but using technology may require a higher level of education and specialized training. Even if new technology is easy to use, someone must be trained to maintain and repair it. For both of these reasons, training has become a major part of the FIEs' hunt for higher productivity.

The process of training is not always smooth, because of a combination of haste, cultural miscommunication, and the magnitude of the task. A Beijing country operations manager put it this way: "Foreigners assume they know everything, and that it is obvious; usually when there is a problem [in running the plant] it is because we haven't trained [the workers] properly. They don't understand many processes; they need to be taught" (#22). A Shanghai-based manager amplified the point, emphasizing that there are limits to how quickly staff can be trained. Foreign ventures so anxious to get into the market that they fail to think through establishment issues are likewise inclined to push through training too quickly (#33). A Guangzhou manager concurred: "This is a very high-specification operation compared to what Chinese are accustomed to, and so it takes a lot of training to get people up to the job" (#38).

Who is hardest to move up the curve toward greater x-efficiency? A large number of interviewees made the same remark: grab the young, let go of the old. Age bias was clear everywhere in China when questions arose of what makes for an efficient plant and what staff will be easiest to train. "No experience is better than bad experience," says Frank Chang, manager of Wuhan Grand Motors, a joint venture producing minivans under difficult circumstances (*Business China*, 31 March 1997, 4). His staffing rules: new hires with a high school diploma should be no older than 20, those with a college degree no older than 25. Chang trained 220 inexperienced, handpicked staff from scratch with the help of only one other expatriate. Managers in Shanghai, where FIEs are very close to the market, felt the same as their inland compatriots. They saw two Chinas: one was poisoned by traumatic experiences in the Cultural Revolution and the preceding famines, stymied by socialist work habits and ingrained conservatism; the other was under 30 years of age, dynamic, open-minded, ambitious, and even easier to train than union employees back in Bordeaux or Ohio.[7]

Deployment and Management of Staff

Interviewees identified impediments to deploying staff geographically and other management control issues as productivity problems. Restrictions on the ability of the firm to reorganize its labor hamper productivity at the plant, an x-efficiency issue. To the extent that dilution of management control makes FIEs reluctant to share appropriate, productivity-enhancing technologies, the technological determinant of TFP growth is affected as well.

As noted in chapter 3, there are implicit and explicit restraints on the firm's ability to move employees around. The existing social insurance system disinclines municipalities from granting the residential permits needed in order to transfer staff, because they are fearful of having to assume ballooning welfare obligations (however, temporary *hukou* holding companies are emerging to help). Some expatriates report needing permission from local overseeing authorities before moving staff among jurisdictions; others claim that they can operate freely in moving senior people. Even when policy does not stop an FIE from moving staff, individual Chinese employees may still be wary of relocation for fear of losing local benefits, especially subsidized housing received by a spouse that might be sacrificed for the sake of a short-term assignment in another city. In early 1998 authorities announced plans to dismantle the system of state-subsidized housing; removal of such entitlements will encourage mobility over time.[8]

---

7. A number of interviewees bemoaned the lack of "initiative taking" by local employees both in management and on the factory floor. They tend to avoid taking full responsibility for decisions, a form of risk aversion also manifest in legal affairs. Exploring this complex sociological tendency lies beyond the scope of the present study; however, respondents believed that younger personnel were as capable of taking initiative as anyone else in the world. So perhaps the long-standing stereotype of responsibility-shy Chinese will disappear as institutional factors change.

8. See "Zhao Chen on Housing Reform," Xinhua News Agency, 29 April 1998.

Other managers saw restructuring management as most important for increasing labor productivity. It was noted that many FIEs have horizontal management structures, while Chinese are more accustomed to those that are vertical and hierarchical (#33). Another institutional impediment may arise when a foreign manager must share decision-making power. Shared management may diminish the FIE manager's most potent tool: providing incentives to JV staff. Until recently, compensation based on performance was infrequent in China, and in many JVs today resentment about pay differentials still remains. Therefore, increasing productivity by better organizing and motivating human resources is hindered by pressures to make foreign investors share management control, by cultural differences, and by the legacy of communist-era industrial organization.

One final factor has been clumsiness and insensitivity on the part of foreign managers. Interviewees admitted FIE missteps in building local organizations and trust. It is clear that some expatriates are unable to understand the psychology and motivations of local staff (and what has shaped them). This is not surprising—given language barriers, a sometimes insular and alien Chinese culture, and wide gaps in material wealth—but it can have disastrous consequences. One interviewee explained what went wrong with a major negotiation over a joint venture arrangement that would have positioned an American firm enviably in the petrochemicals market near Shanghai: "Well, one problem was that the head of our negotiating team hated Chinese people" (#12).

Overstaffing

Overstaffing has attracted much attention in the business literature and mainstream press. There is considerable evidence that FIEs are pressured to take on more staff than needed, and it is a sign of the consuming preoccupation of Chinese leaders with the nexus of unemployment and social instability. As noted in chapter 3, coercion can occur when investors seek approval for establishment, at which time the labor contract must be reviewed by appropriate labor authorities. However, use of incentives—such as debt forgiveness—as an alternative to arm-twisting becomes more common with time. Foreign investors might accept overstaffing for a number of reasons, most of which ("the workers are cheap anyway," or "we will need them in the future as we grow," or "this will build our local credentials") reflect an implicit bet on rapid productivity gains.

As noted in chapter 3, however, FIEs are becoming more realistic about staff size and finding new ways to avoid these obligations. They seem to be succeeding to a degree: managers interviewed for this study rarely identified overstaffing as a first-order concern. Nonetheless, the issue is clearly genuine, the more so the more that a sector is dominated by the state; and it will probably get worse during the accelerated reform of the SOE sector trumpeted at the 15th People's Congress.

Goods Factors

The second input that affects the FIE's productivity in China is goods. First, there are intermediate goods that FIEs use to produce their finished products, whose supply can be difficult to manage. Expatriates must make arrangements with local suppliers (sometimes having to identify sources of local content to meet establishment contract obligations), transport intermediates from afar on a timely basis across a highly uncertain distribution system, obtain these goods undamaged and undiminished by pilferage, and take into account the trade policy variables that can interrupt supply.

Second, choices concerning the plant and equipment to be installed can affect productivity. What is the appropriate technology?—that is, what is readily usable and maintainable in China's industrial environment, given parts shortages, power outages, poor-quality supplies of industrial water, and the like? For example, facilities using coal-fired boilers have had to anticipate residual blasting materials in the coal supply exploding in their firing chambers; it is thus reasonable to use a somewhat sturdier boiler than might be employed elsewhere. There are also pressing questions about protecting the chosen technology, given China's widespread problems related to the piracy of intellectual property.

Third, the FIE's decisions about the scale and capacity of its operation affect the productivity of the venture. Because they are related to the plant and equipment, scale and capacity are also treated in this section.

Intermediate Goods Inputs

Numerous interviewees addressed the importance of creating "value chains" for their Chinese operations, a key to forming secure relationships with local suppliers. A technology firm thus has cajoled its US providers of architectural services and office furniture to open up branches in Beijing, because local substitutes lacked sufficient quality and import duties made using overseas suppliers prohibitively expensive (#31).[9] The firm believes that creating these networks in China is crucial if it is to focus on its core competencies. Another firm included in this study (near Guangzhou) opened a factory with almost the sole purpose of providing in-country product to McDonald's (#38). As a worldwide supplier to McDonald's, this firm had to set up production in China to spare their customer the challenge of—in this case—locating sufficient quantities of honey-mustard sauce. Forming relationships up and down the value

---

9. In fact, even their Feng Shui consultant had to be brought from the United States, since none in China was sensitive enough to their high-tech needs. (Feng Shui, the ancient Chinese belief system used to properly orient artificial structures—such as factories—to energy sources in nature is making a comeback in modern China. Regardless of their own beliefs, expatriates often follow these practices to demonstrate a sensitivity to local tastes.)

Figure 4.1 FIEs in China's trade, 1980-96

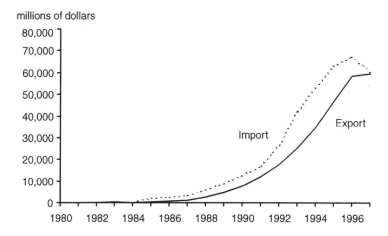

millions of dollars

Source: Australia Department of Foreign Affairs and Trade (1997a).

chain lowers costs, outsources comparative disadvantages, and improves supply dependability. It thus frees management to focus on improving productivity in other ways.

As noted in chapter 2, most FIEs are increasing local content because it makes good business sense. Foreign enterprises are still net importers to China, although the gap is closing (see figure 4.1). By finding local sources of supply, they cut delivery times and reduce uncertainty. They may or may not cut cost; but figuring in China's poor distribution system and high transport costs, one would expect local producers of many kinds of moderately sophisticated goods to be able to compete. Subsidies make some local materials less expensive; yet many subsidized domestic intermediates are of such poor quality that despite their low price and the high cost of imports, FIEs still prefer to import key items. This circumstance will change over time as more local producers develop inexpensive, quality merchandise to compete with the by-and-large premium FIE-produced imports. The alacrity with which some local Chinese firms accomplished this feat is the biggest surprise to FIEs in 1998 according to some sources (#60).

As shown in chapter 2, expatriate managers spend less time trying to increase local content for the sake of complying with formal requirements than for other reasons. Content requirements are enforced with less passion than they are negotiated. There are large economies of scale to be exploited in the Chinese market, which should help to generate reliable suppliers of many inputs (in many countries with small local markets lacking a sufficient scale, only enforcement of performance requirements would guarantee local production).

The unpredictability of the overburdened and inefficient distribution system gives these efforts to secure trusted suppliers particular urgency.[10] Seasonal variables (harvests, holiday times) invariably disrupt transport; corruption both petty and grand delays and diverts shipments (the army, with its own set of commercial imperatives, still controls the rail system); and the capricious state of trade finance and of insurance infrastructure impedes the flow of intermediates into and through the Chinese economy. Depending on how sensitive the FIE plant's productivity is to volatility in the supply of intermediates, these distribution-related problems can range from annoying to bankrupting.

Trade policy variables affect the availability of intermediate inputs as well. The biggest concern in this regard is the customs regime. Duty rates for many inputs can change unexpectedly, sometimes because of sudden reclassification. FIEs have had to hire full-time staff to do nothing but sit at customs departments—making friends, looking for traps for the unwary, and getting goods cleared for import. More generally, FIEs have been concerned with preserving the capital goods import duty abatement—long an investment incentive standby—that permitted them to bring in plant and equipment at reduced or zero-duty rates in order to spur manufacturing and job creation. This policy has wavered since 1995, though it now appears to be secure for "high-technology" capital goods (a term subject to interpretation). Finally, internal trade barriers between provinces or even towns have been a problem throughout China since reform began, and in many instances they persist (Wedeman 1995). These too can make a mess of FIE productivity by interrupting intermediate supplies.

Technology Application

As noted, technological choices can affect productivity in profound ways, influencing both the static x-efficiency of plant operations and longer-term outward growth in the venture's potential to generate a higher level of output per unit of input. Some of the technology injected into a venture is what expatriates refer to as "soft technology": management know-how and human resources innovation. Much is the hard technology that goes into the production process, especially the plant and equipment used. Foreign firms seeking to achieve greater productivity in Chinese operations boil this technology input question down to two sets of issues. First, local staff may have trouble with new equipment and methods; second, new technologies may not mesh with existing Chinese standards (Guo and Akroyd 1996, 40). These technology input questions take place against a background of concerns about China's protection of intellectual property rights.

---

10. Sheard (1997, 524) notes: "Conceptually . . . it is more useful to think of distribution as being another kind of input that the seller uses in producing its output."

So that local staff will use materials more efficiently or to introduce a higher level of technology altogether, managers rework the industrial process at the venture. Expatriate managers have had to draw on not just management science but also cultural insights. An engineer running a manufacturing plant in Shenzhen put it this way:

This is a dynamic, young, not yet institutionalized organization. It has not absorbed corporate culture yet; [that is why the firm] assigned an expatriate [me] to bring the culture, discipline, and standards that [the firm] runs on. This staff has *unconscious incompetence*—they do not yet know what questions to ask; getting them to *conscious incompetence,* that is the first step. (#19)

The "conscious incompetence" that this manager is trying to instill is a matter of soft technology. His approach has been "managing by metrics": that is, getting workers at every level of the production process to identify a quantitative indicator of their performance, so they can gauge movement beyond that benchmark on a regular basis.[11] His parent company has allowed him the luxury of not worrying about profitability for the time being, so he can instruct his staff "not to worry about market share, just learn to control what you can control: costs in the plant." In the past workers would spread a two-hour task out over the day if demand were slack; now they are instructed to work as efficiently as they can, utilize the machines to the maximum, and to be pleased to finish early. To maximize productivity from the technology on hand, they have had to change their psychology.

Interviewees' remarks about transferring tangible technology mirrored those about the intangible know-how: the two go together. The manager of a Guangdong joint venture making food products described getting the factory staff to increase throughput on the line:

There is an American narrow-mindedness about how to transfer technology effectively. Our [expatriate engineers] say, "Why can't these people do it this way, what is wrong with them?" But they are always looking for "the commie behind the bushes." You have to take a hands-on approach, and mentor them, because of the gap between our way and their traditional way; [you cannot just do] demonstrations instead. I refuse to give expatriates any line responsibilities; I saw that they did not know how to manage Chinese workers. . . . Finally we were able to do a sister program with [a US] plant, but when they come here now they are really only observers. (#38)

Foreign firms will find it difficult to increase productivity if they do not select technologies appropriate for the Chinese marketplace. That is, their

---

11. Similar efforts to introduce "management information systems" were reported by a Western banker (#8) recently tasked with taking over the management of a Chinese family's textile firm based in Hong Kong. Traditional hostility to such metrics was strong among the existing upper management, who talked of preferring to manage "by touch," but rapidly eroding profits had prompted the owners to experiment with this novel approach.

facilities must take into account the level of economic development prevailing in China, the special challenges of operating in a developing market (e.g., electricity interruptions), and maintenance needs (e.g., spare parts). Chinese negotiators routinely encourage foreign investors to introduce technologies to China that are beyond the ability of local partners to absorb. Numerous interviewees reported friction over the level of technological sophistication to be used in their China operations. They recognized that technology transfer would be the trade-off for some amount of market access, but they worried that overshooting the local ability to support a technology would lead to unproductive enterprises. And, of course, high-technology installations give rise to concerns about protection of intellectual property rights (IPR).

Judicious technology application is a key means of raising economic productivity. The case studies for this study, however, made clear that firms hold back on transferring technology because they lack confidence in Chinese IPR protection regimes. The irony may be that China is large enough and dynamic enough to attract a higher level of technology transfer than the typical emerging economy. As inflows of FDI to China decelerate in the late 1990s, Chinese authorities will have to make the climate for technology transfers more inviting if they hope to keep open this critical avenue of TFP enhancement.

Scale and Capacity

"Scale economies," a powerful source of productivity in many manufacturing industries, exist when "relatively large producers [can] manufacture and market their products at lower average cost per unit than relatively small producers" (Scherer and Ross 1990, 97). For example, the amount of setup time needed for a process is the same no matter how many units are being produced. Therefore, as the number of units produced increases, the per-unit costs sunk into setup correspondingly decrease, and thus average costs come down. Economies of scale can occur for other reasons as well.

Interviewees identified several impediments to these benefits of scale (and thereby improved productivity) in China. First, larger scale means larger fixed start-up costs. As discussed in chapter 2, many foreign investors insist on entering the Chinese market in a phased manner, in order to avoid the sort of obsolescing bargain situation in which they find they have no leverage to stave off new demands from local authorities. The logic of phasing may conflict with the logic of scale economies. FIEs often operate shy of proper scale, even taking a loss for protracted periods, in order to test the Chinese market before committing themselves fully.

In many cases foreign investments under $30 million in value are permitted without approval from the central government, an extremely important consideration for firms wishing to set up quickly or to locate in an

Table 4.5 DCAC: one year's forecast vs. actual demand, 1996 (units)

	Forecast	Actual
January	300	300
February	1,672	1,372
March	1,372	800
April	1,056	528
May	1,184	0
June	1,520	648
July	784	600
August	480	480
September	552	600
October	2,162	480
November	1,728	288
December	2,304	624

Note: Units of a major automotive component to be supplied to DCAC by a major foreign subcontractor. Original forecast is 18,000 per year. DCAC 96 forecast is 14,500 per year.

Source: Author's interviews.

area not clearly favored by the central Guidelines but in which local officials will welcome the FIE (i.e., provide generous incentives). Some FIEs may acquiesce in subscale operations in order to remain under this approval ceiling. Some firms have set up one phase of operations valued under $30 million with the plan to add another phase separately and thus avoid national-level scrutiny. They have been disappointed to find that local officials promised too much if they endorsed this approach: the central government is taking a hard line on such tactics. Many firms must then choose between subscale operations and a disapproving central bureaucracy.

Reaching effective scale requires that a firm not only tool up to produce at an efficient level but also gain access to buyers: the goods must be moved out of inventory. As a Shenzhen manager pointed out, "You can't produce if there's no demand; drastic fluctuations in the market can be a determining factor on productivity" (#19). Of course factory managers cannot manage the demand for their goods in China. But they can actively anticipate the problem.

Enterprises must first of all estimate accurately the demand for their goods before setting up shop, and then take steps to ensure that they can produce at the scale that makes them competitive. Foreign investors have made errors of judgment in this regard. In their haste to establish, they have insufficiently studied demand patterns or else made overly rosy assumptions. For example, a foreign firm subcontracted with the Dongfang China Automotive Corporation (DCAC) to supply a major car component: table 4.5 and figure 4.2 show the gap between units forecast for 1996 and the actual number ordered (#26). Having built capacity to fabricate

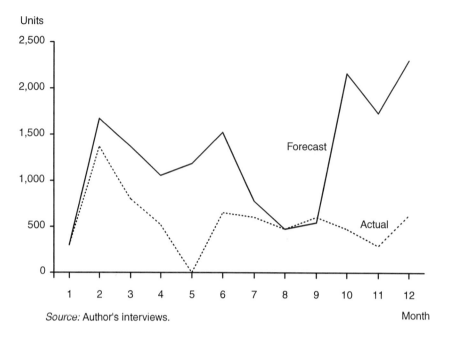

Figure 4.2 DCAC: One year's forecast vs. actual demand, 1996

Units

Forecast

Actual

Source: Author's interviews.

Month

2,000 or more units by the end of that year, the JV found itself at a production level averaging one-quarter of that projected, with devastating results for its productivity (and profitability). In fairness, accurate information (as discussed in chapter 2) in the Chinese market, like all emerging markets, is harder to come by than in mature markets. Yet even some FIEs cognizant of these problems have mistaken the demand picture.

In another case, a Shanghai telecommunications JV was held back from full-scale production by its Chinese parent, because older partners in another city were loath to see their operations become less dominant (#33). Similarly, Shanghai's prodigious efforts to protect local car manufacturers through nontariff barriers have made it difficult for other producers to enjoy potential economies of scale (#46). And as a senior managing director of a telecommunications venture noted (#20), it is hard to get up to scale when units of the investor's foreign parent company compete with the local operations by also selling in China, diminishing the total available market.

Others interviewed made points contrary to these. The president of a large technology FIE in China (#36) stressed that his firm accepted an initial low quota to produce for the local market, because he "had confidence in our partner's wisdom" and believed that they would allow the venture to get to scale over time. A combination of robust domestic demand and an activist local partner (a government entity) did lead to an expanded quota for this firm. The plant manager who said, "Productivity first, profits later," is not unusual. Many firms claim to accept overcapacity now and hope to get scale right later. Jost-HY, a trucking supply joint venture set up outside Wuhan, is reported to be taking the same position: improve quality at 25 percent capacity now, and aim at maximizing use of the plant by 2003 (*Business China*, 31 March 1997, 2). The Guangdong telecommunications joint venture included in this study is willing to "bleed for a while" in order to reserve a space in a rich market, should the economy boom in the future (#20).

FIEs must deal not only with national-level restrictions on distribution (and on other operations essential for better achieving scale efficiencies) but with troublesome local policies. In a normally functioning market with 10 undersized plants producing similar goods, a process of consolidation would take place until a smaller number of larger plants was left. Concentration in the industry would increase, but as long as barriers to entry and exit were low, the reduction in competitors would be accompanied by enhanced productivity at the remaining plants and consumers would benefit. In many markets in China, however, local authorities use protectionism and subsidies to maintain employment and forestall enterprise failure, thereby preventing consolidation and decreasing productivity growth (and, ironically, long-term growth in employment quantity and quality). Welfare gains (i.e., greater aggregate economic growth) after consolidation would surpass the employment benefits of artificially keeping plants afloat, but fear of social unrest drains the will to accept the transition. As a result, some FIEs capable of offering value by operating at greater scale find that they cannot grow normally due to the authorities' management of their market shares. This overcrowding is shockingly evident in table 4.6, which shows the host of auto producers in China, some planning to produce a mere 1,000 cars a year—an absurdly low number in this industry. Indeed, hundreds more vehicle enterprises produce in the hundreds or tens of trucks or buses a year (#46).

Absent from this discussion so far has been the flip side of scaling up toward efficient production volumes: overcapacity. This is widely considered a serious problem in many sectors in China today, inducing deflation, eviscerating profit margins, and fueling some of the clumsy efforts at local protectionism. Lardy (1998) cites Chinese surveys indicating capacity utilization of below 60 percent for over 900 major industrial products manufactured by Chinese entities. He blames this phenomenon—little or no rational exit by money-losing firms—largely on soft-money loans by state banks, without which they could not survive. These in turn are intended to hold back the flood of unemployment that would follow consolidation. FIEs, including many interviewed for this study that reported equally low or lower capacity utilization ratios, survive not because they receive state loans but because they are able to absorb losses while anticipating a more rationally structured market to come.

The case of Pilkington Glass has been widely reported. Pilkington established operations in China early (in 1983), forming Shanghai Yaohua

Table 4.6 Overcapacity? The case of the auto sector in 1996

	Production volume (thousands of vehicles per year)	Production capacity (thousands of vehicles per year)	Excess capacity (percentage)
Santana	200	300	33
Cherokee	26	50	48
Daihatsu	88	150	41
Peugeot	2	20	90
Audi (SRF)	15	30	50
Jetta	27	165	84
Citroen	9	60	85
Alto (Suzuki)	16	50	68
Yunque (Chinese)	1	14	93
Total	385	839	54

Note: Several GM vehicles (Buick models) are scheduled to begin production in 1998.

Sources: Author's interviews and calculations.

Pilkington (SYP) to make float glass. Its success and profitability (gross margins of 59 percent were reported for 1995) attracted competition. Since then, three major rivals have added 450,000 tons per year capacity to SYP's 300,000, with a further 300,000 tons capacity expected in early 1998. For SYP, this means 1998 profits were 20 percent of what they were three years previously, as prices fall and market share crumbles (Overcapacity Hits Pilkington's Chinese Adventure, *Financial Times*, 16 January 1997, A1). Discussions with Pilkington managers (#58) confirmed that the pain of overcapacity was being felt at interior operations as well, where capacity was higher than needed and demand was below expectations. Chinese SOEs that consume intermediates often have not met their original projections, making it impossible for their FIE suppliers—like Pilkington—to reach productivity goals in turn.

Overcapacity is not a problem for everybody. Some FIEs are in uncrowded industries; others have unique holdings (e.g., ARCO, which hit a major gas field in the South China Sea) or technologies (e.g., Motorola, whose early pager product dominated the market, or Boeing). With major investment in place, and scale economies at work already, these firms can afford to develop demand through product innovation and marketing. For many other FIEs, the winning strategy is to start small and keep production offshore until it is clear how large and lasting domestic demand really is (#40). Many firms have mistaken the filling up of supply chains for strong growth in consumption, only to learn that the demand was not there and that they had expanded capacity prematurely.

Whatever the reason for their predicament, managers now looking at serious overcapacity must decide what to do. Having conceded much to Chinese partners and authorities in the negotiations establishing the joint ventures, investors cannot just downsize. Even when FIEs have retained authority to adjust their labor force, there are strong pressures not to lay off workers, pressures that must be respected if the firm has long-term interests in China. Meanwhile, as even more capacity comes on line, firms are increasingly tempted to try to move their product by providing generous credit terms, which in turn has led to problems with accounts receivable.

As with other key problems faced by FIEs, one can assign responsibility for the current overcapacity on both sides of the Sino-foreign divide. On the one hand, the haste with which some foreign firms rushed into China, neglecting to carry out thoughtful market analysis, is partly to blame. Bad data and intentional distortion by expatriate managers eager to lure headquarters staff back to China after the Tiananmen incident also contributed, as did failure to recognize the serious inadequacies of distribution channels.

On the other hand, Chinese policy crowds firms together. Central planners retain a strong role in industrial policy; the "encouraged" and "restricted" categories of the Guidelines for foreign investment distort the pattern of new industrial investment. Restrictions on the reporting of economic news undercut market analysis.[12] At the same time that hurdles in the way of market access keep some FIEs from reaching efficient scale, formal and informal impediments to downsizing prevent efficiency gains for others. Size matters, especially in sectors formerly nestled under the state's wing.

Capital Factors

Like the other factors, capital can affect productivity one of three ways: an increase in absolute amount (normally a useful thing, though too easy terms can lead to inefficiency), more efficient allocation of what exists, or technological evolution in its use. Enhanced allocation (x-efficiency) may result from reducing wasteful spending on nonproductive activities (such as graft). A recent *Economist* essay on Asian banking crises noted: "Bankers failed to examine the financial risks they were undertaking: a lunch or a round of golf would do more to inform their credit decisions than spreadsheets of financial data. This 'Asian Way' of vetting borrowers has proved costly indeed" ("How Far is Down," 15 November 1997, 20). An example of technological innovation is the introduction of computerized scenario planning to identify promising investment opportunities. Interviewees discussed a number of ways in which improving FIE productivity through better capital practices was key. The main themes were keeping costs in line within the factory and improving management of capital within the broader organization.

---

12. Hazelbarth (1997, 13) notes: "Although the trend in China clearly is toward greater media autonomy and diversity and away from government control and intimidation, crosscurrents of resistance persist. Powerful domestic institutions still constrain efforts by the media to become more autonomous and politically diverse."

Cost Control within the Plant

Even small capital expenditures shape the culture and organization of an enterprise. Because labor-intensive activities can be inexpensive in China, there is a temptation not to take seriously the task of keeping them in line with productivity objectives. Factory managers stressed the importance of these costs to overall productivity. If excessive numbers of drivers, guards, foremen, cooks, and janitors are lounging around a facility, even if the wage cost of maintaining them is minuscule (which increasingly it is not), it is difficult to focus on productivity among semiskilled and managerial employees. Costs treated as insignificant by Western managers may be seen as major by local employees, and a dismissive attitude toward them can have a deleterious effect on performance.

Likewise, small costs to buy off rent seekers such as petty officials can create a bad working environment. One plant manager (#26) identified "keeping overhead costs down" (wage bills, "consulting fees," electricity assessments, etc.) as the number one challenge to productivity at his facility in interior China. They threatened to consume all capital resources before they could be used for reinvestment.

Capital performance metrics recognizable to modern managers are being applied for the first time in many enterprises in which foreigners are involved. Such "scientific" approaches to allocating capital resources still appear quite radical in many parts of China. Before one can manage capital use in such a way, there must be professionals in place who have the right skills. This is why FIEs are scrambling so fiercely to attract or train financial professionals, as described in chapter 3.

The challenge of this particular aspect of productivity rests largely with the FIEs and the expatriates themselves, although the transitional nature of the Chinese marketplace and its widespread graft complicate the task. True, the pressure placed on the foreign investor during establishment to give up management control over the joint venture has the potential to stymie efforts at cost cutting. Preventing the release of surplus workers to cut costs is a prominent example. Further, Chinese partners against whom cost cutting might be directed may be either quasi-governmental organizations or else closely associated with policymakers. But investors have increasing choice nowadays of when and with whom to enter into a partnership, and no policy exists to prevent them from finding allies who agree with the imperatives of enhancing capital productivity at the plant—though that effort may delay their entrance into the market.

Financial Efficiency within the Organization

A significant number of managers involved in operations in China were concerned by restrictions on the ability of FIEs to manage financial flows *across* units. Unlike the use of capital at the plant level, the movement of money within the larger organizational structure is shaped by policy. Capital cannot be managed on a unitary basis for various FIE joint ventures organized under a holding company, one method of supporting operations efficiently. Foreign investors are lobbying for holding companies to be granted such rights or else for them to be transformed into "captive finance companies" that could accomplish the same end. This would improve administrative efficiency, foster innovation, and permit resources to be shifted from less productive to more productive endeavors.

Many Chinese partners involved in JVs are reported to have very short time horizons for profitability. While foreign investors accustomed to mature financial plans aim at making ventures profitable within perhaps three to five years (the average in China for profitable ventures, according to surveys by the Economist Intelligence Unit 1995, 1997), Chinese partners often expect dividend payments after a year or two. Perhaps they have less confidence in the long-term behavior of markets, or are suffering short-term cash crunches because they are overextended, or desire liquidity to go after new and unrelated business opportunities. In any case, many (not all) expatriate managers reported having difficulty convincing Chinese partners to defer capital withdrawal until the business was well established. Their focus on the short term has made it possible for some FIEs to buy out shares of their JVs and increase control. Many foreign investors take this opportunity when it arises. But weighing against this creeping shift to foreign control are overseeing authorities that must approve ownership changes (their general practice appears to be to discourage such buyouts, which nevertheless are believed to have become widespread). The conflict reflects China's fundamental ownership problem: it remains unclear (in practice, if not in law) who has ownership rights sufficient to take remedial, productivity-enhancing measures that conflict with social or mercantile imperatives trumpeted by governmental agencies.

This problem is complicated. Intrafirm transfers of capital can be tantamount to providing financial services, an area still heavily restricted from foreign participation. Foreign investors have created Byzantine ownership structures among JVs and holding companies to get around restrictions on services (along with those on distribution). The central authorities have permitted some FIEs to experiment with new structures, as is their habit while pondering whether to legitimate those practices; so far, they are holding the line much more firmly on the use of such arrangements to do finance.

Institutional Factors

Business professionals often talk about "cultural factors" when considering how to raise productivity in China. These points are discussed here along with other phenomena of an "institutional" nature.

Existing Culture and "Resistance to Change"

An Economist Intelligence Unit survey of foreign enterprises (EIU 1997) asked managers to rank the factors they felt most hampered the productivity of their operations. The second and fourth respectively were "language/culture" and "resistance to change." The responses collected for this study gave these problems similar importance. They are "soft" factors, difficult to quantify. Yet the majority of foreign businessmen in China mention these concerns repeatedly and believe that dealing with them is critical to raising productivity at their operations.

To read the literature on joint ventures in China from the early through the late 1980s, one would think that working with Chinese labor and management partners was next to impossible. The most popular work—*Beijing Jeep*, by Jim Mann of the *Los Angeles Times* (1997)[13]—paints a picture of intransigence, complete with deception, manipulation, arrogance, ignorance, and incompetence (not to mention the errors of the Western side of the partnership). Expatriates understand the motivations of their Chinese partners far better now than in the 1980s when that story unfolded.

But that understanding does not necessarily spell sympathy. The head of a major American conglomerate's China company observes (quoted as the epigraph to this chapter), "The biggest problem in China is 50 years of socialism; who cares anything about doing a good job after that?" (#22). He is not alone in his views; many interviewees knew China's commercial history in this century, and while they had learned why things are they did not accept excuses for why they cannot be changed.

The cultural factors in China are not unique. The executive not only perceived Russia as in worse straits but he considered the culture of Washington to be a bigger impediment to his work than that of Beijing (as US foreign policy toward China in the mid-1990s lurched from moralistic to militarist for a time). He and a number of other expatriates perceived less resistance to change in China than in other emerging economies (notably Indonesia).

For each foolish complaint such as "They can't speak English," there was an observation that cultural frustrations resulted from the poor training of both local employees and expatriates. FIE managers focused at length on their efforts to urge regular maintenance at the plant. While this at first sounds paternalistic, teaching repair and neatness seems indeed essential to improving productivity in China. It is widely felt that productivity suffers in China because of a systematic bias against investment in such intangibles. Without adequate maintenance and repair, x-inefficiency grows as excessive downtime is required to do unscheduled maintenance. In the past, performance measures did not include quality of output, time-

---

13. *Beijing Jeep* was first published in 1989.

liness, or downtime; only recently have objective standards to optimize these factors been employed in China to a significant extent. Many plant managers at FIEs fight a daily battle to change negligent maintenance habits.

Corruption and Graft

All expatriates interviewed who were involved in managing factories or field offices noted petty extortion of various sorts as a distraction for managers, and potentially a drain on resources. If managers are spending all their time dealing with shakedowns, they are going to have less time to focus on running a business or a plant. Rent seeking can take the form of requests for preferential supply deals, pilferage, cost padding, plain bribery, and the like, and it affects both productivity and profitability. As Kimberly Elliott notes in the introduction to a comprehensive 1997 collection of essays on corruption, the phenomenon is truly global, present in rich and poor countries alike (Elliott 1997); China presents an excellent example of how productivity can suffer as a result.

Most of those whom the interviewees described as rent seeking were related to the civil service in one way or another. They told of fire inspectors insisting that absurd numbers of lightning rods be purchased from them for a small facility, and police requiring special fees to validate the residence permits of expatriate managers, to guarantee adequate protection for the factory, or simply to not cause trouble. Most pernicious appear to be tax authorities who find "irregularities" that portend serious fines and penalties unless the FIE agrees to use specific "tax consultancies" to assess the situation, at a fee—sometimes petty, sometimes hefty. Such consultancies, usually consisting of little more than a retired local government official, are today a very common means of extracting payoffs.

However, while all factory managers reported corruption (including facilities in Tianjin, Shanghai, Wuhan, Guangzhou, and Shenzhen), local governments do not endorse such practices. Many local investment authorities are trying to reduce these practices (interviewee #55, the director of the Wuhan Foreign Investment Office, was a good case in point). Several interviewees maintained that expatriates (through their comprador agents) propose bribes more often than Chinese officials seek them. Some argued that many charges of bribery reflect misunderstandings of a gift-giving culture. Another faction of respondents stressed the *virtues* of corruption, arguing that petty graft has been the fuel propelling China out of the Stone Age to its present level of high growth and promise. They maintain that the totalitarian grip of the bureaucracy would not otherwise have permitted development.

Without debating the merits of this perspective (which seem to have some validity in a bureaucrat's playground like China), it is clear that the present level and breadth of corrupt practices are very likely to diminish growth in the future, even if they helped to facilitate it in the past.[14] Corruption can distort productivity growth by diverting capital, labor, and goods from their best use, by acting as a discriminatory tax and open-ended risk that requires hedging, and by compromising quality control. Some empirical analyses suggest the "corruption tax on FIEs in places like China can exceed 20 percent" (S.-J. Wei 1997). It is obvious why expatriate managers saw these problems as a threat to productivity.

But many businesspeople derided such talk of "threats" as lacking rigor and in any case lacking relevance in high-growth Asia: Asia prior to the financial turmoil of 1997, that is. The different conditions in Thailand, Indonesia, Malaysia, Korea, and other Asian economies make unitary explanations for the financial trouncings suffered across the region impossible. But as the dust settled, one common thread did emerge: crony capitalism, or the making of noncommercial investment decisions guided not by productivity but by connections. While not explaining the whole of the Asian crisis, this does point to factors contributing to economic fragility in all of these countries, and most certainly in China as well.

Crude financial firewalls (particularly the use of a closed capital account) in the Chinese economy have provided a little more time before the rot of corruption-oriented decision making on investments leads to a productivity failure and subsequent crisis (Rosen, Liu, and Dwight 1998). But evidence supporting the weak position of the portfolios of financial intermediaries in China—public and private—is overwhelming (Lardy 1998). To date, repeated efforts in China to strike hard at corruption have failed. Short of clearly vesting citizens and stockholders with property rights, and then empowering courts to uphold those rights, it is unlikely that the logic of productivity will have sufficient standing to deal cronyism a deathblow.

Discordant Organizational Structures

Interviewees described institutional problems inside FIEs as a challenge to improving productivity. Not surprisingly, such critiques were more likely to be heard the further one moved from the headquarters operation in the home country and the nearer one came to the plant level in China.[15]

---

14. Those who argue that the case for bribery's positive effects has no merit (e.g., Rose-Ackerman 1997, 33) generally note either that in the cases in which high growth and high corruption have gone together the future might nonetheless be grim (a point with which no one could take issue) or that there is more to life than growth—there is equity, too. This second argument ignores cases in which high growth, high corruption, and broad-based economic gains have all gone together: most notably, that of China.

15. Prior to interviews with expatriates in China, there were background interviews with US headquarters personnel of many of the firms examined in these case studies. Only a handful of home-country interviewees acknowledged problems of discord, whether out of ignorance or reluctance to admit them. By contrast, managers in the field focused considerable time on these issues in their remarks.

Similarly, those interviewees further removed from the plant level in China were more likely to try to fit the China operations into the firm's global framework, and thus were less likely to have insights into the important reasons for and implications of incongruities in structure among units in China.

The manager of a Shanghai FIE identified a typical problem (#33). His manufacturing JV is aligned with a partner that is subsidiary to a local government ministry, while his parent firm has a longtime previous alliance with officials in another municipality. For important product lines produced both in Shanghai and at the preexisting facility, this Shanghai manager has the capacity and the orders to expand production to serve the local market and achieve better scale economies. Fearful of stepping on the feet of partners from the other municipality, however, the venture's American parent restrains this plant and lets its older partnership serve the market at higher cost.

This manager was extremely frustrated, having set up a state-of-the-art manufacturing center in record time (about a year). He is aware that the relationships nurturing the firm's fortunes must be respected, but displeased to do it at the expense of productivity. The director of a sales JV in Shanghai (#24) is in a similar situation. The operation's manufacturing JV parent in Tianjin refuses to cede the Shanghai market: it requires all sales in Shanghai to be logged in Tianjin, along with a brokerage fee, and continues to sell spare parts to Shanghai clients directly, undermining the business's Shanghai office (set up with considerable effort). "We screwed up and negotiated neither majority control over decisions with [the Tianjin partner], nor a nonexclusivity arrangement so that [the Shanghai office] could sell directly without going through Tianjin," he explained. Without independence from Tianjin, his office will not be able to operate productively. "We need a nationwide corporate perspective," he lamented.

This American FIE has a sister firm under the same corporate umbrella, a sister that is also established in China (#25). It would make sense for them to consolidate some functions to boost productivity, but that is unlikely: one unit's Shanghai ministry partner is also the partner of the other unit's archcompetitor. This sort of tangled organizational web is pervasive in China today.

The manager of a venture in Wuhan (#26) echoed these sentiments. His suggestion: avoid intrafirm discord and give expatriates the chance to manage the FIE without micromanagement from abroad. This point is China-specific: because they are less standardized with global practice than other overseas operations, ventures in China cannot be fit easily into a worldwide corporate model. He underscored that both expatriates *and* local staff must take the initiative. For example, through his Chinese deputy, this manager entered into a supply arrangement that guaranteed him both on-time delivery and a politically useful relationship with local authorities. Home-country supply managers, however, were seeking economy of scale by sourcing this particular part globally and using it world-wide. But in China, that move would be far more costly: the outside managers took into account neither the value of the relationships earned by using a local supplier nor this FIE's need, as a joint venture, to seek consensus with its Chinese partners to break off a good local relationship. A different calculus applies in China, especially during these years of transition, and bickering within firms is disruptive.[16]

An interesting case of organizations at cross-purposes involves a joint venture that manufactures telecommunications switching equipment near Guangzhou, in Guangdong Province (#20). Aggressive Chinese start-up factories are competing with this JV, producing a product that looks remarkably similar on the outside. In fact, they gained access to the technical details through the "research institute" associated with the JV's overseeing authorities—essentially, they pirated the firm's switch technology. This in itself is an intellectual property problem and came as no surprise to the FIE's general manager—indeed, he expected it. But the story is more complicated.

While the design of the switch can be replicated by Chinese competitors, the result can hardly compete with the JV's product because it lacks the specialized high-technology chip that runs the switch. However, the Western unit of the parent company fabricating these chips is selling them into the Chinese market: the FIE's domestic competitors promptly buy them, plug them into the pirated architecture, and undercut the JV on price. The JV's parent firm appears to be deliberately hobbling its Chinese operation. Headquarters seems to have taken in-country management's recommendation to accept slow market-share growth as a sign that the enterprise is pie-in-the-sky, so it has decided to make a quick profit where it can. On the other side of the organizational structure, the Chinese partner to the venture has taken to informing potential customers of marketing plans and thereby encouraging them to hold out for discount prices.

Scope of Participation

It has already been noted that bottlenecks in supply and distribution channels can disrupt FIE operations and that FIEs face policy restrictions on distribution that domestic firms do not. The Guidelines treat distribution and services as restricted or prohibited sectors. These proscriptions potentially deny FIEs "economies of scope." Less often discussed than economies of scale, these refer to "the impact on total costs, plant-specific and product-specific, attributable to production of more than one product" (Scherer and Ross 1990, 100). Additional products can include intermediate services such as distribution and marketing, as well as final

---

16. This does not necessarily mean that the parent company in this case was wrong for trying to force China in line with its global practice. Indeed, every firm must balance the costs and benefits of such decisions. Rather, it is meant only to illuminate the locus of intrafirm tensions.

Table 4.7 Expanding service operations of a joint venture in Tianjin, 1994-97

	1994	1995	1996	1997
Sole branches	33	50	70	80
Cooperative branches	3	0	0	0
Service offices	14	25	23	26
Sales offices	0	35	83	140
Total	50	110	176	246

Source: Author's interviews.

services such as warranty, repair, and maintenance. These are especially important in China where many basic business services are scarce or underdeveloped (especially outside big cities).

Therefore some FIEs have rushed to create holding companies, joint trading companies, branch offices, joint sales offices, and ever new structures in an attempt to get goods to market, solidify relationships with customers, and respond to logjams before they cause the plant to shut down and productivity curves to crash.[17] Table 4.7 presents the growth in service offices of a Sino-American JV based in Tianjin that has been able to expand beyond manufacturing through its partnership with a well-established Chinese enterprise. These sales and service networks can only support the units that this JV manufactures in China, not the many other models that the firm's US parent manufacturers elsewhere. In addition, important sales subsidiaries are finding it very difficult to operate in other provinces where they do not have manufacturing facilities.

For many firms to achieve a high level of manufacturing productivity, it is important that attendant services grow with sales. Some services the FIE needs to conduct for itself, including finance among units, advertising, marketing, and debt collection; others it provides as a business line to clients alongside the goods it makes—for example, a maintenance contract on an elevator. In some cases, the services at issue may be the firm's primary product, which is sold to other firms. However, foreign firms' ability to participate in China's service sectors is limited, and interviewees identified these scope prohibitions as important barriers to enhancing productivity.

Environment and Productivity: A Note

Environmental externalities underscore the difficulty of measuring productivity. A facility's efficiency depends partly on whether the negative

---

17. Whether absence of scope will directly affect productivity depends on factors such as the customer base (domestic or export) and the industry (pagers are easier to handle than frozen food).

pollution externalities of the production process are "internalized" when a facility's performance is assessed. In an unregulated marketplace, if the pollution streams of a firm were simply ignored, then operating the facility without any environmental controls would maximize productivity. However, if the costs associated with those pollution streams—for example, medical expenses due to coal smoke in the air and mercury in a local lake—are billed to the firm generating them, then a different appraisal of productivity would be necessary.

Currently, foreign enterprise managers (especially Western ones) are looking beyond China's lax enforcement of environmental law and applying a productivity calculus that takes greater account of environmental harms than what is strictly required. Some foreign firms are even leading the way by creating a "positive externality" by raising local awareness of pollution control and demonstrating cost-effective remedial steps. However, there are other foreign operations in China that make little effort to operate a clean plant. (Although adequate rules have been created, enforcement is the problem; in early 1998 China's Environmental Protection Agency was finally given ministerial status, which may be an indication that stricter enforcement will follow.)

Although a company can be the trailblazer, China's central government must take the full initiative to produce the economywide steps necessary (including investment and training) to address the country's looming environmental crisis.

Analysis

The first impression that emerges from this chapter is how deeply expatriate managers are engaged in the economic life of China, shaping the culture of the work environment both directly and indirectly in their efforts to improve productivity. As the reformist clique of Chinese planners intended, foreign enterprises have brought technology both hard (machines) and soft (managerial know-how). These have powerful positive spillovers that accrue to the host country, beyond the simple economic value of the goods produced and the wages paid. Less tangible but equally important is the competitive mind-set that foreign firms have helped to introduce. When able to compete inside the borders of China, FIEs have brought virtuous competitive pressure to bear on domestic firms. Even in sectors in which authorities still limit foreign participation, such as finance, the simple presence of FIEs can force Chinese firms to change as they anticipate future competition. For example, though a major American bank had only a small initial presence in China, domestic institutions were studying it closely and imitating its product-pricing behavior (#60).

Such behavior powerfully supports the thesis that competition can be even more effective than privatization as a spur to economic development and productivity gains. In recent years, many scholars have made this argument with reference to particular sectors, such as telecommunications, whose far-reaching shifts away from statism were under debate:

> While both [competition and privatization] strategies can help liberalize[,] . . . the competition strategy lowers rates and improves quality more dependably. This is because privatized monopolies are likely to focus not only on efficient operations . . . but also on protecting their profit margins. Indeed they may raise prices and oppose new products . . . that would compete [with their existing money-makers]. (Petrazzini 1996, 6)

Li Wei makes the same point with regard to the Chinese reform experience in general, after studying productivity trends in the state-owned sector from 1980 to 1989. Finding a strong relationship between the advent of competition and long-overdue gains in SOE performance, he notes:

> These findings have implications far beyond simply providing a better understanding of the performance of Chinese state enterprises during the reform period. They suggest that enterprise restructuring can improve enterprise performance even without formal privatization and that the marginal economic liberalization as practiced in China can improve resource allocation when barriers to the state-monopolized industries are also lowered to foster competition. (1997, 1082)

Such success has contributed to the resolve of China's leaders to push ahead with domestic reform, even in the face of increasing social anxieties and the possibility that their own authority may diminish. This competition-before-privatization model seems to offer Chinese policymakers a way to escape their current dilemma: ideologically unready to confront the task of privatizing state-owned enterprises but incapable of meeting rising expectations with sluggish productivity growth, policymakers have used competition, partly from domestic entrepreneurialism as provided by township and village enterprises and partly from FIEs, to spur domestic productivity.

As important as these innovations have been to China's reforms and to forecasting the shape of restructuring to come, our focus here is assessing the Chinese scene in terms of foreign investor compatibility. Table 4.8 summarizes the productivity-related issues, assigning them to one or more of the four categories established in chapter 1 with special attention to the policy-related factors.

Transitional and Self-Imposed Variables

Many of the impediments to productivity include a transitional element, a sign of the changes taking place both in the organization of firms in China and in the scope of foreign participation in the economy. It is

Table 4.8 Roundup of issues: productivity

Issue	Category	If policy . . . Level	If policy . . . Priority
Labor			
Availability	Transitional		
Training	Transitional, self-imposed		
Deployment and management	Transitional, policy	Local, central	Medium
Overstaffing	Policy, self-imposed	Local, central	Low
Goods			
Supply networks	Transitional, market structure		
Distribution problems (inputs)	Transitional, policy, market structure	Central, local	Medium
Trade policy swings	Policy	Local, provincial, central	Medium
Technology application	Transitional, self-imposed, policy	Local, provincial, central	Medium
Scale economies	Policy, market structure	Local, provincial, central	Medium
Capital			
Costs in the factory	Self-imposed, transitional		
Financing the organization	Policy	Central	High
Institutional			
"Resisting change"	Transitional, self-imposed		
Corruption and graft	Policy, transitional	Mostly local, provincial	Medium
Discordant organizations	Self-imposed, market and strategy policy	Provincial, central	High
Economies of scope	Policy	Central	High

prominent in labor issues—not surprising, given the shortages of skilled workers and the hindrances to training and deployment. The area of goods inputs, too, has transitional problems because of the evolving distribution system and the time required to build local value chains. The greatest transitional issues affecting capital inputs involve the slow process of changing attitudes toward costs at the plant level. Institutional factors, including corruption and resistance to change, are also likely to become less prominent in the long term, as the marketplace develops and workers and officials are increasingly exposed to new modes of commercial activity.

But FIEs must take responsibility for a good many self-imposed productivity problems as well. In labor, these include training failures, which contribute to the "resistance to change" that expatriates describe. In addition, many FIEs admit inadequate negotiation and planning to address the questions of intermediates and of capital. Many investors argue that the urgency of getting established in China before markets are cornered outweighs the value of making more deliberate preparations for entry. That is their choice; but some investors have avoided these pitfalls, demonstrating an alternative to heedlessly rushing in. Proper staffing levels, cost containment, and training are unglamorous microeconomic details, but the firms with the best performance take them seriously. The choice—so important to productivity—of technology level brought to the Chinese market obviously is in part under the venture's control. While in some cases FIEs made missteps because they tried to employ more sophisticated technologies than the market could accommodate, such errors move more into the realm of policy, because of China's poor record in protecting intellectual property.

Perhaps the most interesting productivity problem for which the firms bear partial responsibility is the phenomenon of conflict within their organizations, which involves policy and market structure complications as well. Foreign investors are steered toward partners in China, but they also court them enthusiastically, hoping (in many sectors) that powerful local partners will spell market control. They have learned the benefits of *guanxi* capitalism—protected or favorable access to market shares and comfortable relations with overseeing authorities—but the drawbacks come as a surprise. The investors find that expanding operations beyond the original jurisdiction, overhauling the management structure and performance goals of the venture, or placing the global profitability of a multinational enterprise ahead of the Chinese company's well-being can be difficult or impossible. The responsibility borne by FIEs for their choices of organizational partners, it appears, will be a key theme of Chinese marketplace studies in the coming years.

Policy Variables

Once cognizant of the importance of transitional and self-imposed impediments to productivity growth, one can better gauge the impact of policy problems on foreign enterprises. Policy factors are discernible in 10 of the 15 themes in this chapter. National restrictions on management control of ventures hamper deployment of labor and lead to overstaffing. Trade policies (including swings in duty rates) and technical policies (such as coerced transfers of technology) influence the availability of intermediates, the plant and equipment the FIE uses to manufacture, and the attainability of scale economies in production. Policies curtailing scope of business interfere with FIEs' efforts to manage capital productively across China-based units. Industrial policy goals force foreign investors into partnerships that often turn fractious and counterproductive. And of course varieties of graft and corruption affect the bureaucracy to a serious degree in China, as even the Communist Party admitted with the very public ouster of Beijing Party chief Chen Xitong.

Three of these matters were seen by the expatriates as high-priority concerns, while the others are mostly medium priority: serious, but somehow manageable or tolerable. The first important policy issue was the problem of organizational finance. Foreign firms want to be able to consolidate and manage money flows among their various ventures in China. Such latitude would permit not only more efficient investing and costing but also better credit management and thus market development. This affects profits as much as productivity, but it can certainly be argued that better control over profitability would also make possible more productive organizations as well (e.g., through economies of scale). For investors that have only a single operation or factory in China, this consideration will not be relevant; for the many larger multinational investors it is a first-order concern—and one attributed to policy alone.

Second was the problem of strife within the organization. To the extent that it results from China's policy aspirations of guiding FIE establishment in ways that simultaneously strengthen specific Chinese industrial giants, it deserves significant attention from China's trading partners. Such policies are neither consistent with the intent of the World Trade Organization (WTO) nor in the long-term interests of Chinese consumers, inasmuch as they act to suppress the productivity-enhancing effects of competition. However, the problem also involves self-imposed and market structure aspects. Many FIEs take the initiative in partnering with a Chinese entity in the hope of gaining a market advantage. In addition, the market structure in China is developing in such a way that fewer firms may dominate important industries such as telecommunications to the detriment of consumer gains, and thus FIEs may be forced to partner their way into the action. Rather than simply applying foreign policy pressure, encouraging the Chinese to take an active regulatory stance in favor of greater market contestability may address this problem more effectively.

Finally, policy restrictions on the scope of FIE business operations were a high-priority impediment to productivity, because operating without distribution, sales, and follow-up business functions deprives modern firms of the feedback they depend on to streamline and optimize production. This topic has figured prominently in ongoing WTO accession negotiations in 1998. Once the central-level policy restrictions are rescinded, impediments to foreign participation in the marketplace will remain, as the following chapter details, but this regulatory aspect is most important. That many FIEs already circumvent these policies by creative interpretation of existing laws is a good indicator that the central government will formalize its endorsement of those practices in the not-too-distant future.

Market Structure Variables

Market structure (competition policy) aspects come into play in the development of supply networks, the distribution problems that stall economies of scale and scope (and hence create barriers to successful competition), and the discordant organization problems that emerge because FIEs can select from among only a limited number of partners. All of these involve the input of intermediate goods into the production process and the movement of finished goods out of inventory after manufacture. The hallmark of a collusive market sector in no need of the efficiency that procompetitive policies promote is reduced productivity. Chinese authorities need look no further than their own SOEs to see the results of too much cooperation and not enough competition. The message sent by most FIEs is that they would rather compete than collude, but they will collude if that is their only option for succeeding in the Chinese economy. Nevertheless, they remain focused on productivity, which puts them a step ahead of many indigenous competitors.

5

Ex-Factory China: Distribution, Marketing, and Services

Invigoration of the domestic economy also means opening the domestic economy. There are, in fact, two open policies: open to the outside and open to the inside.

Deng Xiaoping, 1984 (cited in Wedeman 1995, 1)

[I]f the underdeveloped nature of [China's] distribution system causes a further gap in living standards among regions, we have no guarantee that what we fear most will not occur. . . . Material affluence must be enjoyed, not only in one part of the country but by all citizens. . . . This goal cannot be accomplished without modernization of the distribution system. . . . Chinese distribution systems represent not just a "Dark Continent" but a potential quagmire. Yet I feel that it is my duty as an entrepreneur to help modernize distribution in China, for the sake of peace in China, in Asia, and in the world.

Isao Nakauchi, 7 December 1994
(Drucker and Nakauchi 1997, 20–22)

Distribution Rules: A Domestic Trade Policy

Encountering the almost religious fervor of Isao Nakauchi, a Japanese executive, as he talks about China's distribution systems with his friend and business consultant Peter Drucker, many Americans—in Congress or commerce—might be perplexed. More trucks are needed so that ice cream does not melt en route to Hangzhou from Shanghai, and this threatens world peace? Surely such a claim appears hyperbolic. Yet in the opinion of many of his fellow expatriates at work in China, his remarks are not, in fact, off the mark. The state of the systems of distribution within the Chinese economy is probably the single best predictor of the sustainability and stability of the experiment in economic reform taking place in the People's Republic of China.

For 50 years, the international trade policy regime has been developed and refined, in order to bring freer trade and the accompanying economic benefits to nations. Its embodiment is the World Trade Organization (WTO), whose focus has been border barriers to trade, such as tariffs, quotas, and arbitrary trade bans (e.g., those couched as spurious health concerns). The regime has been fairly successful at dealing with these impediments. Partly because tariffs are lower as a result of the General Agreement on Tariffs and Trade and WTO, and partly because trade with less economically developed countries such as China has increased, attention is turning to the domestic analogue of the open international trade regime: domestic distribution rules, or *competition policy*. Ironically, although the belief that openness in international rules of trade produces rich rewards for everyone involved is almost universal, openness in rules has barely taken hold *domestically* in many countries.

In exploring foreign participation in the marketization of the production process at the plant level in China, the previous chapter provided an essentially microeconomic analysis. But its implications go beyond the enterprise: the market model of economic efficiency also affects the design of commercial policies governing the interaction *among* economic actors, whether the sellers and buyers be firms or individuals. While market forces are reshaping production processes in China, the actual "markets" where goods and services are bought and sold exist *outside* the firm. This may seem obvious; yet even today, many state-owned enterprises (SOEs) in China are loaded with so many functions and tasks that employees could go a lifetime transacting almost all business within their firm—including housing, groceries, education, medical care, entertainment, and burial.

Such concentration of functions resulted from an excessive concern with equity, which led government planners to provide for economic needs entirely by fostering cooperation (the hallmark of activities within a firm). Competition policy, while recognizing the importance of equity objectives, seeks to achieve efficiency goals as well.[1] There is no single proper balance between cooperation and competition as tools to generate economic outcomes, and no society would want to rely on either exclusively.

China is no exception. The 20-year reform period has been, in effect, a time of experimentation during which different implicit competition policies have been applied to different segments of the Chinese economy. Early on, foreign-invested enterprises (FIEs) were introduced to China largely to cooperate with Chinese firms in the domestic economy (by sharing skills, technologies, finance, and work tasks) and to compete in

---

1. The introductory section of this chapter is heavily indebted to the work of Graham and Richardson (1997b) in making competition policy clear and understandable to policymakers and noneconomists.

the international economy (through their exports). Over time this demarcation has eroded; today, FIEs both compete in the domestic economy to a significant extent and cooperate with Chinese firms and regulators in a manner that sometimes fails to serve the best interests of the nation.[2] The ad hoc competition policy regime implicit in China appears to have outgrown its usefulness: the present Chinese marketplace requires a more considered, explicit set of rules for domestic trade. At stake are the fortunes not just of foreign firms but of domestic firms as well—indeed, the aggregate welfare of the Chinese economy is in question.

Before suggesting what the shape of an updated and formalized competition policy regime for China might look like, this chapter picks up the story of the emerging business environment in China where chapter 4 leaves off: it explores the *ex-factory* business functions. Our concern here is everything that happens after the "product"—say, a toaster—is wheeled out of the factory door (see also box 5.1). It must be marketed, advertised, and moved to a point of sale through a set of distribution channels. It must be checked for damage suffered in transit and presented for sale, and perhaps credit terms must be provided to the wholesaler, retailer, or final buyer. The sale must be facilitated and supported through warranty and service. The measure of a market's *contestability* lies in the firms' ability to undertake (to whatever extent needed) these functions—in a word, to sell.

A broad set of factors can block ostensibly productive enterprises within a country from serving demand efficiently, thus denying buyers lower prices and a full selection. These obstacles to market-oriented distribution contribute to losses in potential GDP, per capita income, and productivity growth for the nation. Over the longer term, the lack of feedback and signaling among investors, producers, sellers, and buyers—hallmarks of open domestic distribution—has a deleterious *dynamic* effect; that is, economic development will (at a minimum) proceed more slowly. It becomes impossible to divide labor according to comparative advantage, firms cannot decide what to focus on and what to outsource, and cooperation among producers becomes less certain and therefore less productive. These are efficiency arguments in favor of domestic distribution rules.

As Graham and Richardson (for example) stress, competition policy is also properly informed by equity considerations, or "fairness"—a far tougher standard to measure and one subject almost inherently to different interpretations (1997a, 7–9). Nevertheless, it is clear that FIEs walled off from distribution solely due to their foreignness have an equity bone to pick in terms of Chinese competition policy as well; just as important, so too do the great majority of Chinese firms excluded from domestic mar-

---

2. FIEs, like domestic firms, are forced by the present regulatory environment to engage in collusive arrangements that underperform more competitive models of industrial organization.

Box 5.1 Distribution feedback leading to efficient production

Consider the sophistication of a modern distribution system such as exists in the United States. A small-town retailer notices he is low on a brand of shampoo. Restocking his shelves is a process with many elements, each of which reduces economic waste:

■ An inventory management system, typically computer run, tracks the retailer's stock and changes in demand.

■ A local distributor can supply the store with product in small quantities, often less than a case, in a matter of days (so that low inventories can be maintained, reducing costs).

■ A higher-tier regional distributor is capable of meeting the needs of the numerous local distributors on a timely basis.

■ Physical infrastructure—including dependable roads, communication systems, trucks, and smaller vans—exists to move product to the retail level; bottlenecks along these arteries are instantly identified and circumvented; and increasingly, whole fleets of delivery vehicles are tracked via satellite.

■ The human resources needed to manage the flow of goods and information through each channel down to the buyer are in place, keeping track of stock, making deliveries, and resolving problems, all with a minimum of graft.

■ Financial infrastructure facilitates payment, credit, and allowances among retailers, wholesalers, and manufacturers.

■ Demand (national, regional, or even local) is coordinated with marketing and advertising campaigns that affect product flow.

■ As signals of demand flow up the supply chain from the retail level to manufacturers, quick production and pricing decisions are made in short order, the product mix is adjusted in the medium term, and new products are developed over the long term.

■ Quality assurance and other services, including repair, are available to support the sale—especially for more expensive purchases.

ket opportunities because they are Sichuanese companies in Shanghai or Henan firms in Harbin. It is hardly surprising to find Chinese firms fighting against foreign entry into the domestic market when they themselves are boxed out of the bidding as soon as they leave their hometowns.

The impediments to domestic trade in China fit well into the four categories applied throughout this study. Purely physical problems such as a lack of roads represent daunting transitional impediments to distribution, which will take time to remedy. Unfamiliar with China's many such deficiencies, foreign firms sometimes create problems for themselves by failing to plan ahead for these challenges. Chinese policy plays an explicit and major role in this area. Finally, the market structure emerging in the absence of a formal competition policy is inviting serious collusion in restraint of trade, segmentation of markets, and other problems. National commitments to permit foreign market entry in order to satisfy external pressures are probably the easy part of the solution; uprooting anticompetitive behavior *within* China's many disparate marketplaces will be the real challenge.

Distribution in China

Pre-1949

Debate continues on the extent to which China saw dynamic growth in the prewar period (1890–1930). There is little question, however, that the commercial infrastructure in China before that time was relatively primitive. By the 1930s China's transportation system was comparable to that in the United States prior to the Civil War (Rawski 1989, 223). Its people were more poorly connected than those of any other major economy of the day, a situation rooted in China's expansive geography, overwhelmingly agrarian economy, and low rates of capital formation. As Rawski explains,

> The shortage of financial capital tightly constrained the expansion of production and trade in all sectors of the Ch'ing [1644–1912] economy. . . . The lack of funds restricted the size and scope of mercantile activity. During the imperial era, China's economy spawned a variety of institutions that alleviated the effects of the shortage of capital. Farmers formed revolving credit societies. Merchants employed brokers who performed a variety of services, but whose essential function was to hasten the rate at which commodity stocks could be turned over, thus expanding the volume of trade that could be conducted with a fixed financial base. The urgency of saving time allowed men with no financial assets to begin brokerage careers on the strength of their personal integrity and willingness to spend long hours in search of potential trading partners for merchants who willingly paid fees for successful introductions. (1989, 155)

Two important points can be gleaned from Rawski's observations. First, the lack of mercantile foundations at the start of the twentieth century, though remedied to an extent, continued to shackle the economy. Second, distribution networks and other market-clearing mechanisms would spring up to fill the need, in the absence of pressures otherwise. Unfortunately, violent civil war and the Communist agenda provided just such pressures.

Communist Era

After 1949, the victorious Communists perpetuated the neglect of policies that would support the market. Mao emphasized the precept of "self-reliance" (*zili gengsheng*) above all else (except perhaps national defense). Spurning the notion of comparative advantage that would argue for economic specialization internally (and externally), he prodded the Chinese economy toward local self-sufficiency from the early 1950s onward (see, e.g., Naughton 1996b, 51, 62).[3] In refuting Soviet admonitions to divide labor among socialist nations, Mao declared:

> [Specialization] is not a good idea. We do not suggest this even with respect to our own provinces. We advocate all-round development and do not think that each province need not produce goods which other provinces could supply. We want the various provinces to develop a variety of production to the fullest extent. . . . The correct method is each doing the utmost for itself as a means toward self-reliance for new growth, working independently to the greatest possible extent, making a principle of not relying on others[.] (quoted in Riskin 1987, 206)

Whole industries were transplanted out of developed areas and dropped into the interior, in order to create a reserve "third front" in the event of foreign invasion. The emphasis on self-sufficiency suffocated the tendency for the supporting components of a market economy (such as marketing) to develop alongside production. Connections with international markets were at best severely limited; in most cases they were entirely severed. Incentives to expedite domestic trade were squelched. The physical infrastructure necessary for the efficient flow of goods was neglected, reducing even the potential for interprovincial trade. There is little reason to connect towns and regions and to facilitate trade among them if everyone is supposed to be producing everything for themselves.

Post-1979

The manic commitment to local self-sufficiency largely halted when reform began in the late 1970s. The marketization of the Chinese economy has proceeded apace since then; businesses increasingly grapple with the problems of a working rather than a moribund economy. Yet reform initially had a good number of complications, both residual and new, and many of them remain today.

Prior to reform, state-owned entities, or "state trading companies" (STCs), monopolized the distribution process. STCs tended to be hierarchically organized vertical monopolies, usually with four or five levels of distribution (national, regional, provincial, local, and/or county), and in some cases they controlled retail sales as well. Distributors simply moved preallotted quantities of goods from factories run according to state plan to the selling or consumption points. They had little incentive to improve their efficiency: if goods sat on shelves, no signal to slow production

---

3. Wedeman (1995, 23) notes that during the Mao period, in compliance with the Great Helmsman's penchant for regional and local self-sufficiency, one microeconomy's local roadblocks and trade barriers against the products of its neighbor represented *adherence* to policy, not *violation* of it. Echoes of such behavior still ring through China's economy today, as they have in one form or another since at least the Warring States period (475–221 BCE). Wedeman traces the evolution of the term *guanqia*—roughly, illegal customs posts—back to that ancient time (17).

reached back to the factory; if they sold out, there was nothing to do except wait for the next cycle's allotment. Lacking incentives for higher levels of output, manufacturers had no interest in the odd distributor who might take the initiative to move more product (that would only get them saddled with higher quotas in the next planning cycle).[4] Retailers similarly had little incentive to increase inventory turnover. Moreover, each product generally had its own distribution bureaucracy, precluding any opportunity to bundle complementary products (bagels and cream cheese, dumplings and soy sauce). Few mechanisms were available to signal changes in tastes or demand, distinguish between innovative and obsolescent production, or differentiate between high- and poor-quality output; the distribution infrastructure, which serves these purposes in a market economy, existed almost solely to move products through a linear progression of steps.

One reform permitted manufacturers to distribute their wares directly to customers, thus ending the monopolies of the designated STCs (their fiefdoms had been enshrined in policy; there were no applicable laws). As a result, the various layers of distributor in the old system began competing with one another for business.[5] Soon, entrepreneurs were trying to make a profit by moving goods, as pent-up demand for such services showed the way. Today, state-run distributors compete with small, nonstate upstarts in many sectors; between 1990 and 1994, goods handled in the old manner fell from 85 percent to 40 percent of the total. Sectors monopolized by large STCs are now the exceptions instead of the rule.

As producers were learning to discriminate among distributors, central authorities were promoting greater macroeconomic level competition as well. The designation of special economic zones (SEZs) nourished pockets of prosperity and generated a virtuous scramble among jealous localities to take advantage of the new conditions, either by lobbying for similar status (which would help a jurisdiction to court foreign direct investment [FDI]) or by establishing an office or agent in the SEZs.[6] Yang (1997, 48) traces the internal linkages, or *neilian,* that formed like antpheromone trails between SEZs and interior provinces in the early and mid-1980s. These pronounced enhancements of distribution architecture were a (perhaps unanticipated) consequence of coastal experimentation.

But the competition could be fierce and frightening, too. The central authorities were simultaneously forcing localities to innovate through "fiscal starvation" as they cut back budget resources unilaterally. Early re-

---

4. There are cases of SOEs passing out huge bonuses in order to avoid showing a profit that would cause the state to increase their profit requirements the following year (EIU 1996a, 9.5).

5. The Economist Intelligence Unit's *China Hand* (1996b) dates this change to 1986.

6. In 1991 there were 111 SEZs; in 1993, 8,700 (Yang 1997, 56).

forms invigorated value-adding industries on the coast that relied on cheap, undervalued raw materials and basic heavy-industry inputs from the interior. As provinces were thus split between the more and less favored, those in the disadvantaged regions sought remedial steps such as barriers against the onslaught of products from coastal growth centers. These early advantages, even if redressed by subsequent policy, may have given coastal centers a head start that entitled those in the interior (by their way of thinking) to distort distribution channels in compensation (Wedeman 1995, 29). Local governments were inclined to protect their local resource bases. Many set up interprovincial trade barriers by blocking channels of distribution.

In *Bamboo Walls and Brick Ramparts,* Wedeman (1995) describes China's interprovincial trade wars of the 1980s. In province after province, governments directed investment into the same sectors.[7] The resulting overcapacity was predictable (in hindsight), and it largely caused the rush to local protectionism that followed in the late 1980s. As Wedeman (1995, 197) put it:

> "blind introduction of [manufacturing technology] and redundant construction" in defiance of local comparative advantage worked at cross purposes to increased local specialization and weakened structural incentives to expand trade as local governments in less developed regions sought to expand local manufacturing and localize the production of key industrial productions.

Local protectionism to guard local markets against dumping from next door emerged and spread as provinces reciprocated. As specialization and efficiency were undermined, these severely segmented markets made economies of scale unattainable. Only in sectors without local champions (such as high-technology industries) did modern distribution on a national level develop unimpeded.

Wedeman's study also relates the central government's battle against provincial mercantilism, whose importance the quote from Deng Xiaoping that serves as an epigraph to this chapter makes clear. "Opening to the inside" has in many ways been a more difficult task than opening to the outside.[8]

---

7. The sectors on which Wedeman focused were appliances, beverages, chemical fibers, chemicals, coal, construction materials (extraction), cotton wares, electronics, ferrous metals (extraction), food processing, garments, light machine building, metal products, nonferrous metals (extraction), plastics, steel and iron, textiles, tobacco processing, and transport vehicles and automobiles (1995, 195 n. 11).

8. However, imports still go through a more layered distribution system than do domestically manufactured goods. In many cases the product starts with a Hong Kong transshipper; it next goes to a Chinese trading company and then into the layers of provincial/regional/local wholesaling en route to consumers at the retail level. Avoiding the vagaries of those layers was a powerful motive for setting up FIEs inside China. Nonetheless, for many FIEs and Chinese firms, shipping among Chinese cities produces more headaches than does importing.

Simply rescinding the STC monopolies has not made the distribution system efficient. Central policy still prevents FIEs from distributing any products they do not manufacture in China proper, and the selection of local distributors remains poor even when distribution markets are not heavily concentrated. Where entry is permitted, an oligopolistic market structure often still predominates, owing either to the short time since reforms began or to nontransparent barriers to entry.

The perils of these present distribution problems are fivefold: they aggravate local income inequality, they augment regional disparities, they make administering the Chinese economy more difficult, they are economically costly in the aggregate, and they present an objectionable barrier to foreign firms while failing to offer real protection in return. Reform to remove these undesirable effects is clearly in the central government's interest.

Peter Drucker argues that only "distribution-led economic development can create the *human resources* which China needs more than anything else" (Drucker and Nakauchi 1997, 22). Indeed, the level of business savvy of the average newspaper-stand owner in Beijing or Guangzhou seems to exceed that of the typical SOE manager. It seems likely that the Chinese now rushing into the vacuum left by years of bias against ex-factory commerce will power the country forward in the years to come.

Foreign Investors and Distribution

A "dual economy" has characterized China during the reform period, as Naughton (1996a) has pointed out. Foreign investors, it was hoped, would provide export-oriented growth. Of course, foreign investors more often than not had the domestic market in mind, as had been the case for centuries. As the attentions of FIEs increasingly focus on the local market, the machinery of domestic business operations becomes important. "Distribution" is the most immediate of a group of concerns that arise once the time comes to get manufactured products to market, promote them, and sell them; others include wholesaling and retailing, trade financing, advertising and marketing, service (repair and maintenance), and management of transaction problems. Deng Xiaoping was acutely aware at the start of reforms that long-standing distribution inadequacies were robbing China of efficiency. While that realization set him ahead of preceding policymakers, remedial action is still far from complete.

It is impossible to generalize about foreign investors in China with regard to distribution (such generalizations are equally impossible from the perspective of domestic companies, explored by Wedeman 1995). Foreign enterprises differ markedly in their target customers (many still only export), product, size, and location of operations within China. Even enterprises with similar profiles can face vastly different distribution challenges. Furthermore, it is unclear whether the distribution strategies presently evolving should be considered success stories or evolutionary culs-de-sac, as the central government may yet clamp down on them. Many other practices are not even known yet; by the time the government endorses a practice (or researchers get wind of it), it has usually been in illegal use for three to five years.

This section will describe the regulatory framework that foreign firms confront as they establish operations in China. Central concerns raised by expatriate managers are then examined. While not an exhaustive survey of the stratagems used to control the ex-factory fate of the product, it does focus on recurrent points made by foreign managers, including what they see as sources of problems. It provides a broad sense not just of the distribution challenges but also of the way these shape market development in general and of the considerable progress achieved in this area.

The Regulatory Environment

No law in China governs the activities of FIEs in the area of distribution per se. Rather, the rights of foreign investors to participate in distribution of their products are mentioned in passing in a number of laws. Chinese regulations generally treat distribution as a distinct sector, not an inherent element of a manufacturing business.

The Catalogue for the Guidance of Foreign Investment Industries (see appendix A) categorizes distribution activities among "restricted foreign investment industries," in subsection "B." This means that central-level approval is needed for any foreign participation in distribution as a line of business. The Guidelines make clear that wholly owned foreign enterprises (WOFEs) are not permitted in domestic commerce or foreign trade, reiterating the restriction also found in Article 4 of the 1990 Detailed Implementing Rules for the Law of the People's Republic of China on Wholly Foreign-Owned Enterprises. In joint ventures (JVs) involved in distribution, to the extent they are centrally approved despite their restricted category status, the Chinese side "must be the holding party or play a leading role," meaning it must have a majority standing in the ownership of the venture.

The WOFE Rules (Articles 45 and 46) stipulate that WOFEs are prohibited from domestic or foreign trading generally but can sell in China their own products (Chinese-made, not goods produced by sister units of the firm or parent companies outside China), either directly or through a local agent. However, the Rules limit such sales to product in excess of an agreed on "sales ratio" that specifies what share of WOFE production must be exported (the "export ratio");[9] all other domestic sales must be approved by the overseeing authorities. Joint ventures are generally permitted to distribute their Chinese-made goods as they see fit, without a statutory export ratio, but they similarly may not engage in domestic trading of any product that they do not manufacture. Despite the prohibition on distributing goods in China manufactured outside the country by their own companies, they find more or less legal ways to do so quite often (further discussed below). Firms that are not established in China may not distribute products directly in the Chinese market; instead, they must first sell the goods to a Chinese foreign trading company—the only agents authorized to receive invoices from the sellers.[10] Foreign investors, unable to control businesses engaged in distribution services, can now provide only for their own distribution needs.[11]

The point about invoicing is important, for the illegality of collecting bills without proper standing to ship and sell their products is precisely what makes life so difficult for most FIEs. But, as is the case with every other realm of business law and regulation in China, actual practice is far more complex than national law would suggest. Complexities arise because:

- The regulations are drafted with considerable ambiguity, leading to both legitimate differences in interpretation and considerable legal efforts to find loopholes.

- Central authorities use this ambiguity to privilege favored firms or industries, and to withhold normal rights from firms or industries as a form of protectionism.

- Administrative guidance (from various and sometimes competing sources) can override the basic laws and regulations, either explicitly or unofficially.

- Provincial or local authorities may interfere with the national limits on distribution, being either more generous (to lure investment or meet other local goals) or more restrictive (to protect local interests).

---

9. Although Japanese companies are beginning to focus on the domestic markets, they remain more dependent on exports. Domestic sales made up about 40 percent of their total sales in 1995. This ratio is rising slowly but it remains considerably lower than that of US companies, whose domestic sales were 80 percent of their total in 1994. The Japanese companies rely on exports because they are more profitable; indeed, Japanese foreign affiliates play a similar role in many Asian countries.

10. As described below, many imports are sent through an intermediate channel: Hong Kong trading companies and "converters" are able to get goods into the Chinese market at significantly lower rates of tax, duty, and sometimes theft.

11. However, there already exist a number of foreign-invested distribution consultancies that contribute strategies to—without directly managing—FIE distribution (interviewee #1 operates such a system).

- WOFEs, whose sales in the domestic market are limited by the negotiable and unequally enforced export ratios, may be saddled with high ratios that foreclose domestic trading opportunities.

- Central or local indifference toward enforcement (or impotence) can mean viable opportunities for FIEs to distribute in spite of the law (as has been the case in the retail sector).

New legal structures may soon permit greater FIE participation in distribution. First, a few "joint venture trading companies" have been approved, though with significant qualifications (see footnote 10 in chapter 2).[12] Second, FIE trading companies set up in Waigaoqiao, a section of the Pudong new development area in Shanghai, may purchase products, "export" them into the trade zone from anywhere in China, and then sell directly anywhere in the world. This may be interpreted to mean the companies can sell back directly into China to anyone they want, *after* paying import duties (#1).[13] Furthermore, these firms may be able to purchase worldwide and distribute goods into the rest of China from Waigaoqiao. The firms can invoice in renminbi directly, the trade zone authorities handle the import/export documentation (for a fee), and the renminbi can be swapped for foreign exchange to transact further business. At the moment, this practice seems to be legal.

FIE and Distribution in Practice

While the regulatory regime is being loosened incrementally to allow wider FIE participation in distribution, many foreign firms are already more deeply involved than the law would suggest is possible. Acting in the belief that law follows practice in China, not the other way around as in the West, they have good reason for their bold behavior. First, involvement in the distribution process is key to knowing who a firm's customers are, critical information for marketing purposes. It is also important for ensuring payment, as many local businesses routinely ignore obligations until administrative pressure is brought to bear on them. Second, involve-

---

12. Interestingly, the Shanghai representative of a large American conglomerate (#6) reported that her firm chose to decline an invitation to receive one of the few licenses to establish such an entity. The reasons: a suspicion that profits from the venture would disappoint, and a certainty that some of the firm's strategic business units would refuse to let others elsewhere in the firm take the lead on distributing their wares. This internal fighting was a source of tremendous frustration to the interviewee, a Chinese citizen, who found it difficult to explain to her local government contacts why her Fortune 100 company rejected a much-sought license.

13. Some may interpret (and are interpreting) the Waigaoqiao regulations to permit them to trade and distribute directly, without having to pay duties as though the goods were reimported, but that reading is more questionable.

ment is essential in order to teach (and provide incentives for) shippers and sellers to operate more efficiently and thus to move more product. Third, in the absence of an overarching procompetitive stance on the part of central authorities, many FIEs are worried that firms that fail to seize a distribution channel for themselves now will be closed out later. And fourth, there is an out-of-control aspect to the distribution picture in China that leaves some firms little choice: they must do it themselves or it will not get done. As the Economist Intelligence Unit noted, "The downside of this evolutionary process [of breaking up state distribution monopolies] is that distribution in China has progressed from a tightly organized—if rigid—system to a chaotic system with few rules and little means of enforcing the rules that do exist" (1996b, 9.8). The chaos remains, although the rigidity imposed by limited channels to market may be returning in some sectors as well.

For clarity, the laundry list of concerns raised by expatriates about marketplace conditions will be grouped into four sets of government imperatives:

- *Let go of the bad:* Legal restrictions on scope of business and the ambiguous legality of distribution operations in practice must be redressed.

- *Grab the good:* Domestic firms and FIEs alike are eager to develop more extensive operations addressing specific functions, such as marketing and services; they should be encouraged through the development of good regulations. The physical infrastructure required for efficient distribution also requires attention.

- *Principles, not just policies:* Unless authorities take direct action (beyond mere rule making) to control the behavior of local authorities, ministries allocating market shares, and private and quasi-private companies employing anticompetitive practices to block other firms' access to the market, the benefits of a contestable marketplace cannot be enjoyed. Corruption problems plaguing the marketplace also require executive action.

- *Include the foreigners:* Because of their own choices and their forced adaptation to the Chinese regulatory environment so that they might participate in the marketplace, foreign parties are still distinguished from domestic in the Chinese view. Complex corporate structures and resulting internal organizational problems, failure to plan well, and a predilection to delegate direct involvement in Chinese markets all separate the foreign-invested sector from the domestic. But in reality the distinctions are quickly eroding, in part because external waves of pressure are reshaping Chinese distribution patterns. Authorities must transcend the "who is 'us'" debate (in which all globalizing nations engage) and secure commercial activity, domestic *and* foreign.

This could just as well be called "include the outsiders," as nonlocal Chinese firms are as prone as foreigners to be excluded locally.

Let Go of the Bad

Regulatory Regime

Removing impediments in the existing regulatory structure is the first, most explicit, and probably most important step that FIEs call for to improve the ex-factory marketplace environment in China. The regulations have already been discussed in detail. While they are implemented to serve parochial needs at the local level, they essentially reflect national policy, as local distribution positions derive from top-level directives. If such policies were left to localities or even provinces, sufficient competition would be generated to counteract most anticompetitive barriers. As it is, FIEs are finding back doors into domestic commerce that circumvent the limits set out in law, thereby eroding the utility of the existing regime. In the long term, competition will cut through efforts to base local gains on antilocal policies.

Ambiguity

FIEs complain that central policy is designed to keep them guessing. "The strategy for finding distribution channels," bemoans the government affairs manager for an American firm, "is to explore what you can get away with" (#15). The more fastidious a firm is about adhering to the letter and spirit of the murky law, the more disadvantaged it will be in dealing with distribution issues in China. US firms in particular—bound by the Foreign Corrupt Practices Act—are hindered more than others.

Ambiguity provides room for a government inexperienced at managing a market economy to experiment. As one interviewee put it, the center remains aloof until it can no longer avoid decisive action; then it moves slowly and deliberately. But while this wiggle room on policy makes life more comfortable for Beijing, it frustrates many FIEs. It is hard to be certain what is legal and what is not, and that by itself is a source of frustration to firms concerned about legality. Most FIEs settle for keeping their distribution activities from clear illegality, which is quite different from keeping them legal. Yet other firms distinctly *prefer* legal murkiness to the glacial pace of opening implied by a strict interpretation of national law. So even as many complain about the current state of distribution, many are quietly building extensive networks. Inchcape Pacific, for example, has bundled a variety of licenses together to offer broad logistical services. Proctor and Gamble is envied for the success of its approach, evident in its shampoo being sold on most of the street corners in China.

The general manager of the Beijing-based holding company of an American chemical multinational spoke frankly about how ambiguity on the highest level affected his distribution function. The first task, he explained, is to find out what the existing laws mean, which requires trusted local hires who are politically well connected. The next, more difficult task is to obtain an "interpretation" of the "provisional implementation" of a law or regulation. To Western sensibilities, the process is duplicitous:

> Even a vice premier said China would not open its trading regime for at least five years. If this is the case then fighting to open it will not be wise for the firm. To exist, you must move product. You must find a way, find someone, to help you send an invoice, and then to get paid for it. So you team up with a local company. They can bring in the [imported] product, and resell it. [Our firm] has an agreement with them to pay a certain commission. [Our firm] is doing all the marketing, all the real management of the Chinese company. It's just a front providing the service of shipping. Then that agent has the responsibility to collect payment. The agent often has influence, intimidation, they can use that to extract payment. (#15)

China is more unpredictable than most emerging markets because Beijing has enough leverage over investors to change the rules of the game if it sees fit. And because of the particular hurdles facing central authorities who seek to shape an efficient market structure, the government may see fit to do quite a range of things.

Grab the Good

Collecting

Expatriates stress that distributing product is the key to numerous attendant business functions, ex-factory issues that are essential to tailoring operations to customers, assessing creditworthiness, and developing an ongoing service relationship with customers to secure buyer loyalty and satisfaction. The most critical of these functions are collection/finance, marketing, and service provision. They are not all walled off from FIEs explicitly (FIEs may gather marketing data for their own use), but restrictions on distribution stymie these efforts in practice. In other areas, notably services, FIEs are more directly prohibited from developing a business presence.

Because FIEs need to finance the inventories being expanded by the retailers and wholesalers, they need better control over their property as it moves through the economy. Conversely, a key reason why the existing state-owned distribution channels are folding is their inability to provide and manage the credit needed to make distribution run smoothly (EIU 1996b, 9.6).

The heart of the collection issue is accounts receivable. The interviewees had diverse responses on this topic, agreeing only that dealing with it was a large drain on managers' time. Happy FIEs claimed accounts receivable averages of around 30 days or less, and pointed to deposit or advance payment requirements as essential. Less sanguine finance directors (and less senior officers more generally) reported waiting up to 120 days or more to get paid. Many interviewees saw their receivable periods lengthening, but this could have been a cyclical event.

This state of affairs is complicated, though many firms are driven to offer long terms by cutthroat competition. More important, however, is the point that knowing the customer is absolutely essential to getting paid anywhere in China today—and that knowledge requires intimate participation in distribution. If FIEs must move their wares through state-dominated channels, then they will fare no better than the indigenous dinosaur enterprises to which they are connected through interlocking debt. One finance director put it like this:

> If you don't get paid, you need to make noise at the brother, father, grandpa companies [referring to the interlocking holding arrangements common among new Chinese firms]. Especially it's useful to say, "If your son [subsidiary] can't pay, maybe you can pay me 95 percent [of their debt]." The more you know, the more quickly you can act. (#15)

Scrambling to build market share, FIEs will find such relationships powerful aids to their balance sheets. But these ties cannot be developed unless the foreigner is allowed to face buyers directly and assess their purchasing power.

Marketing

To the extent that restrictions on distribution insulate FIEs from their customers, they lose the ability to carry out marketing research directly, having to rely on less-sophisticated local surrogates instead. For General Motors interns in the Beijing office, this has meant being sent into the streets of the capital to find out who is buying their cars after the middlemen get them, so that GM can set up a relationship with those buyers.

Service Provision

Like the products they distribute, the products that FIEs may service must be from their local manufacturers and not unaffiliated goods. They technically cannot even service products made by their firms elsewhere and imported into China. However, there appear to be exceptions to these rules. First, several expatriates suggested that a handful of firms had secured superregulatory service rights by cozying up to regulators. Second, many FIEs "manage" local companies providing service to their products in parallel to their local manufacturing. As with sales, the implication with service is that the "localness" of these Chinese partners is a ruse; their operations are managed by the FIEs. Third, the products that many FIEs are most concerned about servicing are indeed their local manufactures, and they are expanding their service networks quickly to do that (recall table 4.7).

But for many FIEs that strategy is not yet feasible. High-technology firms must be able to service complicated products that they are not yet able to manufacture in developing China (imagine the complexity of a CAT scanner or a jet aircraft engine). Other firms are simply uncomfortable doing service in China in a "gray" manner and are insisting on clear legal approval. And in a highly competitive environment, many FIEs will be able to differentiate themselves from local and foreign rivals only on the basis of their superior service. Unless subtle (and less subtle) firewalls are removed, they will be unfairly locked out of the market—a market, therefore, that will be dominated by service providers of inferior quality.

Physical Infrastructure

Expatriates talk a great deal about the state of China's physical distribution infrastructure. Despite tremendous growth in recent years, the country still lags far behind in the stock of roads, railways, and other arteries needed for transport and distribution. Delayed infrastructure development is likely the greatest impediment to productivity growth for FIEs and Chinese firms alike. Tables 5.1 and 5.2 summarize basic indicators for physical distribution infrastructure. Table 5.3 shows the retail infrastructure in China, while Table 5.4 compares it to that of more mature markets.

Joe O'Leary of the Polaroid Corporation states his concerns this way: "Polaroid doesn't have a market access problem in China. We're satisfied with the duty rate. It's physical distribution that's the problem. Distribution in China is one of the biggest challenges that Western companies face." In O'Leary's case, the problem is a largely state-owned trucking industry that is subsidized and thus insulated from the market pressures that might force it to be more efficient (quoted in "6-Year-Old Polaroid Venture Gives China Its Best Shot," *Journal of Commerce*, 1 October 1997, 7D).

A large logistics company included in this study (#21) can provide the most basic infrastructure item: a fleet of vehicles owned through its China joint venture. McCormick China gets its product to the Shanghai market through a fleet of small vans that provide marketing materials to retailers as well (Spicing Up the Chinese Market, Catherine Gelb, *China Business Review*, July/August 1997, 25). But outside local markets, roads are rarely developed sufficiently to permit distribution by truck. The few exceptions include the Guangzhou-Shenzhen-Hong Kong corridor; hence the statement by several interviewees that infrastructure was decisive in their decision to locate in Guangdong (##8, 19).

Cross-country distribution mostly relies on the rail system, the only truly national connector. But those using it face serious delays, pilferage, bribery, and other problems (##18, 40). The Chinese and foreign managers of a Sino-American manufacturing venture interviewed together in northern China (#23) decried with one voice the tendency of railroad shipments simply to stop during holiday seasons—or for no reason at all. "International shipment is no problem," they said; "shipping to south China by rail or boat" is the tough job.

Table 5.1 Distribution infrastructure growth: structure of freight volume by transportation type, 1978-96

Year	Railways (percentages)	Highways (percentages)	Waterways (percentages)	Total freight traffic (thousands of tons)	Railway freight traffic (thousands of tons)	Highway freight traffic (thousands of tons)	Inland waterway freight traffic (thousands of tons)	Civil aviation freight traffic (thousands of tons)	Principal seaports freight traffic (thousands of tons)
1978	44.2	34.2	17.4	2,489,460	1,101,190	851,820	432,920	64	198,340
1980	20.4	69.9	7.8	5,465,370	1,112,790	3,820,480	426,760	89	217,310
1985	17.5	72.1	8.5	7,457,630	1,307,090	5,380,620	633,220	195	311,540
1990	15.5	74.6	8.3	9,706,020	1,506,810	7,240,400	800,940	370	483,210
1991	15.5	74.4	8.5	9,857,930	1,528,930	7,339,070	833,700	452	532,200
1992	15.1	74.7	8.8	10,458,990	1,576,270	7,809,410	924,900	575	603,800
1993	14.6	75.3	8.8	11,157,710	1,626,630	8,402,560	979,380	694	678,350
1994	13.8	75.8	9.1	11,802,730	1,630,930	8,949,140	1,070,910	829	743,700
1995	13.4	76.2	9.2	12,348,100	1,658,550	9,403,870	1,131,940	1,011	801,660
1996	13.0	75.9	9.8	12,962,000	1,688,030	9,838,600	1,274,300	1,150	851,520

Source: State Statistical Yearbook, 1997, China State Statistical Bureau.

Table 5.2 Infrastructure development under the Ninth Five-Year Plan, 1996-2000

Sector	Capacity to be added, 1996-2000	Total capacity[a]	Capacity growth, based on 1995 level (percentage)	Total investment (billions of dollars)[a]
Aviation				
Passenger traffic (million)	55	100	122	na
Air freight traffic (million tons)	0.9	1.8	100	19.7[b]
Ports and waterways				
Shipping traffic (billions ton-km)	595	2,300	35	8
Roads (km)	130,000	1,230,000	12	37
Telecommunication				
Exchange lines (million)	70	140	100	60
Power				
Total installed capacity (gw)	90	300	43	64.3[c]
Nuclear power (gw)	18	20	852	na
Coal				
Production (million tons)	230	1,500	18	24
Oil				
Production (million tons)	36	185	24	48.9[d]
Oil refining (million bpd)	0.9	4.6	24	na
Gas				
Production (billion cubic meters)	2.6	20	15	na
Total capital investment	na	na	na	303

na = not available.

a. Estimated.

b. Includes $16.3 billion for aircraft and $3.4 billion for airports.

c. Half of this capital budget is to go to transmission lines.

d. Includes $38.5 billion for oil and gas exploration and $10.4 for oil refining.

Source: Australia Department of Foreign Affairs and Trade (1997a, 237).

Principles, Not Just Policies

Distribution and Local Authority

Authorities at the provincial and local levels of government control the typical FIE's market access to an even greater degree than central rules do.

Table 5.3 China's retail structure, 1980-96

	Retail stores (thousands)	Population (millions)	Retail stores per 1,000 persons	Persons per retail store
1980	1,463	987	1.5	675
1985	7,783	1,058	7.4	136
1989	8,412	1,127	7.5	134
1990	8,710	1,143	7.6	131
1991	9,240	1,158	8.0	125
1992	10,063	1,171	8.6	116
1993	11,570	1,185	9.8	102
1994	12,260	1,199	10.2	98
1995	13,287	1,211	11.0	91
1996	13,963	1,224	11.4	88

Sources: State Statistical Yearbook, China State Statistical Bureau; International Marketing Data and Statistics, 1996, Euromonitor, quoted in Arieh Goldman (1996a).

Table 5.4 Retail structures in five selected markets

		Number of retail stores (thousands)	Population (millions)	Retail stores per 1,000 persons	Persons per retail store
China	1996	13,963	1,224	11.4	88
Japan	1992	1,591	126	12.6	79
United States	1994	1,513	258	5.9	170
Hong Kong	1993	57	6	9.5	105
Singapore	1993	20	2.7	7.4	137

Sources: China Statistical Yearbook, China State Statistical Bureau; International Marketing Data and Statistics, 1996, Euromonitor, quoted in Arieh Goldman (1996a).

As discussed in chapter 2, gaining the local license to operate is generally the most important hurdle that foreign investors need to clear,[14] and doing so requires making compromises. Local authorities know how important distribution is, and they can use their influence over it to allocate and manage market share, protect favored industries from competition, and shape investment patterns. Their power ranges from influencing the export ratio for WOFEs, to approving a labor contract for a JV that seeks

---

14. Recall that as a rule of thumb, projects under $30 million in value can sidestep the need for central-level approval (provided they meet other requirements in the Guidelines—see appendix A). The great majority of FIEs are established under that ceiling.

to shed preexisting distribution staff, to designating what will be considered a "local manufacture" and thus qualify for local distribution rights.[15]

Central authorities increasingly are pushing social obligations (e.g., pensions and other elements of the workers' safety net) down to the localities. Local authorities are heavily invested in local enterprises, and their base of political power is often dependent on their industries as well. Looming SOE and banking-sector reforms (including a bankruptcy mechanism) will bring additional pressure at the local level. Thus, local authorities have potent reasons for using influence over distribution as a tool to deal with the costs that they are responsible for, especially in the absence of any strong procompetitive policy promulgated from above.

Local parochialism is not necessarily bad news for FIEs; some individual firms are enjoying privileged positions. For example, foreign oil companies are eager to get into retail distribution through ownership of fuel-service stations. However, the national Guidelines for foreign investment explicitly state the central government's disapproval of foreign participation in retail service stations (see appendix A, "Restricted Industries," category A).[16] Yet industry representatives interviewed for this study reported:

> Small foreign [gasoline] firms will go directly into distribution, especially in southern China, and not worry about the Ministry of Internal Trade [MIT] cracking down on them; larger firms stand back and use a middleman. The middleman comes to us and says, "I have approval for 200 gas stations." We check it out, and someone at the MIT will confirm to us that this agent does in fact have the right to invite us into business—he somehow got past MIT or whatever ministry. If we trust the guy enough, we will let him use our name; if not, [we will supply the gas and he will] use a local name. (#12)

Once firms crack open the market they become less concerned about, or perhaps even antagonistic toward, further opening for competitors. The FIEs that are first into the market often intend to dominate local distribution. The petrobusiness manager quoted above continued:

> [There are] limited means of distribution in China, and it's a crowded ballroom. People are looking for partners. There is a limited amount of time to partner up. Once these partnerships are formed, it will be an oligopolistic marketplace: a few competitors will split up the retail market—including services—and control it. China is a chaotic, anarchic market trying to find a template, a pattern—a collusive one. Barriers to entry will increase, and the first firms in will make the money. This is not a matter of policy for China, it's just the way it will play out.

To date, his company has far fewer than 200 gas stations around Guangdong; it appears to have about the same number as Mobil, Shell, Caltex,

---

15. "Manufacture" can be used very loosely; rolls of imported plastic were approved for local distribution by a JV simply because they were cut in half in Shanghai.

16. The exception is along "superhighways," where the Guidelines invite foreign participation—a distinction that echoes the separation of advanced enclaves from the main economy.

and Hong Kong-based Fortune appear to have. These firms and others are getting a taste of the distribution process in gas retail, and they are doing so through the permissiveness of local authorities in Guangdong Province. Their local partners, the middlemen with special dispensations to enter into distribution/retail arrangements, are often associated with local governments, or perhaps the People's Liberation Army. Local quasi-governmental entities may collect fees or a share of profits from the stations. Most important, the number of such stations now appears to be capped. Costing only $10,000 or so a station to open up, these venues are cheap; instead of opening markets, these partnerships with local government may now serve to ensure that capacity does not drive down margins for established ventures. Under the guise of better enforcing national law, local officials can thus protect existing players from new competition.

Direct influence at the license/start-up phase of the business (when distribution rights are defined) is just one way in which the behavior of local governments affects FIE distribution. As noted above, local trade wars raged between jurisdictions in China in the 1980s. Tactics included setting up local customs posts (*guanqia,* which are gates across the road) where trade is fined or taxed, attempting to corner resource markets or otherwise prevent raw material from reaching other producers (*ziyuan dazhan*), and engaging in predatory pricing and other anticompetitive practices (*jiage dazhan*) (Wedeman 1995). These aggressive measures attracted considerable criticism from Beijing, and central policymakers have waged campaigns to stop them. Though progress has been made, local distribution barriers orchestrated by subnational governments continue to distort commerce and investment. This occasions much complaint—but many FIEs use the parochialism to their strategic advantage too. An auto-sector specialist in Beijing noted:

> SAIC [Shanghai Automotive Industries Corporation] and, just as importantly, its JV partners—GM and VW—are looking to distribute products nationally. Ultimately, this will be the only way to compete profitably in the market. This does not preclude JVs' using local protection to suit their own purposes at various points in time. Protectionism at the local level in the auto industry is rampant throughout China and will likely remain so for some time. (#46)

An interviewee with a competing auto consortium described a typical tactic:

> Shanghai auto industry authorities had a regulation on their books requiring that all cabs had to have 1.6-liter engines, which happened to be the specification of Shanghai-built VW-model cabs.[17] This effectively was a ban on TJs [a Chinese-built car made in Tianjin] and Citroen [a Chinese JV model made under the Dongfang name in Guangzhou and Wuhan]. The central authorities came out and said Shanghai couldn't do that—but Shanghai continued to do it anyway. The center [Beijing] couldn't stop them from favoring VW in this way. (#26)

---

17. Cab fleets still constitute a major portion of the passenger car market in Chinese cities.

The Beijing-based consultant corroborates:

> The municipal Shanghai government put forth a regulation stating that only cars with engines having a displacement of 1.6 liters or above may be used as taxis. They further stated that cars without trunks (i.e., hatchbacks) could not be used as taxis—these were aimed at the Tianjin Xiali mainly, but also affected the other small cars (the Changan Airto and the Wuhan/Citroen Fu Kang). These cars were making inroads into the Shanghai taxi market as they have done elsewhere. As usual the loser is the consumer. I can't comment on exactly what passed between the central government and Shanghai. Regulations are not always followed. What is clear is that there are fewer and fewer non-Santana [i.e., non-VW] taxis on the road. (#46)

This interviewee also observed that the city of Wuhan retaliated with a carefully tailored set of cab restrictions of its own. The result of such policies, as so often seen, is markets more segmented and collusive than they need to be. Unable to distribute vehicles nationally, auto firms will not attain economies of scale in production. Efficient scale would permit firms to produce more cars with fewer resources, thereby better serving the Chinese market and—ultimately—competing head-to-head with efficient producers worldwide. In an extreme example already noted, there are still many state-owned vehicle factories in China producing a few thousand or even fewer vehicles a year (see table 4.6). Because these facilities need subsidies and their poor-quality product must be absorbed, more efficient producers lose opportunities to distribute better-made products and to lower unit prices by increasing the volume shipped.

Local impediments to efficient distribution take myriad forms, and only a few examples have been presented here. Several qualifications should be added as well, however. First, these issues can affect domestic companies as well as foreign enterprises. One cannot assume that FIEs are singled out at the local level for discriminatory treatment just because central regulations make such treatment possible. Second, these concerns are not unique to China, though they may affect China to a greater degree than elsewhere because of the legacy of Mao's self-sufficiency campaign. Third, the amount of local interference in distribution varies widely across firms, sectors, and regions. And finally, it is worth recalling that the central government has exerted pressure against local protectionism in recent years, though with mixed success.

Allocated Market Share

Some interviewees argued that their total available market was "allocated" by industry authorities whose plan was to nurture not competition or marketplace efficiency but local champions. This protective action seems most likely when a limited number of buyers have budgets directly influenced by central economic authorities: for example, in the area of telecommunications switching equipment. In this sector, a limited number of provincial telecom entities operating under the guidance of the national Ministry of Post and Telecommunications (MPT, in the process of merging with several other ministries) are the buyers and operators (and regulators).[18] Seven Sino-foreign joint ventures, which together control about 60 to 65 percent of the market, offer equipment in this sector, while the remainder is shared among domestic suppliers (five with greater than 1 percent share, dozens smaller than that). The general manager of one of these joint ventures observed:

> The central government has tremendous impact on your [sales] volumes. It's tough for us from North America to understand this. Access to knowing where the jobs will be, and who the customers [with authorization to make purchases] are, is essential. Your "allocated volume"—never in writing—is the key. We were so enamored of the Chinese market, we totally lost perspective that it was a controlled market. We thought we could outmarket the Chinese. We were wrong. It is a market *planned* economy. (#20)

Having learned to pay ubiquitous "rep fees" of perhaps 3 percent of sales price back to the customer (after the sale, never before—*that* would be a bribe!), this manager still cannot get his bids taken seriously in other provinces. Such restriction is this chapter's closest approach to an industrial policy per se. Allocating market share is a way for government either to keep more players in a market than the market would bear or to keep new players from coming in and eroding the margins of existing players. In a system in which Asian values such as the sanctity of doing business based on cozy relationships are held dear, it is easy to imagine that in volatile markets the urge to allocate would be strong, at least in some industries. It is conceivable, however, that the financial difficulties East Asia has experienced since 1997 might alter Chinese attitudes toward industrial policy. Time will tell.

Market Foreclosure

Several interviewees expressed concern that distribution channels would be "locked up" in China by private or quasi-private actors. The expatriates fear not so much constraint by central design, as in allocated market share, but old-fashioned private-sector monopolization, accomplished through control over distribution. They have observed that in some sectors there exist a limited number of distributors, that sometimes the

---

18. Some have questioned whether the national MPT really can control the powerful southern provincial telecom companies that are already half spun-off from their regulatory mothers. However, the ministry has unilaterally announced that Guangdong Telecom and Zhejiang Telecom would be bundled into a China Telecom Company to be offered as an "H-Share" offering to foreign investors on the Hong Kong market (Leah Nathans Spiro, "Goldman: Wired to a Wireless Bonanza?" *Business Week*, 13 October 1997, 94). This may signal a reassertion of national prerogative over cocky provincial authorities.

number is fixed or declining, and that barriers to entry (such as restrictions on foreign participation in domestic trading and retail) prevent new competitors from entering the market. Under such conditions, distributors could employ exclusive dealing arrangements, impose contracts requiring buyers to purchase exclusively from them, and stipulate tying and bundling that would foreclose market opportunities to other producers.[19]

These concerns mostly arise in sectors in which the state retains control of the distribution channels: for example, aerospace, coal, tobacco, and some agricultural goods, such as wheat. To be sure, this list is shrinking as traditional state distribution companies break up and enterprises expand their use of new channels. Nonetheless, limitations on entry into the distribution process are likely to persist, as industrial ministries fight to dampen competitive pressure within their fiefdoms.

But more important than these remaining pockets of statism is the tendency toward greater private concentration of market power when central authorities fail to promote and protect competition. Collusive arrangements involving formal and informal partnerships among local regulators, producers, and distributors permit a few firms to manipulate markets and thus achieve monopolistic profits. One interviewee stressed that such arrangements need not be a function of central government policy (indeed, they may even be seen as undesirable); rather, they will occur naturally (#12)—if there is no counterbalancing antitrust policy. These policies are critical to economic development in a globalizing economy, in fact, though they are only beginning to be discussed multilaterally (Graham and Richardson 1997a, 1997b).

One cannot help noting that private barriers to trade rising from the ashes of public barriers is precisely what has most worried foreign analysts of Japan's marketplace in recent years. The huge Kodak-Fuji case regarding photographic film that went before the WTO concerned private practices that had the effect of closing Kodak out of market opportunities.[20] The Dispute Settlement Body at the WTO declined to find on behalf of the US plaintiff, on the grounds that private restraints are outside of the organization's charter, but the issues raised in the case are certain to return soon. Japan has demonstrated how difficult such practices can be to deal with, once they are ingrained. Of course, the Chinese market differs from the Japanese in important ways, and little indicates that Chinese firms could act so concertedly on a national basis. At the local level, however, they will be increasingly disruptive to competition.

---

19. Analysis of such practices and their implications can be found in Scherer and Ross (1990, 562–69).

20. See Graham and Richardson (1997a, 1997b) for thorough explorations of this case and its larger context of competition policy.

Corruption and Distribution

Expatriates point to another factor complicating the distribution picture: corruption. Firms in many sectors confront "shrinkage"; that is, a portion of a given shipment of product disappearing between the factory door and the point of sale. One interviewee suggested that a 1 to 5 percent theft rate was acceptable to him (#1). Moreover, the quality of remaining product can diminish as a result of pilferage, as opened shipments are exposed to the elements. Similar shrinkage can also occur at the other end of the production process: arriving shipments of intermediate goods or raw materials may be tampered with in transit. Again, these are problems in all developing (and many developed) markets as well; but in China the limits placed on the ability of foreign investors to manage the problem by closely controlling distribution creates more tension than usually occurs elsewhere.

Corruption can also lead to FIE complacency about restrictions on distribution that insulate the firm from the sleazier aspects of the Chinese marketplace. Several managers thought it was just as well that their local Chinese agents handled distribution, as they would be uneasy engaging directly in the practices necessary to make sales, such as bribes, kickbacks, payments through "black accounts," and so on (#19). Almost all interviewees agreed that it was next to impossible in China to both keep one's hands completely clean and prosper at the same time. By situating distribution outside its control, the FIE gains some comfort in uncomfortable circumstances.

The China country manager for a large petrochemicals firm hints at a strategy for dealing with company positions that might be attacked as illegal or unethical: "In the US, what is not explicitly legal to us we worry is illegal; in the Chinese perspective it is the opposite. So our approach is the 'return of the compradors' " (#12). Compradors, as explained in chapter 3, have a long history in China, and the term retains a pejorative connotation of Western imperialism. These intermediaries have always served as a sort of shock absorber between the ethical sensibilities of Western and Chinese businesspeople. Such partnerships are widely used today to skirt charges of corrupt practices, qualify a business for legal status, and otherwise deflect liability. Compradors themselves—even those with foreign citizenship—are not, of course, protected from prosecution if they break Chinese law. Nonetheless, the enterprising Chinese keen to profit from the gap between FIEs' official practice and the compromises required for success in the Chinese market are evident everywhere.

Include the Foreigners

Organizing to Distribute

The original means by which foreigners entered the Chinese market was to buy an existing set of channels through a joint venture arrangement.

The commercial counselor at the US Consulate in Guangzhou remarked: "Yes, you can find a tactical way in, but only if you get in bed with a Chinese partner in order to distribute. . . . Is that what WTO means?" Indeed, this model has been less than satisfying to many FIEs. Chinese partners oversold the capacities of their channels and failed to update them to accommodate productivity improvements on the manufacturing side. In general, they were fearful of change, avoiding confrontation with vested interests that enjoy government patronage and resisting the release to foreign partners of authority to manage distribution assets; they worried that the result would be layoffs, cost cutting, and a loss of their own relevance as firms got to know clients for themselves.

Increasingly, therefore, FIEs have sought greater control over distribution, through partnership with Chinese investors who are more passive, or through more determined negotiation or pressure on Beijing to change the law. They must be able to choose efficient channels. In the words of one manager: "Relationships are important; if you are lacking market share, then you ought to get a better distributor" (#17). Getting a Chinese partner to break ties with a long-standing distribution partner can be very hard indeed if the FIE is confined to traditional organization structures.

The American petrochemical firm mentioned above produces a variety of agricultural chemicals at one joint venture in China, and hence—according to statute—it has the right to distribute those products through the distribution channels of its choosing. The JV's parent firm also produces chemicals outside China purchased by the same Chinese customers. While it is logical to sell the two complementary chemicals together through the same channels—like tablecloths and dinner napkins—doing so is not permitted; an ostensibly Chinese importing company handles the item not produced in China. But the FIE effectively directs the sales, shipment, and marketing of the imported product, too. At the retail level one can hardly tell that the sister products arrive through separate channels. The middlemen receive an "agent fee" (*daili fei*) of 3 to 5 percent of retail price but add practically no value to the chain of commercial processes by which the product reaches the customer. These local "partners" are learning little about how to manage distribution, because the FIE makes all the decisions. Essentially, the Chinese are paid to be a shell.[21]

The firm has had to develop a complicated organization, creating a China holding company, which coordinates with the local JV and a Hong Kong company; "the Hong Kong agents have better control over billing and payment" (#17). While the local JV has a sales force to promote distribution of the locally manufactured products, sales into China of related products manufactured elsewhere must be made (and the invoice sent

---

21. One finance director described a common tactic: "Taiwan firms form a local shell JV, which is local from a legal perspective. As locals they can invoice, they can buy directly and sell locally. There are many of them" (#17).

from) the Hong Kong company (a subsidiary of the US parent). The China holding company—based in Beijing—is not permitted to engage in any sales, only to "coordinate" them by referring customers and otherwise representing the firm.

This arrangement generally has not worked well. At the time the holding company was created, the foreign investors knew that selling through such a structure was not explicitly legal. However, their negotiators were given to believe that in short order such activity would be permitted. In fact, the new regulations clearly barred holding companies from coordinating sales. Thus, the firm is left with an organizational structure that is bulky and not legally useful; moreover, it continues to face the same distribution problems, with retailers being invoiced separately—from local JVs, Hong Kong, and even the home country. However, the firm still hopes to use the promise of future investments as leverage in resolving these problems.

By contrast, the German chemical firm BASF has trumpeted a very similar organizational structure, designed to meet the same challenges, and it claims to have had a better experience. It too is most concerned with integrating its relationship with customers, as its slogan suggests: "one face to the customer." Like the American firm, BASF established a China holding company, which owns 10 percent of each of the firm's ten JVs. Acting as agent for the JVs, the holding company sells for them. Again, however, it is not allowed to issue invoices or collect the bills directly. But BASF uses a computer system to automatically invoice the appropriate JV for each "sale" the holding company makes. Managers at BASF claim this works well and have not expressed anxiety that the legitimacy of their organizational structure will be challenged.[22]

Such markedly different experiences may be explained in part by different relationships with partners and within the firms. Complicated stratagems do not work without a good deal of complicity and cooperation within the organizational family. In order for the holding company to be effective, the JVs must fully consent to the arrangements. If they wish to retain control over customer relations and distribution, they may balk. It is also clear that such arrangements cannot succeed without the acquiescence of central authorities (especially when the firm touts its strategy publicly).

Organizational tangles can become even worse. The general counsel for another major American conglomerate (#7) described no fewer than seven overlapping distribution structures, each one built on top of the last and all still functioning. Thus the firm now has

■ three separate joint venture companies ("to spread our dances around"),

22. This description of BASF's operations is based on reporting by the Economist Intelligence Unit in *Business China*, 13 October 1997, 4–5.

- an import/logistics wholly owned company in Shanghai,

- a wholly owned China holding company that they had hoped could do distribution and service,

- 23 rep offices of the Hong Kong branch of their US-based international operations company, which provide service (technically illegal) on the firm's products, and

- 16 liaison offices set up under the holding company in the mistaken belief that they would be legally permitted to handle service and distribution.

Tasked with ensuring that the firm meets its worldwide commitment to full compliance with local laws and regulations, this general counsel is amply challenged by the China operations structure. He summarized, "The idea is to shut down the Hong Kong-parented branch offices. But in the meantime we have huge overhead here with these multiple layers. We are stuck with multiple distribution channels, none of which is clearly legal."

Firms seek other effective ways—short of achieving integrated distribution like BASF's—to serve the Chinese market. A common approach is to combine direct selling where it is legal and the use of local agents where it is not (or where the market is too small for the FIE). The director of the American chemical company cited above (#16) was realistic: "I am ready to go 100 percent to customers directly. For now, I would be happy with a combination of distributors [for smaller sales] and direct contact with big customers."

The manager of the Shanghai sales office of a high-technology company (a joint venture with the Shanghai Ministry of Post and Telecommunications, though the parent company's China operations are wholly foreign-owned) is trying to enlist the aid of independent distributors while he focuses on the bigger customers. These "independents" are useful because the nearby markets both are too small for the firm to look after and require more "specialized knowledge" (#24).[23] But the parent company in Tianjin, the JV sales office in Shanghai, and the Chinese partner to the Shanghai JV are all distributing products in parallel (#33).[24] The result is a good deal of conflict before a new distribution channel can be put to use by any of the three, but especially by the joint venture in the middle; the

---

23. This particular "specialized knowledge" apparently was in the application of bribes.

24. To further complicate the situation, Shanghai MPT has been instrumental in helping the firm gain entry to far-off Kunming (Yunnan Province) where collusive deals had previously locked them out. So the parent firm in this case has felt obliged to restrain its JV and let the Chinese distributership take the lead in Shanghai. The JV manager sighed, "[This is a good relationship, but] it takes a lot of energy to use relationships this way. In the bottom of our hearts, we'd like to see China a totally opened market."

partners get together regularly to review their distribution patterns and how they affect pricing, but that does not prevent confusion.

Another alternative emerging in China today is assistance from distribution consultancies or logistics companies with global experience. For example, UK-based logistics company Inchcape Pacific now has 2,000 employees in China, only 18 of whom are non-Chinese (and only 2 of those 18 are non-Asian). Inchcape has acquired a variety of trading licenses, which they exploit to the maximum. They have a JV transportation fleet, a JV freight-forwarding license, and a customs brokers license (also JV) that, bundled together, make possible one-stop distribution service to some customers. Focusing especially on fast-moving consumer goods, Inchcape has developed a strong presence in China. As a distribution firm with a foreign face, Inchcape offers other foreign firms a degree of comfort—at a price, no doubt. Other logistics companies are far smaller than this 70-country player; some ply the waters of a single city such as Shanghai (#1), or a single industry. While logistics companies provide a solution within the law (if loosely interpreted) for the distribution needs of some foreign businesses, "converters" operate in a grayer legal area. Converters take title to goods in Hong Kong, get them across the border, and re-sell them (often back to the same firm that brought them to Hong Kong, or an entity associated with it) with a lower markup than the statutory tax and duty regulations specify, including the fee for this service. The trick is to understate either the volume or the value of the goods being brought in. Any import must have a value-added tax (VAT) receipt with it when purchased, and the legal responsibility for its accuracy lies with the purchaser. Regardless of the particular arrangement with a converter, in the end the buyer is burdened with the taxes due on the import.

Some foreign firms believe that they must get a toehold in China but find the statutory duty rates prohibitive. By using converters, they are entering and gaining market share, albeit at risk of "channel shutdown." A logistics firm director interviewed (#21) judged the central government content with the current level of these abuses (or not bothered enough to try to stop them in faraway Guangdong, anyway) and believes that Beijing probably has accurately estimated the costs. He pointed out that as tariff rates fall further, whether unilaterally or as a condition of WTO entrance, converters will become less and less relevant. Even now, they represent only a very small share of total imports into China, being mainly used for high-value, high-duty goods in Guangdong Province. Of course, as long as tariff rates remain high, then ways of circumventing them through shady distribution are likely to persist.[25]

Only a small sample of distribution practices in China has been examined.[26] Especially in southern China, the reality is that a distribution

---

25. In 1998, another in a long line of antismuggling campaigns was announced.

26. See USCBC 1998 for more insight on distribution and the tactics of foreign firms.

regime far more liberal than the official standard is already in place. Business licenses have been approved permitting distribution centers to be set up in local jurisdictions such as Panyu, a wealthy Guangdong municipality in which freewheeling Chinese customers will find foreign firms merchandising almost anything, more or less directly to the public. Such centers, characterized by high-end imported goods, have been joined by distribution powerhouses such as Wal-Mart, which today operates in Guangdong as Sam's Club. These arrangements are generally made possible through a business partnership with a powerful local entity. They are tolerated either because Beijing is interested in seeing whether they work or because there is nothing the center can do to reel them in; indeed, there is truth to both explanations.

Failing to Plan for Distribution

Michael McCune is a young American who has been involved in distribution activities in Shanghai for some years, including the design of distribution strategies for FIEs. He had a clear sense of the weakness of most foreign investors: "China reps typically come to Shanghai with three folders: a negotiating plan, a production plan, and a marketing plan. But since they are coming from mature markets, they do not come with a distribution plan." A Beijing-based expatriate made a similar observation:

> A [foreign] firm took a 95 percent equity position in a pharmaceutical JV, but agreed to give exclusive, open-ended distribution rights to the minority [Chinese] partner. What company would do that in New Jersey, or France, or Chile? The company is now hostage to the minority partner. (#46)

Foreign investors fail to plan for distribution for a number of reasons.[27] First, as McCune stressed, accustomed to mature markets, they simply take for granted the draw of the market in general, ignoring the infrastructure, services, and regulatory framework that undergird it. Such incompetence is a plausible defense only for smaller FIEs without much experience abroad, at least in an emerging market. Furthermore, this naïveté is unlikely in the operations of Hong Kong or other overseas Chinese investors, who are the most numerous of those contributing to FDI.

Second, foreign investors may be ignorant of prevailing conditions in China; for example, they may be overly credulous of the capacity promises of Chinese partners. Consider the subsidiary of a major American auto parts manufacturer included in this study, which operates in interior China supplying components to a major automotive JV. The firm's prospects are tied to the ability of the auto company to sell passenger

---

27. Obviously, this issue is less important for firms interested only in exporting from China and not in participating in the domestic market. However, to the extent that these firms still rely on the distribution system to obtain their raw materials and inputs, it also is a concern for them.

cars, and therefore it suffered when the plan of the venture's Chinese partner to use its access to truck distributorships proved infeasible. Up to speed and ready to supply more than 2,000 units monthly, this American parts supplier is shipping only hundreds while waiting for the auto JV to create a network of dealerships from scratch (#26).[28] Here, too, incompetence is a thin excuse, though perhaps even larger multinationals can be somewhat forgiven for not fully comprehending the specifics of the Chinese market.

Third, investors may intend to adjust or amend their distribution function after setting up their venture, only to discover the difficulty of reconfiguring this aspect of the business once it is running. With distribution rights, like other areas, a well-negotiated contract will not guarantee an FIE a trouble-free existence in the China market; but too many careless assumptions during establishment will almost surely lead to frustration down the line.

A final possibility is that the Chinese economy is changing so quickly that what seem to be assets can obsolesce between the time a venture is negotiated and the time goods are shipped.[29] For example, one American agribusiness firm constructed an expensive food-processing plant in northern China only to have its source of inputs—the region's soybean crop—wiped out by drought. As its existing distribution and supply plans became useless, the firm has had to start over, creating a new use for the plant (#2). This problem is not primarily attributable to a poor distribution system: such larger forces can knock a business plan off track anywhere. Recovering from this change of fortune, however, is tougher in China due to the limited distribution networks, which complicate the task of finding a secondary application for the plant.

Whatever the reason(s) for poor planning about distribution, the results can be paralyzing. Local partners may be content to rely on sluggish statist channels to move product, and reliable providers of distribution services are reportedly hard to find. These problems often damage the product and market development. As their market share stagnates, many FIEs are unable to understand why or to adjust distribution to break the logjam. Intelligence on the activities of competitors, innovations in retailing, changes in demand, and the like fails to flow back to the manufacturer.

---

28. More disappointing still to the foreign investors was the belated discovery that the auto JV is essentially locked out of major markets such as Shanghai by the anticompetitive practices of local governments that favor local producers; in the case of Shanghai the beneficiary is Volkswagen, although the aggressive entry into Shanghai of GM (which, making Buicks, will theoretically be producing for a more upscale market) may bring VW's local dominance to an end.

29. Note that the FIE itself may change between the times of negotiating and shipping, deciding to switch from a focus on exporting to a focus on the domestic market and thereby creating for itself a new set of distribution needs.

Willingness to Participate Directly

The messages from FIE managers are contradictory. Many stressed how essential it is that foreign firms be themselves involved in the distribution process. There is no other way, they insisted, for expatriates to appraise accurately how much product the system can move, where to best allocate resources to spur sales, what competitors are doing (including piracy), what customers want, and how brands and marketing are evolving. The more intermediaries (be they partners or independent distributors) between firm and customer, the more distorted the signals from the market.

Other managers, conversely, emphasized that even if they were totally unfettered by restrictions they would still leave distribution to partners or subcontractors, because there is no way for them—as foreigners—to know enough about the market to do the job effectively. Also, as already mentioned, some intimated that they were happy not to be sullied by the corrupt practices rife at the street level.

How is this paradox to be resolved? The present era is transitional, and most FIEs will employ a variety of strategies to learn as much as they can about this marketplace. At a minimum, laws requiring that aspects of distribution be left outside the FIE must be treated with some respect. FIEs may not be able to operate as far afield as they like, because they have failed to obtain the necessary licenses from the Chinese or because they cannot justify the expense to their parent organization, given all the uncertainties about still-growing markets. Human resource constraints (see chapter 2) hamper far-flung distribution systems. While many poor-quality, old-line distributors remain, competition is generating service providers that FIEs should not ignore (especially as the best among them may be able to move quickly in the current environment to *dominate* channels). At the same time, unless the firm intends solely to export, direct involvement in the marketplace is critical; China is changing so rapidly and business practices there are so idiosyncratic that isolated firms will not have a clue about how to operate effectively.

Many FIEs both run their own distribution and farm it out. In this way they test alternative methods of getting goods to market. At least until the market structure matures, hybrid strategies will likely make the most sense. Other hybrid aspects of the successful FIE are the high proportion of overseas Chinese in management and the push to localize leadership of the Chinese operations.

Internal FIE Problems

Firms with multiple business units commonly establish separate joint ventures with numerous Chinese partners, in order to achieve as much access as possible in each business niche. Because they seek market opportunities in different sectors, they must find existing players who can bring the required influence to bear. This practice also spreads out the risk of becoming entangled with a local partner that turns out to have problems. There are costs to such a complex organizational structure, however, including difficulty in coordinating tasks such as distribution that should be consolidated for efficiency. Interviewees at several conglomerates discussed their frustrations at getting disparate units to agree on common ex-factory distribution and service strategies. Units may guard jealously their own distribution channels, especially when they rely on painstakingly crafted personal relationships.

Even within the same business line, clashes occur over distribution. One example involves a firm with facilities in different cities. In each municipality the firm had associated itself with a local partner to enter the market, and rivalries between the different partners subsequently erupted over cross-penetration of markets. Similarly, a large American conglomerate that has formed a trading company to handle distribution cannot convince one of its most important units to cede management of sales to the trading company (#6). The holdouts prefer to manage their own distribution channels. The multiple couplings designed to broaden distribution in the face of the FIE restrictions make such squabbles common in China.

External Pressures, Regional Disparities

Managers interviewed for this study observed that quantitative and qualitative changes in distribution networks inside and outside China were shaping Chinese development. For example, FIEs that decided to locate in southern China cite proximity to shipping facilities and reliable delivery to overseas markets as critical determinants of their choice. The lack of reliable distribution infrastructure elsewhere dissuades these labor-intensive industries from moving inland to take advantage of cheaper labor. Developments in international shipping and the falling cost of air freight will further alter the comparative advantage of Chinese production, shaping regional economic development in China just as in other countries.

In industries in which time to market is most important, aspects of physical distribution related neither to policy nor to inadequacies of infrastructure can influence the operations of FIEs. Segments of the apparel industry, a sector in which distribution speed is key, provide an example. From the 1960s through the mid-1980s price was of relatively little concern to apparel producers in the Hong Kong–southern China corridor; labor and materials made up an insignificant portion of costs. In the low- to mid-price niche for which these firms produced, delivery times were not a pressing issue either. Attaining basic quality was the factory's main objective.

Today, designs prepared in New York are instantly transmitted to production sites around the world, and getting the new line to stores ahead of rivals is a first-order challenge. From southern China, delivery times to

New York for finished garments today stand at 21 to 24 days, thanks to trucking from the factory, proximity to frequent fast ships, and extremely efficient port services. The fastest freighters, if timed right, can get product to the New York market in 15 days. This distribution access is both a determining and limiting factor in locating factories today. Hence expanding inland to find cheaper labor is out of the question unless a vastly improved distribution system is installed. From competing production sites in Latin America, product can reach New York in only three to four days.

The textile manufacturers interviewed for this study have managed to keep US-oriented facilities in southern China from relocating to Western Hemisphere sites with liberal tariff arrangements by focusing on productivity and quality and by taking no chances on weak, undependable distribution channels. Nevertheless, several managers are all but resigned to shifting a portion of their company's manufacturing to Latin America from Hong Kong-Guangdong (#8).[30] As of this writing, it is not clear how the Asian financial turmoil of 1997–98—particularly the devaluations in almost all the regional currencies except China's renminbi—will affect microeconomic behavior, and hence the distribution channels that grow up in its wake, in the long term. Undoubtedly the effects will be significant.

Analysis

As with the other business functions, distribution issues can be sorted into four categories of cause: transitional, self-imposed, policy, and market structure. Table 5.5 summarizes the issues discussed in this chapter according to that framework.

Transitional Factors

Transitional factors stand behind a number of the concerns expatriates raised about managing distribution and other ex-factory business operations. It is important to recognize that legal ambiguities in the regulatory realm are not all the fault of legislators. The pace of policy formation has in fact been quick over the reform period, especially in light of the virtual absence of earlier laws and regulations. As authorities strive to develop the frameworks needed by the market, clarity of law does not keep pace. There is a policy element as well, addressed separately below, but one can expect uncertainty to subside in the future with or without external pressure on Chinese leaders.

---

30. In April 1996 Mexico surpassed China as the top exporter of textile and apparel goods to the United States, owing partly to shifts in manufacturing sites ("Apparel Sales to US Still High Despite Moves to Other Sources," *Journal of Commerce*, 1 October 1997, 3D).

Table 5.5 Roundup of ex-factory issues

Issue	Category	If policy ... Level	Priority
Regulatory restrictions	Policy	Central	High
Legal ambiguity	Policy, transitional	Central	Medium
Marketing	Policy	Central	Medium-low
Collection, finance	Policy	Central	Medium-high
Service provision	Policy	Central	Medium-high
Physical infrastructure	Transitional		
Local authorities	Policy, self-imposed	Local	Medium
Allocated market shares	Policy	Central	High
Market foreclosure	Market structure, policy	Central	High
Corruption	Transitional		
Organization complexity	Self-imposed, transitional		
Failing to plan	Self-imposed		
Willing to get directly involved	Self-imposed, transitional		
Internal organizational problems	Self-imposed		
External pressures on distribution	Transitional		

A similar logic holds for the deficiencies in physical infrastructure. Pervasive and profound, these will take some time to be fully remedied whether or not the most effective and expeditious strategies for financing are pursued. Economic growth will outpace even rapid infrastructure construction for some time, and it is far from clear that the best choices will be made. To the extent that FIEs tend to be concentrated in the more advanced segments of the economy and not scattered through the hinterlands, they may enjoy some advantages (on average) over domestic companies spread across the country. These gaps affect all firms in China, of course, not just FIEs.

Insofar as corruption is involved in distribution, it is largely a transitional matter: graft and other private corrupt practices by distributors now threaten FIEs. A broader array of distribution options in the future should permit selection of the less corrupt, hence diminishing the importance of this issue over time.

Three of the four "foreigner-specific" topics include transitional elements. Problems of organizational complexity resulting from attempts to circumvent restrictions, foreign willingness to participate directly in markets instead of leaving ex-factory tasks to compradors, and exogenous (overseas) economic pressures on shipment times and product cycles all stand to change naturally over time. Some of this change is a function of learning (how better to work with Chinese partners); some, capacity (availability of qualified local staff to expand service operations); and some, the natural disequilibrium of changing economic patterns and tastes.

Self-Imposed Problems

Not surprisingly, self-imposed problems are predominant in the foreign-specific cluster as well. The failure to plan for distribution in China, the organizational contortions, and the internal squabbling documented in this study make clear that FIEs are responsible for a significant share of these problems. It can be hoped that these, like transitional factors, will recede over the coming years: firms (successful ones anyway) are self-correcting. In addition, the complications that can arise in dealing with local authorities in China to secure control over distribution can be laid in part to the FIEs. Investors have choices to make about the collusive (or privileged) arrangements they enjoy in exchange for the dollars and jobs they bring. While it may be reasonable to argue that such arrangements are a minimal compensation for other disadvantages that FIEs attempting to compete domestically face, they nevertheless are pernicious from the perspective of the next FIE that tries to enter the market—or, for that matter, of the next Chinese firm from a different locality.

Policy-Related Issues

Foremost among policy-related distribution issues are the formal regulatory restrictions on FIEs, along with the ambiguity of the central legal framework (and ambiguous administrative guidance issued from competing camps in Beijing). Conflicting local-level policymaking, tolerated by Beijing, is an additional policy problem facing FIEs, particularly for firms that desire clear adherence to the law. Allocation of market share, in those sectors in which it takes place, directly blocks access to distribution opportunities and markets. Because so many large enterprises in China either remain state-owned or retain a quasi-state status to some degree, the tendency of firms to foreclose markets and restrain trade is not just a "private" problem, as was argued on behalf of Fuji of Japan in an important WTO case in 1997, but a matter of policy.

Market Structure

The market foreclosure problem possesses a policy aspect because so many firms are technically still state owned; nonetheless, it is the case that many are acting privately in their attempts to foreclose markets—and, of course, many Chinese firms acting similarly are truly private (as are FIEs themselves, some of which act anticompetitively). In the absence of an explicit competition policy supported by central authorities, vertical restraints on trade will crop up in markets wherever only a few distributors are able to move products between production points and markets.

Considerably more evidence is needed to measure whether the trend in China is in this direction, and how widespread it might be. Market structures set slowly. Central authorities (and local ones, in a few cases such as Shanghai's) are exploring the utility of a competition policy in guiding China's nascent markets, but it is unlikely that such a framework can be put in place and enforced before significant concentration has occurred in broad swaths of the Chinese economy.

6

Of Laws and Privileges

The nondevelopment of Chinese law along lines familiar to the West was plainly related to the nondevelopment of capitalism and an independent business class in the old China.

John King Fairbank (1983, 123)

Introduction

Law in China today serves primarily, as it has throughout Chinese history, as an instrument of state control rather than as a limit on or obligation of the state. While over the past 20 years rule of law has made strides in China, legal conditions remain difficult for firms, individuals, and foreign governments. The central government itself is concerned with the inadequacy of the existing system as a basis for important future reforms, such as clarification of ownership rights. Each of the earlier chapters has touched on legal issues; this chapter explores questions of law per se, in two categories. Under the first heading are those that concern the firm in securing predictability and ensuring compliance (mostly in its dealings with the state). Under the second are laws that make possible recourse for the firm when disputes arise over transactions or anything else (mostly with private parties). There is a good deal of overlap, as in China the state is often involved in dealings that usually concern private parties alone in the United States. The question of corruption, though undeniably relevant in an analysis of China's legal environment, is extremely difficult to categorize; it therefore is discussed separately.

A final aspect of Chinese law today requires attention. Foreign investors often enjoy superlegal privileges that benefit their operations and profitability; for example, some have exceptional licenses giving them exclusive rights to engage in some generally prohibited activity. It is difficult to compare the privileges enjoyed by some firms with the costs borne by others as a result; only a cursory attempt is made here. However, two things are clear. First, when these privileges are taken into account, the measure of foreign enterprise power in China's seemingly chaotic marketplace changes significantly. Second, to advance economically China must withdraw many of them, putting all firms on an even footing so that they can compete efficiently. This point is well understood as pertaining to state-owned enterprises (SOEs), which depend on subsidies, allocated market shares, and exemptions from procompetitive and other laws (e.g., those protecting the environment); its application to foreign enterprises has been less widely discussed but is increasingly important. Such privileges may be as detrimental to FIEs' interests in the long run as they are helpful in the short term.

China's legal weaknesses stem in part from unavoidable problems of transition and in part from government policy. The choices that foreign-invested enterprises (FIEs) themselves make also contribute to their problems with Chinese law. There is evidence—though only recently—of FIEs successfully using the legal system to achieve their objectives. The interviews suggested not irremediable lawlessness but a fair degree of legal predictability in China. Legal norms and institutions are evolving at a reasonable pace, reinforced by a network of less formal structures that partially fill in the existing gaps.

How quickly China progresses depends significantly on whether foreign enterprises, China's window to the modern business world, choose to promote change or simply to wait for it (or, alas, to resist it). No single firm can alter China's legal regime. But important individual firms are impelling the creation of local "islands" to serve their legal needs; these include compliance offices at the local foreign direct investment (FDI) bureaus. Moreover, the FIEs collectively do have the power to force change. But there is a catch: FIEs are not a monolithic group, and their behavior is almost guaranteed not to be orchestrated—indeed, it hardly can be. These ventures have different interests in reform, according to their market power, corporate culture, risk affinity, and the like. The weight of the foreign-invested community taken together is most likely to lead to change in those areas in which the logic of the market necessarily generates the same concerns among divergent firms: one can refer to these as forced moves in commercial policy.[1]

---

1. Firms exposed to a common external environment (i.e., a competitively ordered marketplace) over time evolve symmetrical characteristics, such as a desire for predictability and avenues of recourse. These wants are not ideological but pragmatic.

China's Legal Environment

China's legal traditions can be clearly traced to before 1000 BCE. Confucian classics drafted around 500 BCE were still central to Chinese law at the beginning of the present century, millennia later; their remnants are easily discerned in everyday Chinese language and culture today. In an analysis of the dynamics of FDI in China, Wang (n.d., 21–31) reviews the traditional characteristics of China's legal environment. It is striking how germane they appear today:[2]

State-centrism: The purpose of law is to serve the state, not to protect abstract civil rights.

Secularism: Little tradition of religious absolutism exists to provide a definitive higher authority; therefore "Chinese legal institutions lacked the sacred and universal quality based on divinity."

Lack of independence: The primacy of the state precludes judicial independence or checks and balances; the main avenue of appeal is through the assistance of patrons with authority.

Rule of man: The weakness of institutions supports the primacy of powerful individuals in the legal system, who judge by analogy the many matters left uncovered by statute.

Primacy of criminal law: The court system is concerned mainly with preserving the state's omnipotence and with criminal cases; it plays little part in civil disputes (including commercial transactions), deferring them to local mediation bodies.

Inequality: The legal presumption is "legalized inequality," as reflected in the Confucian ethic of filial obligation of son to father, and so on; a harmonious society is presumed to require unequal standing among men and women, old and young, gentry and commoners.

Secrecy: "If [the people] knew the content of the legal codes, they would find ways to go around them in order to avoid punishment"; this extraordinary logic was the basis of withholding the content of the law, thereby concentrating discretionary power to enforce the law in the hands of officials.

Informal mechanisms: As noted with regard to civil cases (including commercial transactions), the state preferred to leave noncriminal matters to resolution by local mediators, clans, guilds, and the like.

Expatriates in China today could be forgiven for presuming that this list had been distilled from present conditions in Shanghai or Chongqing. But

---

2. I am grateful to Hongying Wang for permission to provide this summary of her points.

these observations applied equally on the eve of the reform period, at the end of the Cultural Revolution. As Lieberthal points out,

> China . . . had no legal system and no law in a western sense as of 1977. When the PRC was founded, the party declared all Guomindang [GMD] laws invalid, and during the early 1950s it began to develop new legal codes to replace the defunct GMD statutes. This effort, however, came to a halt at the beginning of the Great Leap Forward [1958–61], and it never resumed. As of 1977, therefore, China was governed by decrees, by bureaucratic regulations, and by the personal orders of various officials; it had no code of law at all. In addition, many of the decrees, regulations, and so on were kept secret. The first foreign firms that sought to invest in the PRC signed contracts subjecting their investments to all pertinent rules and regulations, even though they were not allowed to know what these strictures were! (1995, 150–51)

Thus the dominant legal institutions in 1977 were even less compatible with Western commercial norms than those that sprouted up during the Republican period (1912–49).

When China's leaders decided to reform the economy and crack open the door to foreign participation, they recognized that legal reform would be necessary. On the one hand they were under pressure from potential investors and international advisors, such as the World Bank, to fortify early economic gains with legal reform (see, e.g., Jacobson and Oksenberg 1990, 114–16). On the other hand, they were influenced with equal strength by memories of foreign extraterritoriality in China. Prior to the 20th century, Chinese rulers had granted a limited degree of self-regulation to foreign trading communities (Fairbank 1983, 167). However, starting as early as 1784 and formally after the Treaty of Nanjing in 1842, foreign powers— following Great Britain's lead—placed themselves outside Chinese legal jurisdiction. They were frustrated with the often arbitrary Chinese legal system, not only as it applied to criminal cases but also to commercial transactions. Intending to contain inequities, they imposed an imperialist system ultimately no less inequitable to China, opening and legitimizing foreign encroachment that contributed to the dismantling of the Chinese state.

When Communist authorities ventured to invite foreign enterprises back into China in the 1970s, they were therefore excruciatingly aware of their vulnerability to charges of treason should critics later emerge. Loath to risk having to tell investors to go home in order to stave off charges of pandering, a short-term measure that would inflict long-lasting damage to China's reputation, they took the initiative in legal reforms. Under Deng Xiaoping, the government promulgated a large number of laws and codes, framed a new constitution recognizably Western in form, and adopted key principles such as the separation of powers (giving power to the hitherto impotent National People's Congress)[3] and rule of law (e.g.,

---

3. Only in the 1990s did the NPC show (halting) signs of real independence, however. See, e.g., Steve Mufson, "Chinese Congress Vote Shows Surprising Dissension," *Washington Post*, 18 March 1995, page A21; and "A Little Booing from the Audience," *Economist*, 25 March 1995, page 38.

setting term limits on high officials for the first time). From their inception through 1988 the reforms generated 73 laws, 592 State Council regulations, and over 1,000 "local congress" regulations; most of these (71 percent) related to economic matters.[4]

As economic development gathered momentum, the need for a better legal basis for resolving transactional disputes increased no less rapidly, as private property returned and economic incentives were restored. Chinese citizens once again had material things worth protecting, and with increased dynamism and mobility the old, informal modes of legal recourse were insufficient. As property ownership was reintroduced, economic performance appeared to improve,[5] thus bolstering the consensus for even greater protection to spur growth. Growing economic success also made it more important for China to have a legal system comparable to those of foreign countries in order to facilitate foreign investment, to reduce the natural tensions that arise during trade, and to satisfy the demands of the countries on whose open markets China depended. In addition, China has come under pressure to address inadequacies in civil and human rights protections, a task that logically demands extensive revision to the legal regime. The evidence below, however, is primarily concerned with the commercial imperatives of predictability and recourse in the law.[6]

By 1997 a system of law had been more or less restored in China's urban centers, spurred in no small part by those needs of foreign firms. Changes included a broad framework of publicly available laws and regulations, instead of the personal pronouncements of party leaders known only to bureaucrats; attention to training lawyers, judges, and legislators, instead of leaving the Communist bureaucracy to respond with dogma; and a move to sharpen rights and adjudication procedures, instead of avoiding litigation by shunting cases off into arbitration. And yet it is still very much a system in transition, neither fully serving the purposes that reformers had originally envisioned nor efficiently meeting the needs of market-oriented investors.

---

4. The Australia Department of Foreign Affairs and Trade's East Asia Analytical Unit (1997a, 92) cites a paper by Chen Duan Hong given in Sydney in 1995 for these figures.

5. There may be a considerable difference between apparent and actual growth: see table 4.1.

6. Bette Bao Lord of New York's Freedom House has argued that the long-term (or maybe even medium-term) predictability that FIEs desire *requires* them to attend to human rights conditions in China, as social tensions are likely to build and threaten commerce unless democratic reforms are carried out (personal communication). I agree with her both that enlightened self-interest is needed in China and that social conditions in high-growth areas may get worse before they get better. As argued in chapter 3, many foreign firms do exert a positive influence on social conditions by their very presence and interaction with Chinese employees. Whether these firms ought to direct their sales force and engineers to spend more of their time with Communist Party officials advocating for democracy is a question beyond the scope of this study.

As Child (1996, 220) observes from a management perspective, not only do FIEs in China, as in many countries, face special procedures at the border and restrictions governing establishment, but once set up they continue to be controlled by laws distinct from those applicable to purely domestic firms.[7] When legal questions are unresolved by FIE-specific legislation, domestic law applies by default; but for most matters involving transactions and labor, separate rules are in place.[8] Other nations have crafted special rules to govern the activities of foreign firms operating domestically in exceptional sectors (e.g., banking in the United States), but having two entirely distinct regimes is unusual, if not unique. On its face, then, this seems to demonstrate a lack of "national treatment" for FIEs in the context of investment. Or does it?

First of all, while China's foreign investment laws might be said to deny national treatment to foreign investors by virtue of a two-track legal regime, the national treatment obligation in the World Trade Organization (General Agreement on Tariffs and Trade, Article III, paragraph 4) applies only to foreign products, not to foreign investors. In fact, extending the national treatment principle to the investment realm is a key goal of efforts by the Organization for Economic Cooperation and Development (OECD) to negotiate a Multilateral Agreement on Investment, and it was an important element supporting cross-border investment in the North American Free Trade Agreement. So if a bifurcated legal regime in China *were* a hindrance to foreign firms, it would nevertheless be outside the purview of WTO as presently chartered.

More important, it is not clear that the dual legal system is a hindrance. The special rules for FIEs were designed to create a regime closer to Western norms. While it is separate from domestic law, it may well be superior—at least for the purposes of market-oriented foreign firms. The rule of "no harm, no foul" may apply, as no foreign investors in their right mind would prefer to be subject to the vagaries of the system of domestic adjudication with which wholly Chinese firms must grapple. But if a private party is unlikely to challenge the two-track Chinese system within the WTO mechanism, sovereign parties may nonetheless argue that "sep-

---

7. Jeff Schott of the Institute for International Economics points out that other nations acceding to the GATT/WTO have also employed differential legal systems for foreign firms (e.g., Poland) (personal communication). But in those cases, he notes, the applicants' impact on world trade and the system itself was not large and was moderated by geopolitical considerations (Cold War politics); China's impact, in contrast, is both large and entirely conceived in terms of its economic viability.

8. Not only are FIEs subject to these two sets of law, but for contracts ancillary to the main contract setting up the venture (e.g., covering technology transfer agreements, trademark use, distribution, and supply and off-take) foreign laws (US law, most commonly) can be specified as governing. Savvy tactical reference to suitable statutes is critical. See, e.g., Charles D. Paglee's 1998 "Contracts and Agreements in the People's Republic of China," at http://www.qis.net/chinalaw, 20 April 1998 (under "Chinese Law Explained").

arate but equal is inherently unequal" during negotiation of China's WTO accession package, when they can raise any issues they wish, regardless of WTO discipline.

This study has shown that the firewalls dividing FIEs and domestic firms are eroding rapidly. In a number of sectors, foreign and domestic firms are increasingly indistinguishable, and FIEs are transacting more and more business in the domestic economy. Because of the dual system, a transaction covered by FIE-oriented laws under Western contract would be adjudicated by Western norms, but one between an FIE and a Chinese state-owned enterprise might be subject to different norms. In the latter case, Child (1996, 221) points out, a contract can be abrogated as a result of the decision of a planning authority or agency. The partnerships between firms (including foreign firms) and sympathetic bureaucracies make the potential for serious abuse of this power very clear. It is such fears that lead China's trading partners to contest the present legal regime.

The Expatriate Experience

Next to be discussed are the legal experiences and challenges reported by informants for this study. Three senior attorneys for China operations were among the respondents (##7, 14, 28). Many other interviewees had law degrees, and most had significant experience dealing with legal matters in China. Other counsels were interviewed at the US headquarters of firms.

Predictability and Compliance

Most of the FIEs studied for this book had stated corporate commitments not to violate host-country law, wherever in the world they operated. For example, one large American FIE (whose China company is headed by interviewee #36) applies the following—notably unambiguous—standard:

> As part of a global organization, [we] need to respect the laws, customs, and traditions of each country in which [we] operate. At the same time, certain actions violate the Code of Conduct, even if they are legal and customary in some countries. In general, these would be actions that violate the laws of the United States *or* the host country [emphasis added].

This firm suggests to its employees an easy test to guarantee ethical behavior: a major newspaper should be able to report their actions without embarrassing them. The motivation for running a compliance-oriented firm, in addition to fear of exposure (and of litigation), is greater predictability and a more dynamic enterprise. The firm also distributed Paine's *Harvard Business Review* article, "Managing for Organizational Integrity" (1994), to an array of employees brought together in mid-1997 for the sole purpose of focusing on ethics. Paine's thesis is as follows: "By supporting ethically sound behavior, managers can strengthen the relationships and reputations their companies depend on," enabling them to better attain profitability goals.

Nevertheless, expatriates often noted that in China "the law" does not hold the same meaning that it does in OECD countries, insisting that to naively operate as though it did would only squander resources and effort. Many spoke of competitors who, either because they were from home countries with less established legal cultures or because they were smaller and less subject to scrutiny, operated without regard for legal regimes. And many firms uncomfortable with the shakiness of China's legal environment were simultaneously the beneficiaries of the privileges and opportunities that legal ambiguities permitted. Thus their status was often paradoxical.

Deliberate ambiguity has been extremely useful to Chinese reformers. Explicit guarantees for FIEs (e.g., regarding market access) could have provided hard-liners opposed to trade liberalization with ammunition: after all, not even Chinese firms enjoyed such rights in practice. The vagueness of the regulations enabled reformers to push policy beyond the point of reversal while making possible a fair degree of foreign establishment and competition. Therefore, it would be somewhat misguided to simply deride the present faulty legal regime as inadequate, immature, and corruption prone. True, it has those characteristics, but they also served a purpose. Important domestic reform milestones have been realized; and as the still (but more slowly) growing flow of FDI demonstrates, investors have felt sufficiently protected to find China attractive. The obvious challenge now is to make changes that will serve future and not past conditions. Earlier reliance on ambiguity may make the legal reforms needed for the next phase more difficult to achieve.

Seeking Access to the Content of the Law

Clearly, investors who do not know the relevant regulations will have difficulty planning strategically for the Chinese market and elaborating a rules-based culture within the firm. Such lack of information has been a major problem for China-based FIEs in the past. China continues to restrict publication of some legal and regulatory materials, and in some industries market development is devised behind closed doors. Even the new Price Law, which only went into effect 1 May 1998, allows planners to set prices "when necessary," for a range of goods and services. When reform began, the vast majority of economic law was secret, or *neibu* (literally, "inside").

Greater transparency has been a consistent goal of bilateral and multilateral negotiations, and in fact much progress has been made in this regard. By keeping regulations secret, authorities could implement them as flexibly or arbitrarily as they wished. Earlier investors were willing to come to China without having full access to the statutes. But as the economy has matured, policymakers have become more concerned with a diminishing FIE inclination to invest without transparency. China has had to make its rules and regulations more public as a result.

The major commercial laws, foreign investment guidelines, and preferential sectoral policies have now been published and circulated. They are readily available on the Internet and in libraries, and most expatriates interviewed were able to gain access to the laws and regulations they needed. But while instructions that govern the operation of FIEs and the designs of Chinese macroeconomic policy are available, sector-specific management rules in some cases are not. For example, in some sectors policies allocating market share are said to exist outside the reach of expatriates (#20). Furthermore, as discussed below, much in Chinese laws is not made explicit, instead being fleshed out only over time in implementing regulations and opinions that can take years to be elaborated. Therefore FIE managers must regularly return to the authorities for interpretations and clarifications—the bases of which are still often not transparent.

Transparency is clearly a prerequisite for predictability and compliance. Although relationships with high-powered leaders may temporarily substitute for the predictability provided by a sound, transparent legal regime, in the long term these leaders will be gone and a new generation of regulators will take their place. History suggests that such relationships, implicit deals, and bargains will not be honored by those who follow, and the most senior leaders are aware of the instability of this system.

Bridging Gaps in the Law

China has passed a huge number of laws in recent years, but many areas of commercial concern remain uncovered. New laws and implementing regulations must still be promulgated in areas. Until that happens, firms must fill in the gaps. Either they extrapolate by analogy with existing regulations, get an administrative ruling or opinion from a policymaker, or shop around for a jurisdiction that has a track record satisfactory to the firm. When gaps in the FIE-specific laws exist, domestic law generally applies by default. As noted above, this can be problematic when domestic law fails to provide an adequate market-oriented device to resolve disagreements. Other regulatory issues are covered neither by FIE laws nor by domestic laws.

Such lacks increase the risks perceived by investors. For example, because the regulations are incomplete, firms must repeatedly return to approval authorities for clarifications, which can bring other problems. As a Hong Kong-based senior attorney noted:

> The alternative to a litigious system is constantly going back to approval authorities, which opens so much opportunity for corruption. Getting a *legal*, fully vetted

transfer of land [for example] is a very difficult task. So you get local approval, and hope there is not a "rectification campaign." All that worrying significantly raises the costs, and many Americans just pull out. (#14)

Surely the wrong way to bridge gaps in Chinese law is simply to ignore them: foreigners sometimes delude themselves into assuming that what is not there can do them no harm. The lawyer quoted above recalled a prominent American advisor's glee at hearing from the governor of Guangdong that his business associates could "do everything they wanted, in accordance with Chinese law." The trouble is that "People just do not hear the qualifier: 'in accordance with Chinese law.' People suffer from 'Sino-narcosis,'" he explained.

Barring self-delusion about how holes in the law will be filled, FIEs still cannot predict with certainty how policy will unfold. A large US conglomerate developed layers of distribution and service provision offices only to discover that these operations were in conflict with the policies later enunciated to regulate such activities (see chapter 5). This firm is currently considering whether to push for special treatment under a "grandfather clause" or simply to comply with the new regulations, restructuring from scratch (#7). While those at the conglomerate say they were lulled into thinking that legislation would validate the course of action it took, other legal experts (#54) insist that such firms took their chances and knowingly overstepped the guidance that central authorities had offered about the policies to come. The potential costs of misjudging future regulation is significant, but so is the cost of not moving aggressively in the Chinese market and being boxed out by competitors.

Interpreting the Law to Advantage

That the scope of Chinese legal coverage is widening does not by itself answer all commercial policy questions. For a number of reasons, statutes are often vague or intentionally ambiguous, full of room for interpretation. Early on in reforms, decision makers in China realized that they lacked the competence to legislate effectively, but that loosely written policies could be reinterpreted with experience (exemplified by the expression "crossing the stream by feeling the rocks"). Ambiguity also helps to reconcile residual ideological requirements (e.g., that the state must be the primary economic shareholder on behalf of the people) with practical necessities (e.g., that state enterprises must be privatized to meet economic growth targets in the medium term and beyond). A certain lack of clarity is thus essential to maintaining the image of Communist officials as relevant and potent.

As a result of this ambiguity, foreign and domestic firms try—both defensively and offensively—to shape the circulars and decisions that affect them. Beijing pushes decision-making responsibility down to lower levels of government, with admonitions of "don't ask, don't tell." A firm seeking permission to undertake a certain activity will be told just to do it without asking for formal approval (#52). Firms, likewise, push responsibility down to the lawyers and, increasingly, to compradors, all the while preparing contingency plans to deal with regulatory trouble if it should arise. "Right from the start, you need to build a defense against the possibility that [some authority] may challenge your 'approvals' later," said one senior counsel (#28). She went on:

> There is a lot of interpretation. Asking the right person for an interpretation is key. If you get unclear or conflicting interpretations, what do you do then? And if you ask for a written ruling, for someone to put their word on the line, it is nearly impossible. Often, what you end up with is merely a memo to yourself; maybe you can get someone to "chop" it [i.e., to put their personal stamp on the document, indicating it had been seen by them]. The lawyers [for the FIE] are conceivably the ones who will hang, though the chance of getting [sanctioned by the government] is infinitesimal. . . . An American-style lawyer who demands a paper trail for everything will only bring the business to a halt.

One tactic for dealing with the authorization problem is to send authorities notice of a legal position, which is then presumed to be legal unless sent back marked to the contrary (#36). Thus, most of the time it is the task of the legal staff to find a way to justify what has already been done or decided. "Are we 100 percent ethical?" asked one senior respondent. "Within the Chinese system, we are 99 percent pure from the US standard and 110 percent pure from the Chinese standard. Lawyers *are* where the buck stops, but that's their job" (#37).

With experience, foreign firms are more successful at the art of interpreting the permissible, which is one of the reasons why a local presence is essential to having goods consumed in China. Despite restrictions on distribution and service-sector activities, for example, most firms involved in this study were interpreting their way forward into these areas with tacit central approval (not with explicit blessings). As the general manager of a large American chemical company's China operations noted:

> Getting the laws is doable; interpreting the law is what is difficult. It is hard to get [the authorities] on the record. As an American firm we cannot do anything that is not lawful; but taking advantage of the provisional implementation [of a regulation] is the key to success. Being able to interpret your way through this gray area is the key. At first there may be trial and error, but you need to find the way forward. (#15)

Building Bureaucratic Capacity

The legal professionals involved in this study were in agreement that to become compatible with modern corporate legal norms, the Chinese government requires more and better legal professionals and training. One interviewee (#28) had written papers and held seminars for Ministry of Foreign Trade and Economic Cooperation (MOFTEC) officials on the role of an in-house corporate counsel. Only in 1984 had the State Council decreed that firms were permitted to have corporate lawyers, a fact that reflects the prior focus on rule *by* law, as opposed to rule *of* law.[9] Despite such basic steps, authorities continue to abrogate (or bend) laws and regulations in particular cases with such frequency that the process of building legal competence is compromised.

Only 66 percent of China's judges have a college education, by one estimate (although that is up from 17 percent in 1987);[10] a large percentage have no legal background at all, coming rather from careers with the People's Liberation Army (PLA) or the People's Armed Police. Some may well have strong ties with special interests in the economy, interests that the party bureaucracy is not willing to oppose during China's critical time of social transition. Similarly, *China Daily* reported on 20 June 1998 that only 25 percent of China's 100,000 lawyers had undergraduate degrees. Clearly, specific legal training throughout the gargantuan Chinese bureaucracy will fall short for some time, presenting a major problem for Western firms that want to anchor their operations in solid law.

This has obvious implications for FIE compliance efforts, because investors cannot predict whether the commercial logic of ensuring legal enforcement will prevail or if interlocking relationships will instead prove decisive. China has risked major international embarrassment by abrogating contracts in order to satisfy special interests (in one well-known case, a McDonald's in Beijing was forced to move despite its lease). Yet Chinese leaders are aware that a better legal environment is needed to keep economic development on track, especially in the aftermath of the cronyism-induced Asian financial crisis. While an estimated 60,000 Chinese students are presently enrolled at 300 domestic law schools ("Vital for Market Economy: Lawyer's Education Advancing," *China Daily,* 20 June 1998, page 3), these numbers will only begin to supply China's needs.

Meeting Environmental and Labor Standards

Foreign enterprises in China also have legal liabilities related to environmental and labor obligations. Through the 1980s China promulgated and revised environmental protection laws, and as of 1998 a solid regulatory framework had been elaborated.[11] The problem is not promulgation but implementation. For many Chinese firms under the protection of local governmental entities (or, it is said, in partnership with the PLA), compliance with these seemingly noncommercial objectives is absurdly low, and remedial steps are taken only when cost-neutral (if then). FIEs are more

---

9. *Zhongguo Lushi* (China lawyers), no. 11 (1994), 35–37; cited in Wang (n.d., 45).

10. Stanley Lubman, remarks to the Asia Society (19 April 1997); Lubman (1997, 13–14).

11. In early 1998 the National Environmental Protection Agency (NEPA) was formally upgraded to ministerial status as well.

likely to be held to standards, they are by nature less likely to be coddled by authorities, and they are generally better positioned to afford environmental protection than are domestic firms.

For FIEs with large investments in advanced economic areas, basic environmental standards are today fairly well enforced, and environmental impact assessments are taken seriously in the planning stages (though rarely made grounds for rejecting a project). But otherwise—for many smaller FIEs and outside a handful of localities—enforcement remains lax. Those firms in strictest compliance are likely to have their own reasons for operating to high environmental standards. Some firms from home markets such as the United States and Europe have fears about bad publicity that skirting these obligations in China might bring. And managers at some firms can imagine a time in the future when China will develop a "superfund"-style effort of its own to clean up its environment, complete with "joint and several" liability—a corporate nightmare.

Chinese partners sometimes pressure the joint ventures to avoid the expense of obeying environmental laws and to make other decisions that sap their effectiveness. Once again, the question of who controls the firm becomes crucial, affecting management's ability to make decisions on remediation spending, to process investments, and to choose subcontractors to deal with waste streams, one of the trickiest problems facing foreign firms in China today. Firms interviewed for this study claimed to maintain the same standards in China that they would apply anywhere in the world; but in most parts of China the infrastructure such standards require simply does not yet exist. One supposedly "certified" hazardous waste disposal site sits atop the water table a few miles upstream from populous villages.[12] In practice, conscientious FIEs are simply warehousing toxic wastes that they cannot process themselves, while continuing to search for responsible methods of disposal. That course, though laudable, is quite costly; and one expects that relatively few firms say no to the services of officially approved but incompetent waste disposal agents.

Similarly, FIEs are not always in compliance with Chinese labor regulations, which—like environmental laws—often go underenforced. The manager of a US-owned factory in Shenzhen explained,

> [We] are sticklers for law. The government of Shenzhen says to us, "As long as you have a deal with your [workforce], we don't care whether you are in compliance with official regulations." But we want compliance by the book. I am trying to manage between these two positions. (#19)

Despite his determination to comply with regulations, his factory workforce regularly exceeded overtime limits (see table 3.3). Management is working to bring those numbers down, but mostly for reasons of cost and of work-

---

12. This example was reported by policy analysts at the US Council for International Business, who are helping firms to better grapple with environmental policy issues in China.

place safety, not out of concern for violating Chinese regulations (as indeed they are). No one expects that Shenzhen labor authorities will enforce the labor laws locally, absent any pressure on them to do so. Conditions of noncompliance are, however, a lever that can be used against FIEs on other matters, such as technology transfer or subcontracting arrangements.

As with environmental problems, the greatest threat in the labor area may be aspects of the operation outside the foreign manager's control. FIEs that rely on subcontractors may have little idea of conditions up and down the value chain. Under Chinese law they would be unlikely to face any sanction for the behavior of a subcontractor. However, in the eyes of Western business ethicists those subcontractors' practices may be a foreign investor's responsibility as well. Moreover, their initial negotiated contract may have left foreign firms with limited management power; and ethicists certainly hold them accountable for conditions within their own ventures, even if they claim a lack of complete venture control—especially of labor.

Two difficult questions confront FIEs on labor policies. First, how much diligence should be expected of them in discovering abusive practices? And second, how far ought FIEs to go in promoting social policies to aid the workers in their sphere of influence? Like tracing waste streams, monitoring and enforcing compliance with labor standards among subcontractors can be difficult in practice. The sourcing of intermediate inputs can be highly decentralized, making full audits next to impossible. Clothing company Levi Strauss, which withdrew from China on labor rights grounds in the early 1990s and has since returned, sent auditors to inspect 700 contractors worldwide once it decided to commit itself seriously to social activism (Santoro 1998, 39). But this action is extraordinary and costly; and it represents an investment in image that is more clearly justified on commercial grounds for brand names such as Levi's than for the great majority of manufacturers. Codes of conduct regarding employees vary widely in ambition. No consensus exists on this question, even among labor advocates; it seems reasonable to permit FIEs some latitude in deciding how intimately involved with their workers social lives to become.

In general, as FIEs plan for legal compliance with environmental and labor regulations, the threats to predictability come either from the long-term changes that will alter domestic enforcement or from non-Chinese auditors and activists seeking to pressure investors to act in particular ways. The dearth of active Chinese enforcement in these areas has made the work of these activists assume greater relative importance, creating a conflict of interest for firms that would prefer to uphold standards but that must cope with intense competition and low margins in the Chinese market. Some firms in that developing country are reluctant to embrace symbolic gestures that embody the sensibilities of the advanced industrial nations but have no impact in China (beyond antagonizing leaders). Despite the obvious temptation to cut corners, the majority of firms examined chose to comply with higher environmental and labor standards, at higher cost—mostly, it seemed, out of (first world) habit.

Pursuing Recourse

Disputes between firms and buyers, suppliers, and service providers over contracts and payment are very common in China, as elsewhere. Intellectual property protection issues and conflicts between firms and their employees also arise regularly. By far the most common solutions to these problems are administrative or informal remedies, which rely on local brokers and authorities to use their relationships to resolve disputes. But the number of cases brought to more formal proceedings is increasing in part because FIEs are writing precise instructions on arbitration or litigation venues into their contracts. Thanks to such drafting, the China International Economic and Trade Arbitration Commission (CIETAC) now claims to have the second heaviest caseload in the world, while official yearbook statistics show civil and economic cases resolved legally in China to run into the millions (see *China Statistical Yearbook*, 1997, 741–43). Regardless of the quality of resolution in court cases—which still often leaves much to be desired—their sheer volume is significant and demonstrates a clear trend.

Structuring Contracts

Interviewees stressed the importance of both the contract establishing the venture and contracts governing individual transactions; such emphasis contradicts the position that the legal system does not really matter or deserve much attention. FIE establishment has been discussed at various points in this study, and poorly negotiated contracts have often diminished opportunities for recourse later on. They can interfere with the venture's decisions on staffing, incentives, dividend allotment, sourcing, and technology use. Interviewees identified haste, poor information, ignorance, and fatigue as reasons for accepting contracts that were not well designed to protect the foreign investor. Not least, some had assumed that the legal regimes in China were not worth wasting energy on (an attitude particularly common among Japanese respondents).

There is increasing evidence that the structure of the contract does matter. Several factory managers (e.g., ##20, 26) expressed regrets about not having pursued specific goals in the contract, particularly influence over employee salaries and better control over their Chinese partner's access to sensitive technological data. Legal practitioners have stressed the growing utility of properly structured contracts (see Lubman 1998, 38–44). Setting aside the obvious question of securing managerial control (which would in fact obviate some of the need for legal recourse), instructions for procedures to resolve disputes seem to be particularly important.

Expatriates identified four elements to this task. First, disputes must be referred to the appropriate forum; for example, certain of the arbitration boards set up in China (as discussed below) have reputations for greater fairness than others. Second, it is crucial that they be referred to the most effective body of governing laws. For many ancillary contract matters, though not for the establishment of the venture itself, foreign legal codes (including US codes) can be specified. Third, reasonable time limits must be specified for each stage of resolution prior to litigation. Without such limits, it was observed, Chinese parties were known to keep disputes at the conciliation stage indefinitely. And fourth, interviewees noted that investors must be aware that even well-structured contracts can be abrogated by powerful special interests.

Conflict Resolution Prior to Litigation

Interviewees discussed five types of disputes:

- intrafirm management disputes,
- firm-employee problems,
- firm-firm disputes between commercial parties,
- firm-consumer problems, and
- conflicts between the firm and authorities at various levels.

The case studies suggest that problems currently amenable to legal methods of recourse are mostly those between firm and employee, between firm and firm over intellectual property and payments, and to a lesser extent between firm and consumer over product liability. Relying on the legal system to settle intrafirm disputes among partners or disputes with authorities is generally avoided, as local partners and authorities can influence adjudicators and can potentially damage vital relationships. Foreign investment bureaus increasingly try to resolve firm-authority altercations, but their efforts almost always involve the alternative to legal recourse: administrative remedy (i.e., settling a problem in the proverbial smoke-filled back room).

Foreign firms have two legal remedies (short of litigation): consultation and conciliation (mediation) or arbitration. The first, which is less formal, requires the express consent of all parties to the dispute. The second, once agreed to in the contract terms, is supposed to be compulsory and binding.

Mediation services have sprung up in many commercial areas where FIEs gather, particularly in the special economic zones and in provincial capital cities. For example, Jilin Province with national guidance has developed a conciliation center (see their website at http://www.jl.org/ccpit/center). Mediation of this sort is either stipulated in the contract or agreed to by all parties after a dispute arises. Conciliators grapple with the same broad slate of commercial disputes that arbitrators do. In Jilin, the directors of the conciliation center are also heads of the local FDI bureau, the People's Courts at several levels, and other trade bodies. Interviewees (e.g., #7) reported that following a number of successful arbitration and litigation proceedings, conciliation and mediation services were being taken more seriously as an attractive alternative to more formal recourse. For now though, conciliation is usually only the first step in the process of resolving disputes, as it results in decisions that are not binding.

Arbitration is largely the purview of the China International Economic and Trade Arbitration Commission (CIETAC), a quasi-official body that serves to resolve commercial disputes with an international aspect.[13] Though when it was first resurrected in the 1980s after a 30-year holiday it was derided for its partiality, CIETAC is regarded as more objective today. It has units in Beijing, Shanghai, and Shenzhen, and prominent Chinese and non-Chinese sit on its panels. The commission's Shanghai branch has addressed joint venture and cooperation contracts, international purchase and sales contracts, machinery import contracts, and construction deals gone bad.[14] Firms foreign and domestic both make use of the commission's services. Parties to a contract either stipulate in that contract to resolve conflicts at CIETAC or jointly submit in writing to the commission after a dispute arises. Findings are binding and—in theory—cannot be appealed by either side. As China is a party to the 1958 New York Convention on International Arbitration, CIETAC decisions involving non-Chinese firms can be registered for enforcement in 80 countries worldwide.

While CIETAC is useful and operates in a recognizably Western style,[15] it has no power of *enforcement*; for that, plaintiffs must apply to the intermediate People's Court in the jurisdiction of the losing party. Whether the court will accept the application or not is another question, one that can start the dispute all over again and dilute the effectiveness of CIETAC's decisions. While a People's Court is not supposed to obstruct the findings of the commission, innumerable delaying tactics can be employed to serve a special interest. Moreover, there is evidence that Chinese courts

---

13. Paglee (1998) points out that arbitration of contracts governed by Chinese law does not have to take place in China any longer; they can be referred to almost any national jurisdiction. However, if such recourse is in the establishment contract then it must obviously be approved by examining authorities, who might object at the behest of a Chinese partner.

14. See the Shanghai Commission's website at http://www.china-collection.com/shanghai/ccpit/cietac.htm.

15. Though unlike its Western equivalents, CIETAC has powers of investigative discovery, or at least can make independent inquiries. See "Arbitration—Refusal to Enforce CIETAC Award in Hong Kong," *Asian Maritime and Trade Newsletter*, April 1997, at http://www.cliffordchance.com/library (under "Newsletters").

can reject CIETAC decisions. Paglee (1998) reports cases of Chinese judges finding "fraud" in original venture contract terms that CIETAC did not identify and on that basis reversing decisions, even fining a foreign firm that had prevailed before CIETAC. Similarly, one interviewee (#23) reported the mayor of a major city stepping in and voiding the monetary compensation that a firm had been awarded.

Overall, the interviewees were guardedly optimistic that arbitration was improving, but they believed it imprudent to use arbitration when powerful parties were involved or when the case would attract a lot of attention. These are important reminders that legal institutions for recourse have not fully taken hold and that cronyism can still trump quasi-juridical processes. The most successful cases reported involved disputes with individual employees over contract terms and disagreements with other firms over payments due. In order to make these mechanisms more effective still, Chinese authorities must strengthen the link between CIETAC findings and People's Court enforcement, and reduce the tendency for arbitrated cases to be effectively reopened by courts or by individual power holders.

Such capriciousness implicitly adds to the transaction costs of operating in China, making necessary more hedging against legal uncertainties, higher rates of return, shorter time horizons for payment, and shorter credit terms. Local authorities perceive clearly the gains from diluting resolution procedures on a case-by-case basis; the invisible costs borne by the system at large are harder to conceive. The central leadership must take responsibility for this waste, just as it must show initiative in stripping special interests of the subsidies they demand from society in the form of tariffs and exemption from social obligations (e.g., not to pollute).

Litigation

Some firms studied had attempted to resolve problems through litigation (##7, 22, 23, 28). The interviewees described cases involving delinquent payments, disputes with employees, consumer complaints, and piracy of intellectual property. Even firms that had succeeded in litigating stressed that they would not attempt to resolve a first-order problem, such as non-fulfillment of contract obligations by the Chinese venture partner, through the courts, seeking instead an administrative remedy in those cases. The cost of litigation in terms of damaged relationships can overwhelm the value of winning a case. Thus a US commercial attaché advised, "You are an idiot if you go to court with a problem. . . . [I]t is a Pyrrhic victory at best" (#45).

The weaknesses of litigation in China are several. One problem is cultural; China does not have a tradition of civil adjudication, and people generally assume that state judgments are rendered based on personal affiliations, not on the case's objective merits. And as already noted, the court system suffers from the capacity problems that hobble much of the bureaucracy. Moreover, there is a tendency in the court system to avoid strong positions. Judges rely on a heavy consultative process; rather than deciding cases themselves, they confer with senior colleagues. Lower courts consult with higher courts even in advance of hearing cases. "Judges would rather mediate than adjudicate," Lubman notes, "because they do not want to risk being overturned. It is a 'face' type problem" (remarks to the Asia Society, 19 April 1997). Not surprisingly, litigation proceedings were often characterized as corrupt or arbitrary. Even if one wins a case, decisions can be administratively overturned. And even without a formal reversal, getting the decision against the loser enforced, as in arbitration, is a separate challenge.

In sum, litigation has been of limited utility to FIEs so far, but there already exist islands of legal quality on which investors are trying to build. This is likely to increase in the future as competition to secure higher-value-added investment prompts localities to match the legal steps taken elsewhere in China and around the region. The number and quality of lawyers, judges, and statutes must increase accordingly, and superlegal intervention by agents of state power must be limited. Firms themselves (foreign and domestic) must focus on securing legal recourse instead of concentrating on administrative remedies. All this will take time, but progress is already being made. For example, in a highly publicized case Eli Lilly plans to appeal to China's Supreme Court to protect its intellectual property rights over the antidepressant Prozac, and other firms will be watching the outcome closely.

Intellectual Property Rights (IPR) Protection

Protecting intellectual property rights involves both legal obligations to the state and legal agreements with private parties. Transfers of foreign technology have been essential to China's economic reform and development since 1979. Leaders have implicitly and explicitly aimed at promoting technology acquisition as they invited foreign participation in the economy. As discussed, the foreign role has gradually shifted from "cooperate inside, compete outside," to "compete everywhere." Firms have cooperated by sharing managerial and process know-how, hard technology, and intangible property such as trademarks. FIEs are still eager to bring technology to China, but more than ever they intend to use it to compete domestically, not just to barter their way to a designated local niche and access to cheap Chinese labor. If Chinese intellectual property and technology protection practices do not keep up with FIE needs, they risk discouraging instead of facilitating FDI.

Management control over the venture is essential to secure control over technology transfer. The Guidelines on foreign investment explicitly state the preferences to be extended to firms that transfer higher technology, indicating China's degree of willingness by sector to cede independence to the potential FIE in order to assuage concerns about piracy. Once again, pressure can be applied on foreigners not only during the process of establishing the venture but also when a firm seeks new approvals down the road—to recapitalize the venture, for example. The rise in applications for the use of wholly owned foreign enterprise (WOFE) investment structures in recent years reflects—in part—foreign investors' awareness that good intentions are no match for proprietary control. Chinese central authorities are aware that permitting WOFEs is the price to be paid for encouraging the transfer of more sophisticated technology.

Chapter 2 described in detail the trade-offs and characteristics of the establishment negotiation. The point was made that usually the first priority of a potential investor be achieved by compromising on other goals; thus if control over management, including technology policy, were the first priority of a potential investor, then other goals could be compromised in order to achieve it.

Expatriates also report, however, that China's technology regimes are not always strictly enforced. The definition of a "high-technology firm" that qualifies for certain incentives such as preferential tax rates is often liberally interpreted (especially by local authorities, but also by central authorities when a powerful patron intercedes on a venture's behalf). A related point is that the "substantial transformation" of imports needed for them to be considered domestic manufactures often involves lower levels of technology than strictly required. Generally, technology transfer obligations are negotiable.

Bureaucratic pressure to transfer technology is less critical in a firm's overall decision to employ sophisticated machinery in China than is sometimes thought; sometimes more important is the need to raise productivity by raising the level of technology, as discussed in chapters 4 and 5. Effective use of higher technology also requires transfers of soft technology as well as increased capacity to train the labor force that will employ the new machinery. Such innovations require time, and tensions remain widespread between authorities intent on compelling the introduction of higher-tech goods and expatriate managers attuned to the limits of Chinese firms and workers not yet able to put them to effective use. Chinese partners and authorities, often suspecting that foreign firms seek to utilize outdated technologies in China, automatically press for increased transfers as a matter of course, without clearly understanding what they are asking for. As a result, FIE managers observe that technology sometimes goes underused, misapplied and mismatched to China's level of development and thus to the country's needs.

When there is not effective foreign control over the venture, the Chinese partners often share foreign technologies with research institutes designed for reverse engineering. In many firms, this seems to be accepted as the trade-off for access to the domestic market. Some interviewees confided they understood well before the transfer that their technology would be effectively pirated as a result of their bringing it to China. Thus they simply avoided bringing "the crown jewels" to China (#22). Others reported that those responsible for negotiating the technology transfer contract had no idea what they were doing (#20), failing to secure control over technology. Several interviewees (at the factory level) therefore held their firms to blame for many subsequent IPR problems. Another error cited was not checking the backgrounds of Chinese staff with access to sensitive materials. In some cases, other overseas units of the same firm were selling sensitive materials of great use to Chinese competitors directly into China, with no controls, even while the FIE in China was trying to protect the same technology (e.g., the JV manufacturing telecommunications equipment that was discussed in chapter 4).

In their attempts to protect IPR, several firms had explored the utility of formal legal remedies, but most still rely somewhat more heavily on administrative solutions—that is, getting Chinese friends in power to threaten the offenders. The cases described involved trademark and trade name infringement, patent infringement, and wholesale misappropriation of proprietary registered technology by Chinese state companies via technical institutes. Other technology-related problems included trade secrets, industrial designs, and copyright.

Legal recourse was described as a last resort, though it is increasingly tried. Typically, authorities encourage FIEs to approach violators directly and try to negotiate a settlement: for example, by licensing them or making them subcontractors. This appears to be one function of the conciliation and mediation services described in the previous section. FIEs are reluctant to cut deals on these terms; after all, in their view the offender's actions were criminal. Furthermore, a real, contract-oriented commercial disagreement suitable for arbitration seems rarely at issue. Most reported cases involved unrelated parties simply pirating tangible or intangible FIE property. After exhausting mediation avenues (undertaken earnestly or halfheartedly), FIEs have been able with great effort to compel some governmental responses. In some cases, such as the 1995 confrontation over recording products, foreign government pressure has been directly enlisted to force action.[16]

Several interviewees maintained that when an FIE is willing to commit itself to making enforcement a first priority, the firm has a good chance of getting satisfaction. FIEs cannot count on regimes to protect them in the absence of strong external pressure on local enforcement authorities, from allies in central and provincial government, and from local power bases. Trademark and trade name infringement and local smear cam-

---

16. The China head of one large American chemicals company made the point that he would never ask the US government for help with a trademark problem. He believed that Chinese resentment and American clumsiness would lead to more harm than good (#16).

paigns received significant attention from interviewees—more, generally speaking, than "hard" technology issues. For several firms, the rare instances in which they had employed the legal system involved trademark infringement. An illustrative case involved a Chinese start-up firm imitating the trademark of a major US household durables manufacturer. The FIE went through MOFTEC's Business Administration Bureau to stop the infringement and have the pirate's license revoked. The most telling comment came from the FIE's Asia Pacific director: "We don't care about the technology. The barriers to entry in this industry are next to nothing. It was the use of *our name* that irked us" (#25). Reputation can be forever. Trademarks must be defended not because a fly-by-night firm can make money by using an FIE's name for a short while but because as shoddy knockoffs circulate in a market, that name will be damaged.

Thus, the issue of the scope of business arises again. Marketing, sales, and service at the end of the distribution process are points at which IPR violations can be identified, and they are all functions from which FIEs are formally and informally barred—which is clearly frustrating. Several firms complained about Chinese staff breaking away from the venture to establish service businesses offering maintenance of the FIE's products under its name, but not its management, at cut-rate prices. Though FIEs do often participate in after-sales markets through a not illegal but not clearly endorsed organizational stratagem, the ambiguity of their position can leave them at a disadvantage should they wish to contest infringements. Ultimately, only by participating fully in these business activities will firms be able to protect their IPR.

Corruption

"Corruption" is a generic term for a wide array of issues dealt with by foreign enterprises in developing markets such as China. It might encompass bribery, theft, bid rigging, intellectual piracy, and coercive collection engaged in by private parties, public officials at any level, or expatriate businessmen and firms. The universe of the *possibly* corrupt ranges from the clearly corrupt (bribes to get customs duties lowered) to the likely corrupt ("rep fees" to facilitate large government procurement contracts) to the murky (gift giving and extravagant entertainment for official customers or children of high-level officials). FIEs vary tremendously in their attitudes about the ethicality of corrupt practices in developing China. There is no question, however, that many common practices would be judged illegal in Europe or the United States; indeed, many would be so judged in China were the country's own law better enforced.

The greatest share of comments on this subject concerned bribery and bribery-related activities affecting sales and approvals. A significant number of managers bemoaned "consultancies" used as avenues for FIEs to make payments that would be difficult to justify openly; in other words, they sanitized bribes. A case in Wuhan involved purported tax problems discovered with an FIE's value-added tax (VAT) documentation. The problem could be resolved by a consultant paid a fee of 20,000 RMB and put on the firm's staff at 6,000 RMB per year to ensure the firm "doesn't make similar mistakes in the future" (#26). The alternative was a potential fine for tax fraud of up to 3 million RMB. The manager of this venture remarked that he generally tried to resist such demands, which are common, but would negotiate this one down to a onetime 6,000 RMB payment to avoid trouble.[17] During an afternoon meeting at the Wuhan Foreign Direct Investment Administration, ostensibly an ally of FIEs in such disputes, the director promised to find out whether the case "had merit." Such attempts at extortion arise constantly, however, and cannot be aired out with high-level contacts every time. Expatriates save administrative recourse for the more important cases, and either pay up or take their chances ignoring the smaller ones.

Another interviewee complained that the firm's competitors funneled bribes through "nongovernment organizations" to influence bidding—never openly and directly to officials (#4). Yet another noted that as he attempted to get his product onto the official list of merchandise that hospitals were permitted to purchase, he was pressured to buy help from advisors to a provincial Ministry of Health (#7). A factory manager in Shenzhen reported paying $145 a kilogram for an imported input instead of $85 (his estimation of the correct cost including duty) because the Customs Administration was miscategorizing it into a higher tariff class. For the time being, he was paying so that his production line might keep running. The solution proposed to him: a consulting report on whether the rate ought to be lower, to be drafted by friends of the customs authorities (#19). Another interviewee, in Shanghai, who had to purchase "fire-testing equipment" from friends of the fire inspectors, complained that "every watchdog authority has its own consulting firm" (#33).

The manager of a major telecommunications joint venture in southern China explained the nuances of properly funneling money to a customer after the purchase ("a perfectly legal rebate") versus a payment before the purchase ("a bribe, illegal") (#20). Such ambiguity is the modus operandi among FIEs today: the key is to legitimize practices that would be considered plainly corrupt at home, because otherwise it would be impossible to operate in China at all. In this case the "rebates" were 3 percent of

---

17. The business literature is full of these stories. For example, the EIU's *Business China* (4 August 1997, 2) recounts the tale of a Shanghai office building constructed by foreign investors. They were compelled to buy 24 fire doors for their facility from a subsidiary of the Shanghai Fire Department. They proceeded to throw these away and purchase another set from a reputable foreign manufacturer.

the sales price—a not inconsiderable expense in an industry in which overcapacity has already cut profit margins to a minimum; but managers act as though there is little alternative.

Rep fees are widespread. Payments are generally made through "black accounts" that are not registered to the FIEs, and local partners or compradors handle these transactions. American firms in particular are well versed in skirting legality, as violation of the Foreign Corrupt Practices Act (FCPA) can cause them trouble at home. The president of Asia Pacific operations for a big American manufacturer stated:

> Any formal sales reps must sign our FCPA documentation. There are very few of those, though, usually only attached to a big deal. Dealers [who handle most sales and service] are independent businessmen. We don't have control over their business behavior. We try to explain to them the long-term value of the FCPA, but we are not convinced that China is going to have the same ethics and values as us. Plus, we don't see much risk from exposure [of these practices] here. (#25)

Overall, the managers interviewed seemed more concerned about avoiding a reputation as a firm that could be easily shaken down for payoffs than about compliance with home-country anticorruption statutes such as the FCPA. A regime imposed from abroad and aimed at bribery is likely to have little effect over and above the inherent logic among firms to avoid corruption. In fact, several American managers even pointed to the FCPA as a useful excuse to promote anticorruption objectives within their firms, though they did not perceive it as a serious compliance threat.

Some interviewees tempered the general indictment of corruption in China, making two main points. First, some suggested that the corruption problems were more payee driven than official (#4). "Foreigners are often the worst," this executive reported, noting that most of the bribery he hears about comes from competitors trying to sway the bidding for large projects. The other main contrarian argument posits a valuable role for illegality. "There is corruption here, but that needs to be defined in clearer terms. It can be an implicit pricing mechanism; sometimes corruption is useful" (#5). In this view, the market remains so distorted in China (in terms of prices, waiting times for approvals, salaries, and the like) that including corruption brings the costs closer to the real value of goods and services than would otherwise be the case. This is an intriguing possibility and certainly there is evidence for it, such as the movement of exchange rates toward the black-market precursor to the "swap rate" in 1994. Basu and Li (1994) have argued that corruption can serve to "buy out" entrenched bureaucracies that would otherwise impede progress, for example.

Kim Elliott's *Corruption and the Global Economy* (1997) brought together diverse essays on the corruption phenomenon. Several suggest that despite the obvious severity of corrupt practices in a market such as China's, there are several reasons to temper efforts to make this issue a concern of multilateral economic forums such as the WTO. As Rodrik (1997a) notes, first, the corporate use of campaign contributions in many industrialized nations to gain access to key leaders in a position to help companies secure contracts and licenses is too similar to some corrupt developing-world practices to permit comfortable finger-pointing. Second, Rodrik observes that corruption problems affect domestic firms no less than foreign ones, thereby undercutting the argument that corruption denies FIEs the spirit of national treatment (the letter of the principle, to date, applies only to traded products, not investment). Third, he fears that admission of corruption as a legitimate area for multilateral intercession would naturally lead to activism on issues such as (for example) labor standards, which share the deep social roots of corruption problems and which in China would prove equally intractable at this juncture.

Rauch (1997), in a companion paper, explores corruption's roots in bureaucratic processes. His evidence suggests a relationship between bureaucratic structure and outcomes in bureaucratic performance. The argument complements the present study, which identifies transitional factors that are less amenable to foreign policy pressure and thus should not be targeted in negotiations with Chinese leaders. China is rife with influence peddling by officials below the national level who are embedded in a structure that nurtures corruption; thus, only political reforms from within China, not foreign pressure, can accelerate anticorruption reforms. As FIEs act increasingly like "Chinese" companies, they will have a bigger role in fostering change. The commercial logic of avoiding corruption should eventually translate into pressure for stronger anticorruption strategies domestically.

Superlegal Privileges

Inseparable from a discussion of rights and obligations in China's legal system are the privileges and perks conferred outside the law. Most foreign enterprises support efforts to promote the rule of law in China, in a manner that will secure their business and investment. Few if any, however, are keen to see withdrawn the special incentives, advantages, exemptions, and entitlements that they have won. Such patronage is the major currency of politics in China today, as it has been historically. In fact, often expatriates describe with pride the friendships and special dispensations they have secured for their firms in China. Few see the irony in bragging about connections right after railing against corruption and cronyism.

Four kinds of superlegal privilege, examined below, emerged from the interviews: failure to enforce laws, deliberate failure to reform laws, patron-client protection, and market share allocation. Because these privileges are informal and nontransparent, they can be withdrawn arbitrarily—a possibility that must be figured into an estimation of their value; but on balance they greatly enhance an FIE's standing.

The most frequently described upside of China's incomplete legal environment was spotty or absent enforcement of laws and regulations, as frequently shown in earlier chapters. One cannot simply take the letter of the law as a guide to the fortunes of foreign firms. Failing to enforce laws is not the same thing as rescinding onerous or discriminatory regulations. Hazards abound when firms must rely on the favor of authorities who look the other way.

Since reforms began in 1979, Chinese law has been refashioned and upgraded in bits and pieces. Along the way, many foreign firms managed to secure rights that exceeded those available by law or those enjoyed by other firms. Some foreign retailers, for example, have been able to open operations that regulations seem to ban; and many incumbent firms operate for years while their competitors fail to secure licenses.

Incumbent firms often have an incentive to counteract the reforming instincts of the central authorities, and their incumbency usually provides the flow of cash needed to express their preference. While reform might lead to regulations applied uniformly—making administration more efficient and equitable and expanding competition to enhance aggregate economic welfare—existing firms may prefer the status quo. Perhaps they seek special provisions grandfathering in their privileges, or perhaps they wish to block the changes altogether. In either case, the result is at odds with reform. As the treasury liaison to Beijing from one OECD trading partner sympathetically noted:

> The incumbents see enforcement of the law as unfair. But it's understandable that China's leaders should try to tighten [compliance]. They need to build up infrastructure, and that will take [better tax collection efficiency], and that will mean cracking down on loosely treated firms. (#50)

The overseeing authority to which a firm is responsible can be a powerful ally in China. Interviewees reported gaining major increases in production quotas (#32, helped by certain development zone authorities), favorable changes in duty rates (#26, assisted by an office in interior China promoting foreign investment),[18] suppression of local rent seeking (#13), acceleration of payments (#15), and allocation of market share (##20, 33). A very important service that patrons provide is directing investors toward viable commercial opportunities, for they know where the sale is not already tacitly earmarked for someone else's favorite. In this way, they save the FIE "immeasurable time" (#25). Patrons can help see to it

---

18. Naughton (1996a, table 3) calculated that during the first half of 1996 the rate of imports coming in under concessionary terms exceeded 61 percent: i.e., only 39 percent of all imports ended up paying any duty at all. Moreover, the value of customs duties actually collected as a percentage of the value of imports (which does not include smuggled imports, surely a not insignificant addition) had sunk to 4 percent (table 4). The spread between these numbers raises many questions. Clearly, however, patrons play a very important role in getting clients exempted from import duties.

that the "right" interpretations of the law or implementing regulations are made (#28). In short, "You are bound to have nontransparency if you don't have relationships" (#36).

Several interviewees felt that finding the right patron (or patrons, as both central and local connections are important) was the single most critical determinant of the success of the venture. Not surprisingly, then, several market entry consultants had some advice on the art of picking a patron wisely: consider as a joint venture partner an entity related to the People's Liberation Army (#88). In exchange for a share of profits and perhaps other fees, such a high-status silent partner might be an excellent aid to getting approvals, moving products through customs quickly, and collecting accounts due. While one applauds the creativity of entrepreneurs who cut through red tape, the potential for effective immunity of large segments of the economy from central regulatory authority is troubling, both for commercial and for national security reasons. In addition, patrons ask for as much as they provide, a truth that has somehow surprised many FIEs in recent years. More study needs to be done on how a patron-client relationship that can so boost the FIE's legal standing in early years evolves over time, and on whether there is such a thing as graduating to independence from under the patron's wing.

The habit of doling out favors or enticing special investors with allocated market shares threatens to distort market structure and thus diminish the competitiveness of an economy. It is the antithesis of the culture of fair competition that reformers are advocating. While its extreme form consists of direct, nontransparent assignment of sales volumes, markets can also be allocated by discriminating among firms in terms of the rights they are granted to expand their scope or scale of operations.

Analysis

Some Observations

Several conclusions flow from this discussion. First, it must be acknowledged that to date, the volume of foreign investment flowing into China has been so significant that it seems to put in question certain presumptions about advanced legal regimes being essential. Either the flows of FDI into China are not typical of what is expected, or the investment environment in China is not as chaotic as sometimes suggested—or both, which in fact is the case. The biggest contributors to China's FDI have been ethnic Chinese with close ties to China and a strong, patriotic desire to contribute to the mainland's development. Increasingly, however, investors from dissimilar cultures whose profit-maximizing intentions have little personal basis have invested in China; thus the nature of the money flowing into the country is becoming less exceptional. In addition, this chapter has described numerous ways in which FIEs pursue predictability for their investment and seek recourse when they have problems. China's reputation for capriciousness somewhat exceeds the reality.[19]

Thus the vitality of commerce in the People's Republic and the volume of FDI flowing in indicate that China's legal system deficiencies do not fatally impede investment. Nor is it clear that better legal regimes would lead to still more commerce; the prodigious rush to invest in China is due in part to foreigners' fear—discussed here and in chapter 2—that the inadequate legal system could permit those who enter early to secure unassailable positions in the Chinese market. The extent of superlegal privileges lends credence to those concerns. The presence of a Western-style legal system might have inclined FIEs to pace their entrance to China more carefully. Such a system probably also would have afforded greater opportunities for entrenched domestic interests to launch temporary restraints against new competition.

While the effects of China's inadequate legal regime on FDI volume are thus murky, its effects on transaction costs are clear: they are higher wherever predictability and redress are absent. Shang-Jin Wei (1997) calculates that an increase in corruption from the level existing in Singapore to that common in Mexico implies an added "tax" of over 20 percent and that such costs are just as detrimental to East Asian economies such as China's. One example is the opportunity cost of constant schmoozing to secure the relationships needed to guard one's business. Inadequate legal regimes mean less efficient markets than otherwise might exist, as the pricing needed to cover transactional problems adds costs for all consumers (just as a surge in car insurance fraud in the United States adds marginally to everyone's insurance bill).

Second, the legal tactics that FIEs employ in China—even if they approximate Western regimes in the predictability they offer—remain an exotic variant on OECD-nurtured norms. As such, they raise ethical and commercial questions. They make it difficult to integrate China-based operations with global units (and thus to rotate talent through China to build an international corps). That the local marketplace functions in this exceptional manner will also hamper indigenous businesses as they expand abroad, as well as regulators who seek to participate more actively in international economic rule-making forums.

The third conclusion runs counter to the second: a renaissance of jurisprudence is taking place in China, and the trend is convergence toward international standards. The capacity of and interest in the mediation, arbitration, and litigation systems have grown considerably over a rela-

---

19. A significant share of total FDI into China is either money that is funneled out and then back into the country to qualify for incentives and letters of credit or earnings that are retained and reinvested by FIEs in China, in part because they fear being seen to "extract" too much from China's developing marketplace.

tively short period of time. Foreign (and domestic) enterprises are testing these new avenues with increasing boldness. Some are finding that the threat of such proceedings alone is sufficient to compel settlement of cases out of court. It is possible that a functioning legal system will be in place in just a few more years.[20] While providing the training and building the capacity needed are huge tasks, many foreign firms are already leading the way.

Fourth, while some foreign governments (especially the United States) have ceaselessly called for the rule of law in their negotiations with China, foreign firms cultivate special relationships and deals with government entities at all levels. A conflict will remain for some time between the desire of foreign governments to support the short-term needs of their firms, even if that means embracing superlegal privileges, and the need to support rollback of these privileges so that a reliance on impersonal law can emerge over the long term.

One final observation is that rising prosperity is connected to broad societal change, including legal reform. A number of interviewees stressed that they did not expect significant legal changes until China grows wealthier. More wealth creates more transactions among firms, individuals, and governments. The need to resolve natural conflicts over transactions leads to greater interest in rule of law; thus the WTO will be needed to mediate the conflicts between China and its trading partners as the volume of trade continues to swell. Similarly, as people acquire greater material security and property, they become more concerned with protecting it; insulated from a primary preoccupation with shelter and food, they are able to focus on more abstract goods, such as "fairness."

As per capita GDP exceeds about $5,000, environmental pollution tends to fall off: unbridled growth appears less desirable than cleaner air and water (Grossman and Krueger 1993). Change is also driven by economic forces in the legal sphere, as a senior banker in Hong Kong pointed out: no matter how the Chinese government officials feel about a more or a less liberal legal system, the imperatives of commerce will leave them with no choice. "The legal system needs to be more efficient at serving business. That is a practical matter, not an ideological one" (#51).

Some political scientists point out that this progression need not *necessarily* take place. For example, Pearson (1997) presents evidence that new middle classes in Latin America and in East Asia have tended not to build democracy or rule of law. Rather, they often support authoritarian rulers who keep labor docile and emphasize stability that makes possible further economic growth. Pearson finds similarities between China and these nations. The newly rich urban Chinese may be more interested in

---

20. That is, a legal system offering commercial predictability and recourse. Reforming laws and legal structures to provide *civil rights* 27

traditional clientism and collusion with ruling officials than in legal and democratic reforms.

But growing per capita income in China undoubtedly is helping to bring faster legal and political reform; indeed, it is widely believed by expatriates to be sufficient for effecting such changes. This view has become the standard wisdom among US policymakers as well. For example, in her testimony to the Senate Finance Committee on China's most favored nation (MFN) status (10 June 1997), Secretary of State Madeleine Albright argued that

> economic openness can create conditions that brave men and women dedicated to freedom can take advantage of to seek change. It diminishes the arbitrary power of the state over the day to day lives of its people. It strengthens the demand for the rule of law. It raises popular expectations. And it exposes millions of people to the simple, powerful idea that a better way of life is possible.

Such logic has been central to the decision to extend MFN to China despite ongoing value-laden disagreements on matters such as human rights and intellectual property. Prosperity, the US Congress has concluded consistently, is the best way to transplant values. For European and Japanese foreign policymakers, this truth has been self-evident; they find no need for grueling and divisive annual debates on the matter.

Transitional and Self-Imposed Factors in Legal Regimes

There is an important transitional aspect to the general evolution of China's legal system. As the country grows richer and market transactions become more prevalent, the need for a more mature legal regime will grow as well. Six of the eleven themes discussed in this chapter possessed a transitional aspect: securing predictability and ensuring compliance, bridging gaps in the law, interpreting ambiguous laws and regulations, contributing to capacity building, and dealing with corruption (see table 6.1). While these issues are shaped by policy, no amount of good governance could have averted them entirely. In fact, given the near total absence of a legal framework at the start of reforms, the achievements thus far—though incomplete—are fairly impressive. If further progress is made at the same pace, investors will not be disappointed.

The evolution of dispute resolution and litigation mechanisms is in part a transitional matter as well. Recruiting, training, overseeing, and managing the armies of civil servants required to meet China's need to provide legal recourse will take many decades. The enormity of this task— the size of the market to be managed and the rapid pace of change— also limits the ability of the Chinese leadership to address corruption. Of course, Chinese authorities are ultimately responsible for the nation's regular position at the bottom of qualitative indices of commercial environ-

Table 6.1 Roundup of issues: law

Issue	Category	If policy . . . Level	Priority
Access to content of laws	Policy	Central, provincial, local	Low-medium
Bridging gaps in the law	Transitional, policy	Central, provincial	Medium
Interpreting the law to advantage	Transitional, policy, self	Central, provincial, local	High
Building bureaucratic capacity	Transitional, self		
Environmental and labor compliance	Policy, self	Central, provincial, local	Low-medium
Structuring contracts	Policy, self	Central, provincial, local	Medium
Conflict resolution	Policy, self, transitional	Central, provincial, local	Low
Litigation	Policy, self, transitional	Central, provincial, local	Low
Protecting intellectual property	Policy, self	Central, provincial, local	Medium
Moderating corruption concerns	Policy, self, Transitional	Central, provincial, local	Medium
Securing superlegal privileges	Policy, self, market structure	Central, provincial, local	Medium-high

ment; but any regime would find it difficult to deal with these issues during a period of reform.

In the legal realm, as elsewhere, FIEs are not powerless and passive units merely acted on by forces beyond their control; their own choices affect their experiences in important ways. As they interpret laws to legitimate activities, build bureaucratic capacity, and devise strategies for managing compliance with volatile regulatory areas (especially environment and labor issues), foreign investors make their own beds. Each of the recourse-oriented factors considered here—structuring contracts; using mediation, arbitration, and litigation; and protecting intellectual property rights—is partially attributable to choices that firms make about how litigious to be. Conversely, firms are willing, even eager, to embrace superlegal privileges in order to secure the recourse and predictability (not to mention commercial advantages) that they require. Such willingness undercuts efforts to strengthen the rule of law in China, as firms with informal sources of protection grow reluctant to trade them for the promise of formal reforms to come. Their reluctance is ultimately short-sighted, however; as previous chapters have shown, the decision to sacrifice latitude for administrative comity is returning to haunt many firms now keen to expand the scope of their operations, often years after they initiated their partnerships.

That there is a self-imposed element to FIEs' corruption concerns may be the most controversial observation of this study, at least from the perspective of the firms that took part. Some managers vehemently insist that any active role of European or American firms is dwarfed in importance by the indigenous factors. If one views the marketplace as a whole, they are largely correct, if for no other reason than the still-small size of foreign involvement in China in absolute terms. However, focusing on the limited regions where FIEs still spend most of their energies, one finds that foreign investors have an important impact. They must daily either consent to or reject corrupt practices, petty or grave—and they display a range of possible responses. While not automatically passing judgment on practices that would be condemned in a developed economy, one must note that FIEs have choices to make and that some of these choices can contribute to the cloud of corruption often observed to hang over China's commercial environment.

Policy and Market Structure Factors

Aside from the area of building bureaucratic capacity, in which FIEs take a proactive role, every issue in this chapter is shaped by Chinese government policy. From the most general issues such as passing new laws and enabling a soft political landing through gradual legal liberalization to detailed management of the use of arbitration boards, the plans of leaders, national to local, shape the legal environment. But just as important, in all cases but one policy variables are not alone in determining the legal problems that FIEs confront. The areas of highest concern for most firms appear to involve interpreting the law most advantageously and securing the superlegal privileges that undergird their operations: these do not exactly constitute a rousing call for help from foreign governments to push for the rule of law in China.

The influence of Chinese policy on the legal dimension of commercial activities in China differs in character for FIEs and for domestic firms on its face. Yet these conditions are not necessarily more onerous for foreign firms than for domestic ones. In fact, the foreign sector generally enjoys superior protection in terms of contract enforceability and other elements of commercial law, presenting an interesting case for future WTO consideration. The huge flows of FDI into China in recent years must also be taken into account: apparently, firms are satisfied with the level of predictability and recourse they can secure, despite the lack of formal legal rights.

This view of the policy dimension may temper attacks on the quality of reforms of Chinese commercial law, but the tendency to base the system on superlegal privileges implies market structure problems that cannot be taken lightly. Governments at all levels in China have relied heavily on incentives to attract foreign investors, offering a basket of privileges that directly or indirectly provide preferential access to markets, or even allocate market shares. By design or by accident (and inefficiency), segmented markets are generally far from airtight; that is, there is generally a level of competition in China not characteristic of tightly controlled marketplaces, though fair contestability is clearly not the norm either. With each year that privilege rather than real legal reform is relied on, however, the picture stands to deteriorate: anticompetitive rights will tend to be bought by firms, and consumers and others who will suffer from collusive or monopolistic behavior will be unable to appeal through a legal system. Contemplating that possibility, China's seniormost leaders, Western officials, and expatriates alike may find it advantageous to make common cause.

7

Conclusions and Policy Recommendations

[I]n the semireformed system both the major cities and the small townships are developing more a negotiated economy than a competitive market-driven system. Over the long run, this situation is reducing competition and restricting the size of real markets for many goods and services. This system is also creating powerful vested interests at local levels in which local officials and enterprises collude to take resources out of the larger system to serve their own interests. This starves both the central government and the agricultural sector for necessary funds and amounts to a major change in the PRC's overall political economy. Wrestling with this problem without reimposing centralized administrative controls over the economy will be one of the difficult issues confronting Beijing during the coming years.

Kenneth Lieberthal (1995, 265)

For the United States, managing commercial relations with China is likely to become a more complicated affair in the coming years. In the 1990s US policy toward postreform China has revolved around well-recognized modules: Taiwan relations, intellectual property piracy, human and labor rights, missile proliferation, and Congress's annual debate over renewal of most favored nation (MFN) status. A growing bilateral trade imbalance has begun to capture our attention and prompt calls for "market access," but conclusions about causes and implications have relied more on analogies with Japan than on a meaningful examination of the forces shaping the Chinese marketplace.

The analysis in this study explores the experiences of foreign firms in China in order to demonstrate that our commercial concern with China cannot stop at the border. In fact, analysis must go beyond central Chinese domestic policy. Impediments to China's ability to absorb goods have more fundamental causes: the transition from statism to market, industrial market structure problems related to underregulated capitalism, and the behavior of foreign enterprises themselves as they wrestle to secure a position in what may someday be the world's largest marketplace. These factors have been at work at each stage of the value chain within the foreign-invested enterprises (FIEs) in the chapters of this study.

Despite this multiplicity of factors, US policy has generally treated China as a market to be pried open through policy pressure. Perhaps that is unsurprising: China's foreign policy authorities cultivate an image of being gatekeepers to a monolithic entity that would jump if the mandarins so demanded. While negotiations over China's World Trade Organization (WTO) accession approach their 12th year with a focus on, for example, domestic trading rights for foreign enterprises, many (if not most) of those foreign ventures already dabble in such activities. Central announcements of a smaller bureaucracy, fiscal stimuli, enhanced tax collection, and anti-smuggling and corruption campaigns are diluted by foot-dragging at the local level. Policy analysts in Washington admonish trade negotiators to make negotiations over performance requirements their first priority, but again the expatriate managers themselves confide that such requirements are underenforced and of less concern than issues pertaining to scope of operations and partnering.

This study suggests that Beijing officials prefer at this point to face foreign pressure for concessions on some of these issues rather than admit that some local authorities are already making these changes, ahead of Beijing. Furthermore, the fiction that the old restraints on domestic competition still apply fully provides Beijing with a convenient negotiating chip. Many incumbent foreign and domestic enterprises benefit, insofar as it discourages new entrants and they want no more competition in Chinese markets than they already face. And it is useful for US and other negotiators who have a solid objective to target in bilateral meetings—a target that is already half achieved. However, it is dangerous to ignore or forget the ramifications of the central authorities' inability to enforce trading limits on FIEs partnering with local authorities and their unwillingness to acknowledge these practices for fear of losing internal control.

Not all the problems that foreign enterprises encounter in China can be addressed by new policy set forth from Beijing, even if those authorities are willing to meet foreign demands. Throughout this study nonpolicy factors influencing FIEs have been considered alongside policy concerns. Table 7.1, which summarizes the results, demonstrates that there is much more at work in the Chinese marketplace than policy matters alone.

Table 7.1 Roundup of FIE issues

Stage	Transitional	Self	Policy	Market
Negotiation and establishment	6	9	12	3
Human resources and staffing	9	5	9	0
Productivity and running the plant	9	6	10	4
Ex-factory issues, selling and service	6	5	8	1
Legal issues	6	9	10	1
Total	**36**	**34**	**49**	**9**

Conclusions

Chapter 1 argued that the United States needed a new China policy, one capable of addressing the changing profile of the Chinese state and economy and thus US interests. The observations of our set of expatriate interviewees have now been exhaustively laid out in chapters 2 through 6. The interviews were not focused on the ten general questions proposed in chapter 1 but on microlevel commercial concerns and topics. For example, rather than being asked directly "How compatible is China's investment environment with international expectations?" the interviewees discussed their individual experiences and assessments (see appendix B for a simplified version of the questionnaire). Taken together, however, the collected observations of the foreign firms and managers provide much useful information for approaching those larger questions, considered in detail below.

How Compatible Is China's Present Investment Environment with International Expectations?

There is no one answer to the question of what level of Chinese economic openness is acceptable to the major trading nations today, whether the context is preconditions for WTO accession (the target event on which discussions of China's openness have focused) or bilateral policy. The United States, Japan, and the European Union have all expressed different opinions.[1]

Investment conditions are not fully covered by the WTO, it should be stressed; while the Trade-Related Investment Measures (TRIMs) move in this direction, they are not sufficient. Talks on the Multilateral Agreement

---

1. See articles in *Inside US Trade*: e.g., EU-China WTO Principles Include New Understanding on Tariff Cuts, 17 October 1997, 3–4; EU, China Target Late 1999 for Conclusion of WTO Entry Negotiations, 19 June 1998, 8–9; and Japan, China Announce Preliminary Market Access Deal in WTO Talks, 5 September 1997, 4–5.

on Investment (MAI) within the Organization for Economic Cooperation and Development (OECD) have stalled. The international institutions' slow progress on this front belies its importance: a local presence in China is a critical prelude to selling many goods and services of concern to the United States.[2] Failure to establish may be tantamount to a ban on market access. As chronicled particularly in chapter 5, a local presence used to be crucial because restrictions on foreign distribution left an offshore seller without distributors to get their goods to Chinese customers and because of inter- and intraprovincial trade barriers to selling within China. While today this market fragmentation is less acute, and many new distributors are popping up, the quality of their services remains very poor. As competition grows, it is becoming increasingly important that firms manage the quality of their local distribution functions in China. Otherwise, product does not arrive, or is pilfered, or turns up damaged, or else accounts receivable lag because no personal relationship has been established with the consumer. These real problems described by the expatriates underscore the need to permit foreign establishment. They will likely remain even once "state trading" is fully reformed (i.e., when any foreign exporter can sell directly to any Chinese buyer who might want those goods). This study therefore argues that the domestic trading experiences of FIEs is a better gauge of the long-term prospects for trade with China than an assessment of border barriers, and, thus, there must be concern with investment issues beyond those covered by the WTO.

On paper the establishment process in China retains exclusive aspects, but the large volume of utilized FDI demonstrates the country's openness in practice to foreign establishment. Chapter 2 reported expatriates' views on the tendency of local authorities and other partners to undermine the gatekeeping intentions of central authorities. These phenomena led many interviewees to characterize the establishment regime in China as more open than that in Japan or South Korea, where central bureaucrats wield more control over local behavior, even today. This is quite consistent with data on the trade openness of China and its two neighboring countries (see Zhang, Zhang, and Wan forthcoming), where central impotence also results in virtuous outcomes ("virtuous" from a perspective of liberal economics, that is).

Once operating in China, FIEs are exposed to a host of noncommercial forces ranging from partnering pressures to corruption; these certainly would not be considered hallmarks of an open investment environment. Nor would residual restrictions on scope of operation, a critical impediment to efficient plant productivity and ex-factory operations. The magnitude of these problems for foreign firms was examined in chapters 4 and

---

2. The United States hopes that China will absorb its own goods, of course; but there is also concern that China absorb the region's specialty offerings, thus avoiding Japan's failure to consume its share of the region's product.

5, which presented a picture of various experiences and outcomes depending on sector, region, and the firm's approach to dealing with China. Overall the trend appears positive if still not progressing nearly fast enough to satisfy either impatient foreign managers or the needs of a country dependent on regular and dramatic marginal growth from its reform efforts. Chapter 6 added the many legal (and superlegal) privileges enjoyed by FIEs to the balance sheet of complaints more often talked about.

Performance requirements, an important topic in assessing developing-country investment conditions today, are often at issue in China. The analysis in chapter 2 suggests that these are less onerous than generally thought for foreign firms in China; in addition, they are shaped considerably by the choices of the firms themselves as they make trade-offs to achieve goals such as superregulatory levels of management control.

Moreover, in assessing China's investment practices, recall that no one can insist on China's matching, say, Hong Kong's standards of compatibility with international expectation. It is accepted that absolute levels of openness differ among nations, reflecting valid cultural choices and differences in level of development. What matters most is whether the domestic environment for investment by foreign firms passes muster in terms of national treatment and most favored nation status.

China illustrates a problem with the national treatment standard required of WTO members: there is no standard of treatment for domestic firms. Indeed, conforming to regulations can be even more onerous for domestic entities than for foreign firms, which as often as not negotiate privileged treatment by using their power to bring money and technology and jobs into the country. The interviews make clear that foreign firms can enjoy a level of independence from state intervention greater than the typical Chinese state-owned enterprise (SOE) can (per the viewpoint of western commercial norms anyway). Foreign managers are generally less concerned about state-controlled firms, which lack independence;[3] instead, they are focusing on the smaller set of private domestic firms with which the FIEs will increasingly compete in China and which may benefit both from managerial flexibility and from favoritism written into the regulations.

Investment treatment for firms no less favorable than that enjoyed by firms from other countries—that is, the MFN principle—is also hard to assess. Particular firms often receive superior treatment, both on a sectoral basis and within sectors. The policy dimensions of these preferences are legitimate concerns in light of some WTO regulations (such as the Subsidies Code), especially as they seek to support particular industries or favor domestic over foreign firms. However, it would be difficult to find a pattern of specifically *country*-oriented investment privilege. Even US

---

3. Foreign firms do not have *competitive* concerns regarding SOEs; however, to the extent that they are given market shares to keep them barely afloat, they displace production by efficient firms (such as FIEs) that would permit economies of scale.

firms reported little discrimination based on their "Americanness," despite threats and tensions over bilateral political flare-ups. To be sure, there do appear to be advantages along ethnic lines, particularly for enterprises of the overseas Chinese. But these can be explained by referring not to government policy but rather to better knowledge of how to work the system. In sum:

- Expatriates report that the ostensible barriers to investment are negotiable and that establishing is generally easier than in other WTO countries—mostly because local authorities undermine central rules.

- An analysis of the national treatment and MFN principle profile of the Chinese investment environment is not in clear contradiction with expectations; but in any case, no multilateral investment agreement yet exists to cover these issues.

- The enforcement of performance requirements in China, one area that is partly (but only partly) addressed by the WTO, is less pernicious than usually thought.

- China has achieved its present, not-too-shabby level of investment openness very quickly and has committed to continue its rapid progress.

Based on these facts—gathered from the study of expatriate perspectives on the ground and from broader data sources—this study would assign China an acceptable grade for its openness to investment.

Why, Given Its Domestic Worries, Should China Care about the Concerns of Foreign Enterprises?

The analysis of commercial issues presented in this study has been focused on foreign firms and managers, and geared toward those in the United States (and other Western countries) who make decisions about business and policy. But the government of China should and must be concerned about the problems of foreign firms, and thus should heed this study, for the five reasons given below. That Beijing most definitely does care about what FIEs have to say also (and significantly) suggests that the interests of FIEs and of home and host governments are interdependent.

First, the flow of foreign direct investment to China is a primary concern; so far these flows have been as much despite central policy as because of it,[4] but the Beijing authorities must now show greater understanding of

---

4. Consider the extent, described in chapters 2, 4, and 5, to which local authorities have made life easier for FIEs, often in contravention of the spirit—if not the letter—of the central authorities' pronouncements on investment policy.

foreign investors' needs. The early frenzy to secure market share as first entrants has given way to more caution, as investors pay more attention to the difficulties of doing business in China. Furthermore, the Asian financial crisis has both made firms more reluctant to invest in developing Asia generally and diminished China's particular utility (i.e., as a base from which to serve high growth in the broader region). This study will aid Chinese officials eager to understand the priorities of foreign investors.

Second, the distinction between Chinese and foreign firms is quickly eroding. As the clear separations between domestic and foreign interests disappear, Chinese authorities must ask a question heard in the West a decade ago: "Who is 'us'?" Increasingly FIEs and Chinese firms are the same; at least, it is increasingly beyond the ability of the Ministry of Foreign Trade and Economic Cooperation to see any difference in microeconomic behavior (and data). With so many of the most admirable and competitive firms active in China either in the foreign-invested sector or inextricably joined in value-chain relationships with FIEs, it is essential that Chinese regulators take cognizance of the problems they face.

Third, Chinese authorities should pay attention to this study because purely domestic Chinese firms are increasingly calling for many of the same reforms that FIEs desire, feeling the same pressures from the market. As privatization and independent management of Chinese firms continue to spread, these calls will only become louder. If Chinese companies are to compete effectively with FIEs either domestically or abroad, they will need a home marketplace that encourages competitiveness through sound regulation. Chapter 4 documented the difficulties of well-trained foreign managers in creating an environment conducive to productivity growth in China; imagine how much harder the task is for those running indigenous enterprises. Chinese authorities can learn much about what they are doing right and wrong for their home firms by listening to the expatriates.

Fourth, China can no longer depend passively on a "propitious external setting" (see Oksenberg, Swaine, and Lynch 1997, 16); it now needs to contribute to the stability of that setting. Neglecting the interests of foreign firms established in China will set home governments in conflict with China and will ultimately call international rules into play. At the least, China must nurture its foreign market access, and that means attending to the concerns of trading partners' firms.

Fifth, and finally, Beijing's technocrats realize that they must deal with these problems because China's economy must become competitive. Enhancing the rule of law, improving distribution efficiency, expanding human resource training programs: these and other requirements that FIEs seek are the reasonable objectives of China's leadership and are essential for a strong, independent China.

That the authorities are indeed paying attention to FIEs' concerns is clear; expatriates stressed that it is much easier to deal with officials today than it was in the past. Furthermore, the FIEs are contributing to building capacity in the bureaucracy to address their own needs (see chapter 6), demonstrating that Chinese authorities both care about those needs and are in fact learning from their foreign investors.

Has China Really Turned a Corner, and What Should Be the Reaction to Its New Leadership?

The expatriate managers supply considerable evidence that China has broken with past economic and political policies in important ways. In 1997 China restored important import duty abatements,[5] agreed to negotiate trading rights and state trading in the context of WTO accession talks, resisted devaluing the renminbi, and accepted a dramatic increase in the number of wholly owned foreign ventures (WOFEs). Cohesive pressures to overstaff have abated to a degree, and performance requirements appear to be stressed less (see chapter 2). Beijing has committed to a crackdown on smuggling and petty corruption even when the army is involved (see chapters 4, 5, and 6 for the productivity, distribution, and legal problems arising from such smuggling).[6] Western firms are being bombarded with resumes from government officials, who are facing a 50 percent reduction in the total size of the Chinese bureaucracy over the coming years. In follow-up discussions, interviewees expressed strong confidence in Zhu Rongji's leadership—a remarkable endorsement in light of their feelings about former prime ministers. Some of the interviewees involved in finance predicted a major change in the terms required for wholesale foreign buyout of major state industries.

Tangible political and economic developments inside and outside China—not least the Asian financial crisis itself—precipitated these new trends. China's closed capital account provided time to strengthen the economy against the causes of the crisis, but the rigidity needed to micromanage capital flows is costly. Leaders must press ahead with bank refinancing, enterprise reform and recapitalization, and liberalization of the financial services sector (which must be opened to foreign participation) even in a time of external instability. Complaints of FIEs reported in chapters 2, 4, and 5 concerning restrictions on firms' financial practices are

---

5. To the extent that these create a disadvantage for domestic firms (and therefore an incentive to "roundtrip" investment), such abatements are not necessarily advisable. However, they do demonstrate a sympathy with the needs of foreign investors and an awareness that standard import duties can be prohibitively high. The next step is to recognize the disproportionate harm they may do to purely domestic firms.

6. From *China News Daily*'s 20 July 1998 edition (citing Agence France-Presse): "In a frank editorial on Thursday, the People's Daily assessed the involvement of party, government and army organizations, as well as judicial and law-enforcement departments, in rampant smuggling and urged 'relentless punishment' (Agence France-Presse, 07/16)."

mounting, and they will only worsen so long as central authorities try to maintain their capital account controls. Foreign direct investment has peaked (for the moment), and some of China's best customers (Japan, Hong Kong) are stymied by their own economic malaise. If China continues to rely on its precarious ability to stave off external financial pressure without structural and regulatory adjustment, new FDI flows will fall significantly.

Chinese leaders are grappling with novel choices; the new China seen during President Clinton's 1998 summit meeting appears to be more than just a stunt for the cameras. Many expatriate managers perceive major changes in policy, practice, and business culture in a variety of commercial settings. This break with the past can be for the good (more open and fair competition) or for the bad (more private collusion and asset stripping). The sea changes that have taken place in China must be recognized to encourage developments in the right direction.

For Chinese leaders, the Asian financial crisis provided a rare glimpse into their own possible future, a moment before they were to jump full swing into the *chaebol*-making business. The lessons have been burned deeply into Chinese thinking: unlike its neighbors, China has a chance to avoid building shiny skyscrapers on a foundation of shaky industrial policy choices. The changes in Chinese intention and perspective must be reflected in US policy to encourage further reform and to best support US firms competing in China's markets.

Will the Chinese Economy Be More Open to Foreign Participation in the Future?

China's economy is strained by rapid growth, rising unemployment, near-critical environmental degradation, and widening gaps in income distribution along regional and urban-rural lines. Many elements of these largely transitional problems (and their policy aspects too) are discussed in chapters 2 to 6 as they relate to FIEs. As best documented in Nick Lardy's *China's Unfinished Economic Revolution* (1998), financial-sector reform is looming as well, after years of deferral. Interlocking nets of nonperforming loans, inadequately funded pension and social welfare pools, increasingly fragile capital markets, and poor domestic banking habits must be dealt with if China is to unlock further productivity growth and resolve its state enterprise paradox (i.e., a growing share of fixed investment is needed to keep increasingly unproductive and obsolete industrial behemoths afloat). Rightsizing a portion of the bureaucracy alone will release perhaps 5 million workers into sluggish labor markets. As evidenced by the difficulties that expatriate managers are encountering in reengineering plant productivity (analyzed in chapter 4), coping with these challenges is an enormous task. In this environment, can China be expected to be a more open marketplace for foreign firms? The answer is yes—and no.

Consider two characteristics of the marketplace: cooperation and competition. Under the communist experiment, all was cooperation; self-contained corporate entities encompassed all the competition and supporting firms that in a capitalist economy would lie outside a manufacturing company. Housing, restaurants, even crematoria and undertakers were controlled by the state. When foreign firms were reintroduced to China in the early 1980s, their role was to cooperate in the domestic marketplace. Internationally, they competed as usual, exporting aggressively to earn hard currency as they would elsewhere. But within China they were instead expected to bring skills, investment, and technology; they were pressed into the family. While the special economic zones were islands of incentive, they were also holding pens to reduce foreign involvement in the domestic economy. This "dual economy" characterized the experiences of most foreign enterprises (see Naughton 1996a, 1996b).

As foreign firms press ahead inside the economy, external barriers continue to fall. Trade negotiators haggle over a simple average tariff that has fallen to 15 from 40 percent in four years, but leaks and loopholes bring the revealed average tariff rate below 4 percent. But while policy impediments have receded, the nonpolicy problems identified in this study have increased. For example, the shortage of local human resources severely hampers firms in major markets such as Shanghai. Self-created hindrances that once seemed like innovations (e.g., getting a jump on a major regional market by strategically partnering with a local champion company) are coming to the surface (as the firms find it difficult to convince Chinese partners to expand to other regions). And market structure problems are escalating as the healthier SOEs change ownership categories and suddenly command local markets, not surprisingly with a friendly wink from government regulators (their erstwhile owners). Private constraints to commerce will become more common in China in the absence of a procompetitive regulatory policy. FIEs continue to be pressured—with varying effectiveness—to transfer commercial power over scope, technology, and management to Chinese partners, who play an important role in finding opportunities to sell (see chapters 2 and 5). Taken together, these forces could create high barriers to entry and a collusive and segmented market structure. While incumbent FIEs may be beneficiaries of these concentrations of market power (which may create a greater opening for them), those *aspiring* to establish businesses are closed out not by policy but by dominant rivals.

An important contribution of this study has been to demonstrate (particularly in examining distribution in chapter 5) that private and semiprivate restraints to trade are indeed among the greatest threats to economic openness today. Some argue that the large scale of the Chinese economy will spawn sufficient competition even without a strong central policy supporting it. Interviewees' comments—on exclusive distribution arrangements, limited opportunities to partner with local firms that heavily influence local distribution, and informal pressure from allied authorities to sell within a province instead of more efficiently on a national basis—suggest that the question of whether liberal outcomes can be achieved without a concerted policy on competition must be considered sector by sector. Localism could lead to significant market segmentation within regions for some time, even after the most obvious roadblocks to intraprovincial trade are removed. "Openness" to foreign firms, once achieved, can vary considerably in quality. Official openness without the proactive steps to ensure low barriers to entry (and to remove barriers to exit), an outcome that looks ever more likely, would be of reduced value.

Therefore, this study can only highlight this important question, without providing an answer. China's future openness to foreign firms, like the openness of regions within China to firms from other regions, will likely depend on the central authorities' active role in competition policy. If the large scale of operation in China does, as some predict, ameliorate tendencies toward regionalism and localism, then the need for such activism may be reduced. But the trends described in the distribution sector suggest that the ancient local focus is changing only very slowly and that Beijing's willingness to step up to this challenge is the best indicator of whether China will continue its rapid progress in this regard.

Are Foreign Corporations in China Influencing Social Trends in a Positive Way?

When FIEs in China were mainly assembly operations or subcontracting sweatshops, the level of added value that they sought to achieve was low. Necessarily, the typical foreign manager had little opportunity to engage his 20-cent-a-day worker in conversation. In any case, the manager did not speak Chinese and the worker knew no English. Throughout this study (especially in chapter 3), an alternative picture of foreign business culture has been offered.

Some might argue that the terms of the comparison are unfair. The more benign view of FIEs in China, characterized by heavy emphasis on productive growth through training, monetary and nonmonetary incentives (e.g., facilitating home mortgages), and career development, is based on interviews at larger Western manufacturing ventures, not Guangdong textile factories. But the shift in FIE establishments from low-value-added contractual joint ventures to more sophisticated equity joint ventures and wholly foreign-owned enterprises reflects a broad trend across the country. A mix of low-value and more sophisticated manufactures (electronics, power generation, and medical equipment on the one hand, textiles and toys on the other) now dominates US imports from China.[7] Service-sector activities are also expanding, bringing a whole new wave of training as

---

7. See http://www.uschina.org/press/trade7–8.html#trade8 (9 June 1998).

well as much more sophisticated jobs than the exploitative work stereo-typed as "Chinese."

Such changes will necessarily lead FIEs to focus even more on invest-ing in human resources; and "China's new business elite," as Pearson (1997) describes the emerging middle classes of coastal cities, is growing quickly. Foreign firms are not solely responsible for creating the wealth that fuels this enormous socioeconomic leap, but they play a crucial role in setting expectations and providing a template for workplace reform. The number of Chinese employees of FIEs rose from 660,000 in 1990 to 5.4 million in 1996. If only a million of those employees attain at least a lower-level managerial position, they will form the nucleus of the entrepreneur-ial class of tomorrow.

In addition to jobs (increasingly producing higher-value-added goods and services), FIEs bring to China skills, training, and wage and nonwage benefits (again, see chapter 3). But perhaps most of all, FIEs influence Chinese society by bringing a different workplace culture—one charac-terized by initiative taking, career development, and quality control.

Yet for a number of reasons, these efforts have received remarkably lit-tle recognition outside China. Firms in China are inclined to develop their company cultures quietly so as to avoid drawing the attention of nervous overseeing authorities. In urban centers, tensions about foreign firms sim-mer just beneath the surface, as indigenous enterprises compete with FIEs for choice employees and struggle with the new, higher expectations the foreign firms have introduced.

Similarly, those FIEs with a greater scope of operations than simply manufacturing have the most positive workplace environments but func-tion on somewhat ambiguous terms; they rely on such techniques as bun-dling business licenses from unrelated municipalities, interpreting regu-lations more liberally than officials would (publicly) allow, or getting key officials (unofficially) to turn a blind eye to practices that take place out-side the spotlight. Under these circumstances, FIEs can carry out a range of sophisticated sales, marketing, and support functions, with the help of significant numbers of self-motivated, well-trained local employees. To trumpet all their activities in human resource development, however, would jeopardize their positions.

An FIE may also hesitate to call more attention to the virtuous impact of its operations because at even the most hands-on ventures, aspects of the business are unclear to senior management. Nobody wants to make what one manager called the "Gary Hart blunder": that is, to invite inspection of one's actions only to have numerous flaws discovered. While many for-eign firms expend considerable energy to improve the conditions under their roofs, few would be willing to claim that they control or even know of all the related activities around them in the larger Chinese marketplace. Subcontracting relationships, as well as gray sales and supply practices, are often somewhat nontransparent to foreign venture managers.

But it is becoming more important for FIEs to communicate their social impact. Support for commercial policies conducive to foreign investment weakened worldwide in the late 1990s as concern grew about the implications of economic globalization. For example, in the United States in 1997 and 1998, charges leveled against overseas labor practices figured prominently in campaigns against fast-track trade legislation, renewed funding for the International Monetary Fund (IMF), and the planned Multilateral Agreement on Investment. In order to turn these debates back toward engagement and away from protectionism, firms operating in emerging markets such as China must publicize their efforts and encourage attention to their foreign operations. Increased scrutiny is inevitable; better to invite it than be taken by surprise.

Will WTO Accession Address the Commercial Priorities of China's Trading Partners?

The WTO has broader competence to manage international trade today than had its predecessor, the General Agreement on Tariffs and Trade (GATT), prior to 1995. In addition to traditional work fostering the liberalization of goods trade (aimed at border barriers such as tariffs and nontariff measures), the organization has new or stepped-up authority on trade rules (antidumping, subsidies), services (the General Agreement on Trade in Services), investment (TRIMs) and intellectual property protection (Trade-Related Intellectual Property, or TRIPs). An invigorated dispute settlement mechanism (DSM) now has power to enforce findings on members; under the GATT, procedures required defendant concurrence. The WTO has approved working groups on trade and competition policy, and on trade and the environment. A "built-in agenda" is already turning to additional business, having successfully negotiated plurilateral agreements on basic telecommunications and financial services.

Clearly the WTO's coverage has broad implications for the Chinese economy, especially as membership entails a "single undertaking": China must join all at once, not in stages. Furthermore, during accession China must negotiate market access concessions that will cover a very substantial portion of its marketplace immediately, phase in access for other sectors quickly, and leave only very narrow areas unopened to foreign trade and establishment. While in many sectors wide gaps remain between China and her trading partners as of this writing, the magnitude of Chinese liberalization that has resulted from this process is not in debate.

But the WTO cannot be expected to solve all of the world's commercial problems with China. First, though much was accomplished in designing the WTO, certain of its regimes are not fully capable of addressing their targets. TRIMs, which open the door to arbitration over performance requirements on FIEs (see chapter 2), cannot prohibit them and only includes a partial illustrative list of what is not permitted. Neither the government procurement agreement nor certain important sectoral agreements are required of China. Notwithstanding these shortcomings, concessions can still be pressed on China in bilateral accession negotiations; indeed, there is no single template for accession. Second and more important, the WTO does not yet squarely address the area of domestic competition policy. Essentially, any US exporter whose opportunity to sell into China was precluded by Chinese policy could bring a case before the WTO (were China a member) on the grounds of nullification and impairment of an expected benefit. However, no such argument can be made when the sales opportunity is foreclosed not by public policy but by private actions (Graham and Richardson 1997a, 48).

As shown, especially in chapter 5's discussion of distribution, as reforms move forward in China more firms are removed from state ownership, and their commercial problems also become less closely bound to the state. These are not wholly private matters, given the residual involvement of lower-level governments in local enterprises and state policy lending among the SOEs (perhaps 100,000 still remain). But the "corporatization" formula for shedding state ownership exists, though in its earliest stages.

In the absence of procompetitive policies from central authorities, many sectors in China are likely to reflect—on a local basis—the sort of nationwide private closing of markets that foreign firms have complained about in Japan, notably in the auto parts and photographic film sectors. Some have suggested that China's large scale will make such a trend to monopoly impossible; but as long as regional or provincial markets remain physically segmented, the problem will remain. Indeed, this will concern not just FIEs but nonlocal Chinese firms as well, some of which already complain bitterly about being locked out (of the Shanghai auto market, for example). Conversely, it is quite possible that titularly foreign firms able to solidify relationships in China may enjoy the status of forecloser instead of foreclosee. But such privileges will create more difficulties for foreign governments trying to devise a commercial policy toward China, as firms from their home country eager to do business in China will be divided into incumbents and aspirants. This phenomenon is common in developing economies, but China's sheer size makes it necessary to find solutions uniquely suited to the Chinese context, because there is less leverage against such a superpower.

Therefore, the study argues that rather than concentrating solely on the WTO, commercial remedies should be crafted in partnership with progressive Chinese leaders. This recommendation is bolstered by the growing evidence that China is resigned to deferring WTO accession until the dust of the Asian financial crisis is well settled—perhaps after the millennium.

Do Economic Trends Augur Cooperation between US and Chinese Authorities, or Confrontation?

Canada and the United States have had as many bilateral trade disputes as any pair of nations; but it should not be concluded that their commercial relationship is not healthy. The natural growth in transactional disputes as commerce increases explains the focus in chapter 6 on legal regimes for resolving disputes as they arise. Times of transition and adjustment bring even more conflicts than usual. For example, the Asian financial crisis will likely lead to trade maneuvers that will generate a surge in antidumping suits between the United States and Asian nations, including China.[8] But while an increase in disputes between private parties is inevitable, conflict between sovereign overseers over these cases is not. Chinese and foreign authorities have a common interest in creating more stable, efficient, and equitable market conditions in China, and therefore they are joining in a considerable effort to build capacity for dispute resolution. The WTO will provide an important multilateral venue for such cooperation, while its rules will help to forestall the unilateral actions that can themselves be a source of conflict.

The WTO can play these roles only after China's accession, which will be largely motivated by China's own self-interest. Chinese authorities are concerned with maintaining the flow of FDI into their domestic economy, keeping the capital stock from eroding, and lowering the high transactions costs associated with an unpredictable investment climate. Commercial problems have long been remedied by administrative intervention, whose replacement by standard, internationally accepted procedures progressive elements within China are eagerly anticipating. They recognize that the change will not just promote foreign investment but nurture competitive domestic companies as well, better preparing them for the international market. Chapter 6 provided evidence of China's legal maturation, with the views of the interviewees on China's progress toward these goals.

Chinese leaders must be concerned with not only the microeconomic but also the macroeconomic effects of failing to resolve commercial conflicts with reasonable fairness. Recall that the most problematic restraint of trade suffered by FIEs in China may increasingly involve private actions rather than policy (see especially chapter 5), actions that may harm Chinese firms even more than FIEs. By stifling competition, these actions reduce innovation, block structural adjustment, and stall the reabsorption of displaced labor, serving neither equity nor efficiency objectives for China. Such market foreclosure does not even serve nationalistic ends: incumbent foreign firms ensconced in collusive arrangements by virtue of being early

---

8. Just as important, such suits can be expected *among* Asian economies as well. See Noland et al. (1998).

contributors of technology and capital may benefit disproportionately, as compared to nonlocal Chinese firms from excluded jurisdictions.

In some sectors—for example, many consumer electronics and durables—market domination is already creating problems.[9] The evidence in this study suggests that these conflicts are a primary concern of FIEs, as seen in their focus on dominating partners (chapter 2), the productivity challenges arising from restrained market growth (chapter 4), and difficulties in expanding operating scope (chapter 5).

The United States and China share an interest in avoiding further development along these lines. The costs to China are high: exacerbated regionalism and urban-rural division. And such a marketplace—dependent, like Japan's, on exporting because of a multitude of domestic trade impediments—would undoubtedly draw much political fire from the United States, especially from the Congress. This animosity would diminish the ability of China to assume a regional or global leadership position, as the United States and other Group of Seven (G-7) nations are now hoping it can. Therefore, there is strong logic on both sides in favor of Sino-US cooperation, both to build capacity to support each other's procompetitive regulatory functions and to defuse bilateral confrontations. Having a more efficient legal system to serve business, as an interviewee quoted in chapter 6 put it, "is a practical matter, not an ideological one" (#51). The trend since 1997, influenced largely by the desperation with which Asian host governments are seeking more FDI, points unambiguously toward better conflict resolution, not only for firms but between governments; political stability, after all, is an important dimension of economic stability.

Will China's Central Government Remain the Conductor of Chinese Reforms?

Much has been written in recent years about the devolution of power from the central to provincial and local authorities in China. The boldness of southern provinces such as Guangdong, which had integrated deeply with freewheeling Hong Kong even before the latter's reversion to China, has raised the specter of renegade regionalism typical of China's past. FIEs (and many Americans at home) initially viewed this phenomenon positively, since local autonomy allowed greater freedom from bureau-

---

9. See, e.g., Yang 1998, whose work shows market shares in China of 40 percent and above for the dominant firms selling refrigerators, videocassette recorders, and microwave ovens, and concentrations almost as high (25–35 percent) for the market leaders in air conditioners, washing machines, and televisions; the number two firm is also often in an extremely strong position.

cratic constraint. However, the survey of operational problems in this study shows that an impotent Beijing is not in the FIEs' interest. Many interviewees have recently come to this realization, as they have sought to move beyond their compliant local partnerships to take up a more national position—only to find that there is little national framework within which to operate and that unchecked tensions between provinces can interfere with economic opportunity without a strong center.

There are strong tensions between Beijing and the provinces as well. But while localism stands to stifle openness, even in a worst-case scenario the provinces wishing to be strong have to draw on linkages with nonlocal economies. Interviewees described mounting interdependence both among provinces and between provinces and foreign markets; and those foreign links in particular *do* depend on central management and acquiescence. Such interdependence is evident in labor specialization between coast and inland (chapter 3),[10] productivity considerations favoring multiprovince production plans (chapter 4), and the eagerness of FIEs to develop national distribution operations (chapter 5). Coastal China depends on cheap raw material inputs from Southeast Asia; coal, oil and other energy supplies from northern and interior China; and more sophisticated intermediate inputs from Japan, Europe, and the United States (which later make up a large share by value of Chinese exports—i.e., reexports—by value). Dynamic coastal China will be a net consumer of foreign capital for decades to come. In previous eras, a rich province might aspire to be self-contained; but in the new China these provinces will depend on smooth interprovince commerce, and hence on the specialized services of the national government, as never before.

Many expatriates pointed out that the wealthier provinces are sure to respond to the social unrest likely to accompany structural adjustment of the economy over the coming decade by imploring Beijing to maintain a strong position of authority in order to prevent chaos. Poorer provinces, meanwhile, will continue for the foreseeable future to depend on the center for fiscal transfers from the wealthier regions. It cannot be concluded that in important economic sectors regional markets will not be segmented, or that Beijing will find it easy to impose a liberal commercial template on 10 dynamic provinces and 20 more static ones. But Beijing has a strong role to play that cannot be delegated. It is also clearly in the US national interest to bolster Beijing's regulatory power, as bilaterally negotiated agreements are worthless without the command and control necessary for implementation at the local level.

---

10. Because of rising wage pressures, low-value-added industries are already departing the coast for points inland, leaving the port cities to businesses higher up the ladder (i.e., finishing work and services).

What Is the Prognosis for Foreign Firm Performance in China in the Coming Years?

This study has catalogued the range of difficulties that FIEs encounter at each phase of establishment and operations. It has presented evidence and opinions from expatriate managers on which of these concerns are becoming more pressing and which less, which are more important and which relatively trivial. By definition, the removal of impediments will permit the FIEs to perform better; and because their very survival in a complex market such as China's demonstrates strength and determination to expand, they should be expected to perform well, all other things being equal. So in large part their future performance depends on how intractable the complications in the Chinese market are.

Beyond question, a great many of the problems examined here are lessening—including information gaps and ignorance of local culture (chapter 2), constraints to efficient human resource deployment and management (chapter 3), resistance to change on the factory floor (chapter 4), inadequacies in the physical distribution system (chapter 5), and failure of the court system to address transactional disputes (chapter 6). To be sure, the time and effort still required before these problems are resolved are sobering, but they clearly are distracting FIEs from improving performance less now than in the past. Ceteris paribus, as the economists say, these trends augur well for FIE success, just as they are positive for domestic Chinese firms.

Nevertheless, fundamental problems remain. The foremost of these are partnering issues. Many foreign managers remain proud of cozy relationships with regulators and Chinese partner firms, believing that these links provide an inside track to success. In early phases of operating in China, these relationships can indeed make life easier (e.g., in facilitating the approval process). But in subsequent phases the tables turn. Disagreement within the joint organization about how best to measure the firm's performance impedes human resource development, plant productivity, and broader distribution of firm operations. Chinese partners (government and company) continue to emphasize local social objectives that Western firms delegate to national social safety nets that have been in place in advanced economies for many years. The Chinese perspective will not change until the structural economic transition—with its potential for civil unrest—is over, some years (perhaps decades) in the future.

In the long term, forced partnering will not help the Chinese to address these social pressures: FIEs have a different set of performance metrics—namely, those of profitability—and will simply cease to invest in China if they cannot operate profitably. Thus, there has been a dramatic shift away from joint venture arrangements and toward wholly owned foreign enterprise structures in recent years, a trend that is likely to continue. But as this study has repeatedly stressed, partnering decisions are only partly policy driven; many FIEs have tied themselves to Chinese firms hoping to leapfrog competitors or thinking partnership a shortcut to achieving market dominance. The majority of existing FIEs are JVs, and many new entrants continue to join with local partners either by choice or by coercion.

This study has examined FIEs that had moved beyond establishment to the later stages of expanding and toward acceptance as a local entity.[11] These firms are finding it exceedingly difficult to shed the constraints and obligations of partnering that they had accepted during earlier stages of operation; retaining flexibility has become much more important in their negotiations with local powers. For the longer term, expatriates emphasize the need for a "divorce law" (i.e., a bankruptcy mechanism) to make resolution of partnership problems less difficult. As greater exogenous threats to FIE performance appear, such as financial turbulence outside China, Chinese authorities have had to take these concerns more seriously or risk scaring away investors.[12] The second critical encumbrance on FIE performance identified in this study is limitations on scope of operation (see chapter 5); firms are particularly hampered by their inability to distribute or sell directly products not manufactured in China and to manage the financial functions of Chinese operations on a consolidated, countrywide basis. For many, limitations on entry in service-sector activities that support the main business are a problem as well. Progress is being made in these areas, but not enough.

These two factors—partnering dynamics and scope of operation—are, according to this research, the best indicators of future FIE performance. Of course, other factors will have a significant impact. During a time of massive layoffs and adjustment in the state sector, overall social instability could diminish everyone's performance. The slow recovery of the Asian economies from their financial collapse will reduce performance for FIEs in China as well, as the crisis both makes China less attractive to investors as a regional export platform and makes Beijing hesitant to press ahead more quickly with economic reform. However, such variables are beyond the scope of this study.

FIEs already tied up in undesirable partner arrangements have an uncertain future, while firms able to retain more independence, including the next generation of FIEs starting up without such partners, are better posi-

---

11. The proportion of foreign firms that have reached the final phase is still small: most FIEs arrived in China in the first half of the 1990s (see table 2.1).

12. This conclusion rests on the analysis of interviews that preceded the Asian financial crisis. China's own ability to withstand volatility has much to do with the willingness of foreign investors to continue coming to China; Fernald, Edison, and Loungani (1998), Rosen, Liu, and Dwight (1998), and others have analyzed the implications of the crisis for China. Here, note that the crisis will amplify the trends in FIE performance already under way rather than create new problems. Hence meaningful separation of commercial and political interests is all the more urgent if frazzled investors are to stay excited about China. This trend toward separation is in evidence already, particularly in the context of incentives (see chapter 2).

tioned to succeed. For most firms tied up in JVs, their scope of operation depends on their partner. For WOFEs and JVs with significant control, scope is dependent more directly on China's government. Many firms are already creeping quietly into restricted areas. If Beijing either formally countenances this trend or else abstains from cracking down on the pioneers, then performance is likely to improve. Should a crackdown come, then diminished performance can be expected. The United States should clearly focus considerable attention on policies that affect these two variables.

Is China a Source of Endless Excess Capacity That Will Threaten Other Economies?

A major debate in the United States revolves around fear of a "global glut" of supply that would undermine American jobs and wages. According to this thesis, capacity is being added to global production at an unprecedented rate, outstripping demand worldwide. Much of this capacity, the argument goes, is added by multinational firms from advanced economies creating more production facilities than needed (as a result of an imperative to expand), combined with pressure from emerging markets to shift production. Prominent proponents of this view, who argue that host governments like China's turn production back out toward advanced economies through export performance requirements, include William Greider and Jeremy Rifkin. As economic development in China is a leading source of the anxieties fueling this debate, the American policy debate over engagement with China must concern itself with these views. It has even been suggested that the new Chinese capacity, combined with a supposedly cheap renminbi policy after 1994, precipitated the Asian financial crisis in 1997. But these views are incorrect, and the situation within China is misunderstood.

Overall, the theory of global glut does not hold up today any better than it did one hundred years ago when it was first proposed. In the specific case of China, the surge in Chinese exports and share of the US external deficit in the early 1990s that came seemingly at the expense of other economies in the regions such as Hong Kong, Taiwan, South Korea, and Japan should not be seen as taking something from those neighbors. The change marked not so much an addition to capacity as a transfer of capacity along the lines of comparative advantage.[13] Those nations had some years earlier induced many of those industries away from countries such as the United States, and now as they developed they too were forced to move up value chains. Within China, however, the problem of overcapacity has taken on real salience in less traded sectors, as noted with regard to economies of scale (see especially chapter 4).

---

13. See, e.g., Noland (1996, 36) and accompanying text.

Two policy phenomena have contributed to this overcrowding. First, financing was provided without sufficient consideration of the venture's commercial viability. If financial intermediation were competitive and efficient in China, then strenuous due diligence would ensure that serious misallocation of resources into already crowded sectors did not occur. Unfortunately, just the opposite has taken place. Local investments were controlled largely at the provincial or local level, where decisions were made without benefit of a broader perspective on demand and supply. As a result, many provincial decision makers reached similar conclusions about what investments were attractive and acted as if they were members of a herd.[14] Second, weak firms are deterred from selling out or going out of business in China. For fear of the social consequences of increased unemployment, struggling state firms in crowded sectors have been subsidized into hobbling along when their resources should have been redeployed to more promising opportunities. Barriers to exit are a major challenge to the condition of contestability that is necessary for a healthy market structure, although they are often forgotten in the shadow of barriers to entry.

Therefore, there is a problem that is more a Chinese "sectoral glut" than a global one, but the sectors affected happen to draw international attention—automobiles, for example. The FIEs that participated in this study argued that they would survive when competition was finally allowed in China; they believed it was only a matter of time before Chinese authorities would be forced to stop the current practice of supporting all firms indefinitely and allow the unproductive ones to exit the market. Chinese authorities clearly will make such a change not all at once but in phases—which sector will be first? Will the most "important" sectors—say, computer electronics—be the last ones receiving subsidies, by virtue of the power that Chinese special industrial interests wield? Such "luck" would be ironic: the longer real reform is delayed, the further sheltered firms fall behind independent ones. The answer is of acute interest to FIEs, because as long as Beijing or provincial officials support given sectors, the fit FIEs in those industries will continue to suffer unnecessarily, waiting for the day when competition and market exit are the norm.

To date, Chinese policymakers have tried to remedy their sectoral overcapacity by limiting entry to and exit from overcrowded markets. This practice is neither consistent with WTO principles nor an efficient use of scarce resources within the Chinese economy. How quickly Beijing permits the invisible hand to cull the markets of uncompetitive firms depends entirely on the readiness of central authorities for the marginal social strife that these adjustments will cause.

---

14. Chapter 4 considers the present results of such behavior in some of the markets the interviewees compete in; see further extensive background in Wedeman (1995).

Implications

The conclusions above lead to the following four policy recommendations.

Recommendation 1: Refine US Policy Priorities toward Pragmatic Goals

Using a screening device such as that employed in this study to separate problems amenable to foreign pressure from those that are not, the United States must recognize the present limits of Chinese authority and adjust *expectations* accordingly. Consider table 7.2, which lists only those issues from chapters 2 to 6 with both a policy-related aspect and a high-priority rating: its considerable scope suggests that more narrowing down needs to be done. (While understanding issue areas that have been filtered out is also critical to an analysis of Chinese economic behavior, those issues should not be the primary objects of scarce negotiating leverage.) Of the issues in table 7.2, the present analysis (which is clearly subject to debate) finds only seven to be solely policy oriented.

It is worth focusing on these seven priorities, because policy pressure alone will be ineffectual in the many cases in which transitional, self-imposed, or market structure variables are significant. Five of them involve the scope of FIE operations: regulatory restrictions on distribution, financing within the organization, economies of scope, collection, and service provision. Therefore, continued focus on these areas in WTO talks, where distribution, customer services, and financial services are all on the table, is essential; these are basic business functions that must be permitted to foreign enterprises.

The two remaining top priority issues—Chinese efforts to steer FIEs toward specified partners and to allocate market shares—are the most important and intrusive vestiges of state planning and control of industrial policy. They stand to distort an efficient market structure, defeat competitive impulses, and foster habits of collusion and circumvention. Especially in light of the financial crisis of 1997–98, US policy should concentrate on dissuading China from emulating Japanese or Korean orchestration of industrial policy, as the leadership until recently had explicitly intended. It will take years to fully quantify the costs that a now outmoded market structure has imposed on the Japanese people; other developing countries are still in danger of using the same flawed model.

Recommendation 2: Consider the Limits of the WTO

As observed, the WTO is currently limited in its ability to redress the full slate of FIE concerns raised in the course of this study. The future will see the rise of private competition policy problems, as noted especially in

Table 7.2   High priority, policy-related issues

Issue	Category	Level
Negotiation and establishment		
Locating strategically	Policy, market structure, transitional, self-imposed	Central, lower also
Government industrial policy, steering investors	Policy	Central, lower also
Partner issues	Market structure, policy, transitional, self-imposed	Central, lower also
Labor structure	Policy, self-imposed, transitional	Central
Scope of business	Policy, self-imposed	Central
Human resources		
Securing managerial control	Self-imposed, policy	Central
Comprador employment	Transitional, policy	Local
Productivity at the plant		
Capital: Financing the organization	Policy	Central
Institutional: Discordant organizations	Self-imposed, market structure, policy	Provincial, central
Institutional: Economies of scope	Policy	Central
Ex-factory issues		
Regulatory restrictions	Policy	Central
Collection, finance	Policy	Central
Service provision	Policy	Central
Allocated market shares	Policy	Central
Market foreclosure	Market structure, policy	Central
Law and privilege		
Interpreting the law to advantage	Transitional, policy, self-imposed	Central, provincial, local
Securing superlegal privileges	Policy, self-imposed, market structure	Central, provincial, local

chapters 2 and 5—problems that will affect nonlocal Chinese firms as much as FIEs and that thus should be of broad interest to the Chinese government. Ultimately, such market power concentration poses as great a risk to aggregate Chinese welfare as to FIE prospects, given the ability of many dynamic FIEs to benefit rather than suffer from collusion. Therefore, the United States should immediately consider going beyond the current WTO-accession negotiations to address concerns about competition policy, exploring Chinese willingness to pursue such steps in a cooperative partnership. An appropriate venue may be a bilateral, regional (i.e., Asia Pacific Economic Cooperation), or multilateral forum other than the WTO.

Alternatively, the United States and China could agree prior to China's WTO accession to push for a "Shanghai Round" of WTO talks to finally bring competition policy explicitly into serious negotiations; these talks could be agreed on prior to China's WTO accession, either to stand alone or to feed into "Millennium Round" plans (which would bundle a number of multilateral issues). Such a joint statement of preparedness to address this topic would reduce the burden placed on the WTO. If, as at present, the United States tries to negotiate a Chinese accession package that will accomplish more than the WTO is able to handle, it should not be surprising that a "commercially viable" formula has not yet been mutually agreed to. By putting the imperative of competition policy discussions on the table, the worries of "hawks" anxious about China's accession—that domestic competition practices will erode the spirit of China's concessions on international trade—can be assuaged. Equally important, such discussions begun outside the WTO could facilitate, instead of creating a new requirement for, Chinese membership.[15] They would give both US and Chinese proponents of a quicker accession track a major boost.

Certain conditions would have to be present in order to implement this strategy. First and foremost, senior Chinese leaders would have to be convinced both that competition policy is important and that China is ready to aid in constructing a new international regime to address it. These points are far from obvious to many Chinese officials, but Beijing has for its own reasons already started thinking quite seriously about competition policy, with some support from groups such as the OECD and the International Republican Institute of the United States: draft laws are already under consideration nationally and in Shanghai. Policymakers recognize that competition policies embraced by the United States at an intermediate stage of American economic development—from the 1890s onward—were critical to US success. And they also recognize the key role of collusive commercial practices and lack of competition in precipitating the Asian financial crisis.

Making the jump from accepting the need for a domestic competition policy to embracing competition standards at the multilateral level is not easy, but globalization has undeniably changed the rules: policy must change as well. Still, just as a matter of good politics, it is important that this not be construed as raising the bar for Chinese accession. Rather, China here has a chance to address proactively an agenda that is in its own interest, to help neutralize the objections of opponents of its WTO accession, and to demonstrate leadership on an issue whose time has come.

---

15. As with the Information Technology Agreement catapulted from the APEC forum to the WTO in 1996–97, however, these discussions ideally would be moved inside the WTO once progress was made.

A second condition necessary to advance this strategy is that advanced economies, especially the United States, accept that the time is right to develop competition policies for the global economy, as argued by Graham and Richardson (1997a, 1997b). This will not be easy: such nations can be fearful that mature competition regimes will be watered down at the multilateral level. Though these concerns are legitimate, they cannot be allowed to obstruct progress toward a global regime that can prevent unevenness and volatility in the process of international economic integration. Enthusiasm—and pressure—from Chinese authorities may be just the thing needed to break through the misgivings and resistance in Washington and elsewhere of experts on competition policy.

Third, while this study is proposing that a special US-China initiative set out the terms of a "Shanghai Round" of discussions on competition policy, such an effort would of course include other major players as well. One would not expect resistance to this proposal from the European Union or Japan, as they are already more comfortable with China's WTO accession than the United States appears to be (see note 1, above). However, given that Japan was the battleground for some of the most intense skirmishes over competition policy to date (in the now famous Kodak-Fuji case heard by the WTO),[16] it might be wise to secure Japanese participation in a Group of Three arrangement to lead this effort. Should these three markets make significant progress on the international competition policy agenda, it would be far easier then to draw other parties into the discussion. Like China, Japan has strong reasons of self-interest for coordinating domestic economic reforms with an external discussion of competition policy, provided that leaders are prescient enough to attack these issues proactively instead of again waiting for an economic meltdown.

Finally, such a parallel conversation on competition that would ultimately feed into the WTO process would have to be coordinated with the organization's ongoing formal work. Its unfinished business may be addressed in a proposed "Millennium Round," WTO 2000, or a program of less intimidating "roundups" (see Schott 1996a, 1996b, 1998). The formal agenda might range from sector-specific negotiations (driven by the organization's built-in agenda) to the all-encompassing rounds that are the GATT/WTO norm. The former would offer little chance to draw the understandings fashioned among the United States, China, and Japan into the multilateral discussion of competition policy, except in implementing rules for specific sectors.[17] The latter, however, might very well seek to

---

16. See Edward M. Graham, Kodak Reveals WTO Limits, *Journal of Commerce*, 11 December 1997, 6A.

17. The value of such a contribution is not to be underestimated, however. The most useful result of the Negotiating Group on Basic Telecommunications, which undertook to deal with a single crucial sector, was the appendix of Procompetitive Regulatory Principles that emerged (see Petrazzini 1996, 85–89).

"tee up" competition policy, especially if the time were not right to commence multilateral negotiations.[18]

Recommendation 3: Accommodate Impending Political Reform

In every area examined, marketization and the presence of foreign firms create pressure for new reforms in China that go beyond economics: political reform will *necessarily* occur in the wake of economic trends. Such reform is required in order to keep China's economic revolution on track—for example, by strengthening ownership rights (see Steinfeld 1998) and sharing risk more equitably across Chinese society. Furthermore, political liberalization has been shown to correlate well with rising income levels, at thresholds that per capita income in China's major urban centers is already nearing.

These sentiments are pervasive in the expatriate community, though opinions vary greatly on whether the leadership can successfully manage the coming changes. There is a good deal of evidence supporting this picture of China on the verge of political loosening. Democratic elections have already been introduced broadly at the village level, with surprising success (IRI 1997a, 1997b). Chinese intellectuals are already talking about a "soft political landing," and the senior leadership is beginning a program of serious "democracy research" in the aftermath of President Clinton's 1998 summit meeting in Beijing.[19] American observers, convinced of democracy's relationship to stable development, are keenly interested in Chinese political liberalization. Both US and Chinese officials must pay more attention to sustainable economic regulation as the process of political reform unfolds. Only the central authorities in China can shepherd overall commercial development and implement the changes necessary to reinforce the country's economic underpinnings without which political reforms cannot possibly occur.

It is essential that the United States accommodate political reform and political strengthening simultaneously. To date, the common view has been that strong leadership by Beijing and political liberalization are antithetical; but that is mistaken. A model that stresses the responsibilities of the center is critical to the country's continued well-being. The evidence from FIEs in this study underscores this point, though (ironically) by revealing that some foreign firms support devolution of power away from Beijing and toward more pliant local authorities. The United States must

---

18. Schott (1996b, 19) noted, "Clearly, much more work needs to be done in this area before WTO negotiations could be contemplated." The agenda proposed above is precisely the kind of "work" that is needed.

19. See Kathy Chen, "Jiang Zemin Orders Research on Democracy," *China News Digest—Global News*, 23 July 1998 (http://www.cnd.org).

resist the temptation to support these firms' short-term interest in profit at the cost of the nation's interest in a strong and stable China. To accommodate reform in China, the broader American foreign policy establishment must acknowledge that political restrictions are being relaxed, that reform must occur under the existing regime, and that the regime's authority needs to be strengthened temporarily to implement economic reforms (especially those stressed in the discussion of the prognosis for FIE performance, above).

Recommendation 4: Hold Out a Helping Hand

The analysis in this study illuminates several practical ways in which the United States should help cement reform, bolster bilateral relations, and accelerate resolution of the nonpolicy problems with which its firms grapple in China.

First, as chapter 3 described in detail, the resource China most lacks today is human. After years of denigrating market imperatives, China has a relatively small pool of entrepreneurs and businesspeople with experience running enterprises small or large. In order for China's reforms to succeed, a larger share of the population must be involved in marketization and distribution-led growth (discussed in chapter 5). The United States can help transfer employees more quickly from outmoded deployment to new economic activity by making larger contributions of one of its greatest comparative advantages: educational and training expertise.

The European Union cosponsors a major joint venture business school at Jiaotong University in Shanghai, and Japan contributes significantly to scholarships and teaching for young Chinese. While individual American universities are involved in China, and a large pool of Chinese students study in the United States, a concerted government-to-government effort by the United States to support the banner of higher and technical education in China, perhaps along the lines of the EU flagship MBA program, would concentrate resources and public attention where it is needed most. This focus on human capital can generate additional investment in training in China and can also serve to direct Western human and labor rights activism into constructive channels. As much as anything else, this would help to remind us that China's ability to reach toward developed-country standards is determined by the education and experience of its vast multitudes of people.

Second, in many governance areas in which this study advocates building capacity to meet the needs of foreign firms in China, the United States already has regimes in place. A good example is antitrust policy, which falls under the larger umbrella of competition policy. Through government-to-government exchange the US executive branch, Congress, and judiciary can transfer the soft technology of good governance—that is, know-how—to their Chinese counterparts. While many US agencies are already striving to increase interaction with their Chinese equivalents, they must do so ad hoc, without the benefit of a general US budgetary commitment to programs to build capacity in China. To be sure, international organizations—including the World Bank, IMF, United Nations Development Program, and Asian Development Bank—have long been engaged in such activities, and channels exist between the US Treasury Department and Ministry of Finance as well as many other agencies. Yet the reciprocal state visits of 1997 and 1998 made clear (as bureaucrats scrambled to get involved in the action) that many counterpart organizations between these two superpowers had few ongoing, working-level connections and that the gains from such exchanges could be tremendous. Given the effort and money expended on such dialogue with Russia, the relative paucity of US-China institutional dialogue is inexplicable—all the more so in light of significant Japanese and European bilateral programs in China, which many US interviewees considered marginally advantageous to their competitors from those markets.

Finally, the US-China commercial relationship does not take place in a vacuum. Increasingly, the exogenous factors affecting US firms are not whether Taiwan policy will disrupt the relationship or geopolitics push China into a position hostile to the United States, but what China and the United States can do together to better manage the international economic and political currents that affect both.[20] For these two countries, the silver lining to the Asian financial crisis was the discovery of mutual interests, mutual responsibilities, and mutual willingness to take hard positions to nurture stability and growth even as other would-be leaders vacillated. The United States should continue to explore the capacity of China to bear the burden of international economic leadership, with an eye toward China's taking on a new, institutionalized management role in the G-7 or elsewhere. FIEs are the major bridge across which news of this new Chinese role will be transmitted.

---

20. On the opportunities for such cooperation, see "The New Agenda with China," by Fred Bergsten, at http://www.iie.com/news98-2.htm.

Appendix A
"Catalogue for the Guidance of Foreign Investment Industries"

Approved by the State Council on 29 December 1997, and promulgated by the State Planning Commission and the Ministry of Foreign Trade and Economic Cooperation on 31 December 1997.

Encouraged Foreign Investment Industries

I. Agriculture, Forestry, Animal Husbandry, Fishery and Related Industries

1. Reclaiming and development of wasteland, waste mountain, intertidal zone (except those with military facilities), as well as improvement of low- and medium-yielding field
2. Development of new varieties of fine quality, high-yielding crops such as sugar-yielding crops, fruit trees, vegetables, flowers and plants, forage grass and related new techniques
3. Serialization production of soilless cultivation of vegetables, flowers and plants

Appendix A is from *China Daily*, 8 February 1998.

4. Planting of forest trees and introduction of fine strains of forest trees
5. Breeding of good strains of domestic animals, fowls and aquatic fingerlings (not including special, precious good strains of our country)
6. Breeding of famous, special and fine aquatic products
7. New varieties of effective and safe agricultural chemicals and pesticides (over 80 percent insect death rate, safe to people, animals and crops)
8. High-density fertilizers (potash fertilizer, phosphate fertilizer)
9. New technologies for the production of agricultural films, and development of new products (fiber film, photolysis film, multifunctional film and raw materials)
10. Antibiotic material medicals (including antibiotic and chemical synthesis)
11. New products or new forms of anthelmintic, insecticide, anticoccidiosis medicines used for animals
12. Development of feed additive, and feed protein resources
13. New technology and equipment for the storage, preservation, drying and processing of food, vegetables, fruits, meat products, and aquatic products
14. Forestry chemicals and new technology and products for the comprehensive utilization of "sub-quality, small and firewood" lumber and bamboo in the forest area
15. Construction and management of key water control projects for comprehensive utilization (the Chinese party will be the holding party or play a leading role)
16. Manufacture of new-type water-saving irrigation technical equipment
17. Manufacture of new technical agricultural machinery
18. Improvement and construction of ecological environment

II. Light Industry

1. Design, processing, and manufacture of molds for nonmetal products.
2. Paper pulp (with an annual production capacity of over 170 thousand tons of wood pulp and a related raw material base)
3. Post-ornament and processing of leather and related new-tech equipment
4. Production of nonmercury alkali-manganese secondary battery and lithium-ion battery
5. Manufacturing of high-tech involved special industrial sewing machines
6. Production of polyamide film
7. Production of new-type, highly efficient enzymic preparations
8. Production of synthetic spices, single-ion spices

9. Research and popularization of the applied technology of freon substitution
10. Production of diacetate for cigarette making and processing of tows

III. Textile Industry

1. Production of wood pulp for textile chemical fiber (construction of raw material base with an annual output capacity of over 100 thousand tons)
2. Special textiles for industrial use
3. Printing and dyeing as well as post processing of high-emulation chemical fire plus material
4. Production of assistant, grease, and dye-stuff for textile

IV. Communication and Transportation as well as Post & Telecommunications Services

1. Technical equipment for railway transportation: the design and manufacture of locomotives and main parts, the design and manufacture of line facility and equipment, related technology and equipment manufacture for rapid transit railway, manufacture of equipment for communicational signals and transportation safety monitoring, manufacture of electric railway equipment and instruments
2. Construction and management of feeder railways, local railways, and related bridges, tunnels, and ferry facilities (wholly foreign-owned enterprises are not allowed)
3. Design and manufacture of new-type mechanical equipment for highway and port and related designing and manufacturing technologies
4. Construction and management of city subway and light rail (the Chinese party will be the holding party or play a leading role)
5. Construction and management of highways, independent bridges and tunnels, and port facilities (for public wharfs, and the Chinese party will be the holding party or play a leading role)
6. Construction and management of public dock facilities of ports (the Chinese party will be the holding party or play a leading role)
7. Construction and management of civil airports (the Chinese party will be the holding party or play a leading role)
8. Production of the equipment of DCS/CDMA
9. Production of digital serial transmission equipment of phototiming and microwave synchronization of 2.5 GB/S or above
10. Production of metering devices of 2.5 GB/S for photo communication, wireless communication and data communication
11. Production of AMT exchange boards

V. Coal Industry

1. Design and manufacture of coal mining, conveyance and concentration equipment
2. Coal mining and ore-dressing by washing (the Chinese party will be the holding party or play a leading role in the mining and ore-dressing by washing of special and rare kinds of coal)
3. Production of water-coal and liquefied coal
4. Comprehensive development and utilization of coal
5. Comprehensive development and utilization of low-thermal-value fuel and associated resources
6. Pipe-transportation of coal
7. Exploration and development of coal bed gas

VI. Power Industry

1. Construction and management of heat power station with a single machine's installed-capacity of 100 thousand kilowatts or above
2. Construction and management of hydropower station with the main purpose of power generating
3. Construction and management of nuclear power station with the main purpose of power generating (the Chinese party will be the holding party or play a leading role)
4. Construction and management of power station with the technology of clean coal-burning
5. Construction and management of new energy power station (including solar energy, wind energy, magnetic energy, geothermal energy, tide energy and biological mass energy, etc.)

VII. Ferrous Metallurgical Industry

1. 50 tons or above super-high-power electric furnace (equipped with the ability of external refining and continuous casting) and 50 tons or above converter steel-making
2. Smelting of stainless steel
3. Production of cold-rolled silicon steel tape
4. Production of hot-rolled and cold-rolled stainless steel plate
5. Steel pipeline for transmitting petroleum
6. Processing and treatment of steel scrap
7. Extraction and selection of iron and manganese ores
8. Production of direct reduced iron and retailored iron
9. High alumina vitriol earth, hard clay mining and grog production

10. Deep processing of needle coke, hard coke and coal tar
11. Production of dry coke quenching

VIII. Nonferrous Metal Industry

1. Production of monocrystalline silicon (with a diameter of 8 inches or over), multicrystalline silicon
2. Production of hard alloy, tin compound, and antimony compound
3. Production of nonferrous composite materials, new-type alloy materials
4. Copper, lead, tin mining (wholly foreign-owned enterprises are not allowed)
5. Aluminum mining (wholly foreign-owned enterprises are not allowed) and alumina (3,000,000 tons or more a year)
6. Rare-earth application

IX. Petroleum, Petrochemical and Chemistry Industries

1. Manufacture of ion film for caustic soda
2. Ethylene (with an annual production capacity of 600,000 tons or over, and the Chinese party will be the holding party or play a leading role)
3. Corvic (the Chinese party will be the holding party or play a leading role)
4. Comprehensive utilization of ethylene side-products such as C5-C9
5. Engineering plastics and plastic alloys
6. Supporting raw materials for synthesized materials (bisphenol-A, butadiene-styrene latex, pyridine, 4. 4' diphenylmethane, diiso-cyan ester, and vulcabond toluence)
7. Comprehensive utilization of basic organic chemical raw materials: the derivatives of benzene, methylbenzene, (para-, ortho-, or meta-) dimethylobenzene
8. Synthetic rubber (liquid butadiene styrene rubber by butadiene method, butyl rubber, isoamyl rubber, ethyl rubber, butadiene neoprene rubber, butadiene rubber, acrylic rubber, chlorophydrin rubber)
9. Fine chemistry: new products and technology for dye-stuff, intermediate, catalytic agent, auxiliary, and pigment; processing technology for the commercialization of dye (pigment); electronics and high-tech chemicals for paper-making, food additives, feed additives, leather chemical products, oil-well auxiliaries, surface active agent water treatment agent, adhesives, inorganic fiber, inorganic powder stuffing and equipment

10. Chloridized titanium dioxide
11. Production of chemical products using coal as raw material
12. Comprehensive utilization of exhaust gas, discharge liquid, waste slag
13. Production of depurant of automobile tail gas; catalytic agent and other assistant
14. Development and utilization of tertiary oil recovery which can increase the recovery ratio of petroleum (the Chinese party will be the holding party or play a leading role)
15. Construction and management of oil and gas delivery pipes, as well as oil depot and oil wharf (the Chinese party will be the holding party or play a leading role)

X. Mechanical Industry

1. Manufacture of high-performance welding robot and effective welding and assembling production line
2. High-temperature-resistant insulation material (with F, H insulation class) and mould-casted insulation products
3. Manufacture of equipment for mining, loading and transporting in the well, 100 or more tons of mechanical power-driven dump trucks for mining, mobile crushers, double input and output coal grinder, 3,000 cubic meters/h or more bucket excavator, 5 cubic or larger mining loader, full-face tunnelling machines
4. Manufacture of multicolor offset press for web and folio or paper of larger size
5. Manufacture of clearing equipment for electromechanical wells and production of medicals
6. Manufacture of turbine compressor and combined powder machine for the complete set of equipment for an annual production of 300,000 tons or more of synthetic ammonia, 480,000 tons or more of urea, 300,000 tons or more ethylene
7. Manufacture of complete set of equipment of new type of knitting machine, new type of paper (including pulp) making machine
8. Development and manufacture of precision on-line measuring instrument
9. Manufacture of new technical equipment for safe production and environment protection detecting instrument
10. New type of meters' spare parts and materials (mainly new switches and function materials for meters such as intelligent sensors, electrical adapters, flexible circuit plate, photoelectric switches, and proximity switch, and so on)
11. Research, design and development center of important basic machinery, basic parts and important technical equipment

12. Development of proportional, servo-hydraulic technology and production of low-power pneumatic control valve and stuffing static seal
13. Production of precision trimming dies, precision cavity modes and matrix standard components
14. Manufacture of 250,000 tons/day city sewage-disposal equipment, industrial sewage film treatment equipment, up-flow anaerobic fluidized bed equipment, and other biological sewage disposal equipment, slab making equipment of powder coal ash (5-10 tons/year), recycling equipment for waste plastics, equipment for desulphurization and denitration equipment of industrial boiler, large high-temperature-resistant, acid-resistant bag dust remover
15. Manufacture of precision bearings and all kinds of bearings used specially for main engines
16. Manufacture of key spare parts for cars: complete brakes, complete driving rods, gearbox, steering knuckle, fuel pump of diesel engine, piston (including pistoning), valve, hydraulic tappet, shock absorber, seat adjustor, car lock, backview mirror, glass lifter, compound meter, light, bulb, car fastener
17. Manufacture of car and motorcycle moulds (including strike moulds, plastics filling moulds, mould-pressing moulds, etc.) and clippers (welding clipper, testing clippers, etc.)
18. Production of casted and forged semifinished products for cars and motorcycles
19. Car and motorcycle technology research center, and design and development institute
20. Cars for special purposes such as desert cars for petroleum industry
21. Production of key spare parts for motorcycles: carburetors, magnetors, starting motors, lamps, disc brakes
22. Manufacture of new-tech equipment of water quality on-line detecting instrument
23. Manufacture of special machines and equipment for flood prevention and emergency rescue
24. Manufacture of earth-movers for wet land and desilting machines
25. Manufacture of integrated equipment with a feed processing capacity of 10 tons or more an hour, and the production of spare parts
26. Design and manufacture of new instruments and equipment for petroleum exploration and development

XI. Electric Industry

1. Large-scale production of integrated circuit with a line width of 0.35 micron or a smaller line width
2. New-type electronic spare parts (including slice spare parts) and electric and electronic spare parts

3. Manufacture of photoelectric components, sensitive components and sensors
4. Manufacture of large and medium-sized computers
5. Manufacture of compatible digital TV, HDTV, digital videotape recorder and player
6. Development of semiconductor, photoelectric materials
7. Manufacture of new-type displays (plate displays and displaying screens)
8. Development of 3-dimension CAD, CAT, CAM, CAE and other computer application systems
9. Manufacture of special electronic equipment, instruments, and industrial mould
10. Manufacture of hydrological data collection instruments and equipment
11. Manufacture of equipment of satellite communication
12. Manufacture of digital cross-linking equipment
13. Manufacture of air traffic control equipment (wholly foreign-owned enterprises are not allowed)
14. Development and manufacture of high-capacity mass storage of laser disks, disks and parts
15. Development and manufacture of new-type printing devices (laser-printers, etc.)
16. Manufacture of equipment of multimedia system of data communication
17. Production of single mode optical fiber
18. Manufacture of equipment for cut-in communication system
19. New technical equipment supporting communication network
20. Manufacture of ISDN

XII. Building Material, Equipment and Other NonMetal Mineral Product Industries

1. Production line of fine-quality floating glass with a daily melting capacity of 500 tons or more
2. Production line of high-level sanitation porcelain with an annual production of 500,000 pieces as well as auxiliary hardware parts and plastic parts
3. New building materials (materials for wall, decorating and finishing materials, waterproof materials and thermal insulation materials)
4. Production line of new-type dry process cement of clinker with a daily output capacity of 4,000 tons or more (only in the midwest region of this country)
5. Bulk cement storage and transportation facilities

6. Production line of glass fiber (through direct melting process) and glass fiber-reinforced plastics with an annual capacity of 10,000 tons or more
7. Manufacture of nonorganic, nonmetal material and products (quartz glass, artificial crystal)
8. Production of high-class refractory material used in furnaces for glass, ceramics and glass fiber
9. Deep processing technique and equipment of plate glass
10. Manufacture of tunnelling machine, equipment for covered digging of city metro
11. Manufacture of special equipment for cities' sanitation work
12. Manufacture of tree transplanters
13. Manufacture of machines for road planing and repairing

XIII. Medicine Industry

1. Chemical medicines under patent and administrative protection in our country, medical intermediate specially used in medicine which we have to import
2. Analgesic-antipyretic which has to be produced through new technical equipment
3. Vitamins: niacin
4. New type of anticarcinogen and cardiovascular and cerebrovascular medicines
5. Medicines and pharmaceutics: new products and new forms of drugs produced by means of slow release, controlled release, target preparation and those absorbed through skin
6. Amino acid: serine, tryptophan, histidine, etc.
7. Wrapping materials and container for new medicines and other advanced pharmaceutical equipment
8. New, effective and economical contraceptive medicines and devices
9. New technology, equipment and instruments that control the quality of traditional Chinese medicine and change the packaging
10. New analytical and extraction technology and equipment of the effective part of traditional Chinese medicine
11. New medicines which are produced by means of biological engineering technology
12. Development and utilization of new type adjuvant
13. Production of diagnosis reagent for hepatitis, AIDS, and radio-immunity diseases

XIV. Medical Equipment Industry

1. Medical X-ray machine set with medium-frequency technique, computer control technique, and digital imagery processing technique

2. Electronic endoscope
3. Tubes for medical use

XV. Aerospace Industry

1. Design and manufacture of civil planes (the Chinese party will be the holding party or play a leading role)
2. Manufacture of spare parts for civil planes
3. Design and manufacture of airplane engines (the Chinese party will be the holding party or play a leading role)
4. Manufacture of airborne equipment
5. Manufacture of light gas turbine engine
6. Design and manufacture of civil satellite (the Chinese party will be the holding party or play a leading role)
7. Manufacture of satellite payload (the Chinese party will be the holding party or play a leading role)
8. Manufacture of spare parts for civil satellites
9. Development of the application technique of civil satellites
10. Design and manufacture of civil carrier rockets (the Chinese party will be the holding party or play a leading role)

XVI. New Industries

1. Microelectronics technology
2. New materials
3. Biological engineering techniques (not including genetic engineering)
4. Network techniques of information, communications systems
5. Isotopic irradiation and laser techniques
6. Ocean and ocean energy development technology
7. Seawater desalting and seawater utilization technology
8. Development of energy-saving technology
9. Technology for recycling and comprehensive utilization of resources
10. Projects for improving polluted environment and related monitoring and improving technology

XVII. Service Business

1. Information consultation about information on international economy, science and technology, and environment protection
2. Maintenance of precision instruments and equipment, service after sales

3. Construction of new and high technology and building of new product developing centers as well as incubation of enterprises

XVIII. Permitted Projects Whose Products Are to Be Wholly Exported Directly

Restricted Foreign Investment Industries (A)

I. Light Industry

1. Production of washing machines, refrigerators, freezers
2. Production of synthetic emtrol, alcohol ether and alcohol ether sulfate
3. Manufacture of compressors with a shaft power of two kilowatts or less which are specially used for air conditioners and refrigerators

II. Textile Industry

1. Chemical fiber drawnwork of conventional chipper
2. Production of viscose staple fiber with an annual single thread output capacity of less than 20,000 tons

III. Petroleum, Petrochemical, Chemical Industries

1. Barium salt production
2. Refinery with an output capacity of less than 5 million tons a year
3. Cross-ply and old tire reconditions (not including radial tire)
4. Production of sulphuric acid basic titanium white

IV. Machinery Industry

1. Manufacture of equipment for producing long dacron thread and short fiber
2. Manufacture of power-generating units of diesel engines
3. Production of all kinds of ordinary abrasives (containing boule and silicon-carbide), grindstone with a diameter of less than 400 mm and man-made diamond saw bit
4. Production of electric drill and electric grinder
5. Ordinary carbon steel welding rod

6. Ordinary standard fasteners, small and medium-sized ordinary bearings
7. Ordinary lead acid accumulator
8. Containers
9. Elevators
10. Alufer hub

V. Electronic Industry

1. Satellite television receiver and key parts
2. Exchange boards for the use of digital programmer-control bureau and for the use of private branch exchange

VI. Medicine Industry

1. Production of chloramphenicol, lincomycin, gentamicin, dihydrostreptomycin, amikacin, tetracycline hydrochloride, oxytetracycline, acetyle spiramycin, medemycin, kitasamycin, ilotycin, norfloxacinum, ciprofloxacin and ofloxacin
2. Production of analgin, aspirin, paracetamol, Vitamin B1, Vitamin B2 and Vitamin B6

VII. Medical Apparatus and Instruments

1. Production of low- or medium-class type-B ultrasonic displays

VIII. Transportation Service

1. Taxi (the purchase of cars is restricted within China)
2. Gas station (restricted to projects related to super highway)

(B)

I. Agriculture, Forestry, Animal Husbandry, Fishery and Related Industries

1. Development and production of food, cotton and oil-seed (the Chinese party will be the holding party or play a leading role)
2. Processing and export of the logs of precious varieties of trees (wholly foreign-owned enterprises are not allowed)

3. Inshore and continental-river fishing (wholly foreign-owned enterprises are not allowed)
4. Cultivation of traditional Chinese medicines (wholly foreign-owned enterprises are not allowed)

II. Light Industry

1. Product of table salt, and salt for industrial use
2. Production of nonalcoholic beverage of foreign brand (including solid beverage)
3. Production of millet wine and famous brands of spirits
4. Tobacco processing industries such as cigarettes and filter tips
5. Processing and production of blue wet hide of pig, cow and sheep
6. Production of natural spices
7. Processing of fat or oil
8. Paper and paper plate

III. Textile Industry

1. Wool spinning, cotton spinning
2. Raw silk, grey silk fabric
3. Highly emulated chemical fiber and special kinds of fiber such as aromatic synthetic fiber, and carbon fiber (wholly foreign-owned enterprises are not allowed)
4. Fiber and polyester, acrylic fiber and spandex which are not used as fiber (wholly foreign-owned enterprises are not allowed)

IV. Communication and Transportation, Post and Telecommunications Industries

1. Construction and management of main lines of railways (the Chinese party will be the holding party or take a leading role)
2. Transportation by water (the Chinese party will be the holding party or take a leading role)
3. Entry and exit automobile transportation (wholly foreign-owned enterprises are not allowed)
4. Air freight (the Chinese party will be the holding party or take a leading role)
5. General aviation (the Chinese party will be the holding party or take a leading role)

V. Power Industry

1. Construction and management of conventional coal-fired power plants whose single-machine capacity is less than 300,000 kw (with the exception of small power grid, power plants in remote area and power plants of low-quality coal and coal refuses)

VI. NonFerrous Metal Industry (wholly foreign-owned enterprises are not allowed)

1. Copper and aluminum processing
2. Mining, dressing, smelting, and processing of precious metals (gold, silver, platinum families)
3. Mining of nonferrous metals such as wolfram, tin and antimony
4. Exploration, mining, selection, smelting and separation of rare-earth metal

VII. Petroleum, Petrochemical Industry and Chemical Industry

1. Sensitive materials (cartridge, film, PS plate, and photographic paper)
2. Mining and processing of boron, magnesium, iron ores
3. Benzidine
4. Chemical industry products such as ionic membrane caustic soda and organochlorine serial products
5. Radial tire (the Chinese party will be the holding party or play a leading role)
6. Synthetic fiber raw materials: precision terephthalic acid, vinyl cyanide, caprolactam and nylon 66 salt

VIII. Mechanical Industry

1. Complete automobiles (including limousines, trucks, passenger cars, and reequipped cars) and complete motorcycles (the Chinese party will be the holding party or take a leading role)
2. Engines of automobiles and motorcycles (the Chinese party will be the holding party or take a leading role)
3. Production of compressors of air conditioners for cars, electron-controlled fuel-oil injecting systems, electronic-controlled brake and locking-prevention systems, safety aeocysts and other electronic equipment, power generating machines and aluminum radiating machines

4. Reconditioning and disassembling refitting of old cars and motorcycles

5. Fire power equipment: (power unit, turbine, boiler, supplementary machine and controlling equipment) manufacture of units of over 100,000 kw, gas turbine combined cycle power equipments, cyclic fluidized bed boiler, coal gasification combined cyclic technique and equipment (IGCC), pressure boost fluidized bed (PFBC), desulfurization and denitrification equipment (wholly foreign-owned enterprises are not allowed)

6. Hydroelectric equipment: manufacture of hydropower generating units with a wheel diameter of over five meters (including hydropower supplementary machines and controlling units), large-scale pump storage groups of over 50,000 kw, large-scale tubular turbine units of over 10,000 kw (wholly foreign-owned enterprises are not allowed)

7. Nuclear power group: manufacture of nuclear power groups of 600,000 kw or more (wholly foreign-owned enterprises are not allowed)

8. Manufacture of power transmitting and transforming equipment: large-scale transformers of 200 kilovolts or more, high-voltage switches, mutual inductor, cable equipment (wholly foreign-owned enterprises are not allowed)

9. Manufacture of crawler dozers of less than 320 horsepower, wheeled forklifts of less than three cubic meters, and cranes of less than 50 tons (wholly foreign-owned enterprises are not allowed)

10. Manufacture of sheet continuous caster

11. Duplicators and cameras

IX. Electronic Industry

1. Color TV (including projection television), color kinescope and glass shielding

2. Video cameras (including camera-recorder in one unit)

3. Video recorders and magnetic heads, magnetic drums and movement of video recorders

4. Analogue-type mobile communications systems (honeycomb, colony, wireless beeper call, wireless telephone)

5. Receiving equipment of satellite navigation and key parts (wholly foreign-owned enterprises are not allowed)

6. Manufacture of the system of VSAT

7. Manufacturing of phototiming digital serial communication systems of less than 2.5 GB/S and microwave communication systems of 144MB/S and lower

X. Building Material Equipment and Other NonMetal Products Industries

1. Exploration, mining and processing of diamond and other natural gems (wholly foreign-owned enterprises are not allowed)

XI. Medicine Industry

1. Traditional Chinese herb medicines, Chinese patent drug semi and finished products (with the exception of preparing technique of traditional Chinese herb medicine in small pieces ready for decoction)
2. Precursor of narcotics: ephedrine, pseudoephedrine, ergotinine, ergotamine, lysergic acid and so on
3. Penicillin G
4. Production of addictive narcotics and psychoactive drugs (the Chinese party will be the holding party or play a leading role)
5. Production of vaccinums that involve high tech: vaccinum against AIDS, vaccinum against type-C hepatitis, contraceptive vaccinum and so on (the Chinese party will be the holding party or play a leading role)
6. Immunity vaccinums included in the State's plan, bacterins, antitoxins and anatoxin (BCG vaccine, poliomyelitis, DPT vaccine, measles vaccine, Type-B encephalitis, epidemic cerebrospinal meningitis vaccine)
7. Production of Vitamin C
8. Production of blood products

XII. Medical Apparatus and Instruments Industry

1. Disposable injectors, transfusion systems, blood transfusion systems and blood bags
2. Manufacture of large medical treatment equipment such as CT, MRI and accelerators for medical use

XIII. Shipping Industry (the Chinese Party Will Be the Holding Party or Play a Leading Role)

1. Repairing, design and manufacture of special ships, high-performance ships and over 35,000-ton ships

2. Design and manufacture of diesel engines for ships, auxiliary machines, wireless communication, navigation equipment and parts

XIV. Domestic and Foreign Trade, Tourism, Real Estate and Service Industry (Wholly Foreign-Owned Enterprises Are Not Allowed)

1. Domestic commerce (the Chinese party will be the holding party or play a leading role)
2. Foreign trade (the Chinese party will be the holding party or play a leading role)
3. Tourist agencies
4. Cooperation school-running (with the exception of elementary education)
5. Medical establishments (the Chinese party will be the holding party or play a leading role)
6. Accounting, audit and legal consultation services and agent company
7. Agent services (boats and ships, freight, futures, sales, advertisement, etc.)
8. High-ranking hotels, villas, high-class office buildings, and international exhibition centers
9. Golf links
10. Development of pieces of land
11. Large-scale tourist, cultural and recreational parks and artificial landscapes
12. Construction and management of State-ranking tourist areas

XV. Finance and Relevant Trades

1. Banks, finance companies and trust investment companies
2. Insurance companies, insurance brokerages and underwriting agent companies
3. Bond companies, investment banks, merchant banks, fund management companies
4. Financial lease
5. Foreign exchange brokerages
6. Financial, insurance and foreign exchange consultation
7. Production, processing, wholesales and retail of gold, silver, gems and jewelry

XVI. Miscellaneous

1. Printing, publishing and issuing business (the Chinese party will be the holding party or play a leading role)
2. Testing, appraising and attestation business of import and export goods (wholly foreign-owned enterprises are not allowed)
3. Production, publishing and issuing of audio and video products and electronic publication (the Chinese party will be the holding party or play a leading role)

XVII. Other Industries Restricted by the State or by International Treaties That China Has Concluded or Take Part In

Prohibited Foreign Investment Industries

I. Agriculture, Forestry, Animal Husbandry, Fishery and Related Industries

1. Wild animal and plant resources protected by the State
2. China's rare precious breeds (including fine genes in plants industry, husbandry and aquatic products industry)
3. Construction of animal and plant natural reserves
4. Processing of green tea and special teas (famous teas, dark tea, etc.)

II. Light Industry

1. Ivory carving and tiger-bone processing
2. Hand-made carpet
3. Bodiless lacquerware
4. Enamel products
5. Blue and white porcelain
6. Xuan paper, and ingot-shaped tablets of Chinese ink

III. Power Industry and Urban Public Utility

1. Construction and management of electricity network
2. Construction and management of urban networks of water supply, water drainage, gas and heat power

IV. Exploration, Selection, or Processing of Mining Industry; Exploration, Selection, Smelting or Processing of Radioactive Mineral Products

V. Petroleum Industry, Petrochemical Industry and Chemical Industry

1. Mining and processing of szaibelyite
2. Mining and processing of celestine

VI. Medicine Industry

1. Traditional Chinese medicines which have been listed as State protection resources (musk, licorice root, etc.)
2. Preparing technique of traditional Chinese medicine in small pieces ready for decoction and products of secret recipe of traditional Chinese medicine already prepared

VII. Transportation and Post & Telecommunications Services

1. Management of post and telecommunications business
2. Air traffic control

VIII. Trade and Finance

1. Commodity future, financial future and related finance business

IX. Broadcasting and Film Industries

1. Broadcasting stations, TV stations (networks) at various levels, launching stations and relay stations
2. Production, publishing, issuing or showing of films
3. Production, publishing or showing of films
4. Videotape showing

X. Journalism

XI. Manufacturing Industry of Weapons

XII. Miscellaneous

1. Projects that endanger the safety and performance of military facilities
2. Developing and processing of carcinogenic, teratogenic, and mutagenesis raw materials
3. Racecourse, gambling
4. Pornographic service

XIII. Other Industries Prohibited by the State or by International Treaties China Has Concluded or Taken Part In

Appendix B
Methodology

This appendix describes how the study was conducted. The first section outlines the methodology; the second provides a sanitized list of interviewees; the third contains a draft version of the questionnaire used as a starting point for the research; and the fourth supplies the matrix into which the results of the research were entered.

The core information presented in this study derives from extensive interviews with expatriate business professionals in China. Because of the diversity of conditions in China and the complexity of the society, Western writers attempting to understand developments there have often found it necessary to amass a broad group of views and then sift through them. Walder provides a good example of this approach in *Communist Neo-traditionalism: Work and Authority in Chinese Industry* (1986), and his description of it applies equally to the present work:

> The analysis offered here is based in large part on four sources of information: government documents[,] . . . official newspaper accounts[,] . . . scholarly books and articles[,] . . . and over 500 hours of interviews. . . . The last source was by far the most important, and the number of citations does not adequately convey its overall contribution to the study. The interviews, open-ended and ethnographic in nature and at times leading into oral history, were as much a source of orientation and insight as a source of data. Many of the citations in this book are to published documents but the interviews provided the background that led me to frame the questions and structure the analysis the way I have. (xvi)

Methodology

Setting Up the Sample of Informants

Having decided to pursue a broad assessment of the Chinese marketplace and not a single-sector study, I identified a slate of industries in order to elicit a comprehensive range of important views. These included aerospace, agribusiness, automotive, chemicals, consumer goods, electronics, energy resource development, financial services, law and consulting, media, pharmaceuticals, power infrastructure development, retail, telecom, and textiles and footwear.

US firms known to have a presence in China, and preferably firms with a preexisting good relationship with the Institute for International Economics or the Council on Foreign Relations, were identified for each industry.

Invitations to participate in the study as "core companies" were then sent to the first-choice firm in each industry. If the first firm declined, letters were sent to second choices. I promised that the firm's identity would be concealed in the study and I asked for access to senior managers with knowledge of the firm's China activities both at home and in China and for frankness on their part. The invitations were in most cases directed to high-level officers in the companies to ensure access once the firm decided to participate.

In order to explore differences based on home country, firms from outside the United States were also asked to participate. One German firm, two Japanese firms, and one Hong Kong conglomerate joined on this basis. In the course of the research, I realized that it would be too difficult to seriously explore different experiences based on nationality. These firms were therefore treated the same as US firms.

Firms in all industries except automotive, pharmaceutical, textiles and footwear, and retail agreed to participate. The reasons given for not taking part differed; they included strong disenchantment with China (pharmaceutical), preference for a sector-specific analysis (automotive), desire for more control over the content of the study than I was willing to relinquish (textiles and footwear) and no response (retail). However, other firms that did accept included a conglomerate with units in the automotive business in China, a non-US firm involved in textiles, and many firms with considerable expertise on the retail side. The final number of core companies in the sample was 13, although several firms were conglomerates with as many as three separate units in very different sectors that participated individually.

Conducting the Research

Research began in most cases at the firms' corporate headquarters. Usually I traveled to meet with senior home-country China directors in person; in some cases discussions took place by phone. These meetings were very important in establishing a relationship of trust, thereby facilitating greater openness in China. These home-country managers participated in questioning based on a survey that evolved over time; the latest version is reproduced below.

It is important to note that while a questionnaire was used to structure the research and the interviews with informants, not all interviewees responded to all sections of the questionnaires. Because the questions ranged from corporate philanthropy to profitability to legal structure to human resource policy, very few individuals could discuss the whole slate. Rather, multiple responses from the same firm were used to compile a comprehensive picture.

I had originally hoped to include a chapter titled "Profit and Loss" but decided that the small sample could offer a suggestive conclusion at best on a quantitative matter. Furthermore, while the firms were frank about the ways in which profits could be hidden, they were in many cases less ready to provide up-to-date profit figures for their operations.

It quickly became apparent that the China professionals at the core companies knew of other valuable resources for this study. Therefore, a significant number of individuals—in other firms, private consulting, government, or media—were interviewed because of their unique, extensive, or insightful perspective on Chinese commercial conditions. In all cases they were professionals practicing in China.

Twenty-three interviews were conducted with home-country staff before undertaking research in China. These were not drawn on for the issue chapters in this study but rather were used in preparing to work with interviewees in the field in China and in refining the questionnaires. Eighty-eight interviews were held in China during the summer of 1997. Of these, 46 interviews were with those at core companies and the remaining 42 were with the individuals added; they took place in Beijing, Tianjin, Shanghai, Wuhan, the Guangzhou area, Shenzhen, and Hong Kong. This leaves important parts of China unexamined; but it does cover many of the major areas.

Processing the Information

Having completed the interviews, I then organized the information—some of it regarding predicted points reflected on the questionnaires, but much of it unanticipated—into a usable form. This was done with a matrix listing repeated themes and issues across the top and interviewees down the side, with quotes and comments filled into the grid. Under a given theme—for example, distribution—all relevant comments by interviewees could thus be compared and analyzed quickly by going down a column.

From this matrix the priorities involved with managing each of the business functions addressed were identified. These were grouped together and analyzed in the chapters, where other sources of information were also drawn on. However, the specific issues considered were only those identified by interviewees in the research.

Draft tables of the issues in each business function were circulated to all interviewees in the field, and changes and additions were made based on their comments. Furthermore, I followed up with a large number of the interviewees by phone, fax, and (thankfully) email in order to clarify or substantiate points made during the field research. This feedback was used to refine tables of priority issues to their final form. As these are the real focus of the research, a number of interviewees observed that this volume comprises not case studies of firms but rather case studies of how particular business functions are being handled.

Drafts were sent to individuals at each of the firms involved as core companies and to scholars for review. Two study groups, one in Hong Kong, one in Washington, were held to review and critique the findings.

List of Sources

1. Director of marketing, Shanghai-based distribution consultancy.

2. General manager of the China operations of a major American agribusiness conglomerate.

3. Country controller and treasurer for a major American agribusiness conglomerate.

4. CEO of the China operations of a large, diversified American conglomerate.

5. Country manager for a subsidiary of a large, diversified American conglomerate.

6. Government relations manager of a large, diversified American conglomerate.

7. General counsel and government relations manager for the medical systems subsidiary of a large diversified firm.

8. CEO of a holdings company specializing in apparel manufacturing. Based in Hong Kong, it is a Chinese family-owned business.

9. Director of the financing department of a Hong Kong-based investment bank.

10. Ambassador of a European OECD state.

11. General manager of the business development office for a large American energy and chemical company.

12. Corporate representative and regional vice president for a large American energy and chemical company.

13. Vice president of the exploration department of a large American energy and chemical company, operating out of Guangdong.

14. An attorney representing a large American energy and chemical company.

15. General manager of a diversified American chemical company.

16. Chairman of the China/Hong Kong/Taiwan operations of a large, diversified American chemical company.

17. Director of finance for a diversified American chemical company.

18. Deputy general manager of the agricultural products department of a diversified American chemical company.

19. General manager of the holding company of a diversified American chemical company.

20. Senior managing director of a Western telecommunications firm.

21. Chief executive of a Western logistics and marketing services firm.

22. President of the China operations of a diversified American technology and manufacturing conglomerate.

23. Vice president of a subsidiary of a diversified American technology and manufacturing conglomerate.

24. General manager of a subsidiary of a diversified American technology and manufacturing conglomerate.

25. President of a subsidiary of a diversified American technology and manufacturing conglomerate.

26. General manager of a subsidiary of a diversified American technology and manufacturing conglomerate.

27. Executive vice president of the Asia and Americas division of a large American communications and electronics firm.

28. Senior international counsel for a large American communications and electronics firm.

29. Director and deputy manager of China operations for a large American communications and electronics firm.

30. Assistant country controller for a large American communications and electronics firm.

31. Vice president and corporate director of logistics for a large American communications and electronics firm.

32. Managing director of a China plant for a large American communications and electronics firm.

33. General manager for a subsidiary of a large American communications and electronics firm.

34. Vice president and regional director of human resources for a large American communications and electronics firm.

35. Vice president and director of distribution for a subsidiary of a large American communications and electronics firm.

36. President of China operations for a large American communications and electronics firm.

37. Vice president and China country controller for a large American communications and electronics firm.

38. Managing director for the operations of an American food-processing firm.

39. Director of public affairs for a major American high-technology company.

40. Operations manager for an American food and consumer product additives company.

41. Dean of a Chinese university MBA program.

42. Professional choreographer.

43. US Foreign Commercial Service officer.

44. Business development manager for a Beijing-based, Australian-owned human resources consultancy.

45. US Foreign Service officer.

46. President of an Austrian automotive-sector firm.

47. Chief representative in Shanghai for a US-based financial services provider.

48. General manager of the Shanghai office of a US-based shipping and logistics company.

49. Deputy general manager of a Hong Kong subsidiary of a Chinese provincial-level investment agency.

50. Minister-counselor of the financial section of the embassy of an OECD state.

51. Vice president of equity research for a subsidiary of a major American financial services firm.

52. Vice president and chief regional economist for a subsidiary of a major American financial services firm.

53. Managing director of a Beijing-based, foreign-invested market entry consultancy.

54. Practicing attorney with the Beijing office of a US-based law firm.

55. Director, provincial foreign direct investment office (the only Chinese government employee).

56. Former foreign correspondent of a major Western newspaper.

57. Manager of a Hong Kong subsidiary of a major entertainment conglomerate.

58. General manager of a British automotive-sector manufacturing joint venture.

59. Consultant with a Beijing-based, foreign-owned advisory group.

60. Country corporate officer for China of an American financial services conglomerate.

61. Director of a human resources training consultancy and president of an American Chamber of Commerce in southern China.

62. Director of the regional office of an American commercial advocacy group.

63. American commercial diplomat in Beijing.

64. General manager of a major Japanese trading company.

65. Chairman of a major Hong Kong trading company.

66. General manager of the international affairs section of a large Japanese electronics conglomerate.

67. General manager for the China section of a major Japanese commercial bank.

68. Regional director for an American high-technology company.

69. Director of the China operations of a Japanese commercial advocacy group.

70. Finance director of an American automotive joint venture.

71. Managing director of a Beijing-based consultancy.

72. Managing director of an American chemical company.

73. Hong Kong-based financial journalist.

74. Beijing-based financial journalist.

75. Director of the regional office of an American commercial advocacy group.

76. Director of a Hong Kong-based trading company.

77. Deputy general manager of a Sino-American manufacturing joint venture in north China.

78. Vice president of Asia Pacific operations for a division of a highly diversified American technology and manufacturing conglomerate.

79. Marketing director of a Beijing-based information services consultancy.

80. Executive director of a Hong Kong-based trading company.

81. Manager of Asia Pacific operations for a division of an American conglomerate.

82. Managing director of a division of a highly diversified American technology and manufacturing conglomerate.

83. Commercial director of a Hong Kong-owned distribution company operating in China.

84. Managing director of Hong Kong-based electronics firm with operations in southern China.

85. President of the China operations of an American manufacturing company.

86. Former Beijing bureau chief of a Western daily newspaper.

87. Director of a regional office of an American commercial advocacy group.

88. President of a Beijing-based, foreign-invested market entry consultancy.

Questionnaire
Draft Question Set 2: China Operations— US Firms

Senior China Manager

1. General.
   A) Have your plans, on average, overestimated the Chinese market, underestimated it, or gotten it about right?
   B) How do you choose sites? Important factors:
      ■ proximity to market?
      ■ proximity to input sources?

- proximity to quality expat accommodations?
- other expat considerations?
- reputation of local bureaucracy?
- local incentives/environmental considerations?
- presence of foreign community?
- Chinese preference to direct investment toward site?
- other?

C) Discuss.

D) Do you see China as a single market, or multiple?

E) Discuss future expansion of operations in China. What are the Chinese restraints on growth and how are those affecting you? What would the failure of China to undertake reforms mean? Could your operations be placed elsewhere and still serve the same market?

F) Relationship with local, provincial, and Beijing bureaucracies.

Extent to which each plays an active role in the daily concerns of the firm?

Regulatory competence at each level and relative effort spent on each?

Where is policy most and least uniformly applied?

2. Structure. China facilities, date established, type of venture (WOFE, equity JV, etc.).

A) Decision to use JV/WOFE/etc. structure.

B) A holding company for China operations? Why all the interest?

C) Where are China operations run from: China, Hong Kong, United States? What observations on this variable; sector-specific optimality?

D) Changing dynamics affecting structure optimality as firm develops? as China transforms? Is it more of a problem to constantly adapt in China than in other markets?

3. Motivations for China operations.

A) Factors of importance:
- new markets
- regional base
- base for export to United States/other OECD country
- meet competitors
- foreclose competitors
- romantic mistake
- shareholder expectations
- other (explain)

B) Have the strategic motivations for the firm's activities in China changed over time (challenges, goals, profitability, etc.)?

C) What would you say about the motivations of other firms in your sector: long-term vs. short-term outlook?
D) Do you see yourself as an "incumbent"? Does that matter?

4. Negotiations/Setting up operations.
A) Discuss the things characterizing or dominating your negotiations to establish operations in China; what do you think was most important?
- tech transfer commitments (any relevance in banking?)
- relationships with Beijing officials
- relationships with local partners (the "right" partners)
- FDI commitments
- other
B) Have these relationships/commitments/issues been the keys to venture success subsequently?
C) Level of satisfaction with the Chinese commitment to the agreements.

5. Business.
A) What are the key elements of your business operations? Industry niches: what needs to be clustered together in order to achieve optimal business structure?

6. Profitability.
A) Score factors affecting firm profitability
- Chinese domestic market fluctuations
- regional market fluctuations
- markets in United States (or other developed countries)
- presence of competitors entering/exiting markets
- market share arrangements in China
- tax/other nonmarket mechanisms (now same domestic and foreign?)
- other factors?
B) Are your margins better/same/poorer than year before? Attributed to what?
C) Do you expect margins to widen or narrow in the coming years, as more competitors find a way into the Chinese market?
D) Is there concern about vulnerability of profitability to Chinese policy swings?
E) Customers paying on time and interlocking debt problems. What do you think the solution for China is in this regard?
F) A number of nonfinancial firms are getting backdoor (or tacit) permission to do financing and loans to their subcontractors, employees, etc. Do you think this is a long-term issue for your firm? Is there enough business to go around, or does the ability to offer such services create an unfair advantage?

7. Productivity.
   A) Has productivity increased in your venture, on the whole, over the last 12 months?
   B) What are the major barriers to productivity increases in China?
      - local management/skills shortage
      - language/culture
      - not enough sales/business opportunities
      - resistance to change
      - overstaffing
      - supply problems (foreign exchange or RMB)
      - technological constraints

8. Trading regime and market structure.
   A) Latest Chinese WTO offers. Would you be in favor of seeing Chinese reforms accelerated? What effect would that have on your operations? Do you think you have incumbency advantages?
   B) Priority concerns on nontariff barriers, if any?
   C) Competition policy structure in PRC vs. the United States. Concerns about antitrust. Obviously, it is early to talk about competition policy environment in China, but contestability may be an issue in many areas. Discuss.

9. Effect of bilateral political climate on China operations.
   A) Are there concerns about allegations that Beijing presses US firms too much to lobby Washington?
   B) Thoughts on US-China bilateral policy issues; multilateral economic policy stances. Appraise.

10. Globalization debate at home and anxiety about jobs moving to China: a concern?

11. Environmental impact a concern in China?

12. Market information and restrictions on flow of economic data, an issue or a nonissue?
    A) How does the firm meet its information needs?

13. Does firm have a lobbying function in China per se?

14. The fuzzy line between *guanxi* and corruption. Discuss.

15. Human rights, worker relations, social issues in China.
    - How are you keeping the right senior people? A big issue?
    - Wage costs, changing levels. Discuss

16. Public relations/philanthropic activities.
    - Describe extent and experience. How important?

Treasurer/Finance

1. Financial environment.
   A) Remitting profits, dividends, and interest. What has been your experience?
   B) Profitability: discussion of present performance.
   C) Supply/undersupply of RMB, foreign exchange issues.

2. Structure of finance for China operations.
   A) Debt vs. equity.
   B) Limits for FIEs funding their portion of a JV from internal Chinese source is 70 percent? Are such restrictions important? Ignored?
   C) Valuation of tangible inputs to a venture, fees (such as land use fees), and other peripheral aspects of deals. How do you feel about the arbitrary valuation of these things?
   D) Different Chinese accounting practice has been an impediment to correct valuation of Chinese businesses. Are they starting to adopt international practice as a result of interaction with you?

3. Legal and regulatory structures for finance.
   A) Incomplete law governing certain instruments/areas of concern to the firm in the financial area of the China operations? Derivatives, e.g.?
   B) Unattractive mortgage markets because of still poor governance?
   C) Other regulatory issues affecting financial operations of China ventures.

4. Tax regimes.
   A) Discuss tax levels, convergence between foreign tax rates and domestic as a precursor to more wide-open competition. What effect on operations? Similar issues to those in other developing countries?
   B) Incentives' importance?
   C) What percentage of potential tax liability is actually paid at present? Is there a lax interpretation of liability here that plays an important role in determining net margins? Is this a future risk in terms of back liability?

5. Noncommercial cash flow issues (worker-related, etc.). A concern?

Legal Issues

1. What legal resources are required by the firm's China operations? Is mandated use of personnel from FESCO (the government legal firm) or onerous legal reporting and proprietary data a problem?

2. How adequate, in general, is the legal system in China for your operations?
   A) Do you think of incomplete legal and regulatory regimes as a simple commercial risk?
   B) List priority legal and regulatory concerns.

3. Are there examples of gaps/ambiguity in these regimes working in firm's favor? Is that *generally* the case?

4. Experience with mediation/arbitration/litigation. Weak capacity. Political influence.
   A) List of cases the firm has been involved in, and outcome.
   B) Development of mediation services in Beijing and elsewhere; how important?
   C) Discuss pressures to avoid mediation in China.

5. Informal mechanisms for obtaining legal and regulatory needs security: describe.

6. Local vs. provincial vs. central legal structures, interaction; and focus of firm legal priorities.

7. Firm contributions to local/provincial/central regulatory crafting process? Has your firm helped to craft specific regulations? Give concrete examples.

8. Specific topics.
   A) What would an OECD antibribery code do to your operations? What experience have you had with FCPA?
   B) Antitrust, anticompetitive practice concerns?
   C) Export control regulations?

Matrix for Organizing Responses

The following columns in the matrix were used to organize interview responses:

A.   Interviewee name
B.   Business
C.   Base
D.   Motivations for China operations
E.   Negotiation, setup, establishment issues
F.   Incentives
G.   Export, performance requirements

H.   Distribution
I.   Import regime
J.   Services (financial, etc.)
K.   Investment issues
L.   Relationships' importance
M. Industrial policy, central government presence
N.   Market structure
O.   Market trends
P.   Firm structures
Q.   Overcapacity
R.   Tax issues
S.   Profitability
T.   Profit issues
U.   Remittances
V.   Holding companies
W. Productivity
X.   Legal
Y.   Interprovincial trade and barriers
Z.   Beijing-local tensions
AA. Foreign policy pressure effect
BB. Chinese structural reform process
CC. Fiscal and monetary policies
DD. Corruption
EE. Intellectual property rights
FF. Property rights
GG. Employment, labor, and training
HH. Maintenance and quality management
II.   Social initiatives
JJ.   Safety and environment
KK. WTO remarks
LL. Recommendations

References

Abramowitz, Morton I. 1997. *China: Can We Have a Policy?* New York: Carnegie Endowment for International Peace.

Aldridge, A. Owen. 1993. *The Dragon and the Eagle: The Presence of China in the American Enlightenment.* Detroit: Wayne State University Press.

American Conference Institute. 1994. *Doing Business in China and Hong Kong: Into the Next Century.* San Francisco: ACI.

Asia Pacific Economic Cooperation, Economic Committee. 1996. *1996 APEC Economic Outlook.* Singapore: APEC Secretariat.

Asia Society. 1992a. *U.S.-Japan Policy Dialogue on China: Economic Issues.* Report on the First Meeting of the U.S.-Japan Consultative Group on Policies toward the PRC. New York: Asia Society.

Asia Society. 1992b. *U.S.-Japan Policy Dialogue on China: Political Issues.* Report on the Second Meeting of the U.S.-Japan Consultative Group on Policies toward the PRC. New York: Asia Society.

Asia Society. 1993. *U.S.-Japan Policy Dialogue on China: Security Issues.* Report on the Third Meeting of the U.S.-Japan Consultative Group on Policies toward the PRC. New York: Asia Society.

Asian Development Bank. 1995. *Annual Report 1995.* Manila: Asian Development Bank.

Australia Department of Foreign Affairs and Trade, East Asia Analytical Unit. 1997a. *China Embraces the Market: Achievements, Constraints, and Opportunities.* Barton, Australia: Department of Foreign Affairs and Trade.

Australia Department of Foreign Affairs and Trade, East Asia Analytical Unit. 1997b. *The New ASEANS: Vietnam, Burma, Cambodia, and Laos.* Barton, Australia: Department of Foreign Affairs and Trade.

Bai, Chong-en, David D. Li, and Yijiang Wang. 1997. Enterprise Productivity and Efficiency: When Is Up Really Down? *Journal of Comparative Economics* 24, no. 3 (June): 265–80.

Balassa, Bela. 1991. *Economic Policies in the Pacific Area Developing Countries.* London: Macmillan.

Bank for International Settlements. 1997. *The Maturity, Sectoral, and Nationality Distribution of International Bank Lending, First Half 1997.* Basel: Bank for International Settlements.

Basu, Susanto, and David D. Li. 1994. *Corruption and Reform.* CREST Working Paper Series: 94-14. Ann Harbor: University of Michigan.

Becker, Stuart, ed. 1994. *China Power Projects Directory, 1994–95.* Hong Kong: Huge Power International.

Bell, Michael W., Hoe Ee Khor, and Kalpana Kochhar. 1993. *China at the Threshold of a Market Economy.* Occasional Paper 107. Washington: International Monetary Fund.

Bergsten, C. Fred, Thomas Horst, and Theodore H. Moran. 1978. *American Multinationals and American Interests.* Washington: Brookings Institution.

Bernstein, Richard, and Ross H. Munro. 1997. *The Coming Conflict with China.* New York: Alfred A. Knopf.

Birdsall, Nancy, and Frederick Jaspersen. 1997. *Pathways to Growth: Comparing East Asia and Latin America.* Washington: Inter-American Development Bank.

Bloch, Julia Chang. 1997. Commercial Diplomacy. In *Living with China: U.S.-China Relations in the Twenty-First Century,* ed. by Ezra F. Vogel. New York: W. W. Norton.

Boisot, Max, and John Child. 1996. The Institutional Nature of China's Emerging Economic Order. In *Management Issues in China.* Vol. 1, *Domestic Enterprises,* ed. by David H. Brown and Robin Porteras. New York: Routledge.

Broadman, Harry G. 1995. *Policy Options for Reform of Chinese State-Owned Enterprises.* Discussion Paper 335. Washington: World Bank.

Brown, David H., and Mohamed Branine. 1996. Adaptive Personnel Management: Evidence of an Emerging Heterogeneity in China's Foreign Trade Corporations. In *Management Issues in China.* Vol. 1, *Domestic Enterprises,* ed. by David H. Brown and Robin Porteras. New York: Routledge.

Brown, David H., and Robin Porteras, eds. 1996. *Management Issues in China.* Vol. 1, *Domestic Enterprises.* New York: Routledge.

Buckley, Peter J., and Jeremy Clegg. 1991. *Multinational Enterprises in Less Developed Countries.* London: Macmillan.

Burstein, Daniel, and Arne de Keijzer. 1998. *Big Dragon: China's Future: What It Means for Business, the Economy, and the Global Order.* New York: Simon and Schuster.

Callan, Benedicte, Sean S. Costigan, and Kenneth H. Keller. 1997. *Exporting US High Tech: Facts and Fiction about the Globalization of Industrial R&D.* Study Group Report. New York: Council on Foreign Relations.

Central Intelligence Agency. 1996. *The World Fact Book.* Washington: Central Intelligence Agency.

Chan, Anita, and Robert A. Senser. 1997. China's Troubled Workers. *Foreign Affairs* 76, no. 2 (March/April): 104–11.

Chan, M. W. Luke. 1996. Management Education in the People's Republic of China. In *Management Issues in China.* Vol. 1, *Domestic Enterprises,* ed. by David H. Brown and Robin Porteras. New York: Routledge.

Chen Kuan, Wang Hongchang, and Zheng Yuxin. 1988. Productivity Change in Chinese Industry: 1953–1985. *Journal of Comparative Economics* 12, no. 4 (December): 570–91.

Child, John. 1996. *Management in China during the Age of Reform.* New York: Cambridge University Press.

China, People's Republic of, Ministry of Foreign Trade and Economic Cooperation. Various years. *Almanac of China's Foreign Economic Relations and Trade.* Beijing: China Ministry of Foreign Trade and Economic Cooperation.

China, People's Republic of, National Environmental Protection Agency and State Planning Commission. 1994. *Environmental Action Plan of China, 1991–2000.* Beijing: China Environmental Science Press.

China STAFF. 1997. *China STAFF* 3, no. 8 (July/August).

Christopher, Robert C. 1986. *Second to None: American Companies in Japan.* New York: Fawcett Columbine.

Claessens, Stijn, and Thomas Glaessner. 1997. *Are Financial Sector Weaknesses Undermining the East Asian Miracle?* Washington: World Bank.

Clarke, Donald, Nicholas Howson, and Qiao Ganliang. 1997. China's New Partnership Law. *China Business Review* 24, no. 4 (July–August).

Cline, William R. 1997. *Trade and Income Distribution*. Washington: Institute for International Economics.

Cohen, Warren I. 1990. *America's Response to China: A History of Sino-American Relations*. New York: Columbia University Press.

Committee for Economic Development. 1997. *U.S. Economic Policy Toward the Asia-Pacific Region*. New York: CED.

Committee on Scholarly Communication with the People's Republic of China, Office of International Affairs, National Research Council. 1992. *Grasslands and Grassland Sciences in Northern China*. Washington: National Academy Press.

Coopers & Lybrand. 1996. *Tax Primer: Corporate Investment into the People's Republic of China*. 2nd ed. Beijing: Coopers & Lybrand.

Destler, I. M. 1995. *American Trade Politics*, 3d ed. Washington: Institute for International Economics.

Dittmer, Lowell. 1994. *China under Reform*. Boulder, CO: Westview Press.

Dobson, Wendy, and Pierre Jacquet. 1998. *Financial Services Liberalization in the WTO*. Washington: Institute for International Economics.

Donaldson, Thomas. 1996. Values in Tension: Ethics away from Home. *Harvard Business Review* (September–October): 48–62.

Drucker, Peter, and Isao Nakauchi. 1997. *Drucker on Asia: A Dialogue between Peter Drucker and Isao Nakauchi*. Oxford: Butterworth Heinemann.

Dua, André, and Daniel C. Esty. 1997. *Sustaining the Asia Pacific Miracle: Environmental Protection and Economic Integration*. Washington: Institute for International Economics.

Dunning, John H. 1958. *American Investment in British Manufacturing Industry*. London: George Allen and Unwin.

EIU. 1995. *Moving China Ventures out of the Red into the Black: Insights from Best and Worst Performers*. Research Report. Wanchai, Hong Kong: EIU.

EIU (Economist Intelligence Unit). 1996a. *China*. Business Report, 4th Quarter 1996. New York: EIU.

EIU. 1996b. *China Hand*. Vol. 1. London: EIU.

EIU. 1996c. *China's Leading Industrial Companies: The Top 50*. Research Report. Wanchai, Hong Kong: EIU.

EIU. 1997. *Multinational Companies in China: Winners and Losers*. Research Report. Wanchai, Hong Kong: EIU.

Elliott, Kimberly Ann, ed. 1997. *Corruption and the Global Economy*. Washington: Institute for International Economics.

Enright, Michael J., Edith E. Scott, and David Dodwell. 1997. *The Hong Kong Advantage*. Oxford: Oxford University Press.

Fairbank, John King. 1983. *The United States and China*. Cambridge, MA: Harvard University Press.

Fernald, John, Hali J. Edison, and Prakash Loungani. 1998. *Was China the First Domino? Assessing Links Between China and the Rest of Emerging Asia*. International Finance Discussion Papers. Washington: Federal Reserve Board.

Findlay, Christopher, Andrew Watson, and Will Martin. 1993. Policy Reform, Chinese Agriculture, and the Implications for China's Trade. In *Economic Reform, Trade and Agricultural Development*, ed. by I. Goldin. New York: St. Martin's Press.

Findlay, Christopher, Andrew Watson, and Harry X. Wu. 1993. Economic Liberalisation in China: The Impact and Prospects for the "Out of Plan" Sector. *Asian Studies Review* 17, no. 2: 5–20.

Fleisher, Belton M., Yong Yin, and Stephen M. Hills. 1997. The Role of Housing Privatization and Labor-Market Reform in China's Dual Economy. *China Economic Review* 8, no. 1: 1–17.

Fox, Eleanor M., and Robert Pitofsky. 1997. United States. In *Global Competition Policy*, ed. by Edward M. Graham and J. David Richardson. Washington: Institute for International Economics.

Frost, Ellen L. 1987. *For Richer, For Poorer: The New U.S.-Japan Relationship*. New York: Council on Foreign Relations.

Funabashi, Yoichi, Michel Oksenberg, and Heinrich Weiss. 1994. *An Emerging China in a World of Interdependence: A Report to the Trilateral Commission*. Report 45. New York: Trilateral Commission.

Gallup China. 1995. *Gallup China*. Research Report. Beijing: Gallup China.

Gilboy, George J. 1997. China's Hollow Miracle. Photocopy. MIT, Political Science Department, Cambridge, MA.

Gilboy, George J. Forthcoming. Manufacturing China: Industrial Technology and the Institutions of Political Economic Development. Ph.D. diss., MIT.

Goldman, Arieh. 1996a. *Retail Modernization in China: Present State and Future Directions*. CEIBS-Working Paper 008. Shanghai: China-Europe International Business School.

Goldman, Arieh. 1996b. *Supermarkets in China: Entry Limitations and Strategic Dilemmas*. CEIBS-Working Paper 005. Shanghai: China-Europe International Business School.

Graham, Edward M. 1991. Strategic Trade Policy and the Multinational Enterprise in Developing Countries. In *Multinational Enterprises in Less Developed Countries*, ed. by Peter J. Buckley. London: Macmillan.

Graham, Edward M. 1996. Direct Investment and the Future Agenda of the World Trade Organization. In *The World Trading System: Challenges Ahead*, ed. by Jeffrey J. Schott. Washington: Institute for International Economics.

Graham, Edward M. 1998. Globalization and the Multilateral Agreement on Investment. Photocopy. Washington: Institute for International Economics.

Graham, Edward M., and Paul R. Krugman. 1995. *Foreign Direct Investment in the United States*. 3rd ed. Washington: Institute for International Economics.

Graham, Edward M., and Li-Gang Liu. 1998. Opening China's Bond Market. Journal of World Trade 32, no. 4 (August).

Graham, Edward M., and J. David Richardson. 1997a. *Competition Policies for the Global Economy*. POLICY ANALYSES IN INTERNATIONAL ECONOMICS 51. Washington: Institute for International Economics.

Graham, Edward M., and J. David Richardson, eds. 1997b. *Global Competition Policy*. Washington: Institute for International Economics.

Graham, Edward M., and J. David Richardson. 1997c. Issue Overview. In *Global Competition Policy*, ed. by Edward M. Graham and J. David Richardson. Washington: Institute for International Economics.

Grossman, Gene M., and Henrik Horn. 1988. Infant-Industry Protection Reconsidered: The Case of Informational Barriers to Entry. *Quarterly Journal of Economics* 103, no. 4 (November): 767.

Grossman, Gene M., and Alan B. Krueger. 1993. Environmental Impacts of a North American Free Trade Agreement. In *The Mexico-US Free Trade Agreement*, ed. by Peter M. Garber. Cambridge, MA: MIT Press.

Groves, Theodore, Yongmiao Hong, John McMillan, and Barry Naughton. 1995. China's Evolving Managerial Labor Market. *Journal of Political Economy* 103, no. 4 (August): 873–93.

Haiyan Zhang and Daniel Van Den Bulcke. 1994. *International Management Strategies of Chinese Multinational Firms*. Discussion Paper. Antwerp: University of Antwerp.

Harding, Harry. 1997. Breaking the Impasse over Human Rights. In *Living with China: U.S.-China Relations in the Twenty-First Century*, ed. by Ezra F. Vogel. New York: W. W. Norton.

Harrold, Peter. 1992. *China's Reform Experience to Date*. Discussion Paper 180. Washington: China and Mongolia Department, World Bank.

Hay, Donald. 1997. United Kingdom. In *Global Competition Policy*, ed. by Edward M. Graham and J. David Richardson. Washington: Institute for International Economics.

Hayhoe, Ruth. 1996. *China's Universities: 1895–1995, A Century of Cultural Conflict*. New York: Garland.

Hazelbarth, Todd. 1997. *The Chinese Media: More Autonomous and Diverse—Within Limits*. An Intelligence Monograph. Washington: Center for the Study of Intelligence, Central Intelligence Agency.

Hong Kong and Shanghai Banking Corporation (HSBC). 1993. *China*. HSBC Group: Business Profile Series, 10th ed. Hong Kong: HSBC.

Howson, Nicholas. 1997. Wholly Foreign-Owned Enterprises and Holding or Investment Companies in the People's Republic of China. Photocopy. NY: Paul, Weiss, Rifkind, Wharton & Garrison.

Hsieh, Chang-Tai. 1998. Essays on the Measurement and Explanation of Economic Growth. Dissertation. Department of Economics, University of California.

Hufbauer, Gary Clyde, Jeffrey J. Schott, and Kimberly Ann Elliott. 1990. *Economic Sanctions Reconsidered*. Washington: Institute for International Economics.

Hufbauer, Gary Clyde, and Christopher Findlay, eds. 1996. *Flying High: Liberalizing Civil Aviation in the Asia Pacific*. Washington: Institute for International Economics.

IMF (International Monetary Fund). 1993. *China at the Threshold of a Market Economy*. Occasional Paper no. 107. Washington: IMF.

IRI (International Republican Institute). 1997a. *Election Observation Report: Fujian, People's Republic of China*. Washington: IRI.

IRI. 1997b. *Village Committee Elections in the People's Republic of China*. Washington: IRI.

Jacobson, Harold K., and Michel Oksenberg. 1990. *China's Participation in the IMF, the World Bank, and GATT: Toward a Global Economic Order*. Ann Arbor: University of Michigan Press.

Japan-China Investment Promotion Organization. 1997. *Questionnaire for Japanese Companies*, vol. 4. Tokyo: Japan-China Investment Promotion Organization.

Jefferson, Gary H., Thomas G. Rawski, and Yuxin Zheng. 1996. Chinese Industrial Productivity: Trends, Measurement Issues, and Recent Developments. *Journal of Comparative Economics* 23, no. 2 (1996): 146–80.

Johnson, Todd M., et al., eds. 1996. *China: Issues and Options in Greenhouse Gas Emissions Control*. Discussion Paper 330. Washington: World Bank.

Jones, Randall, Robert King, and Michael Klein. 1992. *The Chinese Economic Area: Economic Integration without a Free Trade Agreement*. Working Paper Series 124. Paris: Organization for Economic Cooperation and Development.

Joseph, William A., ed. 1994. *China Briefing, 1994*. Boulder, CO: Westview Press.

Kennedy, Scott. 1997. The Stone Group: State Client or Market Pathbreaker? *China Quarterly*, no. 152 (December).

Khan, Azizur Rahman, and Carl Riskin. 1998. Income and Inequality in China. *China Quarterly*, no. 154 (June): 221–53.

Kristof, Nicholas D., and Sheryl Wudunn. 1994. *China Wakes: The Struggle for the Soul of a Rising Power*. New York: Times Books.

Krugman, Paul R. 1994. The Myth of Asia's Miracle. *Foreign Affairs* 73, no. 6: 62–78.

Lardy, Nicholas R. 1987. *China's Entry into the World Economy: Implications for Northeast Asia and the United States*. Asian Agenda Report 11. Washington: Asia Society.

Lardy, Nicholas R. 1992a. Chinese Foreign Trade. *China Quarterly*, no. 131 (September): 691–720.

Lardy, Nicholas R. 1992b. *Foreign Trade and Economic Reform in China, 1978–1990*. Cambridge: Cambridge University Press.

Lardy, Nicholas R. 1994. *China in the World Economy*. Washington: Institute for International Economics.

Lardy, Nicholas R. 1997. Normalizing Economic Relations with China. *Promoting US Interests in China: Alternatives to the Annual MFN Review* 8, No. 4 (July): 15–21.

Lardy, Nicholas R. 1998. *China's Unfinished Economic Revolution*. Washington: Brookings Institution.

Latham, Richard J. 1997. The Greatest Point of Contact between the US and China . . . Is, and Always Has Been, Commerce. Paper presented at the US-China Business Council Breakfast, sponsored by United Technologies Corporation, Beijing (13 January).

League of Nations. 1931. *Statistical Yearbook of the League of Nations, 1930/31.* Geneva: League of Nations.

Levy, Gina. 1995. *Moving China Ventures out of the Red into the Black: Insights from Best and Worst Performers.* Custom Publishing Report. London: Economist Intelligence Unit/ Arthur Anderson.

Lichtenstein, Natalie. 1993. *Enterprise Reform in China: The Evolving Legal Framework.* Working Paper Series 1198. Washington: Legal Department, World Bank.

Lieberthal, Kenneth. 1995. *Governing China.* New York: W. W. Norton.

Lieberthal, Kenneth. 1997. Domestic Forces and Sino-U.S. Relations. In *Living with China: U.S.-China Relations in the Twenty-first Century,* ed. by Ezra F. Vogel. New York: W. W. Norton.

Lieberthal, Kenneth, and Michel Oksenberg. 1988. *Policy Making in China.* Princeton: Princeton University Press.

Lilley, James R., and Wendell L. Willkie II. 1994. *Beyond MFN: Trade with China and American Interests.* Washington: AEI Press.

Lubman, Stanley. 1997. *Sino-American Relations and China's Struggle for the Rule of Law.* Institute Reports. New York: East Asian Institute, Columbia University (October).

Lubman, Stanley. 1998. Foreign Direct Investment in China: Past Accomplishments, Future Uncertainties. Photocopy.

Madsen, Richard. 1995. *China and the American Dream: A Moral Inquiry.* Berkeley: University of California Press.

Mann, Jim. 1989. *Beijing Jeep: The Short, Unhappy Romance of Western Business in China.* New York: Simon and Schuster.

Mann, Jim. 1997. *Beijing Jeep: A Case Study of Western Business in China.* Boulder, CO: Westview Press.

Maskus, Keith, Sean M. Dougherty, and Andrew Mertha. 1998. Intellectual Property Rights and Economic Development in China. Paper presented at the Southeast China Regional Conference on Intellectual Property Rights and Economic Development in Changging, China (15–18 September).

Mason, Mark. 1992. *American Multinationals and Japan: The Political Economy of Japanese Capital Controls, 1899–1980.* Cambridge, MA: Harvard University Press.

Mastel, Greg. 1997. *The Rise of the Chinese Economy: The Middle Kingdom Emerges.* Armonk, NY: M. E. Sharpe.

McKinnon, Ronald I. 1994. *Gradual vs. Rapid Liberalization in Socialist Economies: Financial Policies in China and Russia Compared.* Sector Studies Series 10. San Francisco: International Center for Economic Growth.

Metzger, Thomas A. 1996. *"Transcending the West": Mao's Vision of Socialism and the Legitimization of Teng Hsiao-p'ing's Modernization Program.* Essays in Public Policy 15. Stanford, CA: Hoover Institution on War, Revolution, and Peace.

Moran, Theodore. 1998. *Foreign Direct Investment and Development: The New Policy Agenda for Developing Countries and Economies in Transition.* Washington: Institute for International Economics.

Mueller, Milton, and Zixiang Tan. 1997. *China in the Information Age: Telecommunications and the Dilemmas of Reform.* Westport, CT: Praeger.

Myers, Ramon H. 1994. *Thoughts on U.S. Foreign Policy toward the People's Republic of China.* Essays in Public Policy 47. Stanford, CA: Hoover Institution on War, Revolution, and Peace.

Naughton, Barry. 1996a. *China's Dual Trading Regimes: Implications for Growth and Reform.* Seminar Paper 96-20. Adelaide, Australia: Center for International Economic Studies, University of Adelaide.

Naughton, Barry. 1996b. *Growing Out of the Plan: Chinese Economic Reform, 1978–1993.* Cambridge: Cambridge University Press.

Noland, Marcus. 1996. *US-China Economic Relations.* Working Paper Series 96-6. Washington: Institute for International Economics.

Noland, Marcus, Li-Gang Liu, Sherman Robinson, and Zhi Wang. 1998. *Global Economic Effects of the Asian Currency Devaluations*. POLICY ANALYSES IN INTERNATIONAL ECONOMICS 56. Washington: Institute for International Economics.

Oksenberg, Michel C., Michael D. Swaine, and Daniel C. Lynch. 1997. *The Chinese Future*. Los Angeles: Pacific Council on International Policy.

Organization for Economic Cooperation and Development. 1996. *Geographical Distribution of Financial Flows to Aid Recipients, 1991–1995*. Paris: OECD.

Ozawa, Terutomo. 1991. The Dynamics of Pacific Rim Industrialization: How Mexico Can Join the Asian Flock of "Flying Geese." In *Mexico's External Relations in the 1990s*, ed. by Riordan Roett. Boulder, CO: Lynne Rienner Publishers.

Paglee, Charles D. 1998. Contracts and Agreements in the People's Republic of China. In *Chinalaw*. http://www.qis.net/chinalaw/contrc1.htm (6 March).

Paine, Lynn Sharp. 1994. Managing for Organizational Integrity. *Harvard Business Review* (March–April): 106–117.

Pearson, Margaret M. 1991. *Joint Ventures in the People's Republic of China: The Control of Foreign Direct Investment under Socialism*. Princeton: Princeton University Press.

Pearson, Margaret M. 1997. *China's New Business Elite: The Political Consequences of Reform*. Berkeley: University of California Press.

Petrazzini, Ben A. 1996. *Global Telecom Talks: A Trillion Dollar Deal*. POLICY ANALYSES IN INTERNATIONAL ECONOMICS 44. Washington: Institute for International Economics.

Pomfret, Richard. 1992. Financial Reform in China. *Seoul Journal of Economics* 5, no. 4: 351–73.

Pomfret, Richard. 1994a. *Locational Competitiveness in East Asia*. Seminar Paper 94-08. Adelaide, Australia: Center for International Economic Studies, University of Adelaide.

Pomfret, Richard. 1994b. *What Can Other Countries in Transition Learn from China?* Seminar Paper 94-01. Adelaide, Australia: Center for International Economic Studies, University of Adelaide.

Pomfret, Richard. 1996. *China's Trade Miracle*. Seminar Paper 96-03. Adelaide, Australia: Center for International Economic Studies, University of Adelaide.

Porter, Michael E. 1990. *The Competitive Advantage of Nations*. New York: Free Press.

Potter, Pitman B. 1995. Foreign Investment Law in the People's Republic of China: Dilemmas of State Control. *China Quarterly* 141 (March): 155–85.

Rauch, James E. 1997. Comments. In *Corruption and the Global Economy*, ed. by Kimberly Ann Elliott. Washington: Institute for International Economics.

Rawski, Thomas G. 1989. *Economic Growth in Prewar China*. Berkeley: University of California Press.

Rawski, Thomas. 1993. *How Fast Has Chinese Industry Grown?* Working Paper Series 1194. Washington: Policy Research Department, World Bank.

Riskin, Carl. 1987. *China's Political Economy*. London: Oxford University Press.

Rodrik, Dani. 1997a. Comments on the Effects of Corruption on Growth, Investment, and Government Expenditure: A Cross-Country Analysis, by Paolo Mauro. In *Corruption and the Global Economy*, ed. by Kimberly Ann Elliott. Washington: Institute for International Economics.

Rodrik, Dani. 1997b. *Has Globalization Gone Too Far?* Washington: Institute for International Economics.

Roett, Riordan, ed. 1991. *Mexico's External Relations in the 1990s*. Boulder, CO: Lynne Rienner Publishers.

Rose-Ackerman, Susan. 1997. The Political Economy of Corruption. In *Corruption and the Global Economy*, ed. by Kimberly Ann Elliott. Washington: Institute for International Economics.

Rosen, Daniel, Li-Gang Liu, and Lawrence Dwight. 1998. Financial Fallout. *China Business Review* 25, no. 2 (March–April): 44–47.

Sachs, Jeffrey D., and Wing Thye Woo. 1997. *Understanding China's Economic Performance*. Working Paper 97/2. Canberra, Australia: Department of Economics, Australian National University.

Santoro, Michael A. 1998. Engagement with Integrity: What We Should Expect Multinational Firms to Do about Human Rights in China. *Business and the Contemporary World* 10, no. 1: 25–54.

Scherer, F. M., and David Ross. 1990. *Industrial Market Structure and Economic Performance.* Boston: Houghton Mifflin.

Schott, Jeffrey J, ed. 1996a. *The World Trading System: Challenges Ahead.* Washington: Institute for International Economics.

Schott, Jeffrey J. 1996b. *WTO 2000: Setting the Course for World Trade.* POLICY ANALYSES IN INTERNATIONAL ECONOMICS 45. Washington: Institute for International Economics.

Schott, Jeffrey J. 1998. *Launching New Global Trade Talks: An Action Agenda.* Special Report 12. Washington: Institute for International Economics.

Schott, Jeffrey J., assisted by Johanna W. Buurman. 1994. *The Uruguay Round: An Assessment.* Washington: Institute for International Economics.

Sheard, Paul. 1997. Keiretsu, Competition, and Market Access. In *Global Competition Policy,* ed. by Edward M. Graham and J. David Richardson. Washington: Institute for International Economics.

Sherwood, Stanley G., Mary Huang, Cassie Wong, Paul Gillis, and Michael Happell. 1998. The Great Wall of Transfer Pricing Becomes Harder to Climb: China's Transfer Pricing Circular and June 1998 Meeting with the SAT. *Tax Management Transfer Pricing Report* (29 July).

Shi Dinghuan, Yang Tianchen, and Mu Huaping. 1997. Proposals to Improve Import of Technology and Accelerate Technological Innovation. *Zhogguo Keji Luntan* (Forum on Science and Technology in China), no. 4 (July): 8–12.

Shinn, James, ed. 1996. *Weaving the Net: Conditional Engagement with China.* New York: Council on Foreign Relations.

Shirk, Susan L. 1994. *How China Opened Its Door: The Political Success of the PRC's Foreign Trade and Investment Reforms.* Washington: Brookings Institution.

Sinton, Jonathan E., ed. 1996. *China Energy Databook.* Berkeley, CA: Ernest Orlando Lawrence Berkeley National Laboratory.

Smil, Vaclav. 1993. *China's Environmental Crisis: An Inquiry into the Limits of National Development.* Armonk, NY: M. E. Sharpe.

Smith, Christopher. 1996. End the Beijing Love Affair Now. http://www.inetport.com/~gra/chinasmith1.htm (Rev. 22 May 1997).

Soled, Debra E., ed. 1995. *China: A Nation in Transition.* Washington: Congressional Quarterly.

Spence, Jonathan D. 1991. *The Search for Modern China.* New York: W. W. Norton.

Srinivansan, T. N., ed. 1994. *Agriculture and Trade in China and India: Policies and Performance since 1950.* San Francisco: ICS Press.

Steinfeld, Ed. 1998. *Forging Reform in China: From Party Line to Bottom Line in the State-Owned Enterprise.* Cambridge: Cambridge University Press.

Sugimoto, Takashi. 1993. *The Political Stability of Ethnic Regions in China: A Methodological Study.* IIGP Policy Paper 105E. Tokyo: International Institute for Global Peace.

Swaine, Michel D., and Donald P. Henry. 1995. *China: Domestic Change and Foreign Policy.* Santa Monica, CA: RAND Corp.

Taylor, Robert. 1996. *Greater China and Japan: Prospects for an Economic Partnership in East Asia.* London: Routledge.

United Nations. 1997. *World Investment Report 1997.* Geneva: United Nations.

USCBC (US-China Business Council). 1996a. *From Chain Stores to Direct Sales: Foreign Participation in the PRC Retail Sector.* Washington: USCBC.

USCBC. 1996b. *Labor Developments in China.* Washington: USCBC.

USCBC. 1996c. *Management Training for Local Hires in the PRC.* Washington: USCBC.

USCBC. 1996d. *US Corporate Practices in China: A Resource Guide.* Washington: USCBC.

USCBC. 1998. Distribution of Goods in China: Regulatory Framework and Business Options. Washington: USCBC.

US-China Information & Service Corporation. 1996. *China's Tariff and Non-Tariff Handbook, 1996.* Manassas, VA: US-China Information & Service Corp.

US Department of Commerce. Various years. *US Foreign Trade Highlights*. Washington: US Department of Commerce.

US Department of Commerce. 1995. *Foreign Direct Investment Abroad 1994*. Washington: US Department of Commerce.

US Department of Commerce, National Technical Information Service. 1994. *China Commercial Guide, 1994–95: A Guide to Doing Business in China and Information on Current Economic Conditions*. Washington: US Department of Commerce.

US Department of Commerce, National Technical Information Service, International Trade Administration. 1994. *The China Business Guide*. Washington: US Department of Commerce.

US Department of Energy. Various years. *International Energy Annual*. Washington: US Department of Energy.

US Department of Labor, Bureau of International Labor Affairs. 1994. *Changes in China's Labor Market: Implications for the Future*. Washington: US Department of Labor.

US Department of Treasury. 1997. *Treasury Bulletin* (December). Washington: US Department of Treasury.

US House Committee on Foreign Affairs, Subcommittee on Human Rights and International Organizations on Asian and Pacific Affairs, and on International Economic Policy and Trade. 1989. *Human Rights and Political Developments in China*. 101st Cong., 1st sess., 13 and 19 July.

US Trade Representative. 1998. *National Trade Estimate Report on Foreign Trade Barriers*. Washington: US Trade Representative.

Vogel, Ezra F. 1989. *One Step Ahead in China: Guangdong under Reform*. Cambridge, MA: Harvard University Press.

Vogel, Ezra F., ed. 1997. *Living with China: U.S.-China Relations in the Twenty-first Century*. New York: W. W. Norton.

Walder, Andrew G. 1988. *Communist Neo-Traditionalism: Work and Authority in Chinese Industry*. University of California Press.

Wang, Hongying. n.d. Law, Diplomacy, and Transnational Networks: The Dynamics of Foreign Direct Investment in China. Photocopy.

Warner, Malcolm. 1996. Beyond the Iron Rice-bowl. In *Management Issues in China*. Vol. 1, *Domestic Enterprises*, ed. by David H. Brown and Robin Porteras. New York: Routledge.

Wedeman, Andrew Hall. 1995. Bamboo Walls and Brick Ramparts: Rent Seeking, Interregional Economic Conflict, and Local Protectionism in China, 1984–1991. Ph.D. diss., University of California, Los Angeles.

Wei, Li. 1997. The Impact of Economic Reform on the Performance of Chinese State Enterprises, 1980–1989. *Journal of Political Economy* 105, no. 5: 1080–106.

Wei, Shang-Jin. 1997. *How Taxing Is Corruption on International Investors?* NBER Working Papers 6030. Cambridge, MA: National Bureau of Economic Research.

Weidenbaum, Harry, and Samuel Hughes. 1996. *The Bamboo Network: How Expatriate Chinese Entrepreneurs Are Creating New Economic Superpower in Asia*. New York: Martin Kessler Books.

Weir, Robin. 1997. In Transit to China's Hinterlands. *China Staff* 3, no. 8 (July/August).

Williamson, John, ed. 1994. *The Political Economy of Policy Reform*. Washington: Institute for International Economics.

World Bank. 1994. *China: Foreign Trade Reform*. Washington: World Bank.

World Bank. 1996a. *The Chinese Economy: Fighting Inflation, Deepening Reforms*. World Bank Country Study. Washington: World Bank.

World Bank. 1996b. *World Bank Annual Report, 1996*. Washington: World Bank.

World Bank. 1997a. *At China's Table: Food Security Options*. China 2020 Series. Washington: World Bank.

World Bank. 1997b. *China Engaged: Integration with the Global Economy*. China 2020 Series. Washington: World Bank.

World Bank. 1997c. *China 2020: Development Challenges in the New Century*. China 2020 Series. Washington: World Bank.

World Bank. 1997d. *China's Management of Enterprise Assets: The State as Shareholder.* World Bank Country Study. Washington: World Bank.

World Bank. 1997e. *Clear Water, Blue Skies: China's Environment in the New Century.* China 2020 Series. Washington: World Bank.

World Bank. 1997f. *Financing Health Care: Issues and Options for China.* China 2020 Series. Washington: World Bank.

World Bank. 1997g. *Old Age Security: Pension Reform in China.* China 2020 Series. Washington: World Bank.

World Bank. 1997h. *Sharing Rising Incomes: Disparities in China.* China 2020 Series. Washington: World Bank.

World Bank. 1997i. *World Development Indicators.* Washington: World Bank.

Wu, Hongda Harry, with George Vecsey. 1996. *Troublemaker: One Man's Crusade against China's Cruelty.* New York: Times Books.

Yahuda, Michael. 1996. *The International Politics of the Asia-Pacific, 1945–1995.* London: Routledge.

Yamazawa, Ippei. 1998. *APEC's Progress toward the Bogor Target: A Quantitative Assessment of 1997 IAP/CAP.* Tokyo: Pacific Economic Cooperative Council/Japan Committee.

Yang, Dali L. 1997. *Beyond Beijing: Liberalization and the Regions in China.* London: Routledge.

Yang, Dali L. 1998. Survival of the Fittest. *World Link* (June): 50–53.

Young, Susan. 1995. *Private Business and Economic Reform in China.* Armonk, NY: M. E. Sharpe.

Yu, Tzong-shian, and Joseph S. Lee, eds. 1995. *Confucianism and Economic Development.* Taipei: Chung-Hua Institution for Economic Research.

Zhang, Jialin. 1994. *China's Response to the Downfall of Communism in Eastern Europe and the Soviet Union.* Essays in Public Policy 48. Stanford, CA: Hoover Institution on War, Revolution, and Peace.

Zhang, Jialin. 1997. *An Assessment of Chinese Thinking on Trade Liberalization.* Essays in Public Policy 18. Stanford, CA: Hoover Institution on War, Revolution, and Peace.

Zhang Shuguang, Yansheng Zhang, and Zhongxin Wan. Forthcoming. *Measuring the Costs of Protection in China.* Washington: Institute for International Economics and Unirule Institute of Economics.

Zhang, Xiaoguang. 1996. Predicting Structural Changes in Asia's Foreign Trade. East Asia Analytical Unit Working Paper. Canberra, Australia: East Asia Analytical Unit.

Index

Page numbers in *italic* refer to boxes (*b*), figures (*f*), tables (*t*), or footnotes (*n*).

303

dispute resolution, 201, 211–18, 226
  arbitration, 212, 213–14, 224–25
  intellectual property rights, 217–18
  litigation, 211, 214–15, 224–25
  mediation, 212–13, 217, 224–25
distribution
  importance of local presence for, 17, 20, 170–71,
    191, 218, 234
  issues for foreign-invested enterprises, 167–68,
    189–90
  market structure issues, 162, 167, 195–96
  policy issues, 162, 195
  self-imposed issues, 162, 195
  transitional issues, 162, 193–95
distribution system
  actual involvement of foreign-invested
    enterprises, 22, 170–71, 185–89
  ambiguity of policy on, 172–73
  changes needed, 171–76
  collection function, 173–74
  corruption and theft in, 184, 191, 194
  current status, 34
  efficiency, 162b
  history, 163–64
  importance for economic reform, 159–60, 167
  for imports, 166n, 169, 185–86, 188
  independent companies, 187, 191
  internal trade barriers, 38, 136, 161–62, 164n,
    166, 180–81, 190n, 244
  interpretation of regulations on foreign
    involvement, 23–24, 173
  investing to ensure access to, 56
  issue categories, 194t
  joint ventures involved in, 184–89
  lack of openness, 160
  logistics companies, 188
  market share allocation, 181–82, 222, 223
  monopolies, 164–65, 182–83
  problems, 136, 162–63, 167, 171
  reforms, 165
  regional disparities, 192–93
  regulation of, 168–70, 172, 177–81, 185
  restrictions on foreign involvement, 23–24,
    60–61, 167, 173, 249
  unpredictability, 136
  See also retailing; transportation
domestic market
  increasing focus on, 127, 167, 235
  proximity to, 37–38
  See also distribution
Dongfang China Automotive Corporation
  (DCAC), 139–40, 139t, 140f
Drucker, Peter, 159, 167
Dunkin' Donuts, 24
duties. See tariffs

economic growth
  historical, 163
  incomes, 120
  middle class, 111, 242

  transitional problems, 239
  uneven, 41, 81, 103t, 104f
economic reforms, 9–10, 153, 160–61, 164–67
  in financial sector, 239
  importance of distribution system, 159–60,
    167
  legal reforms needed, 200–1, 225–26
  link to political reform, 256–57
  progress of, 238–39
Economic and Technical Development Zones
  (ETDZs), 37
economies of scope, 150–51
Economist Intelligence Unit (EIU), 32, 146, 171
education
  of Chinese workers, 93–94
  of judges and lawyers, 208
  MBA programs, 109, 120, 257
  See also training
EIU. See Economist Intelligence Unit
Eli Lilly, 215
employment. See human resources; labor
environmental impacts
  lax enforcement of laws, 152, 210
  omission from productivity measurements,
    124, 151–52
  regulations, 208–9, 210–11, 225
Environmental Protection Agency (China), 152
equipment
  as factor in productivity, 134
  imported, 62–63
  maintenance of, 146–47
  telecommunications switching, 181–82
  See also technology
equity joint ventures
  amount invested in, 49t
  establishment of, 25, 28
  number approved, 27t, 48f
establishment of foreign-invested enterprises
  (FIEs), 17
  evolution of process, 20, 21
  financial structure, 52–53, 80
  human resources issues, 46–47, 51–52, 77, 80,
    81, 89–96
  incentives, 61–63
  industrial policy issues, 39–42
  interpretation of laws and regulations, 61, 62,
    80–81, 173
  issue categories, 75, 76t
  issues for investors, 20–21
  legal environment, 21–22
  locations. See location selection
  management control issues, 46, 50–51, 80, 91,
    94–96
  market structure issues, 82–83
  negotiations, 21, 46–47
  openness of process, 8–9, 234
  ownership forms, 46, 47–49, 48f, 49t, 80
  partners. See partners
  phasing, 46, 53–56, 138–39
  policy issues, 78–81

establishment of foreign-invested
enterprises—*continued*
regulations. *See* Provisional Regulations for
Guiding the Directions of Foreign
Investment
scope of operations, 59–61, 80, 81
self-imposed problems, 77–78
strategic choices, 20, 29*f*, 35–36, 45–46
transitional issues, 77
See also approval process; performance
requirements
ETDZs. *See* Economic and Technical Development
Zones
ethical behavior, tests of, 203
European Union, 233, 255, 257
Evans, Peter, 73
ex-factory business functions, 161
See also distribution; sales; services
expatriates
amenities for, 39
cultural differences with local employees, 133, 146
efforts to groom local managers, 95*b*
limits on number of, 94, 118
list of sources, 282–86
perspective on Chinese situation, 5
relationships with Chinese, 13–14
study of, 3–7, 279–82, 286–92
exports
Chinese, 130*t*
of foreign-invested enterprises, 127, 128*t*, 135*t*
performance requirements for, 30, 65–68,
168–69, 170
processing operations, 28, 38
See also trade
extraterritoriality, 200

FCPA. *See* Foreign Corrupt Practices Act
FDI. *See* foreign direct investment
Feng Shui, 134*n*
FIEs. *See* foreign-invested enterprises
finance
accounts receivable, 173–74
flows within company, 144–45, 156
foreign exchange accounts, 67, 80
See also capital; costs
financial crisis, Asian. *See* Asian financial crisis
financial institutions
expertise in bond markets, 54
reforms, 239
requirement for Shanghai location, 36–37, 79
financial news services, 24, 24*n*, 79
financial structure, negotiating, 52–53, 80
Fordham University, 109
Foreign Corrupt Practices Act (FCPA), 89, 111,
172, 220
foreign direct investment (FDI)
Chinese policies, 236–39
flows into China, 17, 18*f*, 23, 34*t*, 86–87, 223, 234
locations of, 40*f*
size of projects, 23

foreign exchange accounts, 67, 80
foreign-invested enterprises (FIEs)
capital, 59*t*
establishing. *See* establishment of foreign-
invested enterprises
exports, 127, 128*t*, 135*t*
future performance of, 13–15, 248–50
home office control, 149–50
imports, 127, 127*t*, 135, 135*t*
introduction in China, 160–61, 200
new structures, 30, 49, 145
number of, by enterprise form, 27*t*
organizational structures, 148–50
ownership forms, 46, 47–49, 48*f*, 49*t*, 80
phases of development, 14, 55
positive social influences, 11, 86, 113, 114, 120,
241–43
productivity. *See* productivity
profitability, 14*n*, 55, 56
public attitudes toward, 242
strategic choices, 20, 29*f*, 35–36, 45–46
superlegal privileges, 197–98, 221–23, 224, 225,
227, 228–29
See also joint ventures; wholly owned foreign
enterprises
Fortune, 180
Fuji, 183, 195

garment industry
distribution of products, 192–93
employee turnover, 111
labor practices, 112
subcontractors, 112
See also textile industry
GATT. *See* General Agreement on Tariffs and Trade
General Agreement on Tariffs and Trade (GATT),
92*n*, 160, 243
General Motors, 17, 72, 174, 180
Buick plant in Shanghai, 55, 75, 129–31, 190*n*
governments. *See* Chinese government; local and
provincial governments
graft. *See* corruption
Guangdong Province, 39
economic activity, 38–39, 246
export-processing operations, 38
foreign retailers, 24, 189
retail service stations, 179–80
Guangzhou, foreign investment in, 37–38
guanxi (relationships), 13, 31–32
Guidelines. *See* Provisional Regulations for
Guiding the Direction of Foreign
Investment

Hainan, 37
Hewitt East Gate, 109
high technology industries
distribution of products, 187
incentives for, 24, 216
locations, 38
holding companies, 49, 145, 186

Hong Kong
  economic links with Guangdong, 246
  goods imported through, 188
  investments in China, 33*n*
  return of, 10
housing loans, for Chinese employees, 99, 129
huaqiao. See overseas Chinese
hukou (residence permit) system, 101, 102–3, 119,
    132
human resources
  changes needed in labor market, 101
  Chinese employees, 4, 87, 87*t*, 242
  costs. *See* labor costs
  cultural differences in workplace, 88, 117, 132*n*,
    133, 146
  dang an (personnel files), 101, 102–3, 119
  demand for employees, 86, 87–88, 129
  employee benefits, 99, 105–8
  employment levels at joint ventures, 91, 92–93
  factors in productivity, 129–33
  government labor bureaus, 91–92
  hiring staff, 93–94, 110, 116, 118
  hukou (residence permit) system, 101, 102–3,
    119, 132
  issues, 85–87, 115, 116*t*
  issues in establishment of foreign-invested
    enterprises, 46–47, 51–52, 77, 80, 81, 89–96
  local Chinese managers, 95*b*, 99*t*, 100*t*, 173
  management control over workforce, 94–96,
    118, 132–33, 143
  market structure issues, 119–20
  mobility, 100, 102–4, 119, 132
  number of expatriate managers, 94, 118
  operational issues, 89, 96–98
  overstaffing problems, 52, 92–93, 117–18, 133
  policy issues, 115, 117–19
  positive social influences of foreign-invested
    enterprises, 11, 86, 113, 114, 120, 241–43
  preference for young employees, 108, 131–32,
    132*n*
  quotas for Chinese employees, 94
  in representative offices, 54, 90
  retaining employees, 110–11, 116, 129
  self-imposed issues, 116, 117
  shortages of skilled workers, 93–94, 98, 101–2,
    116, 129–31, 240
  training. *See* training
  transitional issues, 116–17
  See also labor; labor practices
human rights advocates, 113–15
  criticism of labor practices in China, 97, 98,
    112–13, 120, 243

IFC. *See* International Finance Corporation
IMF. *See* International Monetary Fund
imports
  converters, 188
  distribution system, 166*n*, 169, 185–86, 188
  equipment, 62–63
  of foreign-invested enterprises, 127, 127*t*, 135, 135*t*

inputs, 62–63, 127*t*, 135
  of state-owned enterprises, 127*t*
  See also tariffs; trade
incentives
  for foreign investment, 61–63
  for high technology investment, 24, 216
  impact of, 64*b*, 81
  from local governments, 37, 41, 77
  tariffs, 62–63
  tax rates, 62
  See also special economic zones
Inchcape Pacific, 172, 188
incomes
  distribution, 100, 103–4, 103*t*
  growth, 120
  See also salaries
Indonesia, 26*f*
industrial policy, 25, 39–42, 143, 156, 252
inputs, imported, 62–63, 127*t*, 135
Institute for Industrial Economics (China), 74*b*
institutional factors, in productivity, 145–51
insurance companies, 79
intellectual property rights (IPR), 215–18
  administrative solutions, 217
  effect of concerns on technology transfer, 138,
    215, 216–17
  enforcement, 73
  foreign government involvement in issue, 217
  international negotiations on, 243
  problems in China, 71, 72, 75
intermediate goods, 122–23, 134–36
International Finance Corporation (IFC), 95*b*
International Monetary Fund (IMF), 243
International Republican Institute, 254
investment environment, 21–22, 35–36, 236–38
  comparison of APEC countries, 26*f*
  future openness, 10–11, 239–41
  international expectations, 233
  openness of, 8–9, 233–36
  transparency, 30–32
IPR. *See* intellectual property rights

Japan, 257
  commercial policy toward China, 233
  investment environment, 234
  investments in China, 33, 39, 57–58*t*, 169*n*
  technology assimilation, 74*b*
  trade with China, 19*t*
  trade disputes, 183, 244
Japanese Overseas Development Agency, 73
Jiang Zemin, 118
Jiaotang University, 109, 257
Jilin Province, 212, 213
joint stock companies, 49
joint trading companies, 49
joint ventures (JVs)
  assembly operations, 55, 126–27
  conflicts with other partners of foreign firm, 44,
    149, 191–92
  contractual, 27*t*, 28–29, 48*f*, 49*t*, 126–27

OECD. *See* Organization for Economic
Cooperation and Development
oil
production and refining, 177t
retail service stations, 179–80
O'Leary, Joe, 175
organizational structures, 148–50
Organization for Economic Cooperation and
Development (OECD), 111, 254
Multilateral Agreement on Investment (MAI),
68, 202, 233–34
overcapacity. *See* capacity, excess
overseas Chinese (*huaqiao*)
investments in China, 39, 223, 236
managers of foreign-invested enterprises, 117
overtime, 96, 97t, 209–10

Panyu (Guangdong), 189
partners, 42–45
absentee or passive, 50, 60
conflicts among partners of foreign firms, 44,
149, 191–92
disadvantages of, 44, 82–83, 248, 249–50
dissolving relationship, 45, 145
employment levels, 91, 92–93
expectations for dividends, 145
friends and relatives of, 94, 118
government influence on choice of, 39–41, 79, 155
individuals, 13–14, 42
management styles, 96
motives, 44
need for, 77
ownership shares, 50–51
problems with, 14
selecting, 144, 155
state-owned enterprises, 39–41
See also joint ventures; management control
Partnership Law, 30, 49
patents, 71, 217
See also intellectual property rights (IPR)
pensions, 105, 108, 108n
See also social welfare system
People's Daily, 108
People's Liberation Army
control of rail system, 136
joint ventures with entities of, 47, 208, 223
People's Republic of China (PRC). *See* China
performance requirements, 63–65, 81, 235
compliance with, 66–67, 69, 72–73
export ratios, 30, 65–68, 168–69, 170
international agreements related to, 68, 70–71,
232, 243–44
for joint ventures, 65–66
local content, 69–71
research and development, 71
technology transfer, 30, 71–75, 215–16
for wholly owned foreign enterprises, 30, 65,
66, 168–69, 170
personnel files. *See dang an*
phasing investments, 46, 53–56

loss-leader ventures, 55
reducing project size under threshold for
central approval, 56–59, 138–39
Pilkington Glass, 141–42
plants. *See* productivity
Polaroid Corporation, 175
policy issues, 7
distribution, 162, 195
in establishment of foreign-invested
enterprises, 78–81
highest priorities, 253t
legal environment, 228–29
productivity, 155–56
recommendations, 252–58
pollution. *See* environmental impacts
ports, 38, 177t
power infrastructure, 52–53, 177t
PRC (People's Republic of China). *See* China
Price Law, 204
Proctor and Gamble, 172
productivity
capital factors, 143–45
of collective-sector firms, 124–26, 124t
components, 128–29
definitions, 122–24
effect of training, 131–32
environmental impacts and, 124, 151–52
of foreign-invested enterprises, 122, 126
goods factors, 134–38
increases and wages, 99
institutional factors, 145–51
issue categories, 153, 154t
labor factors, 129–33
market structure issues, 157
policy issues, 155–56
scale economies, 138–41
self-imposed issues, 154–55
state-owned enterprises (SOEs), 124–26, 124t, 153
technology and, 123, 131, 134, 136–38
total factor (TFP), 123, 124
transitional issues, 153–54
property rights, 201, 225
protectionism. *See* trade barriers
provincial governments. *See* local and provincial
governments
Provisional Regulations for Guiding the Direction
of Foreign Investment (Guidelines), 22–25
distribution restrictions, 168, 179
encouraged sectors, 22, 259–69
industrial policy reflected in, 39, 143
interpretation, 23–24, 62
labor quotas, 94
ownership share regulations, 50, 95
prohibited sectors, 22–23, 276–78
restricted sectors, 22, 23, 269–76
restrictions on wholly owned foreign
enterprises, 29, 47, 118
technology transfer requirements, 72, 215–16
text, 259–78
Pudong area (Shanghai), 36–37, 62, 79, 170

quality, consciousness of, 108, 109–10

railroads
controlled by army, 136
distribution of products, 38, 175
regulations. *See* Provisional Regulations for Guiding the Direction of Foreign Investment
regulators
need for training, 13
partnerships with, 42, 248
patron-client relationships, 222–23, 225
relationships. *See guanxi*; partners
representative offices, 53, 54, 90
research and development performance requirements, 71
residence permits. *See hukou*
retailing
foreign companies, 24, 79, 189
industry structure, 178*t*
joint chain stores, 49
service stations, 179–80
roads, 175, 177*t*
Rubin, Robert, 24*n*

SAIC. *See* Shanghai Automotive Industries Corporation; State Administration for Industry and Commerce
salaries
caps on increases, 80, 95–96, 99–100
differences between foreign and domestic firms, 99–100
differences by location, 99*t*, 100–1
gap between skilled and unskilled workers, 98–99, 101*t*
increases, 98, 99*t*, 100*t*, 116
performance-based, 133
sales
importance of local presence for, 17, 20
See also distribution
Sam's Club, 24, 189
Sanyo, 65
Sasser, Jim, 2
scale economies, 138–41
Schwab, Susan, 78
scope of operations
effects on productivity, 150–51, 156
expanding through affiliations, 112
limits to economies of scope, 150–51
negotiating, 59–61, 80, 81
restrictions on, 59, 249, 250
services, 150–51, 151*t*, 241–42
of state-owned enterprises, 160, 240
self-imposed issues, 6–7
distribution, 162, 195
in establishment of foreign-invested enterprises, 77–78
human resources, 116, 117
legal environment, 227–28
productivity, 154–55

service stations, 179–80
services
marketing, 174
provided by foreign-invested enterprises, 150–51, 151*t*, 174–75, 187, 241–42
SEZs. *See* special economic zones
Shandong Rizhao Power Project, 52–53
Shanghai
financial institutions in, 36–37, 79
foreign investment in, 37–38
General Motors plant, 55, 75, 129–31, 190*n*
Jiaotang University, 109, 257
port, 38
protection of local automobile companies, 140, 180–81
Pudong area, 36–37, 62, 79, 170
taxis, 180–81
textile industry, 38
wages, 99
Shanghai Automotive Industries Corporation (SAIC), 180
Shanghai International Trust and Investment Corporation (SITIC), 50
Shanghai Ministry of Post and Telecommunications, 187
Shanghai Yaohua Pilkington (SYP), 141–42
Shantou, 37
Shell, 179–80
Shenzhen, 37, 107, 209–10
Shinn, James, 13
Singapore, 32–33
SITIC. *See* Shanghai International Trust and Investment Corporation
smuggling, 188
social welfare system
current problems, 51, 108, 118–20
obligations of employers, 105–6, 106*t*, 107
reforms attempted, 105
SOEs. *See* state-owned enterprises
special economic zones (SEZs), 37, 41, 79, 165, 240
State Administration for Industry and Commerce (SAIC), 74
state economic planning, 252
productivity effects, 125
See also industrial policy
state-owned enterprises (SOEs)
corporatization of, 12, 238, 240, 244
employee benefits, 105, 106
employment reductions, 118
imports, 127*t*
overstaffing, 92–93
partnerships with, 39–41
productivity, 124–26, 124*t*, 153
scope of operations, 160, 240
state control of, 235
subsidies, 107, 251
State Science and Technology Commission, 74
state trading companies (STCs), 164–65, 169
STCs. *See* state trading companies

subcontractors, 89, 111, 112, 114, 119
  compliance with labor regulations, 210, 242
suppliers
  foreign-invested enterprises as, 134
  relationships with local, 134–36
  technology and know-how transfer to, 73
SYP. See Shanghai Yaohua Pilkington

tariffs
  on capital goods, 136
  on imported materials, 62–63, 136
  rates, 188
  reductions, 10, 240
  as subsidies, 125
  See also trade barriers
tax authorities, corrupt, 147, 219
tax rates, 62
technology
  contribution to productivity, 123, 131, 134, 136
  selecting, 136–38
  training in, 74b, 131, 137
technology transfer
  assimilation of, 73–74, 74b
  Chinese policies, 71
  intellectual property rights concerns, 138, 215,
    216–17
  know-how, 73, 152
  negotiations on, 55, 71–75, 138, 215–16, 217
  performance requirements, 30, 71–75, 215–16
  piracy, 216–17
  standard model of, 75
telecommunications
  capacity, 177t
  cellular networks, 23–24
  protectionism in, 181–82
  provincial companies, 182, 182n
  restrictions on foreign investment in, 23–24
textile industry
  locations of companies, 38
  See also garment industry
TFP. See total factor productivity
Thailand, 26f
Tianjin, 38, 75
total factor productivity (TFP), 123, 124
trade
  Chinese exports, 130t
  Chinese trading partners, 19t
  growth in Chinese, 247
  international regime, 160
  Japan-China, 19t
  smuggling, 188
  US-China, 12–13, 17, 18t, 231, 241
  See also exports; imports; World Trade
    Organization
trade barriers
  employment maintained by, 141
  as subsidies, 125
  within China, 38, 136, 161–62, 164n, 166,
    180–81, 190n, 244
  See also tariffs

trade disputes, 12–13, 183, 244, 245
trade names, 71, 109–10, 217–18
  See also intellectual property rights (IPR)
trademarks, 71, 73, 217–18
  See also intellectual property rights (IPR)
Trade-Related Intellectual Property (TRIPs)
  agreement, 243
Trade-Related Investment Measures (TRIMs)
  agreement, 68, 70–71, 233, 243–44
training
  effect on productivity, 131–32
  employees, 108–10, 117, 120, 146
  foreign government aid for, 257
  legal, 207–8, 226, 257–58
  in new technology, 74b, 131, 137
  See also education
transitional issues, 6
  distribution, 162, 193–95
  in establishment of foreign-invested
    enterprises, 77
  human resources, 116–17
  legal environment, 226–28
  productivity, 153–54
transportation
  for exports, 38
  freight volumes, 176t
  history of system, 163
  infrastructure development, 177t
  problems, 136, 175
  railroads, 38, 136, 175
  roads, 175
  trucking, 175
Treaty of Nanjing, 200
TRIMs. See Trade-Related Investment Measures
  (TRIMs) agreement
TRIPs. See Trade-Related Intellectual Property
  (TRIPs) agreement
trucking industry, 175

unemployment, 90–91, 90t, 118
unions. See labor unions
United States
  Clinton's China summit (1998), 2, 10, 239, 256
  communication between government agencies
    and Chinese counterparts, 258
  competition policy, 254, 257–58
  critics of Chinese labor practices, 243
  Foreign Corrupt Practices Act (FCPA), 89, 111,
    172, 220
  foreign policy toward China, 1–3, 256–58
  trade with China, 12–13, 17, 18t, 231, 241
United States commercial policy toward China,
  1–3, 231–32, 233
  importance for businesses, 4
  issues, 8–13
  most favored nation status, 226
  potential for cooperation, 245–46
  recommendations, 16, 239, 252, 253
universities, MBA programs, 109, 257
urban areas. See coastal cities

Other Publications from the
Institute for International Economics

POLICY ANALYSES IN INTERNATIONAL ECONOMICS Series

54 **Real Exchange Rates for the Year 2000**
Simon Wren-Lewis and Rebecca Driver/*April 1998*
ISBN paper 0-88132-253-9   188 pp.

55 **The Asian Financial Crisis: Causes, Cures, and Systemic Implications**
Morris Goldstein/*June 1998*
ISBN paper 0-88132-261-X   77 pp.

56 **Global Economic Effects of the Asian Currency Devaluations**
Marcus Noland, Li-Gang Liu, Sherman Robinson, and
Zhi Wang/*July 1998*
ISBN paper 0-88132-260-1   104 pp.

BOOKS

IMF Conditionality
John Williamson, editor/*1983*   ISBN cloth 0-88132-006-4   696 pp.

Trade Policy in the 1980s
William R. Cline, editor/*1983*
(out of print)   ISBN paper 0-88132-031-5   810 pp.

Subsidies in International Trade
Gary Clyde Hufbauer and Joanna Shelton Erb/*1984*
ISBN cloth 0-88132-004-8   302 pp.

International Debt: Systemic Risk and Policy Response
William R. Cline/*1984*   ISBN cloth 0-88132-015-3   336 pp.

Trade Protection in the United States: 31 Case Studies
Gary Clyde Hufbauer, Diane E. Berliner, and Kimberly Ann Elliott/*1986*
(out of print)   ISBN paper 0-88132-040-4   371 pp.

Toward Renewed Economic Growth in Latin America
Bela Balassa, Gerardo M. Bueno, Pedro-Pablo Kuczynski,
and Mario Henrique Simonsen/*1986*
(out of stock)   ISBN paper 0-88132-045-5   205 pp.

Capital Flight and Third World Debt
Donald R. Lessard and John Williamson, editors/*1987*
(out of print)   ISBN paper 0-88132-053-6   270 pp.

The Canada-United States Free Trade Agreement: The Global Impact
Jeffrey J. Schott and Murray G. Smith, editors/*1988*
ISBN paper 0-88132-073-0   211 pp.

World Agricultural Trade: Building a Consensus
William M. Miner and Dale E. Hathaway, editors/*1988*
ISBN paper 0-88132-071-3   226 pp.

Japan in the World Economy
Bela Balassa and Marcus Noland/*1988*
ISBN paper 0-88132-041-2   308 pp.

America in the World Economy: A Strategy for the 1990s
C. Fred Bergsten/*1988*   ISBN cloth 0-88132-089-7   235 pp.
                                 ISBN paper 0-88132-082-X   235 pp.

Managing the Dollar: From the Plaza to the Louvre
Yoichi Funabashi/*1988, 2d ed. 1989*
ISBN paper 0-88132-097-8   324 pp.

United States External Adjustment and the World Economy
William R. Cline/*May 1989*   ISBN paper 0-88132-048-X   392 pp.

Free Trade Areas and U.S. Trade Policy
Jeffrey J. Schott, editor/*May 1989*
ISBN paper 0-88132-094-3   408 pp.

Dollar Politics: Exchange Rate Policymaking in the United States
I. M. Destler and C. Randall Henning/*September 1989*
(out of print)   ISBN paper 0-88132-079-X   192 pp.

SPECIAL REPORTS

WORKS IN PROGRESS

Explaining Congressional Votes on Recent Trade Bills:
From NAFTA to Fast Track
Robert E. Baldwin and Christopher S. Magee
The US - Japan Economic Relationship
C. Fred Bergsten, Marcus Noland, and Takatoshi Ito
China's Entry to the World Economy
Richard N. Cooper
Toward a New International Financial Architecture: A Practical Post-Asia Agenda
Barry Eichengreen
Economic Sanctions After the Cold War
Kimberly Ann Elliott, Gary C. Hufbauer and Jeffrey J. Schott
Trade and Labor Standards
Kimberly Ann Elliott and Richard Freeman
Leading Indicators of Financial Crises in the Emerging Economies
Morris Goldstein and Carmen Reinhart
The Exchange Stabilization Fund
C. Randall Henning
Prospects for Western Hemisphere Free Trade
Gary Clyde Hufbauer and Jeffrey J. Schott
The Future of US Foreign Aid
Carol Lancaster
The Economics of Korean Unification
Marcus Noland
International Lender of Last Resort
Catherine L. Mann
A Primer on US External Balance
Catherine L. Mann
Globalization, the NAIRU, and Monetary Policy
Adam S. Posen

Australia, New Zealand, and Papua New Guinea
D A. INFORMATION SERVICES
648 Whitehorse Road
Mitcham, Victoria 3132, Australia
(tel: 61-3-9210-7777;
fax: 61-3-9210-7788)
email: service@dadirect.com.au
http://www.dadirect.com.au

Caribbean
SYSTEMATICS STUDIES LIMITED
St. Augustine Shopping Centre
Eastern Main Road, St. Augustine
Trinidad and Tobago, West Indies
(tel: 868-645-8466;
fax: 868-645-8467)
email: tobe@trinidad.net

People's Republic of China (including Hong Kong) and Taiwan
(sales representatives):
Tom Cassidy
Cassidy & Associates
470 W. 24th Street
New York, NY 10011
(tel: 212-727-8943;
fax: 212-727-9539)

India, Bangladesh, Nepal, and Sri Lanka
VIVA BOOKS PVT.
Mr. Vinod Vasishtha
4325/3, Ansari Rd.
Daryaganj, New Delhi-110002, India
(tel: 91-11-327-9280;
fax: 91-11-326-7224)
email: vinod.viva@gndel
http://globalnet.ems.vsnl.net.in

Mexico and the Caribbean
(non-Anglophone islands only)
L.D. Clepper, Jr., sales representative
Publishers Marketing & Research
    Associates
79-01 35th Avenue #5D
P.O. Box 720489
Jackson Heights, NY 11372
(tel/fax: 718-803-3465)
email: clepper@pipeline.com

South America
Julio E. Ernod
Publishers Marketing & Research
    Associates, c/o HARBRA
Rua Joaquim Tavora, 629
04015-001 Sao Pãulo, Brasil
(tel: 55-11-571-1122;
fax: 55-11-575-6876)
email: emod@harbra.com.br

Canada
RENOUF BOOKSTORE
5369 Canotek Road, Unit 1,
Ottawa, Ontario K1J 9J3, Canada
(tel: 613-745-2665;
fax: 613-745-7660)
http://www.renoufbooks.com/

Central America
Jose Rios, sales representative
Publishers Marketing & Research
    Associates
Publicaciones Educativas
Apartado Postal 370-A
Ciudad Guatemala, Guatemala, C.A.
(tel/fax: 502-443-0472)

Western and Eastern Europe (including Russia), as well as the Middle East and North Africa
The Eurospan Group
3 Henrietta Street, Covent Garden
London, England
(tel: 011-44-171-240-0856;
fax: 011-44-171-379-0609)
email: orders@eurospan.co.uk
http://www.eurospan.co.uk

Japan and the Republic of Korea
UNITED PUBLISHERS SERVICES, LTD.
Kenkyu-Sha Building
9, Kanda Surugadai 2-Chome
Chiyoda-Ku, Tokyo 101, Japan
(tel: 81-3-3291-4541;
fax: 81-3-3292-8610)
email: saito@ups.co.jp

Puerto Rico (School/College/Academic markets)
David R. Rivera, sales representative
Publishers Marketing & Research
    Associates
c/o Premium Educational Group
MSC 609 #89 Ave. De Diego, Suite 105
San Juan, PR 00927-5381
(tel: 787-764-3532;
 fax: 787-764-4774)
email:drrivera@coqui.net

Visit our website at:
http://www.iie.com

E-mail orders to:
orders@iie.com